THE ASSASSINATION OF
YITZHAK RABIN

THE ASSASSINATION OF YITZHAK RABIN

EDITED BY YORAM PERI

STANFORD UNIVERSITY PRESS

Stanford, California   *2000*

Stanford University Press
Stanford, California
©2000 by the Board of Trustees of the
Leland Stanford Junior University
Printed in the United States of America

Library of Congress Cataloging-in-Publication Data

The Assassination of Yitzhak Rabin / edited by Yoram Peri.
   p.   cm.
   Includes bibliographical references and index.
   ISBN 0-8047-3835-1 (cloth : alk. paper) — ISBN 0-8047- 3837-8 (paper : alk. paper)
   1. Rabin, Yitzhak, 1922—Assassination.   2. Israel—Politics and government—
1993.   3. Right-wing extremists—Israel.   I. Peri , Yoram

DS126.6.R32 A87   2000
956.9405'4—dc21   00-024100

This book is printed on acid-free, archival-quality paper.

Original printing 2000

Last figure below indicates year of this printing:
09 08 07 06 05 04 03 02 01 00

Typeset in 10/13 Galliard by John Feneron

Contents

Contributors

MAJID AL-HAJ is Professor of Sociology in the Department of Sociology at Haifa University.

NACHMAN BEN-YEHUDA is Professor of Sociology and the Dean of the Faculty of Social Sciences at the Hebrew University.

LINDA-RENÉE BLOCH is Professor of Communication in the Department of Communication at Tel Aviv University.

HAIM HAZAN is Professor of Social Anthropology in the Department of Sociology and Anthropology and the Director of the Herczeg Institute on Aging at Tel Aviv University.

TAMAR HERMANN is Professor of Political Science at the Open University and the Director of the Tami Steinmetz Center for Peace Research in Tel Aviv University.

RUTH MALKINSON, Ph.D., teaches at the Bob Shapel School of Social Work, Tel Aviv University.

ISRAEL ORBACH is Professor of Psychology and the Chair of the Psychology Department at Bar-Illan University in Ramat-Gan.

YORAM PERI is Professor of Political Sociology and Communication in the Department of Communication at the Hebrew University, Jerusalem.

TAMAR RAPOPORT is Professor of Sociology of Education in the Department of Education at the Hebrew University.

AVIEZER RAVITZKY is Professor of Jewish Thought and the Chair of the Department of Jewish Thought at the Hebrew University.

EHUD SPRINZAK is Professor of Political Sciences and the Dean of Lauder School of Government at the Interdisciplinary Center in Herzliya.

ELIEZER WITZTUM is Professor in the Division of Psychiatry, Faculty of Health Sciences, at Ben Gurion University of the Negev and Director of Psychotherapy Supervision, Mental Health Center at Beer Sheva.

GADI YATZIV is Professor of Sociology and the Dean of the Communication Department at the Natanya College.

EPHRAIM YUCHTMAN-YAAR is Professor of Sociology in the Department of Sociology and Anthropology and the head of Tami Steimnetz Center for Peace Research in Tel Aviv University.

BARBIE ZELIZER is Professor of Communication in the Annenberg School of Communication at University of Pennsylvania.

THE ASSASSINATION OF
YITZHAK RABIN

Introduction: The Writing Was on the Wall

YORAM PERI

In the late-night hours of September 13, 1993, the 71-year-old Yitzhak Rabin felt a sense of elation uncharacteristic of this dry, pragmatic, and introverted man, elation that had nothing to do with the altitude of his plane on its flight out of Washington, D.C. That afternoon on the White House lawn, a circle had begun to close as he and Yasser Arafat set down their signatures on a historic political document. These representatives of the two national movements that had clutched at each other's throats for almost a century had begun to transform that grip into a handshake of partnership. Rabin knew it was only a beginning, he was not at all sure that the deed would lead to peace and he imagined there would be violent repercussions. But what never entered his mind is that one result would be a political assassination, and that he would be its victim.

I looked at Rabin, contemplative in the dim blue light at the front of the plane. In the war of 1948 to establish the state of Israel, Rabin had been a young commander ordered to break through the siege of Jerusalem. As chief of staff in 1967, he sought to prevent President Gamal Abdal Nasser of Egypt from carrying out his promise to "throw Israel into the sea." Now, in the dusk of his years, this conservative, cautious, and pessimistic man was joining a select group of leaders—Charles De Gaulle, Mikhail Gorbachev, Frederick William DeKlerk—who, with their own hands, had seized the reins of history and forced it to change direction. In this moment of elation, hope was revealed. "If by Israel's fiftieth anniversary I can reach a permanent arrangement with the Palestinians and an agreement with Syria," and here he used Israeli slang taken from Arabic, "I would be *mabsut*—satisfied."

Rabin's intense desire to close the circle was so patently clear that even his closing words, spoken in his flat, prosaic way, sounded matter of fact: "What I wouldn't do for that." Was Rabin so convinced that nothing would happen to him, despite his efforts to change the course of history? Or was this again his constrained style, the unembellished report of a soldier, the understatement of a realist? On the night of November 4, 1995, after taking three bullets and being rushed to the hospital in his state car, he managed to utter only one sentence, "My back hurts, but it's not so terrible." These last words were chillingly reminiscent of the final words spoken 70 years earlier by Joseph Trumpeldor, the first mythic hero of Zionist history. "It's not terrible," are the words attributed to the one-armed pioneer-soldier wounded by Arab gunfire in a battle in the Galilee, "It's good to die for one's country." After "not so terrible," Rabin's head fell slack and he lost consciousness.

Seen from a distance, the assassination should not have been so surprising. Scholars know that human history is rife with political murder. With the exception of periods when it ebbed—Athens in the fifth century B.C., the first centuries of the Roman Empire, feudal Europe from the first half of the eleventh to the early fourteenth century, and again Europe from the seventeenth to the late eighteenth century—political violence was an almost acceptable practice of political life.

Indeed, the belief that the march of human progress diminishes the number of political murders is not well founded. On the contrary, the twentieth century was one of the bloodiest. And this wave, worse than those prior, is not yet over. Although there were only 100 attempted political assassinations in the nineteenth century, 30 of them successful; from the early twentieth century until the end of the 1980s, no fewer than 700 such attempts were made, and 70 achieved their objectives. And those who would believe that the end of World War II ushered in a more enlightened era will also be disappointed by the numbers. More than half the political assassinations perpetrated in the twentieth century took place in the second half (Ford, 1985: 29).

The fate of Yitzhak Rabin was thus no different from that of many world leaders on all the continents. In the United States, a president (John Kennedy in 1963) and a presidential hopeful (his brother Robert Kennedy in 1968) were assassinated; in India, a prime minister (Indira Gandhi in 1984) and the son who succeeded her (Rajib Gandhi, three months later) were the victims of assassination that began with the founder of independent India (Mahatma Gandhi, killed in 1948). In modern Europe, there were acts of assassination in the cold North (Swedish prime minister Olof Palme in 1986, although it is still not known whether this was a political assassination or the victim merely happened to be a politician), to the warm South (Aldo Moro in Italy in 1978). In Africa, heads of state were assassinated from the South (South African president H. F. Verwoerd in 1966) and the North (Egyptian president Anwar Sadat in 1981). Similar events occurred from Latin America and the Far East to the Middle East, where first kings (Abdulla in 1949 is one of many) and then militarymen who became politicians lost their lives in a manner unnatural, though not uncommon, to the region. The assassination of heads of state, noble or ignoble, is deeply ingrained in human society. And perhaps the noble ones suffer more: "Good kings would be likely to be slain more often than tyrants," said Thomas Aquinas (cited in Ford, 1985: 125), "for the rule of good kings was hard on evil-doers and evil men are more likely than good men to resort to such a desperate measure as tyrannicide."

In nondemocratic societies, political assassination has been a rather efficient means of changing government, whether the assassination of tyrannical or nontyrannical leaders (George, 1988). But the phenomenon continued even in societies that agreed about due process for transferring authority, and indeed earned its own name—"regicide." Thus social thinkers looked for an explanation of the phenomenon at deeper levels. In Totem and Taboo, Freud suggested the concept of patricide as the origin of the political community. Rene Girard developed the theory of assassinating a political leader as sacrifice of the scapegoat, necessary to expunge the potential of destructive internal violence in society (Girard, 1977). Freud and Girard are not alone; consider the works of Mirceau Eliade (1959). In the spirit of the explanation that sees sacrifice as the necessary basis for society even in modern times—nationalism does this by way of wars, not ritual sacrifice—Marvin and Eangle explain the assassination of Rabin in totemic terms. The Oslo Accords undermined the territorial boundaries of society and eliminated the traditional ritual enemy, plunging it into a totemic crisis. The ritual of Rabin's assassination recreated national unity and restored the damaged self-identity (Marvin and Eangle, 1996).[1]

Without traveling too far afield in history or regions of the unknown, clear thinking should have been sufficient to warn Israelis of the possibility of regicide in their backyard. Since the 1970s it has been observed that solutions to the Israeli-Arab conflict will provoke internal political violence.

Would someone willing to give his own blood to redeem the homeland hesitate to shed the blood of another who is about to give up holy land? Political violence in Israel has not just been a hypothetical possibility. Whether rationalized as a reaction to Palestinian violence, vengeance, or a cynical political tactic—as was usually the case—illegal political violence became a normative phenomenon among many Israelis—directed against Palestinian inhabitants of the territories,[2] Palestinian citizens of Israel who are innocent of all wrongdoing, and even against Jews: in 1983, Emil Gruenzweig was killed by a hand grenade tossed by a Jew into a Jewish peace demonstration in Jerusalem.

As 1996 approached, it should have been clear that in all matters related to political violence against Arabs, Israeli society had loosed its restraints and its compunctions. Proof was the reaction of Israeli society to the massacre of Muslim worshipers in Hebron by Baruch Goldstein, a settler driven by a sense of divine mission. Public reaction was passive, but some—including Member of the Knesset (M.K.) Hanan Porat from the National Religious Party—did not conceal their joy. Afterward, the murderer became an admired hero, his ornate grave became a pilgrimage site, and a book praising his deed became a bestseller among the extremist right. Although the act was condemned by the authorities, nothing more was said or done: "The prosecuting authorities refrained from bringing the full weight of the law down upon the fanatic rabbis who supported the deed" (Moshe Negbi, *Ma'ariv*, January 10, 1997).

It is not surprising that in the six months before Rabin's asassination, signs proliferated that a physical attack was possible not just against Palestinians, but against Jews too, including top political leaders. In retrospect, it is hard to shake the feeling that Rabin's murder could have been expected. There were red lights and warning bells, and still the system did not believe that it was possible. A retrospective reading of the newspapers in the months preceding the assassination reveals how the stage was set, step by step: first verbal invective, then symbolic behavior, then ritual murder and actual physical violence, and finally the assassination. Even the words "the writing on the wall" appeared. Except that whoever was supposed to read it simply did not.

In the first stage came the discrediting and delegitimization of the government. Some of the epithets: "a government of blood . . . wicked and cruel . . . that could create a new Tiananmen Square in Israel. . . . All means are kosher to bring it down" (*Nekuda*, a settlers' publication, July 1995); "a mad government that is shrinking Israel to the size of Auschwitz," "a lawless government . . . submissive, confused, traitorous" (M.K. Rehavam Ze'evi, *Ha'aretz*, October 6, 1995); "a sick government" (M.K. Arik Sharon, ibid.); "a government of thieves," "a licentious government," "a government lacking honor" (writer and former M.K. Moshe Shamir in the May issue of *Nekuda*); and "a bunch of judenrat, Quislings" (M.K. Raphael Eitan, January 1995).

This invective was accompanied by a campaign to delegitimize Rabin, to undermine his self-confidence and dehumanize him among the wider public. Participating in this campaign were not just extremists but also popular members of the Knesset and upright public figures. Rabin was defined as a "pathological case" who is leading the nation to surrender, which is "worse than death" (Shamir, *Nekuda*, July 1995) or "a schizoid cut off from reality" (Dr. Neta Dor-Shav, *Yediot Aharonot*, October 13, 1995). Several leaders of the right compared Israel to France occupied by the Nazis, and Rabin's government to the Vichy regime of Marshal Pétain. Pétain's fate—execution by the betrayed nation—was frequently mentioned in this analogy.[3] In one demonstration, an effigy of Rabin appeared in the uniform of an SS officer, and two days before the assassination, Leah Rabin came home to find the regular weekly demonstrators outside her door calling out, "Next year we'll hang you in the city square like Mussolini and his mistress."

There is a great danger in stereotyping political figures, which makes their assassination look like the murder of a symbol, not a human being. Through stereotyping, explain Weisz and Taylor, the assassin dissociates the individual from the role and kills the stereotype, not the human: "An illogical process that identifies a stereotype with the whole personality of the leader is a precursor to the distorted thought of physical elimination" (Weisz and Taylor, 1969).

In the wake of the shouting or written declarations that "Rabin is a traitor/murderer" came the call to action, "Death to Rabin" (*Yediot Aharonot*, August 22, 1995). In September, Orthodox rabbis in the United States compared Rabin to Arafat and Hitler, calling him an "informer," "traitor," and moser (a Jew who betrays another Jew to the enemy) (*Yediot Aharonot*, August 11, 1995). Radio Seven, the settlers' station and the main organ of the clerical-nationalist camp, expressed agreement with these epithets. On October 19, Benny Allon, one of the two leaders of the radical right Zo Artzenu movement (who became a member of the Knesset after the assassination), asserted, "Rabin is leading the state to civil war. If he's not careful, he's liable to get killed. . . . Things can get so bad that just as Goldstein killed 40 Arabs, someone will kill 40 left-wingers. . . . You have no idea how many people feel contempt for the government, and they have no qualms about doing something about it" (*Ma'ariv*). The possibility of political assassination was explicitly raised (Sylvie Keshet, *Yediot Aharonot*, October 20, 1995), and Yosef Lapid wrote, "Do we need some sort of madman killing Yitzhak Rabin for the state to insist on respect for law on the street?" (*Ma'ariv*, October 17, 1995).

After the word "death" became routine in political slogans, symbolic expressions of political murder began to appear: In Haifa, currency came out of an ATM bearing a call to murder Rabin. In early September, demonstrators appeared carrying memorial candles, signs against Rabin, and a coffin covered by black cloth. In October, dead doves were sent to the Office of the Prime Minister, with letters threatening, "We're going to rub you out, your end is near" (*Yediot Aharonot*, October 26, 1995). Indeed in the wake of these expressions, the deeds also come: assault of ministers' vehicles and Rabin's car, and later, at a violent conference in Netanya, a physical assault on Rabin himself (on symbolic assassination, see Kirkham, Levy, and Crotty, 1970: 355).

Participating in the campaign against Rabin were illegal extremist groups (Kahanists and other racist groups), upright public figures (the man who assaulted Rabin in Netanya was none other than Natan Ophir, rabbi of Hebrew University), and even leaders of parliamentary parties (Tzachi Hanegbi, later minister of justice, who commandeered the loudspeakers at a rally in the Western Wall plaza). A careful and sophisticated division of labor emerged between the nonlegitimate, extraparliamentary bodies and the parliamentary opposition, and the latter used the former as it suited them. On October 20, two weeks before the assassination, *Ha'aretz* columnist Arye Caspi wrote, "Who's on the firing line," condemning the slogan "Rabin is a traitor," which could encourage someone from the right to follow through. Caspi described how he had met Rabin in a hotel, where "every person in the lobby could have easily picked off the prime minister with a gun from a distance of five meters."

The writing on the wall was not invisible to the General Security Services (GSS). Immediately after the Oslo Accords, the GSS assessment was that there was a possibility of Jews killing other Jews. After Goldstein's rampage in Hebron, the GSS decided to more closely monitor extremist Jewish elements. In mid-August, the police and the GSS weighed the possibility of forbidding armed settlers from attending rallies (*Yediot Aharonot*, August 16, 1995). In May and June, after receiving information about the possibility of an attempt on the life of ministers or even the prime minister, the GSS considered possible scenarios but concluded that the danger would become imminent only upon the evacuation of settlements (Zeev Schiff, *Ha'aretz*, April 5, 1996). The GSS leaked its assessments to the media, but Shimon Romah, a retired GSS officer, said in a newspaper interview, "Conditions currently obtain in which an extremist will try not only to humiliate the prime minister, but to do more. I'm afraid that the motive exists for an attempt on the life of Rabin" (*Ma'ariv*, October 12, 1995).

Despite this, and even though the subject was discussed, professionals and lay citizens alike refused to believe that a political assassination was possible. The conclusions of a government investigative commission opened with the words, "The GSS had considerable information about the increased threats to the lives of high level officials, headed by the prime minister . . . [but it] did not sufficiently act to impress this threat upon the bodyguards of these officials."

The False Collective Israeli Consciousness

Why was murder considered so unlikely? Why was the writing on the wall not seen? The answer stems from the false collective consciousness of Israeli society. Despite its ongoing preoccupation, if not obsession, with itself, especially its collective identity, Israeli society has a distorted self-image, reflected in four components of its consciousness.

One was the false perception of the sources of social evil. The myth of the victim, the persecuted people, which has been fostered by the Jewish nation for hundreds of years—the "objective" basis for this, as for any myth, is irrelevant (Ohana and Wistrich, 1996)—created a situation in which evil is always perceived as coming from the outside. After all, the victim of violence surely cannot be the root of the evil. The Holocaust served as the ultimate justification for this ethos. Jews were the ultimate victim and the Nazis the embodiment of absolute evil. This historical proclivity of Jews to see evil as stemming from the outside obstructed the ability to identify internal sources of evil, even when the alarm bells were sounding.[4]

A second element in the false collective consciousness is Israeli society's nonviolent self-image. This is related to both the Jewish ethos of being a victim and the Jewish image of being powerless. The powerless, it is presumed, cannot be violent. Although the Zionist revolution took place years ago, and since then the powerless have become very powerful and the state of Israel a military superpower, the self-image remains that Jews are not violent collectively or individually. Thus when Israel became a conqueror, it viewed the occupation as "enlightened." Violence against a civilian population was rationalized as the need to maintain law and order, and shocking abuses of Palestinians by Israeli soldiers during the intifada were defined as "aberrations." Typical for "frontier societies," vigilantism was ignored.[5]

The third component of the false consciousness relates to the power and stability of Israeli democracy. The view of Israel as "the only democracy between the Mediterranean and the Indian Ocean" was fostered by the Israelis as part of their battle with Arab states over world opinion. This ethos made it difficult for the public and politicians alike to acknowledge the weaknesses in it: that Israeli democracy is "thin" and not "thick"; that the cohesion of society has diminished (Horowitz and Lissak, 1990); that there is a broad social periphery that does not accept democratic values (Peres and Yuchtman-Yaar, 1992); that Israel is undergoing a crisis of legitimacy (Aronoff, 1989); and that it is actually not as stable as it appears—having had no fewer than 27 governments in 49 years up until the assassination. Contrary to the analysis of Shapira (1977) that Israeli democracy is formal, not liberal, it turns out that there is a weakness not just in the ethos, but in the democratic process. The Israeli democracy is conditional, and many "call into question its moral and even procedural validity" (Yatziv, in Chapter 14). The belief that Israeli democracy is strong and stable led to indulgence about violence toward Palestinians and also downplayed the possibility that violence would be directed against Jews. Only a year after the assassination did Attorney General Michael Ben-Ya'ir admit that "the basic principles upon which democratic rule is based did not sufficiently trickle down to all strata of the population in Israel. This means that Israeli democracy is much more fragile than we thought a year ago" (Ma'ariv, October 25, 1996).

Finally, the false consciousness tended to attribute omnipotence to the Israeli security forces. The kidnapping of Adolf Eichmann and the nuclear plant whistle-blower Mordechai Vanunu, the rescue of hostages in Entebbe, sabotage of a nuclear plant in Iraq, and the thwarting of various terrorist activities by Israeli security services all reinforced the belief that even if someone planned to harm the head of government, the all-powerful security services would easily prevent it.

This false collective consciousness is also what led Rabin to reject the reports he received that some 2,000 Jewish residents of the occupied territories and another 4,000 right-wingers within Israel were liable to resort to violence. In a survey from late August 1995, 0.7 percent of the respondents made explicit that "a political assassination would be a correct deed if it would halt the peace process." The classified report received by Rabin noted that there were approximately 100 people with the "potential to carry out an assassination."[6]

It therefore becomes clear why Yitzhak Rabin belittled the warnings of the GSS. "Take the pressure off me," he told Carmi Gillon, head of the GSS, when security was beefed up after the assault on him on October 10 (Yael Gvirtz, *Yediot Aharonot*, September 13, 1996). He refused his bodyguards' requests to wear a bulletproof vest in public, even after Minister Ben-Eliezer, whose own car was damaged by demonstrators, warned him, "there will be a murder here," and he waived use of an armored car brought from the United States.

The desire to psychologically analyze Rabin's disregard for the danger is understandable, and the conclusions of such an analysis are fascinating. In a complex psychoanalytic explanation that rests on the conceptual world of Jacques Lacan, Gabriel Dahan asks how the assassination could have been so expected and yet not enter the imagination? "Tyche and Automaton, the expected and the unexpected, create an amazing drama in their encounter, in the paradoxical realization. They are possible only where there is a divided subject, a subject that desires. The expectation is charged with desire and the mourning ritual is an act of unification" (*Pulmus*, no. 7 [1997]: 49–51). Explanations from social psychology sound less imaginative but perhaps more persuasive than the psychoanalytical analysis. Shlomo Breznitz speaks of the mechanism for self-deception, which helps the individual and society endure a sense of vulnerability by paralyzing the antennae that identify the expected danger. This mechanism denies the immediate danger by fostering the belief that "although there are symptoms of danger, my case is special and different, and therefore I am not vulnerable," or by denying personal responsibility ("Although there is danger, what can I do to prevent it? Let someone else take care of it").[7]

Without disparaging these explanations, I believe that an analysis drawn from the cultural, especially political, sphere is more meaningful. In other words, what caused the inability to see the writing on the wall was the distorted, paralyzing influence of overpoliticized Israeli society, the intrusion of excessive political considerations on all spheres of life. The advantage of this explanation over others will become clear in Chapter 1, which examines the impact of the assassination on Israeli society, and in the final chapter, which addresses the fate of the memory of Rabin and the acts of commemorating him. At this stage, let us remain in the period preceding the assassination, when the anticipated and ultimate course of events might have been prevented.

The enormous political tension between the Labor-Meretz government and the opposition—the Likud, the religious parties, and the extreme right-wing parties—is what constructed the attitude toward political violence and the threat of political assassination from the illegitimate extraparliamentary right. Spokespersons for the government treated this violence as socially and politically pathological, the behavior of an extremist minority that should be handled by the police, the GSS, and the judicial system. What the government perceived as a more serious problem, the "real" political danger, was the struggle of the legitimate right against it, its policies, and its very right to exist. Although Rabin was accused of disdaining and belittling the settlers and the extraparliamentary settlers' organizations, this is a misreading. His behavior was not instrumental, but expressive. Rabin had no desire to humiliate or insult, but ignoring them only reflected his belief that the extremists were unimportant and hence not worth giving undue consideration. Thus, Rabin himself raised the threshold of sensitivity to the threat of an attempted assassination.

Although the legitimate right benefited consciously and deliberately from the game played by the extremist right, it is very hard to suspect it of having intended or even imagined that the verbal and symbolic violence would lead to an actual physical assassination. They rode a tiger in the belief that the tiger could be tamed. Thus accusations by government spokespersons that the legitimate right encouraged violence were perceived by it as demagogic incitement intended to defame and hurt them politically. On August 31, *Yediot Aharonot* published responses to the question, "What are the chances of assassination against the leaders?" Replied former prime minister Yitzhak Shamir, "It is not the left in danger today, but the national camp." He reminded readers of the mysterious assassination of Labor leader Chaim Arlosoroff in 1933, and the claims then made by the right that the left falsely accused it of murder to strengthen the right's claim to power. "We are worried that some madman will do something that we'll be accused of exactly when we are on the way up. If God forbid something happens, the finger will be pointed at us." As a result, the left concentrated on the legitimate right and scoffed at the security analysis of extremists, while the right, insulted by accusations and wanting to use the extreme right for its purposes, did not accurately assess the destructive potential of their deeds or distance itself from them.

In this light, the reaction of right-wing leaders to warnings issued by the GSS that they restrain the extremists can be understood. They attributed greater importance to attacks from the left than to the danger from extremists. Benjamin Netanyahu and Limor Livnat accused the Labor Party of "waging a campaign of organized incitement against the Likud" (*Yediot Aharonot*, October 13, 1995), and M.K. Uzi Landau said, "Labor is spreading a blood libel against the Likud. This is character assassination in the best Bolshevik tradition, and I suggest that it not be scoffed at" (*Yediot Aharonot*, October 19, 1995). Arik Sharon even noted the blood libel that had preceded Stalin's purges (*Yediot Aharonot*, September 1, 1995). The left regarded these responses as demagoguery, but right-wing leaders believed their rhetoric and suspected that the heads of the GSS were collaborating politically with the left. Later, the GSS director admitted, "Transmitting the message was difficult, and met with a psychological block," (Yael Gvirtz, *Yediot Aharonot*, September 13, 1996).

The final question remains: Why did the media—which reported on this violent process as it unfolded, explicitly contemplated the possibility of political assassination, and even noted that Rabin was the target—treat the anticipated event with equanimity? The answer is related to its professional norms and the modus operandi. In an age of multiple channels and high commercial competition, the media prefer events that have a dramatic character. This tendency causes protest groups that wish to draw attention to themselves to increase the drama of their behavior. Protest groups know, for example, that the media will not send reporters to a routine demonstration if they do not expect some disturbance of the peace to take place (Clutterbuck, 1981). The media, for their part, try to milk the maximum drama from the event, and thus a symbiosis develops between political protest groups and the media (Wolfsfeld, 1991). Through this process of spiraling extremism, politicians get more coverage and journalists get a better story. The assassin noted this in his police interrogation: "The root of all this extremism is lack of media coverage. All the vandalism in Hebron and those other places of allegedly extremist organizations are all due to the lack of attention. It all stems from the desire to attract media attention."[8]

But because politicians and journalists alike were aware that they were exaggerating the drama, among themselves they did not give much credence to the messages. Thus even senior journalists were blind to the obvious in the months preceding the assassination. "The debate about a political assassination of public figures is not logical and carries a dangerous message," wrote Ron Miberg (*Ma'ariv*, September 1, 1995). In the rival newspaper, Amos Carmel wrote, "The feeling remains that someone is trying to sow hysteria. . . . Someone is trying to introduce devils to tip the balance in the public debate. If attackers against the elected government are hiding behind every bush, and if the GSS is unable to catch them, then we should be defending the threatened ministers and not disagreeing with them. On the other hand, whoever disagrees with them under these conditions is virtually supporting Jewish terrorism, which invalidates his opinions (*Yediot Aharonot*, August 31, 1995).[9]

Did the assassination that shattered Israeli society cause it to reflect upon its false collective consciousness? Definitely not on an institutional level. The mandate of the committee of inquiry appointed by the government after the assassination did not include the social, cultural, and political aspects of the assassination, but only the functioning of the GSS. No wonder the results of its investigation met with criticism by left-wing intellectuals. "The report ignores the fact that the assassination was the product of hatred, racism, and religious barbarism, and not because the field of vision of the security man was under 360 degrees," wrote civil rights lawyer Avigdor Feldman (*Ha'Ir*, April 3, 1996), however the committee and its report were saved from falling into the mire of a political debate. The murder trial was almost a routine criminal proceeding. Because the judges were determined not to turn the courtroom into a political arena, they avoided any discussion of the ecology in which this assassination had evolved.

Since the assassination, the Israelis have indeed been going through a hurtful soul-searching process. But before we examine it and analyze its consequences, the first subject to be addressed in this book is this: what processes prepared the ground for a political assassination? Rabbi Yoel Bin-Nun, one of the more moderate leaders of the settlers' group Gush Emunim, asserted, "The assassination of a prime minister is civil war." Perhaps not an actual war, but the assassination was one element in a violent collision between systems of thought and culture. How did this latent civil war develop and what characterized it?

Although there is a tendency to study political assassination through psychological analysis of the assassin (Rothstein, 1966; Weisz and Taylor, 1969; Weinstein and Lyerly, 1970; Crotty, 1971; and Socarides, 1982 are but a few examples), I believe that assassination should be seen as a product of the historical milieu and social political context: "The origin of political assassination is the collective human existence and not the soul of the individual" (Wilkinson, 1976: 7). It is a social and cultural phenomenon that emanates from a wider system and requires a broader social perspective as described by "thick description," in Clifford Geertz's terminology. To understand the assassination of Rabin, one must embark upon an anthropological journey into Israeli society, exploring the forces at play and the rules of the game, which will reveal the underground currents and motivating mechanisms.

In his analysis of the assassination of John Kennedy, Sidney Verba notes that social crisis provides an exceptional opportunity to observe political institutions, which can then be viewed under pressure. A conflict like this also permits the examination of political processes, because it "makes apparent certain patterns of political belief and commitment that in ordinary time remain latent and unobservable" (Verba, 1965: 351). But more than the political is under scrutiny here. Understanding the assassination requires the deconstruction of cultural structures, in order to reveal and analyze the ethos and myths that drive society, as well as its representations and symbolic order. Thus, sadly, the assassination provides a unique lens for observing contemporary Israeli society and democracy.

The second pervasive theme in the book concerns public reaction to the deed. The assassination placed Israeli society in a liminal state (Turner, 1969; 1974)—a reflexive situation in which society "looks at itself and asks not just what it is, but what it should be." This rite of passage of Israeli society is characterized by feelings of being deeply moved, intense emotional relations, and a profusion of communication, fear, and sacredness. In this special situation, political rituals and civil ceremonies take place, the thin tissue enveloping society seems to be retracted, and basic questions arise about its character, identity, mission, hopes, and longings.

In examining public reaction to the assassination—a moment of great flux in which systems crumble and new ones evolve—the moment of "blink" in the language of Gramsci—a process evolves for formation of the imagined community (Anderson, 1987), the invention of tradition (Hobsbaum and Ranger, 1983), and the shaping of the social memory.[10] How does the field (to use Bourdieu's terminology, 1993) look, in which a struggle is being waged about the creation and definition of national culture? This is also a good opportunity to scrutinize the significance of the holy in contemporary secular society, following the processes of deification, iconization, and commemoration of a contemporary martyr.

A third constellation of themes revolves around the impact of the assassination on Israeli society. Was it "the first shot in the civil war," as noted by some? Or a warning shot intended to prevent a volcanic eruption? While the assassination revealed flaws in Israeli democracy, did it also bring about their repair? In particular, did it halt or slow down the crisis of legitimacy in the political system? To understand this, one should ask if Israelis held the assassination narrative in common, or are there counternarratives for various cultural groups? If so, what meanings are ascribed to them?

On the comparative and theoretical level, analysis of the impact of the assassination on Israeli society touches on two topics that have traditionally kindled the imagination of thinkers and scholars. First, does the assassination constitute an integrative element, or, conversely, strengthen the process of social disintegration? In other words, was the assassination a transformative element in Israeli society? If so, how has the character of society changed? Second, is assassination effective in changing the course of history? Or perhaps Bismarck was right that "political genius consisted in the ability to hear the distant hoof-beat of the horse of history, and then by a superhuman effort, to leap and catch the horseman by the coat-tails" (Berlin, 1980: 25). Genius like this can exist only among those murdered — Rabin apparently had it — but not among murderers.

The Structure of the Book

This book is an academic project, but it also has a personal dimension. Like many Israelis, I was shocked but not surprised by the assassination. As a student of the postcolonial era, I knew that Israel's separation from the occupied territories would entail violence. I told this to Rabin in one of our talks, as I expressed concern about the tactics he was using in his information campaign. In their desire to sell the Oslo Accords to the Israel public, he and Shimon Peres used the argument that the agreement would reduce Palestinian terrorism. This was not only an erroneous historical assessment, but also a political mistake. The history of colonialism teaches that as the hour of agreement and separation draws near, violence increases. This is the moment when the extremist opponents of the agreement realize that the twelfth hour is at hand, and the only thing that remains to prevent its realization is the escalation of terrorism. This happened in Algeria: in the last months of the war in 1962, the OAS (Organisation de l'Armée), which had attempted to prevent the Evian agreements, killed three times the number of people killed by the FLN (Front de Libération Nationale) in the seven previous years of war. "You must not promise a drop in terrorism, because it will increase and will include terrorism of Jews against Jews," I told Rabin. He did not like these words.[11]

At the time, I expected not just a wave of Muslim terrorism, but also Jewish vigilantism; however I believed that Israeli Defense Forces (IDF) soldiers would be the target. I never imagined that Rabin himself would be harmed. What is more, I believed that most of the threats about civil war were part of the brinkmanship intended to deter the government from implementing its policies. I was wrong. I also forgot lessons learned from research about the link between the rhetoric of violence and violent deeds, the cumulative impact of ongoing vilification, and the processes that this creates—dehumanization of the victim and transmuting him from a human being into a symbol (Weisz and Taylor, 1969; Kirkham et al., 1970: 355; Sprinzak, 1995). I even forgot the importance of the word in Jewish culture.

My interest in the assassination—the conditions that led to it and its repercussions—extended beyond scholarly curiosity; it was a kind of therapy, a way to continue my connection with the man I knew and worked with. The close connection between us began when he returned to Israel after serving as ambassador to the United States in 1973. He joined the Labor Party when I was then its spokesperson. Together with my friend Dov Tzamir, a kibbutz member in the Negev, we set up Rabin's campaign headquarters for leading the party after Golda Meir's resignation. After Rabin's election victory, I became his political adviser. Later, when he was prime minister and I was Labor's political representative in Europe, I facilitated meetings with leaders of Social Democratic parties in Europe, Harold Wilson, James Callahan, Willy Brandt, François Mitterand, Olof Palme, Bruno Kreisky, and others.

With the fall of Rabin and the Labor Party government in 1977, I turned my attention to academic research. After completing my doctorate at the London School of Economics, I wrote a book about civil-military relations in Israel (Peri, 1983). Again Rabin played a starring role—as chief of staff who had become prime minister. In the third cycle of our relationship, he was a member of the Knesset, head of the opposition, and later prime minister, and I was editor-in-chief of the daily newspaper *Davar* and president of the Newspaper Editors' Committee. He did not like the criticism that I published in my newspaper—there was a great deal—and he even once canceled his subscription. But it did not affect our personal relationship. In short, my relationship with Rabin evolved in the three spheres of my professional life: politics, journalism, and academia. And at every angle from which I viewed Israeli society, Rabin was at the center of the picture.

This book examines the assassination with the broadest possible lens through writing by the best minds in Israeli political science, sociology, anthropology, history, psychology, communication, and education. Though interdisciplinary, the book is constructed as a unit, with four parts. Part one provides context, with Chapter 1 presenting the story of the assassination from a panoramic, integrated view. It describes Israeli society on the eve of the assassination—the liberal-democratic versus the clerical-nationalist camp, in the context of the peace process and starting the transition from an epoch of war to one of "secular democracy," and the crisis of legitimacy of Israeli democracy. Next, the chapter examines the cultural process of ascribing meaning to the assassination, ending by analyzing the repercussions of the assassination for Israeli democracy and social fabric.

Chapter 2 offers a historical perspective of the Rabin assassination by sociologist Nachman Ben-Yehuda, author of *Jews Killing Jews* (1995). This chapter places the assassination of Rabin into the context of almost 100 political assassinations carried out by Jews through 100 years of modern Zionist history. A more specific chronology is provided in Chapter 3 by Ehud Sprinzak, a political scientist and an expert on right-wing extremism in Israel. He reviews the processes that led up to the assassination among extremist groups.

Part two of the book examines how Israeli society grappled with the assassination, opening with a chapter by psychologist Israel Orbach, who sees Rabin's assassination as an expression of the Israeli suicide wish, a traumatic crisis that is a delayed reaction to the Holocaust. This is followed by analyses of how three sectors in Israeli society responded to the event. Avi Ravitsky, a professor of Jewish philosophy, trains his lens on the religious community and the three stages of trauma it felt at the assassination. In Chapter 6, political sociologist Majid Al-Haj looks at the response of Israeli Arab citizens to the assassination, their efforts to demonstrate membership in Israeli society, and how these efforts were received. Chapter 7, which I wrote, examines the role of the media in the first week after the assassination and their centrality in creating the political ritual and the myth of Rabin, used by hegemonic elites to forge the collective Israeli identity.

Part three has a more anthropological orientation. In Chapter 8, Tamar Rapoport scrutinizes the reaction of young Israelis, particularly the gap between the image of how young people reacted to the assassination and what really took place. Anthropologist Haim Hazan takes this one step further in Chapter 9, grappling with the dilemmas of the Zionist ethos and the process of globalizing this ethos through mourning patterns. The patterns described by Hazan are directly related to the work of psychologists Witztum and Malkinson, who examine in Chapter 10 the cultural and social construction of mourning patterns after Rabin's death.

The commemoration of Rabin was characterized by a profusion of visual devices from popular culture. Stickers in unprecedented variety and numbers are examined by media observer Linda-Renée Bloch in Chapter 11. This is followed by an analysis by Barbie Zelizer, author of *Covering the Body: The Kennedy Assassination, the Media and the Shaping of Collective Memory* (1992), who examines the frames used by the U.S. media when covering the Rabin assassination, and asks why they drew a comparison with the Kennedy killing. Her study adds to the theoretical research about how journalistic needs affect the coverage of dramatic events.

The three final chapters, in part four, though rooted in the past, look toward the future of Israeli society. In Chapter 13, political scientist Tamar Hermann and sociologist Ephraim Yuchtman-Yaar make a quantitative contribution to the anthology, presenting survey data about the attitudes of Israelis before and after the assassination toward violent political protest. In Chapter 14 sociologist Gadi Yatziv examines the assassination in the context of the "last moment"—Rabin's peacemaking activity at the close of an era marked by modernity and enlightened rationalism, before the discursive communication is replaced by the new, postmodern, and derationalized discourse. And in the final chapter, I consider the problematic nature of commemorating and canonizing Rabin in a deeply divided society, and an era when the metanarrative fails.

This is the place to thank the many people who helped me in the preparation of this book. Special thanks are due to my students in the Department of Communication at Hebrew University Jerusalem, who took part in three seminars and assisted me in my research. I am indebted to my colleagues in the department, especially Professors Elihu Katz and Tamar Liebes, for their helpful comments on the manuscript. Several chapters were read by other colleagues in the Faculty of Social Sciences, and I thank them for their comments. Some of the chapters benefited from careful scrutiny by experts in the field in other universities, including Barry Schwartz of Georgia University, who commented on the chapter dealing with the collective memory of Rabin, and Abraham Cordova of Tel Aviv University, a real intellectual and a friend, who contributed many ideas. Thanks are due to the Smart Institute affiliated with the Hebrew University Communication Department, the Truman Institute for the Advancement of Peace, and the Research Committee of the Social Sciences Faculty, headed by Shmuel Zamir, for their assistance in funding the research and production of the book. Gratitude is due to all of these, but none of them is responsible for the final text. An earlier version of Chapter 7 (on myths and the media) was

published in the *European Journal of Communication* in 1997. The deepest
debt of all I owe to my wife, Pnina, and my children, Daphne, Jonathan,
and Alma, who continue to pay the price of the long hours devoted to my
work.

The assassination of Rabin was neither an integrative nor a transformative factor in Israeli society. On the contrary, this event brought to light
how deeply riven the society is. Political assassinations are an expression of
the high level of delegitimacy of the democratic order. The future level of
political violence in Israel will depend largely upon whether this segmented
society will be capable of developing a new pattern of integration. As long
as the national debate rages about the future of the occupied territories and
the fate of peace—a debate that reflects the deep schism regarding the desired collective identity—it is doubtful that a new integrative pattern will
emerge that is democratic and pluralistic. Indeed, several of the authors
note the increased probability of another political assassination, now that a
precedent exists. Thus, the memory of Rabin will also remain a memory
that divides rather than unites. But the collective memory continuously
raises details from the past and erases others, tries on new forms and rear-
ranges the old forms of events, places, and people. And if, in this constant
state of flux, we cannot know the past, can we presume to know the future?

Notes

1. Similarly, Tamar Elor sees the assassination as "killing for the honor of the
family." This is murder that takes place among traditional Arab societies, whereby
the father or one of the bothers kills the daughter or sister whose sexual behavior
was considered to be inappropriate and to bring disgrace upon the family (see
Meimad, vol. 13, 1998).

2. See the annual reports of various monitoring agencies, such as B'Tselem,
Law Enforcement Vis-a-vis Israeli Civilians in the Occupied Territories, Jerusalem,
March 1994.

3. A list of quotations that make the analogy has been compiled by Akiva Eldar,
Ha'aretz, October 24, 1996.

4. My thanks to Yaron Ezrachi for his original contribution to this subject.
On the use of the Holocaust, see Yehuda Elkana, "Thanks to the Forgetting,"
Ha'aretz, March 2, 1988.

5. According to B'Tselem, The Israeli information center for human rights in
the occupied territories, 133 Palestinians were killed by Israeli civilians between the
beginning of the intifada in 1987 and 1997. See B'Tselem Report of January 1998,
Jerusalem. On violence in Israeli society see, for example, Lehman-Wilzig (1983)
on the high frequency of protest activity; Kimmerling (1995) on militarism in civil

life; and also Hermann and Yuchtman-Yaar in Chapter 13 on the attitude of Israelis toward violence. Only in recent years did the realization begin to dawn that there are violent elements in Israeli society, but many perceived that revelation as part of the process of myth-shattering, a reflection of the self-loathing of academics, intellectuals, and "left-wingers."

6. The report was given to Rabin by his personal survey researcher, Kalman Gaier. Personal communication from Kalman Gaier, July 1996.

7. From a presentation at the first international conference of the Rabin Center for the Study of Israel, "The Modern State and Political Assassination," Tel Aviv University, March 1997.

8. The transcription of Yigal Amir's interrogation by the police, December 25, 1995, p. 89.

9. The analysis of escalation resembles the analysis of the mechanism of habituation made by Breznitz in the lecture cited in note 7. Repetition of the same message (that serious violence might erupt) transformed the information into background noise to which no attention is paid. To this was added the principle of gradualism: because the symptoms appeared gradually, there was no sense of deterioration until everything suddenly appeared to be tottering at the abyss, but by then it was too late.

10. On the distinction between social memory and collective memory, see Chapter 18 and also Zelizer (1995).

11. Chilling evidence of this principle, in exactly the same language, appeared in the second week of August 1997 in the deliberations of the Truth and Reconciliation Committee in South Africa. The white extremists who murdered Chris Hanny, the black Communist Party leader, admitted that the 1993 murder had been intended to sow havoc that would thwart the democratic transmutation in their country.

References

Anderson, Benedict (1987). *Imagined Communities*. London: Verso.

Aquinas, Thomas (1985). *De Regimine Principum*. Bk. I, Chap. 6 (cited in Ford, p. 125).

Aronoff, Myron (1989). *Israeli Vision and Division*. New Brunswick, N.J.: Transaction.

Ben-Yehuda, Nachman (1993). *Political Assassination by Jews: A Rhetoric Device for Justice*. Albany: State University of New York Press.

Berlin, Isaiah (1980). *Personal Impressions*. London: Hogarth.

Bourdieu, Pierre (1993). *The Field of Cultural Production*. Cambridge: Polity.

B'Tselem, the Israeli Information Center for Human Rights in the Occupied Territories (1994). *Law Enforcement Vis-a-vis Israeli Civilians in the Occupied Territories*, Jerusalem. March.

Clutterbuck, R. (1981). *The Media and Political Violence*. London: Macmillan.

Crotty, William J. (1971). *Assassination and the Political Order*. New York: Harper and Row.

Eliade, Mircea (1957, 1959). *The Sacred and the Profane*. New York: Harper and Row.

Ford, Franklin L. (1985). *Political Murder: From Tyrannicide to Terrorism*. Cambridge, Mass.: Harvard University Press.

Galnoor, Itzhak (1996). "The Crisis of the Israeli Political System: The Parties as the Central Factor." In Moshe Lissak and Baruch Kne-paz (eds.), *Israel Towards the Year 2000*. Jerusalem: Magnes, pp. 144–76 [Hebrew].

George, David (1988). "Distinguishing Classical Tyrannicide from Modern Terrorism." *Review of Politics* 50, no. 3: 390–419.

Girard, Rene (1977). *Violence and the Sacred*. Baltimore: Johns Hopkins Unviversity Press.

Hobsbaum, Eric, and Terence Ranger (eds.) (1983). *The Invention of Tradition*. Cambridge: Cambridge University Press.

Horowitz, Dan, and Moshe Lissak (1990). *Trouble in Utopia*. Tel-Aviv: Am Oved.

Kimmerling, Baruch (1993). "Militarism in Israeli Society." *Theory and Criticism*, no. 4: 123–40 [Hebrew].

Kirkham, James F., Sheldon G. Levy, and William J. Crotty (1970). *Assassination and Political Violence*. New York: Praeger.

Lehman-Wilzig, Samuel (1983). "The Israeli Protester." *Jerusalem Quarterly*, no. 21: 127–38.

Marvin, Carolyn, and David W. Eangle (1996). "Blood Sacrifice and the Nation: Revisiting Civil Religion." *Journal of the American Academy of Religion* 64, no. 4: 767–80.

Malkinson, Ruth, Robin S. Simon, and Eliezer Witztum (1993). *Loss and Bereavement in Jewish Society in Israel*. Jerusalem: Kana [Hebrew].

Naveh, Eyal (1990). *Crown of Thorns*. New York: New York Unviversity Press.

Ohana, David, and Robert Wistrich (eds.) (1996). *Myth and Memory*. Tel-Aviv: HaKibbutz HaMeu-ad; Jerusalem: Van Leer Institute [Hebrew].

Peres, Yochanan, and Ephraim Yuchtman-Yaar (1992). *Trends in Israeli Democracy*. Boulder, Colo.: Lynne Rienner.

Peri, Y. (1983). *Between Battles and Ballots: Israeli Military in Politics*. Cambridge: Cambridge University Press.

Rothstein D. A. (1996). "Presidential Assassination Syndrome: II. Application to Lee Harvey Oswald." *Archives of General Psychiatry*, no. 15: 260–66.

Shapira, Jonathan (1977). *Israeli Democracy*. Ramat Gan: Massada [Hebrew].

Socarides, C. W. (1982). "Why Sirhan Killed Kennedy: Psycoanalytic Speculations on an Assassination." *Psychoanalytic Inquiry*, no. 2: 133–51.

Sprinzak, Ehud (1995). *Ilelalism in the Israeli Society*. Tel Aviv: Sifriyat Hapoalom [Hebrew].

Turner, Victor (1964). *The Ritual Process*. Chicago: Aldine.

—— (1974). *Dramas, Fields and Metaphors: Symbolic Action in Human Society*. Ithaca, N.Y.: Cornell University Press.

Verba, Sidney (1965). "The Kennedy Assassination and the Nature of Political Commitment." In Bradley S. Greenberg and Edwin B. Parker (eds.), *The Ken-*

nedy Assassination and the American Public. Stanford, Calif.: Stanford University Press, pp. 348–60.

Weinstein, E., and O. Lyerly (1970). "Symbolic Aspects of Presidential Assassination." *Psychiatry* 32, no. 1: 1–11.

Weisz, Alfred, and Robert Taylor (1969). "American Presidential Assassination: The Role of the Social Environment." *Diseases of the Nervous System* 30, no. 11: 659–68.

Wilkinsson, Doris Y. (ed.) (1976). *Social Structure and Assassination Behavior.* Cambridge, Mass.: Schenkman.

Wolfsfeld, Gadi (1991). "Media, Protest and Political Violence." *Journalism Monographs,* no. 127.

Zelizer, Barbie (1992). *Covering the Body: The Kennedy Assassination, the Media and the Shaping of Collective Memory.* Chicago: University of Chicago Press.

PART I

The Road to Rabin Square

CHAPTER I

The Assassination:
Causes, Meaning, Outcomes

YORAM PERI

Causes: The Ecology of Political Violence

Political assassination is a human phenomenon so common that there seems to be no point in asking why it happens. Indeed, scholars prefer to formulate the question differently: Under what conditions does assassination become more frequent? The wave of political violence that swept the United States in the 1960s enriched the literature with speculation. True to the positivist paradigm of the period and the popularity of quantitative studies, Rummel (1963), Tanter (1965), and others searched for correlations between political and other forms of violence, such as guerrilla warfare, revolutions, muggings, or demonstrations (Havens et al., 1970: 12–14). Others examined the correlation between political violence and other social, political, and economic variables: the level of modernization and development, the level of satisfaction with the system, social and economic change, permissiveness or cohesiveness of the regime, the degree of external violence, the status of minorities in the society, the proportion of murders, and even the rate of suicides (see, e.g., Feierabend and Feierabend, 1969).

In light of the modest contribution made by these studies to understanding the phenomenon, qualitative studies were introduced to provide historical perspective and interpretive analysis. Thus links were found between political assassination and a postwar or postcolonial situation, intense social change, revolutionary periods, formative stages of nation-building, and various ecological variables (Kirkham et al., 1970: 172–99; Ford, 1985). Of particular interest are cases in which violence is carried out in the name of religion, nation, or a combination of the two, which corresponds closely with the situation in Israel. To understand how the Rabin assassination evolved, we need to view its historical context.

As Israel approached its fiftieth anniversary, it seemed to be entering a new age, bathed in optimism. The historic reconciliation with the PLO and Palestinians brought about a dramatic change in Israel's international status. It had diplomatic relations with almost ten Arab states, from the Maghreb to the Persian Gulf. Israel had emerged from diplomatic isolation, with the number of Israeli embassies in the world increasing from 100 to 150. The dream of full international recognition, true acceptance into the "family of nations," was about to be realized.

The "peace process" also contributed to unprecedented economic prosperity: annual growth of over 5 percent for five years, a dramatic increase in foreign investment (from $50 million before the Oslo Accords to $2 billion in 1995) and tourism (from fewer than 1½ million visitors in 1992 to over 2½ million in 1995), and a wave of Jewish immigration from Russia added almost a million to a population of 4½ million within only five years, bringing about intense economic activity and raising the GNP to $15,000 per capita in 1995, from $8,000 only ten years earlier.

But beyond the physical, profound social and cultural changes took place. Israel was poised between two periods: the apparent end of the age of war, controlled by a collectivist-religious and nationalist conception, and the dawn of a new age of democratic, liberal individualism (Ezrachi, 1997). It was moving away from being "a pioneering, heroic society" and toward becoming "a consumer and media society" (Ohana and Wistrich, 1996). Almog refers to this new cultural direction as a shift from "the ethos of nation and Zionist homeland" to "the secular rite of capitalist democracy," or a "new national religion" with the emphasis on "democratic faith" that includes "codes of peace, universalism, and cosmopolitanism" (1996).[1] All these are ideal types, of course, but they reflect a process, the beginning of a new Israeli secular identity.

The dawn of a new era and the seeming triumph of the social groups that led it, identified with it, and profited by it, generated dialectical processes among other groups. What appeared to be the decisive victory of one school of thought, "the peace camp," appeared to the "national camp" to be a catastrophe.[2] The political process was significant not just in the relationships between Israel, its Arab neighbors, and the entire world, but above all in shaping the Israeli collective identity. Setting geographic borders also meant resolving issues concerning the social boundaries between the Israeli collective and the "other," defining the nature of that relationship. The integration of Israel regionally and internationally was perceived by the nationalist camp as the loss of particularist Jewish uniqueness and assimilation into a foreign culture. In the historical struggle between opposing schools of Zionism, the universalist, democratic-liberal approach was about to carry the day over the particularist, exclusivist approach supported by the nationalist camp (although we should not forget that the democratic-liberal wing combined universalist principles with a nationalist approach, resulting in a complex view characterized by more internal tension than was produced by the unidimensional exclusivist approach). As the moment of resolution neared for a conflict almost a century old, one option remained that could halt the process with one fell swoop before it reached the point of no return — violence. Political assassination.

Two processes have produced political changes in Israel since the 1970s: political-ideological developments among the religious-nationalist groups, and social developments among the disadvantaged in Israeli society, primarily Mizrahim, who feel a great affinity to religion and tradition. The peace process linked these two developments by arousing antagonism among both populations, thus laying the groundwork for political assassination.

Within the religious camp, the first political change concerned the Israeli-Arab conflict, with the retreat of many from moderate, dovish political views and adoption of militant, hawkish stands (Hayerushalmi, 1997). This has a deep and complex theological grounding, from Rabbi Zevi Judah Kook's interpretation of redemption, the trauma of the Yom Kippur War in 1973, and analysis of the role of this war in the messianic process, through the crisis generated by return of the Sinai Peninsula to Egypt in the early 1980s, following the Camp David accords. This agreement "cut deeply into the view that sanctified the state and its institutions, as they ceased to be redemptive and no longer served to house the divine throne in the world." The surrender of land was regarded as so grave that disobeying orders and actively resisting military evacuation was justified, as long as Jewish blood was not shed (Horowitz, 1996).

In the mystical atmosphere and in a context loaded with symbols and rituals with which to interpret the hostile reality of withdrawal, many in the Zionist-religious camp began to hope that divine intervention would prevent the withdrawal. Among extremist groups such as Gush Emunim, ideas such as martyrdom and suicide appeared, in hopes of shocking heaven. Thus, the "Jewish underground" emerged and even managed to strike at

Palestinians before it was exposed and its members sentenced, and there were plans to explode mosques on Jerusalem's Temple Mount "to gain leverage in the process of redemption."

The alienation of most Israelis from the settlers fostered messianic ideas among some groups that deviated from the original teachings of Rabbi Zevi Judah Kook, which sanctified the state. Rather than affirm the state, some felt alienation from it and denied its legitimacy. As withdrawal began from parts of Judea and Samaria following the signing of the Oslo Accords, it was not surprising that radical groups such as Rabbi Meir Kahane's Kach movement and its offshoots took the next step and began to attack Jews. "Even if not everyone in the Zionist-religious camp goes all the way and is somewhere on the continuum, we cannot ignore the fact that the latent potential of political violence exists within them, i.e., those who follow Rabbi Abraham Isaac Kook [the father]" (Horowitz, 1996).

A second change that affected the religious camp in Israel was the reduction of the autonomy of the political domain, while rabbinical authorities—limited in the past to the realm of Halakha—penetrated daily political life. In the past, the distinction had been clear: Halakha for the rabbis, politics for the politicians. From the 1980s, however, the politicians of the National Religious Party (NRP), who in the past had decided political, even fateful, questions on their own, now deferred to the rabbis, a practice that had hitherto prevailed only among the ultra-Orthodox.

A third change was related to the internal rift that had divided the religious camp since the beginning of Zionism: "religious Zionists" wanted to integrate religious tradition with acknowledging modernity, support for the Zionist movement, and cooperation with secular parties within it; in contrast, the ultra-Orthodox rejected modernity, Zionism, and cooperation with the seculars. These two groups converged when Zionists adopted extremist religious and when the formerly dovish ultra-Orthodox began to internalize hawkish nationalist views. Thus emerged a nationalist ultra-Orthodox alliance.

Another development occurred where the nationalist secular and the religious bloc overlap. During the prestate days of Israel, the religious bloc (with its internal rift) was one of three independent camps in the consociational structure—the other two being the Labor movement and the right-wing camp—and it was more aligned with Labor. From the 1970s on, however, the religious drew closer to the right-wing nationalist bloc to the extent that in the 1990s, on issues of foreign policy and security as well as definition of the collective identity, there were two dominant blocs instead of three. Counterpoised to the liberal-democratic peace camp was an integrated political-ideological religious-right sector—the clerical-nationalist camp. Nationalist and religious ideologies dovetail well in many countries, particularly in Israel. Even secular Israelis define their nationalism in Jewish terms; because modernity did not spawn a civil society in Israel, religion is nostalgically omnipresent even among secular parts of the Israeli collective.[3]

In light of the inherent weakness of the secular camp, reconciliation of the nationalist and religious components created a synergism of political theology with immense internal power. First, the belief in Jewish uniqueness, of being the chosen people, approached and even crossed the lines of racism (such as publication of Halakhic rulings that permit the murder of defenseless citizens if they are Palestinian). Second, a messianic perspective culminated in the "Messiah Now" movement of the Lubavitch ultra-Orthodox.[4] Finally, the Land of Israel was so glorified that it outweighed the sanctity of life or the unity of the people, which had once been perceived among the Orthodox as of equal importance.

The three principles of clerical nationalism generated a pattern erosive of Israeli democracy. The absence of a universalistic component in the definition of modern Judaism opened the door to a xenophobic, fascist, and militaristic conception that grants Jews special rules of behavior, indifference to reality, and a free hand to use force.[5] If soul-searching about the use of force had been the identifying feature of Israeliness (Peri, 1996), this restraint seemed to be falling away in the clerical-nationalist camp. The new civil religion that emerged in Israel was anathema to the clerical-nationalist theology, and the peace process that strengthened the secular democratic ethos increased the fear of the clerical-nationalist camp. Peace became enemy number one; the democratic institutions came second.

The clerical-nationalists opposed making peace with the Arabs not only because of the cost in ceding territories, but also because peace would lead to contacts with them and hence to assimilation. "The state of war between us and the Arabs is the hand of divine providence guarding the integrity of the nation," wrote a religious educator from the National Religious Movement (Rubinstein, 1998: 147). Their attack on democracy targeted democratic institutions as well as democratic principles and procedures, placing Halakha above Knesset law and rabbis above elected officials; casting doubt on the legitimacy of a government held in place by Arab votes; excluding Arabs—one-fifth of Israeli citizens—from the Israeli collective; and making explicit that democracy is acceptable as long as it does not interfere with the Jewish character of the state.

As the cultural war escalated, they portrayed parliamentary democracy and the state itself as protagonists and challenged them both. The clerical-nationalists launched a campaign to undermine the foundations of the state and to foster contempt for its symbols and representations—shirking army duty, disrespect for the flag, ignoring the sirens calling for two minutes of silence on Remembrance Day for fallen soldiers, a rabbinical ruling removing from the prayer book the blessing on the state and a special prayer for Independence Day. The legitimacy of the state was undermined in practical ways, not just in rhetoric, especially in the occupied territories, where vigilante groups, paramilitary activity, and Jewish settlers took the law into their own hands.

For its part, the state did not sufficiently challenge these forces. Ineffectual law enforcement mechanisms further subverted state authority and its monopoly on the legitimate use of force.

In the perceptive formulation of Michael Walzer, Israeli politics is total politics and is lacking in secular and pragmatic culture (Walzer, 1998). The extreme system of proportional elections prevented the creation of a mechanism that could ease ideological tension between parties and did not allow the parliament to fulfill its integrative function. In the final analysis, the outcome was much worse than just the weakening of democracy: more than 50 years after its establishment, the work of constituting the state is still incomplete, while the level of stateness has deteriorated (Nettle, 1968), with powerful social groups seeking to sabotage its institutions, laws, constitutional provisions, and symbolic system. Assassinating Yitzhak Rabin meant destroying the signified by killing the signifier.

Three positions held by Rabin in his lifetime placed him on the front line between rival Israeli camps. In 1948 he was the 26-year-old commander of the Palmach unit that attacked the Etzel weapons ship *Altalena* as the crew attempted to unload its cargo against government orders. This was the closest Israel came to a civil war between the left, which controlled the national institutions, and the revisionist right. The "holy cannon" is how David Ben-Gurion referred to the shell that sank the *Altalena*, in the belief that the government had saved the infant democracy from violent takeover by a political military unit that refused to accept the democratic rules of the game. For the nationalists, however, this cursed cannon symbolized the tyranny of the left, which was willing to risk civil war to ensure its continued rule. They could never forgive Rabin for his role at that historic moment (Rabin, 1979: 566–69).

In the mid-1970s, Rabin again headed a rival camp, this time as prime minister, when he signed the interim agreements with Syria and Egypt that, for the first time since 1967, included retreat from the Sinai and part of the Golan. This shock led to the founding of Gush Emunim during Rabin's first term as prime minister (1974–77); the religious-nationalist party underwent an upheaval during this formative period, moving from its alliance with Labor to a nationalist, annexationist, and messianic ideology.

Two decades later, Rabin reached the third stage of his life, as the prime minister who steered Israel through a historic turning point. In contrast to the image of the British monarch in Bagehot's classic description, in Israel the prime minister is a double symbol—head of the executive branch, reflecting the instrumental, political, and party dimension, and also expressive of the symbolic dimension of the state. Rabin was then also the manifest representative of one group, the peace camp, though concurrently the representative of the state and statism. Thus criticism of him was double-barreled—the nationalists versus the peace camp, and antistatist forces versus the icon of the state.

Rabin's alienation from tradition and Jewish symbolism, his antireligious sabra-ness, widened the gap between the camps and in the eyes of the right turned him into a symbol of the secular, Hellenist, non-Jewish Jew—a concept rooted in Jewish collective memory from the Second Jewish Commonwealth and attributed to Jews who prefer the humanistic, universalist culture of Athens over the Jewish particularism of Jerusalem. The man who had symbolized "Mr. Security" for most Israelis was accused of throwing Israel's security to the winds and selling the homeland to foreigners. The road from there to "death to traitors" was short.

The peace policies of the Rabin government evoked opposition not just from the clerical-nationalists but also from the disadvantaged groups, those who come out on the bottom in the process of social distribution of the public goods. Their stand against the peace camp should be seen in the context of the struggle between classes and social strata in Israeli society—competition for control over and distribution of resources, but also for a voice in shaping the collective identity and symbolic order of Israeli society.

The globalization process created two subcultures within each of the societies experiencing it: on the one hand, the have's, who enter the new world order and enjoy the benefits it offers; on the other, the have-not's, who are left out of the political process and enjoy no financial benefit from it. The widening economic gap between the top deciles and those at the bottom is one expression of the split in national societies, and it generates reactions also on the level of political values and beliefs.

"Peace is for rich Ashkenazim" was the succinct language of Knesset member Aryeh Deri, political leader of the Shas Party (*Ha'aretz*, July 28, 1977), thereby linking the political process with social issues. Shas voters and the down-and-outers who support other parties had reservations about Rabin's peace process because of their resentment of the Ashkenazi establishment and its symbolic order. The secular, universalist values of the peace camp are foreign to many of them. Their culture, which emphasizes Jewish traditional values and the ethnic basis of collective identity, brings them closer to the nationalist camp. To them, peace seems to serve the economic interests of the well-heeled elite that does business with the Arab world. Peace is perceived as something cold and alienating, like democracy in general. In this sense, the reaction of the low-strata Mizrahim to events in Israel resembles what all liberal democracies are grappling with at the turn of the twentieth century. The cold, rational, and individualist values of the "internationalists" do not speak to the gut or the heart; nor are they capable of providing the warmth and security of the community, especially one based on religion (Hermann and Yuchtman-Yaar, 1997).

The uneasiness of the have-nots in Israeli society explains their political protest. Whichever model of protest is adopted, it is clear that the exclusion of these social groups intensified their denial of legitimacy to the entire social order and even led to violence.[6] The link between the lower class and the willingness to use political violence has been examined in the past (Kirkham et al., 1970: 512–14) and lately also in Israel (Hermann and Yuchtman-Yaar, 1997, chap. 13). As we shall see, it is no coincidence that Rabin's assassin came from the ranks of a marginalized Mizrahi group, which merges the political with the class struggle. For these people, Rabin was the focus of all negative references.

To the combination of the two factors—the crystallization of the clerical-nationalist world view that delegitimized the democratic order, and the deep sense of deprivation and anger of the "have-nots"—a third factor was added, all three together creating fertile ground for an attempted assassination. The third variable in the ecology of the assassination is the normative sanctioning of violence in Israeli society. Even though in its false collective consciousness Israeli society perceives itself as not violent, violence is legitimized. There is an indulgent, normative attitude toward the use of violence as a political tactic in public space (Lehman-Wilzig, 1983) and tacit approval of a high level of illegalism and disregard for laws (Sprinzak, 1995). Discourse in Israel is violent. This is the style of debate in the Knesset and on television, and this is the cause for the extremely high accident rate on the roads.

The ongoing occupation further legitimized the use of violence on the national level, and the equanimity with which the government accepted violence against Palestinian inhabitants of the territories—failing to bring offenders to trial or pardoning many—only added to this. Among certain social groups for whom religiosity is the most salient characteristic, political violence is not a negative value at all. Some of the influential rabbis among the settlers in the territories even published learned essays and books clearly implying that killing of non-Jews is a meritorious act. The book *Baruch HaGever* [a play on words: "baruch," meaning "blessed," was the name of the man, Baruch Goldstein, who cold-bloodedly murdered a group of Palestinians while they were praying], thousands of copies of which were distributed in the territories; it included, among others, an article by Rabbi Ido Elbah, "Clarification of the Laws Concerning the Killing of Gentiles," and this is just one example. Thus it was only natural that the prime minister, who represents the social order more than anyone, would be the victim of someone who wishes to overturn it.

A Search for Meaning

Political assassination, like death on the battlefield, cannot pass unremarked but demands the bestowal of meaning. Bestowing meaning upon assassination is vital not only for solving questions of theodicy but also because of social needs of the collective, without which its confidence in social cohesion and the existence of society as such are undermined. Thus, in a society in which God cannot supply meaning, profanization develops and death is justified in secular terms as something that promotes its modern, national goals (Sivan, 1991: 197).

Political assassination is traumatic and will always be accompanied by intense preoccupation with the question of its meaning: "In pagan and archaic societies, the death of kings was perceived as the death of gods, and this was perceived as part of the cyclical cosmic order. Death also expressed birth and was necessary to ensure continuity. Without the 'death' of the moon, it could not be reborn. Just as death is part of the cosmic order, so too is the death of leaders" (Naveh, 1997). In modern society, the pattern of secular martyrology developed. Thus Lincoln became a martyr in heralding the justice of freeing the slaves and uniting the country; Indira Gandhi a martyr of democracy; John F. Kennedy a martyr of the younger generation who wished to create a more just and free society. Myths constructed around the victims give meaning to their murder and lead to their canonization.

As soon as the assassination was announced, the mass media in Israel and especially television, the high priests of modern culture, began to address the question of its meaning. The interpretation of the assassination—a grasp of what happened, why it happened, and what it meant—was done through choice of a "media frames." This is "a central organizing idea for making sense of relevant events and suggesting what is at issue" (Gamson, 1989: 35).

From the first broadcast and throughout the coming days, one could discern the semiotic struggle over shaping the canonical narrative of the event, constructing its authorized interpretation. It was done by preferring one of several media frames: "incitement," which claimed that the assassination was the result of ongoing provocation against Rabin; "religious incentive," which saw the assassination as a product of religious education and membership in a religious community; "extremism," in which the assassination was the fruit of extremist groups; "insanity," in which the deed was carried out by a lone, crazed individual; or "security failure," which highlighted the failure of the security forces and even accused them of having perpetrated the assassination (Wolfsfeld, 1996).

The media in Israel preferred the incitement frame, as Wolfsfeld explains, because this was the most convenient context (for the U.S. media, see Zelizer's analysis in this volume). The advantage of this frame for the general public was that it most closely conformed to the climate that prevailed before the assassination, the atmosphere of deep political rift.[7]

Another way in which meaning was attributed to the assassination was through ontological definition of the victim. Whereas the above frames deal with the question of *why* Rabin was killed, this asks *who* was killed. Content analysis of the public discourse in the Israeli media in the first year following the assassination reveals five different answers to this question: (1) the victim was a Jew killed by a Jew; (2) Rabin was the victim of a political assassination; (3) the person killed was the prime minister; (4) the murdered man was an individual named Yitzhak Rabin, killed by Yigal Amir; and (5) Yitzak Rabin was an ordinary murder victim.[8]

The first context—the killing of a Jew by another Jew—was the most prevalent among the religious camp and slightly less so among the nationalist camp. It almost ignored the political dimension of the assassination and condemned the deed as contravening the spirit of Judaism. This analysis also appeared frequently among spokespersons for the nationalist camp, which condemned the deed for causing a rift in the nation—not so much because it opposed the principles of democratic rule, but because it harmed the national organism. Hence, those who evoked this framework often raised historical examples of civil war, especially the schism in the Jewish community before the destruction of the Second Temple in ancient times.

Spokespersons for the nationalist camp also frequently described the assassination according to the second framework—as a political assassination in conflict with democratic principles: in societies that use the electoral process and abide by majority rule, decisions should be made at the ballot box, not with the a gun. This context also served many in the peace camp.

The third context noted that the murder victim was not only a political personage, but one who stood at the helm of a political system. Every political murder is forbidden, especially of one who heads and symbolizes a state. The fact that Rabin had also been defense minister only reinforced this image—security, more than anything else, epitomizing statism (Giddens, 1985).

The fourth context highlights Rabin's special personality. Murder of a prime minister is a heinous act, but Rabin's murder was even more serious because of what he represented. This context presented Rabin's life and image as the epitome of the values and symbolic order that the assassination sought to bring down. Naturally this context was used primarily by Rabin's colleagues in the Labor movement and by his partners to the Zionist perspective.

The final context, which views Rabin's assassination as a murder like any other, is completely different from the others, with its intent to deny its significance and singularity. Equating this to a routine murder was a way to take exception to the angry public reaction to the assassination and sometimes camouflaged support for the assassin and understanding of his motives. In the final analysis, the very choice of the context in which to describe the assassination of Rabin constituted a political strategy in the semiotic struggle between different interpretive communities.

But there was another avenue for the semiotic struggle. This can be illuminated by Louis Althusser's concept of *"problematique"* (1970: 45–47, 67–69). What is the theoretical or ideological context in which the discourse of the assassination took place? How has meaning been attributed to it by setting it within a certain social universe of content?[9] According to Althusser, the *problematique* can be revealed by a "sympathetic" or "diagnostic reading," used by Freud to understand the utterances of his patients. In the case of Rabin's assassination, the *problematique* was created by identifying the killing with other political assassinations in history. Comparing one event with another assumes that both have a common denominator. By raising the *problematique* of the previous event, a context or ideological space is created that dictates what can be seen and identified in the new case, and how to interpret and understand it. This comparison need not be open or explicit; it may be an obscure manipulation intended to probe something deep in the collective memory, to arouse conditioned associative stimuli, to create a feeling or atmosphere that will determine the attitudes of the listener toward the new killing.

The assassination of Yitzhak Rabin was compared to a great many other assassinations in history: more than a dozen and a half were cited, and half a dozen were given frequent public mention, especially in the media. The most frequent image evoked was the assassination of Kennedy, and it is easy to see why: Many Israelis still remember and can directly relate to that assassination; like the Kennedy assassination in the United States, the Rabin assassination was the first televised assassination in Israel. Rabin himself was compared to Kennedy more than once, though the Israeli prime minister was politically and even dispositionally closer to Republicans like Richard Nixon in his views and style (Peri, 1996).

Another political killing that was compared to the Rabin assassination was that of President Abraham Lincoln in 1865. The *problematique* of that assassination was the Civil War, the deep division in American society, with the head of state leading the nation to a military resolution, followed by a process of healing. As with Kennedy, the differences between Rabin and Lincoln are considerable, but those who saw a resemblance believed and hoped that, as with Lincoln, the assassination would move Israel toward canonization of the leader's image and habitus (Ofer Shelah, *Ma'ariv*, October 18, 1996).[10]

Another *problematique*, related to questions of nationalism, national minorities, and undermining consensus on democratic norms, emerged in comparisons with European leaders who were assassinated between the two world wars. The 1920s saw a rash of political violence and assassinations of political leaders, but the ones most frequently referred to were of Walther Rathenau, the Jewish foreign minister of the Weimar Republic, and Gabriel Narutowicz, socialist president of Poland, both killed in 1922. The historical context was the existence of a strong nationalist movement in an infant, weak, and unstable democracy. The fragility of the democratic fabric, lack of a constitution, sectorization of the education system, intensity of the religious factor in defining the boundaries of the collective, and lack of legitimacy for the state were all part of the context in which these murders evolved. In the case of Narutowicz, special attention was given to the fact that he was elected president of the Sejm by a bloc of minorities in which Jews were the largest group.

The resemblance between Rabin and Rathenau is especially salient. Both underwent a political transformation from hawkish views to support for a realpolitik solution. Both were perceived by the nationalist right to be engaged in the politics of surrender and betrayal. In the case of Rathenau, this was the Rapallo Treaty with the hated Bolsheviks from the east: "In the irrational atmosphere which then prevailed—a glorified, racist, nationalist, utopian, and imaginary past which moved from the margins to the mainstream of the national agenda—an ideological assassination did not appear out of the ordinary (Oded Heilbruner, *Ha'aretz*, December 24, 1995).

Another European mentioned was Jean Jaures, the socialist and humanist French leader who was assassinated in 1914 by the young nationalist Raoul Villain through the window pane of a Paris coffee house. Rabin and Jaures shared a socialist background, but the main commonality was their attitude toward peace: "Jaures struggled valiantly against the rising nationalism of his era in an effort to prevent the first world war, for which he was killed and martyred. Rabin met—and will meet—a similar fate" (Eli Bar-Navi, *Ha'aretz*, November 17, 1995).

Closer to Israeli reality, and hence more transparent, was the assassination of Chaim Arlosoroff. As noted in the introduction, Arlosoroff's assassination was cited by the Likud leader even before Rabin was killed, in the context of what he believed to be a blood libel of the left against the right in the 1930s (e.g., Yoram Hazani, *Nativ*, 1 [1966]: 53–55). After Rabin was killed, spokespersons for the right repeated the accusation of a blood libel, although Arlosoroff's name was evoked more frequently by the left as evidence that only the right uses methods like assassination. Citing Arlosoroff thus raises the opposite *problematique* to that of Kennedy or Lincoln—not the hope for unity, but accusations of violence and divisiveness by the political rival (Aviva Carol, *Shishi*, December 1, 1995).

Divisiveness combined with fanaticism was the *problematique* of another attempted political assassination soon after the birth of the Zionist movement. This was the 1903 attempt on the life of Max Nordau, right-hand man of Theodore Herzl, the founder of Zionism. The perpetrator, Chaim Selig Luban, fired two shots at Nordau, whom he erroneously accused of supporting the idea of settling Jews in Uganda rather than Pales-

tine. The very attempt at assassination—the first in the Zionist movement—in the context of national fanaticism caused a great stir in the new
movement (Shlomo Nakdimon, *Yediot Aharonot*, October 28, 1996). In this
case, the *problematique* is the danger of nationalist extremism.

A comparison with the many assassination attempts on French president Charles De Gaulle, especially in 1961–62, raises another *problematique*.
Here the context was the process of decolonization by France, and the conclusion was that religious fanaticism, political cleavage, and the weakness of
the democratic infrastructure were all secondary to the central issue of a
colonialist situation. Thus the assassination attempts on De Gaulle were
not cited by those who opposed withdrawal and the peace agreements, but
by academics and intellectuals who opposed the continued occupation
(Ariel Merari, *Ma'ariv*, December 1, 1995; Emmanuel Sivan, *Ha'aretz*, September 6, 1996).

Less frequently mentioned were other assassination victims in Middle
Eastern states, with the *problematique* being that peace is not easy to achieve
and entails bloodshed because of the character of the region. This was the
fate of President Anwar Sadat of Egypt in 1981 after he signed the peace
agreement with Israel, and of King Abdullah of Jordan in 1951, following
peace talks with Israel after the War of Independence. The latter comparison, made by King Hussein of Jordan, resonated deeply in the dramatic
epilogue to his eulogy of Rabin, when he expressed his personal wish to be
remembered at his death as one who sought peace. In a similar context the
names of two other "prophets of peace" were mentioned, both killed in
1983—Dr. Issam Sartawi, one of the PLO leaders killed because he called
for recognition of and negotiation with Israel, and Peace Now activist Emil
Gruenzweig, killed by a hand grenade in Jerusalem (Hayim Baram, *Kol
Ha'Ir*, November 10, 1995).

Some surprising biblical comparisons were made by the Ministry of
Education in a pamphlet issued to schools with guidelines for commemorating the first anniversary of Rabin's assassination ("On the Agenda: Yitzhak Rabin: A Year After His Death"). It was a story not familiar to most
nonreligious Israelis. According to Kings II 25: 24, Gedalya Ben Ahikam,
the Jewish governor of the Land of Israel under the Babylonian occupation,
declares, "Fear not to be servants of the Chaldeans, dwell in the land and
serve the king of Babylon; and it shall be well with you." Militants who
objected to Gedalya's peace policies and Ishmael Ben Netanyahu, a scion of
the Jewish royal family, assassinated him. "Following this assassination in
which a Jew arose and killed a Jew in power," explains this Ministry of

Education pamphlet, "the sages declared a fast day for generations to come."

Although the Ministry of Education (under the late Minister Zevulun Hammer of the National Religious Party) had intended to portray the severe reaction of Jewish tradition to the killing of a Jew by another Jew, the very mention of this ancient assassination aroused ire in several quarters. Members of the Association of Secular Humanistic Judaism believed that it minimized the assassination of Rabin (*Journal of the Association of Secular Humanistic Judaism*, December, 1996: 4), and M.K. Ephraim Hoshaya of the Labor Party raised the issue in the Knesset, noting that Gedalya was appointed governor by a foreign power, the Babylonians, making the comparison with Rabin insidious.[11]

And other analogies were drawn. The plethora of comparisons illustrates the many interpretations given to this assassination and the absence of a common universe of political discourse. Various sectors of the Israeli population conduct discourse on different levels, and dialogue between them is difficult, as each asserts the dominance of its *problematique*.

Consequences of the Assassination

The time that has elapsed since the assassination is insufficient to allow for evaluation of its long-term repercussions. Nevertheless, we can already relate to one key issue that preoccupies researchers of political assassination: Did the assassination achieve its ends? What was its impact? Is assassination an effective way to achieve political ends? Opinions on this are divided. On the one hand, one could say, as historian Eli Bar-Navi said at a 1997 symposium: "Caesar's assassination did not prevent the rise of the principate, nor did the killing of William of Orange prevent the independence of the Netherlands. French absolutism survived the killing of Henry III and IV, and Marie-Anne-Charlotte Corday's knife killed Jean Paul Marat in July 1793, but not the Jacobin Revolution" ("The Modern State and Political Assassination," Tel Aviv, March 3, 1997).

But in the late twentieth century didn't the assassination of Salvador Allende in 1973 change the direction of Chile and perhaps even prevent the growth of democratic socialism in Latin America? Most researchers believe that murder does not ultimately change the course of history, but one has the impression that ethical and noble considerations influence that conclusion.

The main difficulties are how to define impact, what variables to choose for measuring the results of assassination. Without delving into the theoretical and comparative debate (for which see Havens et al., 1970; and Ben-Yehuda, this volume), let us here use Ford's useful distinction: "What should by now be clear is that while assassination has generally failed to direct political change into predetermined channels, it has repeatedly demonstrated the capacity for affecting, often in the most drastic fashion, situations which, in the absence of lethal violence, might conceivably have developed very differently" (Ford, 1985: 381). Let us then examine the Rabin assassination according to the following five criteria.

1. IMPACT ON THE PERSONAL LEVEL

The assassination led to a change of prime minister. However, having Shimon Peres step into Rabin's shoes could not be considered a major change. Their policies, despite differences in nuance and style, were identical. It is more interesting to contemplate what would have happened if the assassination had not happened and Rabin rather than Peres had headed the Labor Party in the 1996 elections. Would that have prevented Benjamin Netanyahu from winning the elections?

Speculations of counter-history are complicated, but here is the scenario that seems most feasible to me. Israeli society, divided almost equally between the peace camp and the nationalist camp in the months before the assassination, showed a slight leaning toward Netanyahu, according to public opinion polls; hence this advantage might have remained on election day. The assassination brought about a significant change in the attitudes of the Israeli public, shifting some 20 percent of right-wing voters to parties on the left, primarily Labor.[12] However, the series of terrorist attacks in early 1996 toppled this support and returned most right-wingers to the Likud and other home parties (Liebes and Peri, 1998). There is no reason to assume that these bombings would not have occurred if Rabin had continued as prime minister. Thus it could be argued that if Rabin had been the candidate for prime minister, the level of support for him would also have decreased following the bombings. His leaving the stage did not fundamentally affect the results of the 1996 elections.

2. CHANGES IN THE POLITICAL SYSTEM

Dramatic events have tended to leave their mark on Israel's political system. The Six Day War at the end of the 1960s not only transformed political discourse but led to the emergence of new political movements, the salient examples of which are the settlers of "Gush Emunim" and "Peace Now" on the two sides of the political divide. The Yom Kippur War in 1973, after a delay of some years, brought about the fall of the Labor Government after 33 years in power; and the interim agreement with Egypt in the 1980s resulted in the rise of new parties, such as "Tehiya," which was founded by some members of the Likud and others who opposed withdrawal from Sinai.

In the days immediately following Rabin's assassination, it seemed as if such a dramatic event was bound to generate change. But it did not happen. The old political parties did not change, and new political movements or organizations did not arise, with the sole exception of "Dor Shalem Doresh Shalom" ("an entire generation demands peace"), a peace movement initiated by the "candle children" that took as its leader Yuval Rabin, the unassuming and introverted son of the murdered prime minister. However, this movement has remained fairly marginal, although it conducts certain educational activities.

The assassination of Rabin ignited the two poles that had formed in Israeli society in previous years. But the trauma of the assassination, which drove home to Israelis the intensity of the cultural antagonism, did not lead to retreat from the "latent civil war." After November 1995, many believed that the assassination would lead to catharsis, sobriety, and reconciliation between the rival camps. Indeed, after the assassination, attempts at rapprochement were made between the two camps, including efforts to integrate more Jewish components into the nonreligious Jewish collective identity in formation, but the process came to a halt. The assassination and its lesson fell victim to the overpoliticization of Israeli society.

Before the 1996 elections, hopes to create a political center by separating the right from the extreme right were foiled because of the new electoral system, the direct election of the prime minister. In his battle with his rival from the left, Shimon Peres, the right-wing candidate, Benjamin Netanyahu, needed all the votes of the right and could not forgo even the most extreme members of this camp. It is not surprising therefore that Rabbi Benny Elon, a leader of the "Zo Artzenu" movement, which had organized violent demonstrations against the Rabin government throughout 1996, entered the Knesset on the extremist Moledet list that called for transfer of the Palestinians.

This does not mean that nothing changed in the political system in the 1990s. On the contrary, the administration was replaced twice, once when Netanyahu was elected in place of Shimon Peres in the 1996 elections, and again in 1999, when the left camp headed by Barak replaced the right headed by Netanyahu. In addition, Israel's political system underwent much more far-reaching changes in the 1990s as a result of demographic and cultural processes, but these changes were not related to the assassination and were not a consequence of it.

The growing self-consciousness of the Mizrachi population led them to abandon the Likud, strengthening their own political and social movement, Shas, which became the third largest party in Israel. Similarly, the growth of self awareness among the Palestinian Israelis brought about a new political consolidation around their national parties. In addition, the arrival of almost one million immigrants from the former Soviet Union (amounting to almost 20 percent of Israel's population) changed the cultural equilibrium, invalidated the old "melting pot" pattern of immigrant absorption, and created the infrastructure for a pluralistic, if not multicultural, society. Political reforms, particularly the introduction of primaries and direct election of the prime minister, translated these demographic and cultural changes into the language of politics: in the 1996 elections, the old Israeli elite at the head of the Labor Party was ousted from political power and replaced by a "coalition of minorities," a coalition of social movements that had hitherto been on the periphery of Israeli society. Even when a center-left coalition returned to power following the 1999 elections, the trends of social segmentation and the process of forming a sectarian society, a society composed of fairly closed cultural groups, continued. But, as stated, these processes were not directly connected to Rabin's assassination.

3. SYSTEMIC CHANGES: THE DEEPENING CRISIS OF LEGITIMACY

Political assassination can create such deep social trauma that it wreaks change well beyond the political system. It may bring about social revolution, or even be a factor in the dissolution of the political systems. The expectation of such change, especially in the political discourse, hung in the air in the second week of November 1995: "Israel will never return to what it was," said the national poet Hayim Guri. Instead, it was the change that never happened. At a rally on the first anniversary of the assassination, Yitzhak Rabin's grandson said, addressing his grandfather, "I ask forgiveness from you; a year has passed and nothing has changed." The basic character of Israeli politics as total politics, an ethno-nationalist politics of absolute truths, of the sacred, national honor, and other absolute values, made such a dramatic shift quite difficult.

To cite just one example, the Israeli Arabs who shared the pain of Rabin's assassination (as shown by Al-Haj, this volume) and believed that it would change the exclusive Jewish nature of the Israeli collective have realized that Israeli ethno-nationalism has remained unchanged. No change occurred in the way they were perceived by the Jewish citizens of the state. After the assassination, 59 percent of Israeli Jews believed that the prime minister should be elected by Jews only (*Yediot Aharonot*, October 22, 1996). And when the possibility arose in December 1999 of holding a referendum on the peace treaty with Syria, many Knesset members supported the attitude that only Jewish citizens and not Arabs should be included in the referendum.

If the assassination might have been expected to lead to collective spiritual stock-taking and generate systemic change in at least in two clear areas—the attitude to the democratic rules of the game and the use of political violence—no real change took place in either. In the three years of the Netanyahu government, the campaign to discredit the democratic and constitutional framework continued unabated. It came from both components of the clerical-nationalist camp, the former labeling it as foreign, western, and opposed to the spirit of Judaism, and the latter arguing that the government institutions were controlled by the old elite to serve its needs. Therefore this camp was ready to challenge the very legitimacy of all these institutions: the police, the prosecution, the entire judicial system, the military top echelons, and the civil service—so long as it hurt what they saw as the power base of the leftist camp.

The most clear-cut battle over the democratic and constitutional framework was in fact waged with the judicial system, especially the Supreme Court, the most prominent political and symbolic keeper of the democratic rules in Israel. The religious wing demanded a change in the method of appointing judges in order to strengthen the court's links to Halakha, undermine the constitutional arrangements, and sidestep court decisions through legislation. Calumny of the Supreme Court chief justice was no less intense than the defamation of Rabin before his assassination, and included expressions that could be construed as incitement to murder (*Yated Ne'eman*, August 27, 1996; *HaShavua*, August 23, 1996; also see Shulamit Hareven, *Yediot Aharonot*, August 28, 1996). A year earlier, a reporter from the ultra-Orthodox publication *HaShavua* had asserted that Rabin was "a murderer," "a traitor," and "insane" and that *din rodef* applied to him.

Although the murder of the man whose private body symbolized above all Israel's political body was committed, according to the evidence of the murderer himself, in the name of religion and the nation, after the assassination the attempts to delegitimize the democratic parliamentary game continued, both from religious quarters, claiming that Halakha, the religious law, overrides Knesset law, and from secular nationalists, who perceived the nation as above civil society and the political community. One year after the murder, rabbis (including Druckman and Waldman, expositors of the religious Zionist position) repeated their admonition to soldiers not to evacuate occupied territories, even if this meant disobeying orders. This position gained indirect support from an official decision of the NRP, published on the first anniversary of the assassination, which states that "majority rule is one of the fundamental principles of democracy, but not the only principle. Fundamental ethical and national tenets are also the lifeblood of democratic society" (*HaTzofeh*, October 24, 1996).

The moderate religious group Oz VeShalom/Netivot Shalom has warned the public that "placing religious law in conflict with democracy and the government also leads to public sacrilege . . . as if the prime minister were not murdered because of distorted religious thinking" (leaflet, February 2, 1997), but this view was limited to a small section of the religious public. A survey of religious adults described a situation of conflict between religious law and the laws of the land: only 39 percent responded that the laws of the land must be obeyed, 32 percent said they would abide by religious law, and about one-third did not respond (*Meimad*, no. 24, December–January 1996). Michael Walzer put his finger on the source of the weakness in Israeli democracy when he suggested that "politics without God" be instituted (*New Yorker*, November 20, 1995, p. 8).

The second vector in the parallelogram of power that continued to deplete the Israeli democracy was related, not to the religious camp, but in fact to the secular. The hair's breadth success of Netanyahu's government in 1996 (Netanyahu won the premiership by a majority of 14,729 votes) was perceived by half of Israeli society in terms of "Have you killed and also taken possession?" (I Kings 21: 19). A cartoon in the Tel Aviv weekly *Ha'Ir* captured the change cynically, showing the king from a deck of cards—pictures of Rabin and Peres, the two defeated kings, in the two lower corners, and Netanyahu and Yigal Amir, the victorious kings, in the upper (May 31, 1996).

Netanyahu himself did not use the strategy of national reconciliation and uniting the nation; he continued to strengthen his camp by exacerbating the contention between the two camps, using the methods of the negative campaign. The criticism, even hatred, that was felt toward him by those who had not voted for him enabled him to argue that the left refused to come to terms with the verdict of the electorate and conducted an anti-democratic campaign of discreditation against him. The tele-populist style of Netanyahu's government and his battle in the name of "the people" against the elite groups and what he called "their control of the state machinery" further undermined the democratic game. This was a novel phenomenon: if before the assassination there had been some who questioned the legitimacy of the political institutions in the name of religion, now the legitimacy of the system was being challenged by the man at the heart of the regime, its actual head.

As with democratic principles, so too with repect to political violence, no real change took place. The recognition of how far political violence could go put the subject at the head of the agenda of public debate for many months. Immediately after the assassination, a campaign against violence, political violence in particular, was launched in Israel. Within a few months it became clear, however, that the assassination had little impact. The style of political debate did not alter, and perhaps became even more fierce: a year and a half after the assassination, Knesset Speaker Dan Tichon expressed concern for the fate of the government itself, noting that "the Knesset has crossed the red line. . . . One who calls the prime minister crazy or an alien subverts the democratic order" (*Ha'aretz*, August 18, 1997). Even views in support of political violence were again heard publicly, and as the first anniversary of the assassination rolled around, the existence of a Yigal Amir fan club was exposed. A special commission appointed by the Ministry of Education found this phenomenon to be fairly pervasive in religious schools.[13] Similar findings appeared in public opinion polls reported in the press (e.g., *Kol Ha'Ir*, December 6, 1996).

Particularly striking were threats against the lives of several public figures, including prime ministers Netanyahu and later Ehud Barak. In one case, a plot was exposed to murder former prime minister Shimon Peres while he was traveling abroad. This revelation was received in Israel without public turbulence, governmental condemnation, or parliamentary reaction. A wave of death threats from religious groups against Aharon Barak, chief justice of the Supreme Court, led to increased security around him, other justices, and the courts. In August 1998, an envelope containing a rifle bullet was sent to a judge and threats against the lives of judges increased. A senior security official noted that never before had the security services accumulated warnings in such quantity or severity (*Yediot Aharonot*, October 20, 1996). Israeli society seemed to be reconciling itself to a high level of violence.

Political violence, at least in its verbal manifestations, did not abate, and the prestige of the security forces, already undermined by their failure to protect Rabin, remained tarnished. The security forces' failure was the main issue investigated by the state commission of inquiry into the assassination, and the damage was compounded by the exposure of internal weaknesses in the security system and the traumatic resignation of many of its leaders. The revelation that Avishai Raviv, one of the leaders of the extreme right and friend of assassin Yigal Amir, was an agent of the General Security Services further undermined people's trust in the institution, particularly in the nationalist camp.

After the assassination, the security services reorganized and they adjusted the way they protected political figures. In the past, the open and informal character of Israeli society had enabled unmediated contact between the public and its leaders. Ministers, even the prime minister, could walk freely in public and were accessible to passers-by. After November 1995, ministers were cordoned off by security people even in closed places like the Knesset, and a ring of security guards around them denied all access to them in public places. Concerns about assassination were so great that when Prime Minister Netanyahu visited military bases, the soldiers were required to unload their guns.

4. CHANGES IN THE COLLECTIVE CONSCIOUSNESS

Political crises may bring about collective agitation and create a new ethical vector, the way the Watergate crisis in Washington created public effervescence that led to a post-Watergate morality.[14] An analysis of the academic and intellectual discourse and its manifestations in art reveals that, at least among the reading classes, the insight was growing that evil was also anchored in the Israeli psyche. The fact that the assassin came from within Israeli society is repeatedly cited in many reflexive analyses of the event.

Recognition of the fact that the rate of violence in Israeli society is high and that it influences politics undermined a major component in the collective consciousness—belief in the cohesiveness of society, and particularly the pre–November 1995 belief in the strength and stability of Israeli democracy. The self-image of a homogeneous, democratic, and internally strong society marked by internal cohesiveness gave way to the recognition that Israel has a fragmented and weak social fabric, and that the foundations of the democracy are rather fragile.

Although the trauma of Rabin's assassination was expected by some to turn the tide of violence in Israeli society, the opposite seems to have occurred—an echoing effect as in Finland in the early 1900s (Auttila, 1976). There is a sense that the ice of political assassination has been broken and that the first assassination will not be the last. Indeed, in 1996 the media discussed "the profile of the next assassin" and who the next victim would be (*Yediot Aharonot*, September 22, 1996).

For some, the assassination was reality's cruel slap in the face of the false collective consciousness. It enabled them to reach a more sober understanding of the national character. This was described as a loss of innocence for many and a deep spiritual crisis. In the harsh words of philosopher Asa Kasher at an international conference on political assassinations (March 3, 1996): "We thought that we were on another moral plane, and we realized that we were not. . . . The assassination broke down the shame barrier of Israeli society. It did not delineate the red lines that must never be crossed, but rather the opposite—it burst the dam. Now there is no self-restraint, but rather an absence of shame."

But even those who did not fear continued violence were aware that Israeli society had deteriorated. Added to this was the growing tension between the two political camps during the period of the Netanyahu government and a long list of flaws in the administration of the state during this period. The growing power of the religious camp, for example, increased the secular society's sense of suffocation. The new social chasm that had formed, this time between the ultra-Orthodox Mizrahi population of Shas and the immigrants from the former Soviet Union, was another expression of the demoralized social situation. After the electoral loss of 1996 and during the period of Netanyahu's government, the feeling in Rabin's political camp and among the old elite could be summed up in the words of Rabin's assistant, Shimon Sheves, on the night of the assassination: "the state is finished."

But it was not just the disappointment of those who had lost the elections. The sense that the seams of Israeli society were coming apart deepened in all the political camps. In a Gallup poll in summer 1998, 62 percent of the Israelis thought that the division between the various social groups had grown, only

6 percent believed that it had decreased, and 25 percent estimated that there had been no change (*Ma'ariv*, August 7, 1998). This figure repeated a trend that has been marked since the 1996 elections.

In fact, since the beginning of the Oslo process Israeli society has been sunk in a long twilight. Half of the nation believes that this is the light of dawn, heralding a new day, and the other half is convinced that it is dusk. After Rabin's murder and the elections—the two sides swapped angles of vision. Their differences were not just over policy, but over the whole nature of the social order and the collective identity, and the reactions of the losing side were extreme. Whereas before the 1996 elections the nationalist camp had responded with political mobilization and violence, the reaction of the left after these elections was despair and helplessness; some even spoke of "internal emigration."

Within three years the situation was reversed again. Flaws in the Netanyahu administration, effective political organization of the left camp and disappointment among the new population—the Russian speaking immigrants—with the government's treatment of their affairs returned the left to power. Now the smile returned to the faces of its supporters while the supporters of the right were filled with gloom.

5. IMPACT ON PEACE POLICY

But in the end the key question remains—the assassination and peace. Since the primary goal of the assassin was to halt the peace process, which entailed withdrawal from occupied territories, what, in fact, was the effect of the assassination on this process? Over Rabin's grave members of his political camp swore to fulfill his testament: "With his death he bequeathed us peace." But the wave of terror strikes in the first half of 1996 and Shimon Peres's peace policy, which was perceived as conceding too much, brought the government down in 1996. Benjamin Netanyahu, the representative of the camp that opposed the Oslo Accords, now took the wheel. But during the next three years he encountered powerful processes that demonstrated once more the truth of the old saying about the irony of history.

Netanyahu's government was torn between two opposing poles: one pole is the ideology that does not believe that Israel can live in peace with its Arab neighbors in the foreseeable future, that in fact rejects recognition of the PLO and refuses to give up parts of the beloved homeland. The other pole is the public's weariness with ongoing war and its desire to end it, added to powerful international and global forces, above all American policy, pushing the wagon of peace forward and forcing Israel's prime minister to climb aboard against his will. Throughout his three years in office, Netanyahu's policy was to maneuver between these two poles, veering now one way now the other, according to the forces operating at any given moment.

From this point of view it may be argued that the assassination succeeded to a certain extent. It blocked what the right called "the mad rush to peace" of Rabin and Peres, ushered in a government whose approach was much colder and more reserved toward the peace process, or in Netanyahu's words, "a government that does not abandon security on the way to peace." But Netanyahu's zig-zag policy finally led to his fall after he signed in November 1998 the Wye agreement, which included further withdrawals. When he saw the extent of the opposition to it among his own supporters, Netanyahu retracted on his commitment. In doing this, he roused against him the supporters of the peace process, both in Israel and abroad, while on the other hand he had already lost the support of the opponents of the peace process who had put him in power. These voted no-confidence in the government and brought him down. The center-left government that followed, headed by Ehud Barak, came in on a ticket of fulfilling Rabin's testament, and the peace process took on new impetus. The assassination thus resulted in the slowing down of the peace process and stalled it for a while, but in the end did not bring it to a halt.

This description of the process largely matches the attitude of the Israeli public toward peace. The Peace Index—a series of public opinion surveys carried out periodically by the Tami Steinmetz Center for Peace Research in Tel-Aviv—indicates that there has been no change in the long run. After the assassination, support for the peace process increased sharply, but this gradually and steadily declined thereafter until stabilizing more or less where it had been before the assassination. During 1995, the level of support for the peace process was between 50 and 60 percent. On December 8, a special survey held immediately after the assassination measured the level of support at 73.1 percent; by the end of the month it had fallen to 65.7 percent; and during 1996 it fluctuated above 60 percent. In December 1999, it was 62.4 percent. Similar patterns emerge for other related questions, such as the belief that a comprehensive peace agreement can be reached with the Palestinians (rising from 43.3 percent to 64.6 percent after the assassination and later leveling off at about 50 percent and 54 percent in December 1999). Since the assassination the split between the ideological camps has deepened, with religious background and political views being the most significant factors. While 78 percent of Israelis who define themselves as nonreligious supported the peace process in August 1997, only 43 percent of the self-defined religious and no more than 20 percent of the ultra-Orthodox, supported it.

Support for peace is one indicator, the assessment that eventually it will arrive is another. This assessment too, that peace will come, did not change in principle but underwent a regression following the assassination and resettled afterwards. The Oslo Accords and Rabin's policies roused hopes that dissipated to a large extent after the assassination and the elections. Whereas before the assassination over 70 percent of the Israelis thought there was a high or moderate probability that peace would be sustained in the next three years, after the assassination and the elections this rate dropped to approximately 60 percent and in 1998 to 58 percent (Arian, 1998), but in 1999 it went up to the level before the assassination, 68 percent (Arian, 1999). The change in the composition of the government and its policy and the acceleration of the peace process inspired a new assessment that peace would materialize.

But in retrospect it may be argued that the rise of Netanyahu's government and the assassination of Rabin that preceded it not only did not disrupt the peace process but acted dialectically to strengthen it, in total contrast to what the two things were designed to achieve. In the case of Netanyahu, his policy ended up by causing fatal damage to the political camp that raised him to power. The fact that the prime minister who rose to power as representative of the opponents of the Oslo Accords was forced to continue with the implementation of the Accords and defend his policy, which they considered erroneous, actually strengthened the legitimacy of the peace process. Netanyahu, who in the 1996 election campaign portrayed Shimon Peres as collaborating with Arafat, himself met with the latter, shook his hand warmly, spoke of him in positive terms, and signed further agreements with him.

But when Netanyahu signed the Hebron agreements and implemented the withdrawal from the city that he had described as the second most sacred city to the Jews, he destroyed the ground under the feet of his historical party, the bearer of the ideology of the Greater Land of Israel. This was the first time that a right-wing leader in Israel had accepted the principle of dividing the country, the principle over which the two main Zionist movements had been divided throughout the twentieth century. Menahem Begin before him had withdrawn from the Sinai peninsula, which was not perceived by the revisionist camp as an integral part of the Land of Israel. If Netanyahu, the nationalist prime minister, gave up sacred parts of the homeland, what could they say about Rabin in the past, or a future left wing leader, who would pursue the policy of division? Netanyahu's contribution to Israel's history is thus enormous, although the opposite of what he was elected for and what he believed in: under his leadership the Likud lost its political raison d'être—the battle for the Greater Land of Israel, the principle of not dividing the land.

It was not, indeed, by chance that the disappointment with Netanyahu was so deep in the nationalist camp that he was called a traitor, just like Rabin before him. On the eve of the 1999 elections, some of the leaders of his party, headed by Benny Begin, the son of the legendary Likud leader, quit the Likud and founded a new party, more faithful to its historic principles, calling it the National Unity (*Ichud Leumi*) party. But the 1999 election results exposed the crisis of the right in Israel: the Land of Israel Movement lost a substantial part of its public support. The strength of the Likud in the Knesset shrank. The nationalist right won a smaller number of votes than its various components had received before the elections. In the other right-wing parties too, such as the NRP, the more moderate wing was strengthened. Knesset Member Benny Begin himself—who was the prime ministerial candidate on behalf of the extreme right—acknowledged the new reality and resigned from political life. So did Knesset Member Hanan Porat, who in the past was one of the leaders of Gush Emunim and of the NRP.

The irony of history was not only expressed in the fact that the right's ascent to power led dialectically to the expansion of public recognition of the peace process that requires territorial concessions. It also decreased the potential for violence that was liable to be used in order to prevent the accomplishment of the decolonization process. Israeli society has, in fact, become aware that it contains an inner reserve of violence. Expressions of violence in politics, as in other areas of life, have not decreased but have, perhaps, grown. But in relation to the peace process and the fate of the territories, Rabin's assassination had significance that cannot be overestimated: it dealt a fatal blow to the possibility that the Land of Israel zealots will use violent measures to prevent withdrawal.

Soon after Rabin's assassination, when the premiership was still in the hands of Labor, Israel implemented another stage of the agreement and the IDF withdrew from Tulkarm and Qalqilya, two towns in the north of the occupied territories. After the shock of the assassination this withdrawal went almost without any reaction from the nationalist camp. Anyone who remembers the inflamed atmosphere in the streets before the first withdrawal may rightly assume that if the Rabin government had carried out the second withdrawal, violence would have escalated and likely produced bloodshed. But this time, against the background of Rabin's assassination, all the predictions of soldiers' refusing to obey evacuation orders, of settlers' responding to the rabbis' orders and bodily preventing the evacuation, of their provoking Palestinians to a round of bloodshed that would force the government to stop the withdrawal—none of this happened.

The restrained tone, the moderately expressed criticism, and above all the absence of physical violence were repeated once more when the IDF evacuated Hebron, the stronghold of Jewish nationalism in the territories, this time under the administration of the Netanyahu government. And even if the rhetoric against withdrawal continued for the entire term of his government, there was clearly a gap between the words and the deeds. It was enough to warn the hotheads against incitement in order to lower their tone, if not to silence them partly. In fact, the word "incitement" became the strongest weapon of the peace camp in the political debate after 1995. Israel's political culture, which in the past had tolerated very extreme language, continued to do so in every other matter (particularly in the struggle between religious and secular), but could not tolerate such expressions in the context of peace and withdrawal.

When the Barak government continued the withdrawal according to the agreements with the Palestinian Authority, and in the winter of 1999 even dismantled a number of settlements—which had been declared illegal—it all went fairly smoothly. Even the extreme opponents of the evacuation felt the need to make it clear that they would not use illegal violence, and used only passive resistance to oppose the withdrawal. When the Barak government renewed the negotiations with Syria and the battle over public opinion against the withdrawal from the Golan Heights was reopened in the last months of 1999, the opponents of the withdrawal again declared: we will fight this policy, but we will not use illegal methods; we will accept the opinion of the majority, we will not use violence. The very mention of the Rabin assassination served to bind the feet of the nationalist camp.

This was expressed very well by Rabbi Yoel Bin-Nun, a settler from Efrat. This rabbi, who was one of the leaders of Gush Emunim and headed educational institutions of the National Religious camp, underwent a severe personal, spiritual, and political crisis following the assassination. He even accused the rabbis of his camp of giving moral and Halakhic support to the dreadful act. In 1999 he publicly admitted that the battle over the Greater Land of Israel had been ignominiously lost, and that what had caused this more than anything else was Yitzhak Rabin's assassination. "We have resigned ourselves to the historic process, the withdrawal, and what decided the issue was the murder of Yitzhak Rabin," he said. "The vile creature [the assassin, Yigal Amir] does not understand that his gun not only destroyed a person but also the idea of the Greater Land of Israel, because after that there is no possibility of fighting for it. No longer will there be battles (to prevent the withdrawal) like those that preceded the assassination, but only attempts to improve positions" (interview in *Yediot Aharonot*, 19 September, 1999).

This dialectic fact, that the horrifying political assassination in fact served as a barrier to even more severe political violence, does not come as a surprise to sociologists of religion, who are aware of the concept of blood sacrifice ritual, or surrogate victim, totem crisis, and the theory of the leader as a scapegoat (Marvin and Ingle, 1996; Girard, 1977). "A totem crisis occurs when there is uncertainty about the essential borders that demarcate our group, when territorial borders are breached and no longer differentiate Us from Them," write Marvin and Ingle (1996: 774). The Israeli government's signature on the Oslo Accords led to just such a totem crisis in Israel. Peace, and even the process itself, weakened the borders that separate the Israeli collective from the Them, the Palestinians. This happened on the territorial level, but even more on the level of the collective identity. This is the reason why Yitzhak Rabin was described and portrayed by his opponents dressed in Arafat's keffiyah or in SS uniform. The prime minister of Israel, the Israeli who was described as the ultimate sabra, was now blended with the figure of Israel's most terrible enemies throughout history.

A totem crisis, argues Rene Girard (1977: 39—67), constitutes an existential threat to the integrity and cohesiveness of society, and the way this dangerous crisis is dealt with is by blood sacrifice. To resolve totem crisis, the totem must re-create its exclusive killing authority out of the very flesh of its members. And what does successful ritual sacrifice accomplish? "After enough blood-letting, the slate of internal hostilities is wiped clean. The group begins again. The external threat is met. Our bad feelings toward one another are purged. Time begins anew, space is re-consecrated. The group basks for a while in the unanimity of its effort, until internal hostilities accumulate once more" (Marvin and Ingle, 1996: 775).

When the peace process was perceived by half the nation as a real existential threat, creating a totem crisis and brought Israeli society to the verge of civil war, there was a need for ritual sacrifice to stop the outbreak of potential violence. In this situation the person who fills the role of surrogate victim par excellence is the political leader. The sacrifice of the political leader may also take a less extreme form than physical murder, for example surrogate murder—defeat in elections. But when the leader is perceived as himself having helped to create the totem crisis, it may take the physical form of bloody assassination. Such assassination is immediately perceived as an event with ritual significance. The shock and horror it arouses may act at once to restore national unity, reduce violence in society, that same potential violence that might have torn it apart from within. The language used by the Israelis after the assassination in fact revealed this thematic structure: Rabin's death was called a sacrifice, and his blood, which was displayed to the public on a blood-stained piece of paper bearing the words of the Song of Peace, acquired the meaning of the blood of the sacrifice on the altar, thus becoming a political testament—no to violence, yes to peace.

Was the Assassination a Transformative Event?

Not every blood sacrifice, however, succeeds in its ritual role; some imperil rather than consolidate the group bond. In order for the blood ritual sacrifice to really fill the function of uniting the nation and creating cohesion, some conditions must be fulfilled. One of the most important is that the victimage must be unanimous, that there must be collective agreement about it. And this was clearly not the case with Rabin's assassination, neither before nor after it. Therefore, the assassination succeeded in stopping the escalation of political violence in the context of the process of withdrawal and separation from parts of the Land of Israel, but it did not succeed in repairing the internal disunity.

In the liminal interlude in the fall of 1995, hope was kindled that the assassination of Yitzhak Rabin would bring about national unity and create a better society. This was an understandable longing, but not necessarily a logical one. Sidney Verba claims that "crisis may, therefore, have major integrative effects on society or major disintegrative effects. They are likely to reinforce whichever of the two tendencies is stronger in society" (Verba, 1965: 357). Thus, for example, crises in Italy, from the Risorgimento until establishment of the republic after World War II, alienated social groups from the political elite. On the other hand, claims Verba, crises in the United States, especially those related to the institution of the presidency and foreign relations, strengthened integrative trends in that society. Indeed, the crisis following Kennedy's assassination did not lead to anomie, but to a reaffirmation of fundamental values, and this reaffirmation was part of the reintegration of American society.

Like all liberal democracies since the French revolution, Israeli society grapples with the dilemma of how to create a coherent body politic based on a multitude of particularist political wills. Unlike Western societies, Israel must engage in this while it addresses difficult struggles—a solution to the colonialist situation and the need to adapt its collective identity to the new situation upon completion of the first stage of the Zionist revolution. The difficulty is even greater because at this complex historical moment, divisiveness and fragmentation are increasing in Israeli society, strong cultural groups that conduct a politics of identity are solidifying, and integrative mechanisms that were effective in the past are weakening. Politicization of the Rabin assassination and the struggle over the meaning of his memory have intensified rather than muted the factionalism within Israeli society.

Rabin's assassination was not a transformative event, despite the hopes and longings expressed in the transitional phase that followed. Although there were changes in attitudes and behavior during this period, these quickly returned to the status quo ante. The theoretical formulation of Murray Havens and others seemed to be written specifically about the Israeli case. The assassination deeply shocked people, but what happened afterwards was more of a reaction to the shock than to the murder itself: "A high degree of shock and its responses permit a system to absorb the assassination of a leader," but the trauma turns into the ritualistic replacement for systemic change (Havens et al., 1970: 35–36). The fundamental character of Israeli society and democracy, including the existence of an antidemocratic ecology, remained the same after the assassination as it had been before. The assassination exposed the fact that Israeli society is at a crisis in its ability to abide by the rules of democracy at a crucial moment of decision.

This is not the first time that Israeli society has come to a crossroads, or that its ability to abide by constitutional arrangements has faced a challenge. The first time was at the founding of the state during the *Altalena* crisis. This was a twilight zone when the voluntary structures of the prestate period were being replaced by the new institutions of a sovereign state. The debate then revolved around the right of the new government to make decisions that would be binding on all. The crisis was not resolved before the government was compelled to use force—lawful violence—against the opposition. The second time the question arose concerning the stability of the democratic structures was in 1977 when Labor, the dominant party in Israel for 33 years, lost the election, and there was concern that the transfer of power would not be carried out. On that occasion, reality was more benign.

National resolution over the peace issue and the fate of the occupied territories has more explosive potential than the previous cases, because the struggle also has religious dimensions. The current debate is not just about the political issue, but has become a duel over the shaping of the collective identity. In 1948 there was a strong political center of the dominant party; in 1977 the political center rested on two powerful parties; with Israel having passed the half-century mark, a strong centrifugal force is weakening this center and society is becoming more fragmented and segmented.

The literature identifies periods or situations in the lives of societies in which there is a higher potential for political violence. These are postrevolutionary periods, after a war, or postcolonialist situations (Ford, 1985: 383). The common denominator in these conditions is intensified social change at a critical stage of the nation-shaping process. And characteristic of them is the diminished legitimacy of the regime, the political system, and above all the constitutional arrangements.

The crisis of legitimacy in Israel was also intensified by the colonialist condition extant since 1967 and Israel's great difficulty extricating itself from it. If a crisis of legitimacy characterizes all contemporary democracies, Israel is suffering from a double crisis—both late modernization and the colonialist condition. And as in the case of the Fourth Republic in France, the necessary conclusion is that without an end to the second, Israeli society will find it very difficult to emerge from the crisis of legitimacy. Indeed, in the summer of 1998, for the first time in the history of the state the General Security Services' annual report presented to the Cabinet stated, "The continuation of the political process and withdrawal from territories is liable to lead to armed assaults on the government and its institutions" (*Ha'aretz*, July 10, 1998).

The U.S. National Commission on the Causes and Prevention of Violence, established in 1968, stated in its conclusion, "We have not found a specific remedy for assassination and political violence in a democracy apart from the perceived legitimacy of the government and its leaders." This is a necessary, but not a sufficient, condition. The new social reality that has arisen in Israel demands redefinition of the rules of the game that do not match the former sociopolitical structures. In the language of Durkheim, it can be said that "a group becomes a group by agreeing not to disagree about the group-making principle."[15] In Israel this precondition has not yet been achieved; debate still rages about the organizing principles of the collective.

In the last two decades of the twentieth century, the collective Israeli text faded. The classic Zionist master-narrative disintegrated, and a new text, common to all, has not been created. In the past, too, the Israeli meta-narrative was not congruent. The canonical Zionist narrative contains contradictions between the humanistic universalistic dimension and the ethnic-religious particularistic dimension, between Jewishness and democracy. But the power of the canonical discourse and practices used by the elite formed a centripetal force that prevented social fragmentation.

The fact that the Israeli mosaic has become more varied and the identity of the different co-cultural groups has strengthened may mean that a common text will never be created. In that case, the need to recognize pluralism will be even more imperative, the need to recognize the legitimacy of a plurality of voices, of the right of each part of the mosaic to interpret the common narrative in its own way, or even to maintain its own story. The strong groups that still exist in Israeli society are not reconciled to the right of others to their own interpretation. They demand a monopoly over interpretation of the text, even at the price of physically eliminating the others. Thus, agreement about the new rules of the social game appropriate for the new situation is a second condition. Even if that is achieved, internal tensions and contradictions may remain in the Israeli story; the tension between the democratic and the Jewish character of the state may abide for many years. However, agreement about the rules of the game can ensure the coexistence of those with differing views.

These are the two issues that the Rabin assassination presents to Israeli society. Rabin himself wanted to solve the first—to put an end to the occupation and thereby complete the task of creating a state, and only later, he believed, could we turn to the work of building a better society. What Rabin never imagined was that the severity of the second problem would not enable him to address the first; that opposition forces would overwhelm him personally at the first stage of the task. The two questions that preceded Rabin's assassination became even more critical afterward: How will Israel ultimately extricate itself from the morass of the colonialist condition, and will the factions in Israeli society reach consensus about the rules of the democratic game? These two questions remain open. How Israel answers them could make the morning of November 5, 1995, the beginning of national healing or the first shot in the Israeli civil war.

Notes

1. Almog (1996) presents no fewer than 30 indicators for measuring a national religion and examining such changes in Israel. An extensive bibliography provides an excellent survey of studies about cultural developments in Israeli society from the formative 1920s and 1930s until contemporary times.

2. Israeli political jargon uses the "left" versus the "right," or the "peace camp" versus the "nationalist camp." In terms of parties, this means Labor and Meretz versus the Likud, small right-wing parties, and the religious parties. However, there is also a correlation between geopolitical ideology and socioeconomic indicators: The "peace camp" has a higher proportion of the more established sectors of the population—Ashkenazim, seculars, and those with higher income and higher social status. The "nationalist camp" has a greater representation of Mizrahim, religious, and lower-income strata; under-represented in this group are the professional, cultural, economic, and government elites. The distinction is also geographic, between center and periphery, and therefore some call the two camps "northerners" and "southerners," such as Motti Regev in "An Introduction to Israeli Culture" (in the forthcoming *Research into Israeli Society*, Ephraim Yaar and Zeev Shavit (eds.), Tel Aviv: Open University). I use these terms here, although it should be noted that the definitions are not completely congruous. Because of the key role played by secular ideology and democratic principles on the one hand, and religion and nation on the other, I shall refer to these two blocs primarily as the "democratic-liberal camp" and the "clerical-nationalist camp."

3. See Ravitsky, 1997, and also a detailed survey of the research that examines the religious structure of Israeli secular existence in Levi, Levinson, and Katz, 1993.

4. Although utopianism was a salient component of all streams of the Zionist movement, the historian Yosef Gorny claims that in the past the subcurrents of realistic utopianism were dominant, whereas fantastic-utopianism dominates today.

5. A detailed review that illustrates the extremes these perceptions had reached—the apex of which is the perception that "Thou shalt not kill" refers only to Jews—can be found in Rubinstein, 1988, pp. 138–82.

6. See, for example, Tilly's "inherency model" and the "contingency model" of Gurr in Eckstein, 1980.

7. No other media frame suggested itself in the first days and weeks after the assassination, so no others were included in Wolfsfeld's study, but one began to appear shortly thereafter. This is the media frame according to which Rabin brought the assassination upon himself because of the infuriating way he dealt with the right and the settlers; see, for example, *Nativ*, August 1997. "When a leader creates such painful delegitimization for the Jewish majority which viewed itself as high quality among Israeli citizens on the Jewish and Zionist criteria, he becomes a certain partner to the blame. Massive pressure ultimately ignites an explosion" (Yeshayahu Steinberger, *Ha'aretz*, October 21, 1996).

8. These content analyses were carried out as part of a seminar about the Rabin assassination and the media that I conducted in the Communications Department of Hebrew University in 1997. Print and electronic media were examined, both

general and sectoral, including religious and ultra-Orthodox, Arabic, Russian, and others. The material was compared chronologically and diachronically for various cultural groups and by other criteria. The content analysis also examined the frequency that each format was cited according to the medium in which it was said, as well as the source—journalists, analysts, politicians, intellectuals, etc.

9. "A word or concept cannot be considered in isolation. It only exists in the theoretical or ideological framework in which it is used. A related concept can be seen at work in Foucault's *Madness and Civilization*. It should be stressed that the *problematique* is not a world view. It is not the essence of the thought of an individual or epoch which can be deduced from a body of texts by an empirical, generalizing reading; it is centered on the absence of problems and concepts within the *problematique* as much as their presence; it can therefore only be reached by a symptomatic reading [*lecture symptomale*] on the model of the Freudian analyst's reading of his patient's utterances" (Althusser, 1970: 254–53).

10. The assassination of Rabin was also compared to that of Martin Luther King (*Naveh*, 1997: 23–35). Salient here was the fact that both men spoke in the name of the "other"—King for blacks, Rabin for the Palestinians. But the ethnocentrism of Israeli culture and its unwillingness to accept the Palestinians as equals disqualifies the parallel to King, who belonged to the other, and comparisons with King virtually never returned to the public discourse.

11. Personal interview with Knesset member Ephraim Hoshaya, October 1997.

12. The shift was especially prevalent among young people. In the 1992 elections, 52 percent supported the Likud; after the assassination, 55 percent said they would vote for Peres (Amnon Barzilai, *Ha'aretz*, May 7, 1996).

13. The Ministry of Education committee reached the conclusion that the identification of schoolchildren with the assassin Yigal Amir "is not a unique phenomenon or one at the 'margins of society,' but a troublesome expression of the zeitgeist among a minority of youth, of apathy about the assassination and sometimes even identification with it." The committee also noted that the phenomenon existed primarily among those with "feelings of social, economic, or political deprivation" (Ministry of Education, Chair, Pedagogical Secretariat, Report of Committee Findings, November 17, 1996).

14. See Schudson, 1992: 154–59, which also addresses the work of Jeffrey Alexander.

15. Quoted in Marvin and Ingle, 1996: 771.

References

Almog, Oz (1996). "Secular Religion in Israel." *Megamot* 27, no. 3: 314–39. [Hebrew].

Althusser, Louis (1970). *For Marx*. London: Vintage Books.

Arian, Asher (1999). *Israeli Public Opinion on National Security 1999*. Tel Aviv: Jaffe Center for Strategic Studies.

Auttila, Inkert (1976). "Assassination in Finland." In Doris Y. Wilkinson (ed.),

Social Structure and Assassination Behavior. Cambridge, Mass.: Schenkman, pp. 140–41.

Barzilai, Gad, Ephraim Yuchtman-Yaar, and Zeev Segal (1994). *The Israeli Supreme Court and the Israeli Public*. Tel Aviv: Papyrus [Hebrew].

B'Tselem, the Israeli Information Center for Human Rights in the Occupied Territories (1998. *1987–1997: Ten Years of Human Rights Violations*. Jerusalem: B'Tselem, January.

Durkheim, Emil (1915). *The Elementary Forms of Religious Life*. Glencoe, Ill.: Free Press.

Eckstein, H. (1980). "Theoretical Approaches to Explaining Collective Political Violence." In T. R. Gurr (ed.), *Handbook of Political Violence*. New York: Free Press.

Ezrachi, Yaron (1997). *Rubber Bullets*. New York: Farrar, Straus and Giroux.

Feierabend, Ivo K., and Rosalind L. Feierabend (1969). "Cross-National Comparative Study of Assassination." Quoted in Havens et al., *The Politics of Assassination*, p. 13.

Ford, Franklin L. (1985). *Political Murder, from Tyrannicide to Terrorism*. Cambridge, Mass.: Cambridge University Press.

Gamson, William A. (1989). "News as Framing." *American Behavioral Scientist* 33: 157–61.

Giddens, Antony (1985). *The Nation-State and Violence*. Berkeley: University of California Press.

Girard, Rene (1977). *Violence and the Sacred*. Baltimore: Johns Hopkins University Press.

Greenberg, Bradley S., and Edwin B. Parker (1965). *The Kennedy Assassination and the American Public*. Stanford, Calif.: Stanford University Press.

Gurr, Ted V. (ed.) (1980). *Handbook of Political Violence*. New York: Free Press.

Havens, Murray C., Carl Leiden, and Karl M. Schmitt (1970). *The Politics of Assassination*. Englewood Cliffs, N.J.: Prentice-Hall.

Hayerushalmi, Levi Yishak (1997). *The Domineering Yarmulke*. Tel Aviv: HaKibbutz HaMeu'had [Hebrew].

Hermann, Tamar, and Ephraim Yuchtman-Yaar (1997). "Is There a Mandate for Peace? Israeli Public Opinion and the Peace Process." In Dan Caspi (ed.), *Communication and Democracy in Israel*. Tel Aviv: Hakibbutz HaMeu'had. [Hebrew], pp. 191–222.

Horowitz, Neri (1996)."The Illumination of Rabbi Kook for the Darkness of the Plazas." *Meimad*, no. 10 (January): 4–12 [Hebrew].

Kirkham, James F., Sheldon G. Levy, and William J. Crotty (1970). *Assassination and Political Violence*. New York: Praeger.

Lehman-Wilzig, S. (1983). "The Israeli Protester." *Jerusalem Quarterly*, no. 21: 127–38.

Levi, Shlomit, Hanna Levinson, and Elihu Katz (1993). *Beliefs, Religious Practicing and Social Relations Among Israeli Jews*. Jerusalem: Guttman Institute for Social Research.

Liebes, Tamar, and Yoram Peri (1998). "Electronic Journalism in Segmented Societies: Lessons from the Israeli Election 1996." *Political Communication* 15, no. 1: 27–44.

Marvin, Carolyn and David W. Ingle (1996). "Blood Sacrifice and the Nation: Revisiting Civil Religion." *Journal of the American Academy of Religion* 64, no. 4: 767–80.

Naveh, Eyal (1997). "Assassination of American Leaders: Trauma, Tragedy, and Meaning." *Zemanim* (January): 23–35 [Hebrew].

Nettle, J. P. (1968). "The State as a Conceptual Variable." *World Politics* 20, no. 4: 599–92.

Ohana, David, and Robert S. Wistrich (1996). *Myth and Memory: The Transfiguration of Israeli Consciousness*. Tel Aviv: HaKibbutz HaMeu'had [Hebrew].

Peri, Yoram (1996). "Afterword—Rabin: From Mr. Security to Nobel Peace Prize Winner." In Yitzhak Rabin, *The Rabin Memoirs*. Berkeley: University of California Press, pp. 339–80.

——— (1996). "The Radical Social Scientists and Israeli Militarism." *Israel Studies* 1, no. 2: 230–66.

Rabin, Yitzhak (1996/1979). *The Rabin Memoirs*. Berkeley: University of California Press, 1996; Tel Aviv: Maariv, 1979.

"The Rabin Assassination: The Ontological Sign" (1996). Discussion between members of the editorial board and Professor Marcello Daskal. *Metafora: A Philosophical Journal*, no. 4: 7–38 [Hebrew].

Ravitsky, Aviezer (1997). "Religious and Secular Israelis: A Post-Zionist Cultural War?" *Alpayim*, no. 14: 80–96 [Hebrew].

Rubinstein, Amnon (1998). *From Herzel to Rabin, 100 Years of Zionism*. Tel Aviv: Schoken.

Rummel, R. J. (1963). "The Dimensions of Conflict Behavior Within and Between Nations." *General Systems Yearbook*, (8): 1–50.

Schudson, Michael (1992). *Watergate in American Memory*. New York: Basic Books.

Sivan, Emmanuel (1991). *The 1948 Generation: Myth, Profile and Memory*. Tel Aviv: Maarachot [Hebrew].

Sprinzak, Ehud (1995). Between Extra-Parliamentary Protest and Terrorism: Political Violence in Israel." Jerusalem: Jerusalem Institute for Israel Studies [Hebrew].

Tanter, Raymond (1965). "Dimensions of Conflict Behavior Within and Between Nations 1958–60." Journal of Conflict Resolution, no. 10: 41–64.

Verba, Sidney (1965). "The Kennedy Assassination and the Nature of Political Commitment." In Bradley S. Greenberg and Edwin B. Parker (eds.), *The Kennedy Assassination and the American Public*. Stanford, Calif.: Stanford University Press.

Walzer, Michael (1998). "Democracy and the Politics of Assassination." In Charles S. Lieberman (ed.), *Political Assassination*. Tel Aviv: Am Oved. [Hebrew], pp. 13–21.

Wilkinson, Doris Y. (1976). *Social Structure and Assassination Behavior.* Cambridge, Mass.: Schenkman.

Wolfsfeld, Gadi (1996). "Critical Events and the Struggle over Meaning: Competing Media Frames of the Rabin Assassination." Unpublished.

Zelizer, Barbie (1992). *Covering the Body.* Chicago: University of Chicago Press.

CHAPTER 2

One More Political Murder by Jews

NACHMAN BEN-YEHUDA

Political Assassinations

In Israel, one of the most commonly heard reactions to the news that Rabin was assassinated was, "But that can't be—Jews don't kill other Jews." But was the assassination of Yitzhak Rabin really an exception in Israeli political tradition? To answer this question, we studied the pattern of political assassinations carried out by Jews in recent history in this part of the world and tried to understand the assassination of Yitzhak Rabin within the historical context of other slayings.

The great majority of studies about political assassinations have been conducted from the perspective of political science, history, or clinical psychology-psychiatry. Very few have examined the criminological and social aspects of political assassinations.[1] And because systematic research is scarce in this field, there is considerable lack of clarity about both the definitions of political assassination and the nature of the methodology that should be used.

Previous research about political assassinations falls into two main categories: those that focus on the killing of an individual, such as the assassinations of John F. Kennedy (1963), Abraham Lincoln (1865), Aldo Moro (1978), Mahatma Gandhi (1948), Martin Luther King (1968), the Archduke Ferdinand (1914), Anwar Sadat (1981), and others; and those that summarize extensive data about a large number of political assassinations in various cultures.[2] Two other types of research, though less common, provide extensive detail about a small number of assassinations,[3] or examine the legal aspects of political assassination in one particular society.[4] These different approaches are sometimes confusing since they do not provide a solid comparative basis. Ted Gurr (1988) points to the sorry state of research about terrorism and political assassination in particular. Although terrorism and political assassination should be distinguished, as will become evident later, Gurr's criticism is still valid about both.

This is one of the main reasons why the assassination of Yitzhak Rabin should be examined in the context of all the known political murders in Israeli Jewish culture, and these compared to assassinations in other cultures. When the assassination of Rabin is viewed in the time frame of a century of Jewish life in Palestine and then Israel, the act gains meaning and depth that would otherwise be indiscernible.

There are three main reasons for placing the Rabin assassination into this broad but circumscribed perspective of known cases: access to data; the ability to study a pattern of deviant ideological and political behavior in a given culture in depth over time; and the fact that during this period, an attempt was made to forge a new Jewish society and culture. This attempt necessitated some fundamental changes—political, social, and cultural—in the collective life of Jews who lived here, with far-reaching consequences for their personal and national identities.[5] Looking at the assassination of Rabin in this context is important, because this violent act represents a cultural clash of the first order between two diametrically opposed identities— democratic, liberal, and secular versus antidemocratic, fanatic, and narrowly religious.

There is a wide variety of definitions of political assassinations, some of them contradictory.[6] This difficulty is somewhat resolved by a two-step approach to the definition. In the first step, we can adopt the approach of Kirkham, Levy, and Crotty and use the expression "political assassination event" rather than "assassination" or "political murder." This term has great value in that it permits us to distinguish between the event itself and its cultural interpretation. They write that a "political assassination event" is "an act that consists of a plotted, attempted or actual, murder of a prominent political figure (elite) by an individual (assassin) who performs this act in other than a governmental role. This definition draws a distinction between political execution and assassination. An execution may be regarded as a political killing, but it is initiated by organs of the state, while an assassination can always be characterized as an illegal act."[7] Now we can ask. What makes a political assassination event a special form of taking someone's life against his or her will? How is this act interpreted in a social context? I suggest the following:

> The characterization of a homicidal event as a political assassination or execution is a social construction. It is a rhetorical device that is used to socially construct and interpret (i.e., to make culturally meaningful account of) the discriminate, deliberate, intentionally planned, and serious attempt(s), whether successful or not, to kill a specific social actor for political reasons having something to do with the political position (or role) of the victim, his or her symbolic-moral universe, and with the symbolic-moral universe out of which the assassin(s) act(s). The universe generates the legitimacy and justifications required for the act, which are usually presented in quasi-legal terms. Efforts are often made to present this legitimacy and justification in quasi-legal terms. However, decisions to assassinate are typically not the result of a fair legal procedure based on "due process."

The above definition distinguishes political assassination from other forms of killing. It also makes clear that what may appear to one side as political assassination can be interpreted by the other as homicide. Political assassination almost always embodies a clash between diametrically opposed ideological views. The definition also distinguishes between a terrorist assassination and a political execution. In the latter, the goal is always specific, while in terrorism the goal is collective.[8]

The Impact of Political Assassinations

The literature is divided concerning the results and effectiveness of political assassinations. Quite a few researchers tend to confuse the evaluation of impact of a slaying and a moral judgment of it.[9] Havens, Leiden, and Schmitt point out the enormous difficulty of evaluating the impact of political assassination.[10] They distinguish between (a) the immediate impact of the assassination and its significance in a historical perspective; and between (b) its personal and systemic-social impact. They list six possible results of political assassinations:

1. No change at all.
2. Personal changes that would not otherwise have happened (for example, Lyndon B. Johnson taking over the U.S. presidency after the assassination of Kennedy).
3. Changes in specific policies.
4. Far-reaching changes in the political system (e.g., following the as-

sassination of Rafael Trujillo Molina in the Dominican Republic in 1961; or the assassination of Patrice Lumumba in the Congo in 1961; or the assassination of Julius Caesar).

5. Inspiration for a profound social revolution (e.g., the assassination of Álvaro Obregón in Mexico in 1928).

6. Causing an entire political system to topple (e.g., the assassination of Engelbert Dollfuss, chancellor of Austria, in 1934; the assassination of the Archduke Ferdinand in 1914).

Perhaps it makes more sense to deal with results than with impact. As David Rapoport claims, "The lone assassin can set furious political forces in motion, but only conspirators have a reasonable chance of controlling them, and the best way to exploit the opportunity provided by the assassination is to usurp the powers of government."[11] In other words, for an assassination to be most effective from the assassin's point of view, it should be framed in a meaningful political setting. Rapoport and many scholars examine a range of dramatic systemic changes that may result from an assassination. These include damaging the credibility of the ruling order, feelings of vengeance, large-scale propaganda, a change of leadership, cultural warning, elimination of a tyrant, forcing the government to take tough measures, self-hate of the population, and preventing specific activities (such as cooperating with a regime defined as hostile or foreign)— clarifying that almost any political assassination has some sort of result. Thus, the question is not whether political assassinations have a result, but what type of result.[12]

It is not difficult to see that although the small band of conspirators around Rabin's assassination was not in the mainstream of Israeli political activity, the assassination set off a critical political dynamic. A group of dovish, secular, left-wing parties lost power to a right-wing coalition buttressed by several fanatic religious parties. The importance of this change for the public atmosphere and discourse in Israel should not be minimized. In this sense and in the short-term historical perspective, the assassin Yigal Amir had a concrete accomplishment. Within several months of his deed, a group of parties came to power that are much nearer the heart and mind of the assassin than of the assassination victim.

Some of the literature that deals with political assassination compares terrorism and political assassination, correctly concluding that assassination is one form of terrorist activity, with similar goals. Some examples: the desire of a group for political recognition; recruitment efforts to the group;

and damage to the morale and prestige of the government. The Western world is familiar with three archetypes of legitimacy for assassination:[13] (1) instrumental justification—the end result morally justifies the means; (2) political assassination as a necessary evil that seeks to prevent a worse evil; and (3) justification of killing as a form of terrorism.

Note that in most cases, the justification for political assassination does not represent the killer as irrational or a madman. And yet what Clarke in his legal work about political murder calls "a pathological theory of assassination"[14] is corroborated by several studies that have shown that most assassins or attempted assassins of American presidents are emotionally disturbed.[15] The consensus of research today is that political assassination should be seen as a systemic characteristic of cultures. The cultural conditions in which this characteristic is expressed thus become a key issue.[16]

The Present Study

The historical context for understanding the assassination of Yitzhak Rabin is based on a survey of the known political assassinations carried out in this region by Jews, from the beginning of the modern Zionist settlement (in the 1880s) until the end of the 1980s, a period of approximately 100 years. This is more or less the period of the formation of the state of Israel and the creation of a new national identity, personal and collective, for Jews. Although I also examined political executions during the course of this research (from the founding of Israel in 1948), the information openly available to the public about such cases is very limited. I do not believe that I managed to create a research model for political executions in this study; nevertheless, the model that emerges from the few cases that are known corroborates the findings from the known political assassination events.

The methodology was based on the use of primary and secondary sources, and only publicly known cases were included. The most obvious shortcoming of this is the possibly incomplete coverage of political assassination events, and partial coverage, problematic and sparse, of political executions. Nevertheless, I had no access to classified sources, and if I had, it would undoubtedly have made the research vulnerable to pressure about what to publish, when, and how. The price of censorship and the inability to publish the findings seemed to me to be a heavy one. In light of this decision, I tried to locate biographical and autobiographical memoirs of those active during this period, and descriptions available in secondary sources. All the relevant archives for this period were examined, as well as newspaper archives in Israel and sometimes abroad. I interviewed every relevant figure who could be located and agreed to talk. Several of these interviews, such as those with past assassins, were very valuable and gave insight into the period and the forces at play.[17]

A typology of political assassination events was developed that is based on the operation itself, regardless of the motivation of the assassins. It resembles an old typology that asserts that an assassination has two stages: preparation and execution.[18] The current typology has four categories; the first two belong to the stage of preparation and the latter two to the stage of execution:

1. The "prepreparation" category examines the deliberations of the assassin(s) and is based on the seriousness of their discussions and decision. Not every threat—or empty threat—enters this category, such as the proposal by Zionist leader Berl Katznelson in 1939 to murder Robert Friar Jardin, the British mandate official then in charge of settlement and lands in Palestine, and Hajj Amin Husseini, the mufti of Jerusalem—two prominent figures perceived as extremely hostile to the Zionist cause. David Ben-Gurion demurred, and the idea never passed the discussion stage.

2. The second category is "preparation" and includes cases in which a decision was made to assassinate, including detailed plans, but for various reasons (either technical or substantive), the plan was never executed. For example, in spring 1920, several members of HaShomer, a Zionist paramilitary organization, planned to assassinate Sir Ronald Storrs, British military governor and district commissioner of Jerusalem. Although the planning reached an advanced stage, the idea was abandoned. The plan to kill the Jordanian king Abdullah by the militant Zionist group Brit Habiryonim, apparently in 1933, is another example. Internal dissension among the conspirators led to cancellation of the scheme.

3. The third category, "Failure," includes cases in which attempted assassinations failed and the victim remained unhurt, sometimes even unaware of the attempt. The reasons for failure were usually technical: a mine that did not explode, a gun that did not go off, a mailed bomb that failed to reach its destination. For example, in August 1939 the militant Zionist underground Etzel tried to take the life of a Jewish officer named Gordon. The assassin pulled the trigger twice, but the gun did not fire and Gordon escaped. Lehi, a group that split off from Etzel, tried to assassinate Sir Harold MacMichael, British high commissioner (1938–44), seven

times without success. Several attempts on the life of General Sir Evelyn Barker by Lehi also failed.

4. The category "Success" includes cases in which the assassination was actually carried out and the victim was injured or killed. Partial success derives mostly from technical and not substantive reasons. Examples of success include the killing of Tufiq Bay in 1923 by the HaShomer movement; the killing of Jacob Israel de Haan in 1924 by the Haganah, the largest Zionist underground in the prestate period; the killing of Commissioner Ralph Cairns by Etzel in 1939; and the killings in 1944 of Lord Moyne, the British minister of state in the Middle East, and in 1948 of Count Folke Bernadotte, both by Lehi.

It should be clarified that the names of the categories are, of course, from the point of view of the assassin. In that sense, there can be no doubt that the assassination of Yitzhak Rabin falls into the category "Success."

Research Findings

The assassination of Yitzhak Rabin is one of 92 political assassination events planned and carried out by Jews in the past hundred years.[19]

Clearly, the political assassinations examined here have meaning in the historical context of Zionist settlement. Most of the cases cited here are of the killing of Jews by Jewish underground fighters in the context of the struggle for national liberation, and not the killing of non-Jews by Jews. Most of this lethal aggression was then aimed by Jews against other Jews, as 60 percent of the victims were Jews. Figure 1 shows that political assassinations were at a peak between 1939 and 1948 and dropped sharply thereafter. Political executions since 1948 do not appear in the graph. The years with the greatest number of political assassination events were 1939, 1944, and 1947, 40 percent of all such killings taking place in these three years. Although it is harder to explain the increased number of cases in 1944 (and 1946), the years 1939 and 1947 are more easily explained.

In 1939, World War II began, as did the ideological struggles between the Haganah and Etzel, and this was one year before Lehi split off from Etzel. Etzel was especially active—some 60 percent of the political assassinations that year are attributed to it. Of all the political assassination events that year by the Haganah and Etzel combined, 70 percent were targeted against other Jews (five were killed by Etzel and two by the Haganah). One of the more interesting cases in the contemporary context was the assassina-

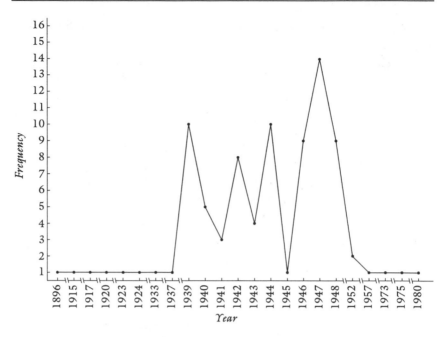

FIG. 1. Years and Frequencies of Political Assassination Events

tion of Arieh Polonski, who immigrated to Palestine from Poland with his wife in the 1920s. At the request of the Jewish Agency, Polonski joined the British police in 1931 as the agency liaison with the British criminal investigations unit. Accusing him of treason, Etzel killed Polonski in Jerusalem in 1939. The father of the victim wrote an open letter to the head of Etzel demanding an explanation for the killing of his son. Etzel replied that the Jewish Agency was responsible for his son's death because it had sent him to inform on his own people. This killing shocked the leaders of the Jewish community in Palestine. A number of outraged prominent figures, including S. Y. Agnon, Henrietta Szold, and Berl Katznelson, signed and published a letter headed "Thou Shalt Not Murder," demanding an immediate end to this activity: "We appeal to the Jewish community with a warning: Stop this evil while it is at the beginning! The community must isolate the inciters and those incited!" This 1939 appeal sounds contemporary in the context of the assassination of Yitzhak Rabin.

The year 1947 was also a difficult and complex year. There were fourteen political murders that year, in which eight of the victims (57.1 percent)

TABLE I

Who Was Responsible for the Political Assassination Events, 1882–1988?

Responsible party	Number	Percent
Isolated individual	5	6
HaShomer	3	3
Etzel	15	17
Lehi	42	48
Haganah	16	18
Other organization	6	7
TOTAL	87	99

NOTE: Percentages are rounded to the nearest whole number

were Jews (four were killed by Lehi and four by Etzel). During this year, the struggle over the definition of the state-in-the-making reached new heights (see Table 1).

One of the most striking findings is that only a tiny minority of cases (6 percent) were carried out by an individual acting alone. The vast majority of political assassinations (94 percent) were not carried out by a lone assassin but were planned by a group, even though the killing itself was sometimes done by one person. Also, the group was not necessarily a large one, as in the assassinations of Rabin and of Israel Kasztner in 1957. This interesting finding suggests one way that the Israeli-Jewish model of political assassination is markedly different from that of many other countries, though it resembles the cases studied in Europe. The group provides the individual with moral support, motive, justification, material means, ideology, and often physical refuge as well.

In the case of the Rabin assassination, one should distinguish between two levels of groups. The immediate small group includes those with whom the assassin was in intense interaction, those with whom he felt safe enough to share inner thoughts, ideas, and plans in a continual exchange of views. And this small group is invested in the social and ideological milieu of a much larger group from which it draws inspiration, ideas, and the psychological and rhetorical tools to interpret the world. This larger group has a world view that combines theology with politics, that sees the "Greater Land of Israel" as the ultimate value, and that therefore regards territorial compromise as treachery. Defining Rabin as a "traitor," "collaborator," and "terrorist" can be understood and meaningful only within this context. Thus the assassination of Yitzhak Rabin was only the final act in a long process undergone by the assassin in which he not only became convinced that he had to carry out the deed, but—as noted by Sprinzak in the next chapter—also developed the justification for it.

As in other cases of Jews assassinating other Jews, both Rabin and his government were the target over an extended period of severe, unbridled incitement, generally from parties on the right, and the religious right. These were not just efforts to undermine the moral and political legitimacy of the government, but taunts aimed personally at Rabin, depicting him as a traitor and threatening that he would eventually stand trial for his crimes, just as other traitors—Vidkun Quisling and Lord Haw Haw (raising associations from World War II)—were tried and punished. The emotional, sophisticated, cynical, and venomous use of rhetoric inflamed passions and fomented violence. In this atmosphere, in the opinion of many, Rabin was transformed into a "stranger," not "one of us." Slogans whose main goals were the delegitimation of Rabin and his government through vilification, invective, and defamation appeared publicly. Right-wing demonstrators stood at intersections throughout Israel carrying signs that incited against the prime minister. Left-wingers who attempted counterdemonstrations were the butt of curses, defamation, and even blows. Two examples may suffice: a rally in which pictures of Rabin in Nazi uniform were borne aloft, and a demonstration outside Rabin's home in which threats were made that after the election Rabin and his wife would stand trial "like Mussolini and his mistress" after World War II (both hanged for treason following a kangaroo trial). Thus in the minds of a substantial number of Jews, Rabin was transformed into a deviant, a traitor, and an outsider. The political and ideological differences provided the framework for more concrete incitement. And the hate campaign prepared the psychological grounds for the slaying.

Right-wing groups have no monopoly on incitement in Israel; during the so-called *sezon* (hunting season) in the 1940s, for example, the left-wing incited opinion against the right. Since the end of the 1970s and early 1980s, however, it was the ideological campaign of right-wing elements that provided the background for a significant number of terrorist activities: the deadly activities of the "the Jewish underground" in the late 1970s; Yona Avrushmi who threw a hand grenade into a Peace Now rally, killing Emil Gruenzweig in February 1983; in October 1984, David Ben-Shimol launched a Lau rocket into a bus carrying Arabs, killing one and injuring another ten; in April 1985, Danny Eisenman, Gil Fux, and Michal Hallel killed Hamis Tutanji, an Arab taxi driver; and in February 1994, Baruch

TABLE 2

Identity of the Victims of Assassination Events, 1882–1988

	Pre-preparation	Preparation	Failure	Victim killed	Victim injured	Total	Percentage
Jewish	4	1	10	35	2	52	60
British	2	2	12	6	0	22	25
Arab	0	3	0	3	1	7	8
Other	0	0	2	4	0	6	7
Total	6	6	24	48	3	87	100

Goldstein killed 29 Arabs and injured 125 more in the Cave of the Patriarchs in Hebron. There is no doubt that those who carried out these activities (all of them acts of terrorism) were influenced by what could be termed "the atmosphere."

As in other cases of political murder, transforming the prime minister into the "other" and a potential victim stemmed from a desire for revenge and to abort the peace process. Amir found political and ideological justification for his deed among some elements of the social network in which he lived. The broader group supplied the psychological and rhetorical tools that provided motivation and ambience and did not negate the desire to carry out a political murder. In this sense there is a similarity between the assassination of Rabin and that of Zionist leader Chaim Arlosoroff (though it is not clear that the murder of Arlosoroff was politically motivated)—in both cases, the killing revealed the deep cleavages in Israeli society.

The fact that most of the political assassination events took place in the years 1939–48 and that organizations were involved raises several interesting questions concerning the identity of the victims in symbolic political terms, and the nature of the process that led to their assassination.

The most striking finding is that most of the victims (60 percent) were Jews (see Table 2). Since most of the killings were carried out by the three Jewish underground movements active before the establishment of Israel, claiming that assassination was justified in order to bring an end to British rule over Palestine, how can we explain the fact that "only" 25 percent of the victims were British but that 60 percent were Jewish? How many Jews were victims of each movement—Lehi, Etzel, and the Haganah? Out of 42 political assassination events in which the Lehi was involved, 20 (48 percent) were directed against other Jews. Out of 15 acts in which Etzel was involved, 14 (93 percent) were directed against Jews. And out of the 16 acts carried out by the Haganah, 10 (63 percent) were against Jews. Thus, although Lehi was the group involved in the greatest number of political assassinations, fewer than half its intended victims were Jewish. In many cases, by the way, the potential victim was warned, sometimes more than once. This was certainly true of Rabin's assassination.

A Special Case of Killing: Profile and Rationale

From the data analyzed in this research, a specific profile of killing emerges, both in criminological and in social terms. Exactly as in the case of Rabin's assassination, the typical political assassination event usually takes place on a weekend in the morning or the evening. The weapon of choice for most assassins, as in the case of Rabin, is a revolver or a bomb. Characteristically, political assassination events take place in one of the large urban centers—Tel Aviv in first place, followed by Jerusalem and then Haifa. In the great majority of cases, including Rabin's assassination, the assassins did precision work, striking only their intended victims. When the weapon of choice was a mine, bomb, or mailed explosive, however, the number of innocent victims was significantly larger. The vast majority of victims (97 percent) were men; most were over the age of 40 and married, though few served in important positions. Only in several instances did the victims hold positions of real importance, such as Count Bernadotte and Lord Moyne. Among the Jews killed, Rabin was a significant exception in this regard: in the entire period examined in this research, none of the Jews assassinated held high positions (with the possible exception, of course, of the murder of Chaim Arlosoroff in 1933, if it was political, but even then there was no parity between their positions). Only a very small and insignificant portion of the victims (about 3 percent) were women. And only once (or possibly twice) was it clear that a woman was in the actual team of assassins.

The findings also oblige us to examine the justifications for these activities in the language of the perpetrators. How did these groups rationalize their deeds? What reasons did they give?

The claims given by the assassins ranged from very detailed, specific accusations to sweeping general rationale. In order of frequency, the justification that the victim was a "traitor/informer" was overwhelmingly the most frequent (91.2 percent) regarding Jewish victims. "Revenge" was most frequent justification (63.2 percent) regarding British victims and less so (20.4 percent) for Arab victims.

During the prestate period, Jewish groups that felt directly involved in the struggle for an independent state and the shaping of a new national identity (to distinguish it from the diaspora identity) used political assassinations to demarcate the boundaries that in their view differentiated "our people" from those regarded as "against us," to distinguish between "us" and "them." In this context, the accusation "traitor" is almost a necessity, and recourse to the motive of "revenge" is also to be expected. In the absence of a formal system of political and social justice, an informal social system like this seeks the same effect.[20] In a struggle of this nature, the use of murder is very specific—particularly against Jews—and can be perceived by the assassins as an attempt to purge the inner group of competing ideologies and commitments and to redefine the moral boundaries.[21]

Use of the terms traitor, informer, collaborator, and spy were routine in political murders. The dawning and painful awareness in the Jewish community of what happened in Europe during World War II forced the Jews in Palestine to examine in depth the subject of cooperation with the conquering power. Thus, the choice of an activity like political murder on suspicion that someone was informing, betraying, collaborating, or spying had a clear meaning, to those involved in making these decisions to murder, to the perpetrators, and to the culture and society in which these acts were carried out. The accusation "traitor" in the historical context of 1939–48 had a distinct meaning. It helped create and define moral-ideological boundaries between fundamentally different world views. The assassination of Rabin conforms to this social model.

The geopolitical setting in which Rabin and his assassin lived is sharply divided over a question of national import: how to resolve the Jewish-Arab conflict, and the Jewish-Palestinian conflict in particular. In Israeli society, the terms "left" and "right" refer to different approaches to resolving these blood-soaked conflicts, and the groups are intensely polarized and buttressed by religious elements (especially on the right). Yitzhak Rabin's policies were intended to resolve this conflict by political negotiation for mutual political and territorial concessions. Yigal Amir refused to accept this path. From his point of view, Rabin betrayed what he and his allies took the undemocratic liberty of defining as "the homeland."

Accusations of Rabin's treachery appeared in right-wing rallies in Israel; they were shouted from the rooftops and uttered with varying degrees of openness. Rabin's assassin lived in and imbibed this atmosphere. From Amir's point of view, murdering Rabin meant eradicating someone who betrayed his world view. There was no clinical pathological element involved. Yitzhak Rabin and Yigal Amir represent two polarized political and moral universes—secular versus religious; liberal versus ethnocentric; tolerant versus fanatic; democratic versus theocratic; one who seeks solutions to conflict through negotiation versus one who uses violence. From a sociological point of view, it is not at all surprising that Amir found himself on the right side of the Israeli political spectrum, comfortable among those who speak his language, share his faith, study in the institutions of higher learning where he did, and live a style of life resembling his. In this sense, Amir is the product of one sector of Israeli-Jewish society, just as he is also a shaper of that segment and expressed it.

Scrutinizing the clash between the two ideological and moral universes also enables us to understand why, after the assassination of Rabin, there are segments of Israeli Jewish culture that publicly identify with Yigal Amir and his deed and feel that the assassination was correct. When those on the right are asked to condemn the assassination, the efforts made by some to avoid answering or to give ambiguous replies reinforce this conclusion. Moreover, after the slaying, elements of the political right and the religious in Israel began a campaign to pry loose the connection between the right-wing religious and the assassination of Rabin. It is interesting how they recruited language for this purposes, such as the debate over whether to use the word "murdered" or "killed" in discussing the "death" of Rabin. The Orwellian use of language about Rabin's assassination demonstrates the gaping ideological chasm between the political camps. Again, the rationale for this behavior is the sharp polarization of Israeli society, of which Rabin's assassination was more a symbol than a cause.

Motivations of "vengeance" and "retaliation" are also of importance in justifying a political assassination event: "Revenge is a universal pattern of behavior. It is a feature of our emotional lives that cannot be eradicated."[22] The desire for revenge is, without doubt, a very strong emotion, and the situations in which there is a desire to "get even" are those in which the potential assassin feels a powerful hurt, deprivation, injustice, and inability to achieve justice otherwise.[23] Thus, revenge is a powerful motivation in a social system that is considered to be fundamentally unjust.[24]

There is no need to espouse the untenable position that an act of revenge can be understood only in psychological terms. This research, as well as that of Rieder,[25] shows that what is presented as a need for revenge or retaliation and its implementation are systemic features of a large number of cultures. The cultural infrastructure on which the social construction of revenge and retaliation is based has a strong moral orientation, guided by a simple and simplistic principle of justice. This principle claims that symmetry and balance should be created in a nonsymmetric and unbalanced situation. Thus it should not be surprising that revenge and retaliation are guided by principles of social construction, by values and norms defined socially, and are not the product of an internal drive, supposedly involuntary or uncontrollable, of isolated individuals. Revenge is a rational, non-emotional reaction (though it is not presented this way), equivalent in the logic of its activity to forms of social control such as punishment. As Rieder argues, the desire for revenge or retaliation against what is perceived as injustice reveals the logical nature of these acts. Therefore, "The rationality of vengeance as a method of social control, not its unreasoning revenging, emerges as one of its striking signatures."[26]

Collaboration, Betrayal, and Alternative Systems of Justice

The 73 political murders carried out from 1939 to 1948 can be seen in the context of a critical turning point in the efforts of the Zionist movement (especially the three Jewish undergrounds before the founding of the state) to establish an independent, national home for Jews. These underground groups saw themselves as intensely involved in what they defined as the struggle against the British occupying power and the Arabs and Palestinians for establishment of a new Jewish state. From what is known about prestate underground movements in other parts of the world, it is clear that the national aspect of political assassination is a universal feature of a struggle of this kind, and not unique to the founding of Israel.[27]

The assassination of Rabin in 1995 can be seen in a similar context. More than anything, this assassination dramatically symbolized the deep cleavage in Israeli-Jewish society between the religious right and the nonreligious left. Those who wondered after the assassination if this deed would engender significant change have come up with a generally perplexing answer. On the one hand, the assassination changed absolutely nothing about any of the key conflicts or institutions in Israeli society; and on the other hand, many feel that something fundamental has taken place. This is a paradox, which can be explained by the fact that what has changed is consciousness. Until the assassination of Rabin, most of the secular, liberal majority in Israel, and certainly the left wing, was aware of the existing cultural conflict, but Rabin's assassination forced this sector to confront the fact that for some Jewish factions, this is a heart-wrenching conflict over which blood will be shed. Although the assassination of Rabin did not change anything concrete, it greatly sharpened the conflict and shaped a new awareness. Some of the kulturkampf underlying the assassination of Rabin is not just a secular-religious rift, but a conflict around the solution to the Jewish-Palestinian strife and, in the longer run, a conflict around the type of culture that will dominate Israeli Jewish society—theocracy versus democracy. Thus, just as the political murders between 1939 and 1948 grew out of a conflict-ridden setting that resembles the one in which Rabin was assassinated and focused on the key question, "Are you with us or against us?," the perception that Rabin was "against us" was translated by Yigal Amir (and others) not into a subject for legitimate debate and political engagement, but into terms of treachery against Israel's national interest. Formulating the issue this way illuminates the path that leads a person or group to perpetrate a political assassination of the type carried out by Yigal Amir. It also leads to the conclusion that additional assassinations are possible if the basic parameters of conflict are not satisfactorily resolved.

If we accept that the primary rationale for assassination is revenge against a traitor or informer, that revenge and retaliation are considered acceptable motives, that most of the victims were Jewish, and the collective character of the assassins, a logical conclusion is that assassination is part of a social pattern that seeks to provide an alternative system of justice—not justice in the criminal or legal sense, but justice in the broad political and social sense.

Jacoby notes that "justice is a legitimate concept in the modern code of civilized behavior. Vengeance is not."[28] Thus, to make the demand for revenge acceptable in modern Western culture, it must be formulated in terms that cannot be interpreted as revenge. Instead of demanding "revenge," the correct and cultured way is to focus the rhetoric on "justice."

The idea of exploiting the concepts of justice and revenge in the rationale of political assassination is not new. Kirkham, Levy, and Crotty noted this in their 1970 research, although not in an entirely explicit and systematic way.[29] These researchers attempt to explore the sense of injustice felt by the individual, as well as the potential for anger experienced by individuals and groups who live in a society they perceive to be politically unjust. They claim that a relatively high frequency of political murders is closely related not just to the sense of political injustice of society but also to the lack of political faith in that society.[30]

Perpetrators of assassinations have claimed that "political assassination" should be recognized as a special type of killing that is justified as a legal proceeding. This is done, for example, when assassins feel that their hopes of getting political or social justice are blocked, or that they are prevented access to legitimate avenues.[31] This concept was applied by the so-called Jewish underground from the late 1970s, who claimed that their security concerns were being ignored, or and by the group of assassins of Israel Kasztner (a Zionist political leader of Hungarian Jewry in World War II, accused of collaborating with the Nazis). Thus, the rationale given by Amir to explain the assassination of Rabin is an application of this concept. Because Amir believed that his political views were not given proper expression in the policies of the country of which Rabin was leader, or that they were given expression in a way that endangered the state, he took the step of political murder.

Another application of the concept is the tendency of assassins to use legal jargon. We often hear, "The underground court passed a death sentence on traitor X" or "The death sentence passed against traitor X was executed." It should be emphasized that evidence of the existence of a court like this is scarce. In some cases, even when we know that a deliberation about the victim has taken place (a discussion that assassins call a "trial"), there is little resemblance between these deliberations and a trial. The more known examples are the Lehi "trial" against Yehuda Arie Levi (the Lehi weapons-supply officer who wanted to leave Lehi for the Haganah and was killed in 1948), or the ludicrous "trial" supposedly held by the IDF (actually by the Haganah) for Captain Meir Tubianski, accused of treason and killed in 1948. There are more extreme examples. In 1942, Lehi set a booby trap that killed three officers in Tel Aviv. Their intention had been to eliminate two British secret policemen particularly hated by Lehi—Jeffrey Morton and T. I. Wilkin. The bomb did explode but accidentally killed others, including two Jews—Shlomo Schiff and Nachum Goldman—who worked in the British police. In a document published by Yair Stern, Lehi is commander, he wrote, "Officers Schiff and Goldman were sentenced to death by the supreme court of the organization. This sentence was approved by the leader and commander of Etzel in Israel and carried out on January 20, 1942 at 01:20 . . . in Tel-Aviv." (At that time, Lehi still called itself "Etzel in Israel.") There is no evidence of the existence of any court, supreme or otherwise, or any legal proceeding by Lehi with regard to the killing.

It should also be noted that the expression "political assassination" was too charged for both Lehi and the Haganah. Haganah preferred "elimination," and Lehi "individual terrorism" (although the term was generally applied retrospectively). Also, the assassins frequently compared their deeds to actions in the Bible perceived as completely justified—Jael's murder of Sisera, or the killing of King Eglon of Moab by Ehud from the tribe of Benjamin. The imagery of the language and the use of Biblical figures reinforced the assassins' belief in the correctness of their ways, and that they were part of a system of justice. Thus, when Yigal Amir searches for Halakhic justification and Biblical figures to identify with, this search can be seen as part of an effort to "legally" justify the action. Although there was no justification of the type and intensity described above, efforts were certainly made to find one.

The idea that political assassination should be accepted as an alternative system of justice, both internally and for external consumption, is not far-removed from other research in the field. The most prominent among them are that of Hobsbawm (1959) and studies from the late 1980s by researchers of the British school.[32] These studies examine popular systems of justice from various angles and what Hobsbawm called "primitive rebels" operating within those systems. In societies with problematic and biased formal justice systems one would expect "rebels" to develop more informal systems and mechanisms of political, social, and criminal justice. The example of Robin Hood is well known, but there are many other cases of bandits who maintain systems of informal and alternative justice that win great affection and appreciation.[33] One of the key ideas that comes out of research in this field is that "crime under certain conditions serves equivalent functions to such recognized political forms as protest and resistance."[34]

Another field of research that developed in recent years is based on the work of Donald Black about social control:[35]

> Focusing upon the concept of self-help criminal justice, Black argues that: "There is a sense in which conduct regarded as criminal is often quite the opposite. Far from being an intentional violation of a prohibition, much crime is moralistic and involves the pursuit of justice. It is a mode of conflict management, possibly a form of punishment, even capital punishment. Viewed in relation to law, it is self-help. To the degree that it defines or responds to the conduct of someone else—the victim—as deviant, crime is social control."[36]

The organizations mentioned so far did indeed create a system of social control. In most cases, the type of justice they conducted was not formal but based on self-help. This type of justice is focused on guarding the moral boundaries of what is defined by them as the collective. In many senses, this conceptual system was also valid for analyzing and understanding political executions by the state.

A more general sociological observation is that an alternative and popular system of justice that operates according to the principles of political (not criminal, civil, or legal) justice can be understood as a system of social control. The ascent of this system to dominance happens in the historical context of what is perceived as a national struggle, and hence also as part of what is perceived as a process of nation-building—against political groups and forces defined as conquerors, hostile and foreign. This is actually the reason that the conceptual system used by the recent Jewish underground and Yigal Amir to describe political assassination is meaningful and revealing. Concepts such as "elimination," "individual terrorism," "justice to traitors," and "justice to collaborators" confirm our observation that those who used these expressions saw themselves as participants in a process of seeing that justice was done in a system of social control. These procedures draw the boundaries of "symbolic-moral universes" at the heart of the ideological struggle of nation-building and forging an independent national identity. Again, it is clear that the assassination of Yitzhak Rabin by Yigal Amir fully conforms to this cultural interpretation.

Gwynn Nettler, a leading criminologist, has made comments about this that merit thought: "Killing for justice translates homicide as execution rather than as murder. This is a translation that appeals to groups that regard themselves as legitimate possessors of moral authority. Thus, both government-in-power and revolutionary challengers of that power refer to their killing of enemies as homicides rationalized by their sense of justice, a sense that fluctuates between demands for revenge, retribution, deterrence, and submission."[37]

From an analysis of cases of political assassination, it is clear that this system functions with very little information, sometimes based on "confessions" or on decisions made by commanders or administrators.[38] In this system, the potential victim has no real chance to prove his or her innocence. It is a system based on claims, images, rumors, partial information, and a strong social construction of "guilt," "collaboration," "treason," and "revenge"—with the use of clichés, slogans, and invective an intrinsic part of the rhetoric, exactly as in the assassination of Rabin.

The matter of collaborators is important. "Collaboration" is related to the concept of betrayal: one who has broken a trust has violated a commitment to a certain symbolic-moral universe. Betrayal is universally perceived as a crime, and in all cultures known to us, punishment for it is generally severe.[39]

An interesting issue is the attitude of Jewish culture toward collaborators and perpetrators of political murder. In Jewish tradition, informers and collaborators are called *mosrim*. Many years in the diaspora taught that the existence of informers can be of grave danger to the welfare of a persecuted minority. The consensus was that if someone was known to be an informer, he or she should be killed before the actual informing took place (there is a debate about whether the person should first be warned). It should be emphasized that it was not enough to suspect someone of being an informer; evidence had to be provided. Determining who exactly was an informer was no simple matter—particularly because of the severe punishment exacted for it. To punish an informer it was necessary to convene a legitimate court with the authority to issue a death sentence. Judaism has a strong tradition of avoiding the death penalty, and there are stringent limits on its application. Only rarely does a Jewish court have the authority to issue a death sentence. Nonetheless, there is evidence that some informers were executed.[40]

Although Jews planning a political murder could appeal to the concepts of "collaborator" and "informer" to defend their intentions, historically they usually have not. With the exception of the killing of Jacob Israel de Haan by the Haganah in 1924, there is no evidence of even one other significant attempt to use the Halakha to justify political murder.[41] Perhaps those involved in assassinations did not know the Halakha; or perhaps criticism of the use of Halakha to justify the killing of de Haan proved to the planners and implementers that they should not appeal to it to justify the killing of those suspected of being informers. Moreover, the prestate Jewish undergrounds and those involved in political murder after 1948 (with the exception of one) saw themselves primarily as secular-political, nonreligious organizations.

We have no conclusive evidence that Yigal Amir found formal Halakhic justification from any religious authority for carrying out the slaying, although a documentary film claims that he did. At the same time, the pattern of half-truths, innuendoes, and other rhetoric used by the assassin and his supporters, as well as his political and ideological affiliation, do support the claim that a search for such justification did take place. The fact that this question evoked evasive responses indicates the reluctance to publicly justify this act in Halakhic terms. Nevertheless, Amir may have concluded from things he heard and to which he was exposed that his deed would receive religious approval, or he may have actually thought that he had such justification (though he never said this explicitly).

Creating a Deviant Identity

Most of the political assassination events before 1948 were carried out by Lehi, Etzel, and the Haganah. These groups take pride in having fought the Arabs and having helped bring about the expulsion of the British from Palestine. It is therefore difficult to explain the fact that the deadly aggressiveness of these groups was also directed against Jews. The assassination of Rabin, however, is easily explained by the words of the assassin and his political-ideological background. There is no doubt that Amir believed his deed was justified by the fact that it could change Israel's policies in a direction more palatable to him.

Political murder events are selective and specific. The prestate underground organizations killed many more Arabs and British by indiscriminate and nonspecific terrorism than Jews. Thus the narrow focus of political assassination events must not obfuscate the more general picture. Moreover, it was easier technically to gather information and kill members of the internal group—other Jews.

Another explanation for the proliferation of Jewish victims of political slayings requires a preliminary discussion of why these prestate underground organizations and Rabin's assassin chose to use the method of assassination. The answer is necessarily functional; from their point of view, they had no choice. Preceding most of these events were extensive debates about the boundaries of what is permissible and forbidden ideologically, about identity and the evolving character of the state-in-the-making, and about how to achieve it. Physical elimination of the adversary was sometimes perceived by the participants as one possible solution. For Lehi, which undertook a greater number of assassinations, these were the principal method of operation; Etzel and the Haganah exercised more restraint.

Indiscriminate and nonselective terrorism is generally directed toward a collective perceived as "foreign" in Georg Simmel's interpretation of the concept—an individual or collective physically close to us but mentally and culturally distant. [42] It was easy to define the British and Arabs as "foreigners." It did not require fine distinctions toward those perceived collectively as hostile and foreign, simply because they were defined as the enemy. Thus, with several reservations and exceptions, fatal aggression was directed toward them in an almost indiscriminate manner.

But defining large numbers of members of the "inner" group or organization as enemies was much more difficult. Thus, actions of indiscriminate terrorism by Jews against other Jews were impossible theoretically (and practically). Political murder is very specific and therefore a powerful tool for coping with the moral limitations of the struggle for independence. When a suspicion of betrayal was raised, the words "traitor," "informer," and "collaborator" were used to define the potential victim and to draw the lines crossed in the eyes of the conspirators. Humiliating words and sometimes rituals levied against the victim were part of the process of stigmatization in which vilification and defamation were key elements. This procedure was supposed to transform "one of us," someone with a legitimate reputation, into someone lacking legitimacy. In this procedure, the victim is spurned and given a stigmatic social identity, defiled and tarnished. Those from the inner group who undergo this are described as representing an immediate and terrible danger to the very existence of the symbolic-moral universe of the group and its members.

In fact, the operating procedure here is the creation of deviant identities. If we remain with Simmel's terminology, we can call it a process of "strangerization." This means taking a member of the group and transforming him or her into a stranger for the other group members. When the process of strangerization is also accompanied by vilification and stigmatization, the result transforms the group member into a stranger, deviant, defiled, disdained, humiliated, and dangerous.[43] This person can no longer be a member of the group that estranged him. This process includes not only strangerizing and distancing the individual, but also dehumanization, which will make it easier ideologically to kill that person, if a decision is made to do so. The procedure becomes more harsh when the conflict is defined as a nationalist struggle—interpretations of the past and future of the society, the rules of conduct in it, its collective identity and boundaries, the identity of its members, and the style of their lives.

At the same time, paradoxically, it has to be clear that in a society characterized by a struggle of this kind, the very meaning of the word "traitor" is problematic. In a situation in which two ideologies or more find themselves on a collision course, interpreting the term "traitor" consistently and reaching consensus about it often become impossible. Indeed, relating to Rabin as a traitor was characteristic of a very specific sector among the Israeli Jewish right and some of the religious. In the eyes of many others, Rabin cannot be transmuted into this. Nevertheless, the process of strangerizing Rabin, presenting him as a traitor, and the no-holds-barred defamation all clearly conform to what is described above. Rabin was subject to an extended campaign of defamation and vilification that delegitimized him and his government. Indeed, this moralistic campaign, which included rationalizations for his death, were continued by some political groups even after his assassination.

A Cross-Cultural Perspective

The founding of the state of Israel marked a dramatic turning point in the frequency of political killing as the state established and institutionalized national systems of critical importance: the justice and the political systems. Through these, various ideological groups could find a direct, fair, and open channel within the formal public framework for their views, aspirations, and values. Hence the need diminished for an alternative system of justice. But when in the late 1970s and early 1980s a group of young, right-wing militants felt that it did not have access to the justice that it deserved, its members organized a direct action group that became known as the Jewish underground.[44]

In a sovereign state, there can be two alternative types of systems. One system may exist because its adherents say that the state failed in one of its goals. A system of this kind (such as the Jewish underground) claims that it is capable of doing things that the state cannot. The second system opposes the very existence of the state, and this opposition provides the moral justification for its actions. Both these systems can flourish in situations where the very authority of the state becomes problematic, vague, or doubtful. The Haganah, Etzel, and Lehi (as well as the group believed to have murdered Kasztner) erected alternative systems of the second type, and so did the group in which Yigal Amir participated.

After the founding of Israel, political murder was carried out by groups of vigilantes—that is, groups that use violence to preserve the order that they believe should exist. The assassination of Rabin fits this interpretation. The pre-1948 Jewish undergrounds were groups of revolutionaries whose use of violence was intended to undermine and eliminate British rule. In both cases, an alternative populist system of control was used.[45]

Although the link between political murders and political executions is somewhat removed from the subject of Rabin's assassination, brief mention should be made of the fact that the interpretation of such deeds is similar. Political executions by the state of Israel have taken place outside the country. To the best of my knowledge, political executions by Israeli agents have not been directed toward Israeli citizens. If this assumption is correct, it places this category of events completely outside the framework of political assassinations in terms of justification, method of operation, and objectives. Nonetheless, it is clear from the known cases (e.g., the slaying of Black September members after their terrorist attack on Israeli athletes at the Munich Olympics) that these are a form of retaliatory action and fit the pattern of political assassination events presented and elucidated in this paper, even corroborating it.

Research of this scope has never previously been conducted, and comparison with other cultures is not at all simple. The data that exist indicate that justice systems similar to the one described above do exist among underground groups in similar circumstances. The French underground during World War II maintained such a system, as did the Kikuyu tribes in Kenya during the revolt of the Mau Mau against British rule. According to one conservative estimate, the Mau Mau killed some 11,500 other Kikuyu and only about 95 Europeans. These data again show that most of the energy and aggression found in political assassination events, including the Mau Mau revolt, is directed inward, toward members of the inner group.[46]

Another example comes from the period of the Arab Revolt in Palestine (1936–39). According to one estimate, approximately 6,000 Arabs were killed during this period, only 1,500 of them through British or Jewish actions; the remainder—approximately 4,500—were killed as a result of internal terrorism (or purging) among various Arab groups.[47] In the seven years between 1980 and 1986, only 23 Arabs were killed by other Arabs in the West Bank and Gaza Strip.[48] By contrast, during the following six years, from December 1987 to November 1993 (the period of the intifada), different sources say that between 771 and 942 Arabs were killed by other Arabs.

Internal political killings, accompanied by widespread use of the terms "traitor," "informer," and "dangerous political and ideological adversary," also characterized some of the political struggles in Europe. Some examples: the organization known as Narodnaya Vesprova[49] (revenge of the people) in Russia in the mid-nineteenth century, the nationalist struggle in Macedonia (and the involvement of the IMRO, Internal Macedonian Revolutionary Organization) in the early twentieth century,[50] the fascist Iron Guard in Bucharest, Romania,[51] the unrest in Germany in the 1920s,[52] and the activities of the FLN (Front de Libération Nationale) and OAS (Organisation de l'Armée Secrète) in Algeria in the 1950s and 1960s.[53] Underground groups in Northern Ireland also made use of a similar system of justice.[54] Ford reports that in February 1972 a group (of the Japanese Red Army) holding out in an abandoned hotel in Karuizawa was surrounded: "When the Karuizawa 'fortress' was stormed by the police, the bodies of 14 defenders were found already dead, killed as deviationists by the survivors in what one writer has described as 'an orgy of self-purification.' "[55]

Clark claims that out of 696 actions of the Basque ETA (Euzkadi ta Askatasuna) in the years 1968–90, about 50 percent were directed against a specific target.[56] He also notes that out of 287 victims of ETA attack, some 6 percent were killed for spying or informing. Indeed, Clark notes that the only source of information about accusations of treason in the ETA is the ETA itself. In almost all the cases, according to Clark, the families of the victims denied the charges and demanded that evidence be presented.

Clearly, the available information supports the conclusion that the model of political assassination that developed in Israel is not unique but is similar to models developed in other places in the world. In every country studied, there existed a phenomenon that could be interpreted as an alternative justice system, in the context of which these events were seen as delineating the moral-ideological boundaries of various assault groups, especially in justifying acts of murder intended to purge or cleanse the groups or culture from "contaminating elements."[57]

Conclusion

In this chapter we examined the assassination of Yitzhak Rabin in the context of research into political murders by Jews over a period of almost 100 years. Surveys of all these events in Palestine and later Israel produced a list of 92 cases (87 net, excluding Rabin) in the Jewish cultural community in the region. The findings reveal that most political assassination attempts were initiated by groups steeped in moral ideology. Although the vast majority took place before 1948 and involved the Haganah, Etzel, and Lehi, the model continues to apply.

Most of the political assassinations were directed by Jews against other Jews who underwent a process of strangerization, humiliation, and defamation. These victims were generally termed "traitors," "informers," or "collaborators" and were perceived by the groups to represent a real and serious danger, not just to their world view but to what they regarded as "the nation." Another frequent motive in justifying political murder, and one related to the first, is revenge and retaliation for deeds that the victim allegedly perpetrated.

In comparison with other societies and cultures, and despite the fact that 88 cases (including Rabin) were identified during this 100-year period, political murder is not a key feature of the Jewish-Israeli culture that evolved in Israel. Perhaps acts of assassination were curbed by severe cultural inhibitions. Membership in an ideological group and acceptance of the ideology of that group enable an assassin to release some of these inhibitions. The group supplies the infrastructure as well as the psychological and moral tools that make it possible to pull the trigger. It is very possible that the collective character of Israeli culture leads the assassin to belong to a group, rather than to act as a lone wolf.

That most of the victims of political murders were Jewish stems from the fact that these assassinations delineated the moral, symbolic, and ideological space of the groups, which view themselves as engaged in a pitched battle for defining the identity of what is evolving in the region, as well as its geographic borders. I used Simmel's term "strangerization" to describe the process undergone by the victim before he or she can be eliminated.

The general conception of political assassination events as it emerges from this study is of an alternative system of political-social justice in which the groups that initiate the assassination events function. When a formal justice system was established after the founding of Israel, the number of such events dropped sharply.

Like other political murders, the assassination of Yitzhak Rabin on November 4, 1995, was carried out by a Jew who was part of a group that identified with the political-religious right wing in Israel. In almost all the important senses, the murder perpetrated by Yigal Amir fits the model of political assassinations that developed in Israel. Like the others, this slaying too was carried out for political and ideological reasons—Rabin was attacked because of his political views and actions. It was the product of deliberate planning, not a temporary loss of control. As in other cases of political murder, an alternative system of justice was in operation. The assassin took steps to attain political justice that he felt he could not attain otherwise and to draw attention to his political ideology. Again, the assassination of Rabin fits the model of political murder that emerges from this study.

And yet the assassination of Rabin deviates in one major respect from other political murders. In the history of political assassinations by Jews in the twentieth century, never before Rabin was a Jew killed who held such a senior political post. What is the significance of this?

The assassination of Rabin took place in a deeply divided and segmented Jewish society in Israel, in which religion and politics are intertwined in a dangerous and sometimes fatal embrace. Rabin's death did not and could not alleviate even one of the conflicts derived from these cleavages. These cleavages are between ideological groups whose political goals are diametrically opposed to each other, with the religious-secular conflict particularly volatile. In the context of these rifts, the significance of the exception in the model of the Rabin assassination is problematic. Is this assassination a harbinger of still more serious rifts? This question is hard to answer, because a large part of what might happen depends on the steps taken by the political system in Israel and the degree of restraint and change in the rules of the game that it will be willing to adopt. But the fact remains that the assassination did nothing to heal most of the major cleavages dividing Israeli society—between Jews and Arabs, and between Jews and Jews regarding geopolitical (left versus right) and religious issues (and perhaps also ethnic and economic). The ability of Israeli society to cope with these conflicts and to process them in a nonviolent manner is key to predicting whether we are headed toward continued violent clashes and perhaps even a civil war, or toward a new flowering of tolerance and acceptance of clear boundaries for negotiating conflict. If we look at the statements of various political and ideological groups since the assassination of Rabin, the picture is not a particularly optimistic one. The level of verbal threats and incitement is considerable. More political figures and senior officials in Israeli society have become the target of threats (including nonreligious judges), and the assassination of Rabin has become a precedent, a threatening rhetorical device for various political groups. The legitimacy given to Rabin's assassination by various segments of Israeli society certainly increases the probability that such a murder could happen again, either by people from these sectors or by those who oppose them. The inability to contain the religious-secular conflict, like the left-right conflict, can lead to violent clashes, open and turbulent, in Israeli society. The geopolitical significance of this confrontation is patently clear.

Notes

I would like to express my thanks to Gideon Aran, Zali Gurevitch, Cyril Levitt, Dennis Peck, Hagit Rosenfeld, and Ehud Sprinzak for their useful comments. My deep appreciation goes to my two research assistants, Einat Yusant and Vered Winitzky-Seroussi, who contributed significantly to this research, and whose efforts enabled collection of the data. This chapter is based on several previous studies of mine (1990a and 1985), especially *Political Assassinations by Jews: A Rhetorical Device for Justice* (1993) and "Saturday Night, November 4, 1995, Kikar Malchei Israel," Tel Aviv: Political Assassination in Eretz Israel, *Alpayim* 12 (1996): 181–210 (in Hebrew). This research was funded by the Israel Association for Research Grants, budget 86-01-007; and the Social Sciences Faculty Research Fund of the Hebrew University of Jerusalem.

1. See, for example, Wilkinson, 1976; Wagner-Pacifici, 1986; and Turk, 1983.

2. See Ford, 1985; Kirkham, Levy and Crotty, 1970; and Lentz, 1988.

3. See Havens, Leiden, and Schmitt, 1970.

4. See the unique work of Clarke, 1982.

5. The theoretical approach of this research is based on contextual constructionism, which emphasizes the existence of a reality as measured or described by observers who are part of the consensus, as opposed to the social construction of that reality. See, for example, Best, 1995; Goode, 1989: 329–30; Rafter, 1990; and Goode and Ben-Yehuda, 1994.

6. See, for example, Kirkham, Levy, and Crotty, 1970: 1; Padover, 1943: 680; Havens, Leiden, and Schmitt, 1970: 2–6; Hurwood, 1970: 1; Crotty, 1971: 8; Lester, 1986: 216; Ford, 1985: 2; Ivianski, 1977: 50; Turk, 1983: 83; and Rapoport, 1971: 4. See also Ben-Yehuda, 1990c.

7. Kirkham, Levy, and Crotty, 1970: appendix A.

8. See also the reservations of Wardlaw, 1982; Hyams, 1974: 15–17, 166–67; Clutterbuck, 1977: 31, 96.

9. See, for example, Hyams, 1974: 4–17; and Ford, 1985.

10. Havens, Leiden, and Schmitt, 1970: 36–39.

11. Rapoport, 1971: 22.

12. See also Kirkham, Levy, and Crotty, 1970: 9–10; Ford, 1985: 387; Snitch, 1982; Crotty, 1971.

13. See Rapoport, 1971: 7.

14. See Clarke, 1982: 5.

15. See Kirkham, Levy, and Crotty, 1970: 78.

16. Ibid.: 148–211. Also see Crotty, 1971; Clarke, 1982; Feierabend, Feierabend, Nesvold, and Jaggar, 1971; Feirabend and Feierabend, 1976; and Ben-Yehuda, 1993.

17. For additional methodological information, see Ben-Yehuda, 1990d.

18. The original typology was most probably developed by Machiavelli. For a discussion of this, see Rapoport, 1971: 12–22.

19. Only 87 were actually analyzed, because four were not clear-cut cases: one involving the Jewish underground (1980); the possible attempted assassination of Member of the Knesset (M.K.) Meir Vilner (1967); the murder of Chaim Arlosoroff (1933); and the murder of Yedidia Segal (1948). Of the 87 cases, 6 were in the prepreparation category (7 percent), 6 in the preparation category (7 percent), 24 in the category of failed attempts (28 percent), and 51, a majority, were "successful" (59 percent). The assassination of Rabin was not included in the aggregated data.

20. This is similar to what is called blood revenge. See, for example, Wilson, 1988; Ginat, 1984; and Daly and Wilson, 1988: 221–25.

21. See Ben-Yehuda, 1985.

22. See Bar-Elli and Heyd, 1986: 68.

23. Similar feelings can also exist in the context of blood revenge.

24. See Marongiu and Newman, 1987.

25. See Rieder, 1984.

26. Ibid.: 134.

27. See Kirkham, Levy, and Crotty, 1970.

28. Jacoby, 1983: 1.

29. For a general discussion, see Kirkham, Levy, and Crotty, 1970: 241–95. For more specific conclusions, see 257–58.

30. See, for example, R. Cohen, 1986.

31. See Abel, 1982.

32. See also Wilson, 1988; S. Cohen, 1986; and Crummey, 1986.

33. See, for example, Kooistra, 1989.

34. See S. Cohen, 1986: 470.

35. See Black, 1983, 1984a, 1984b.

36. See Weisburd, 1989: 5, 10, whose interesting book deals with vigilantism and violence among Israeli settlers. Weisburd interprets this violence as deviant behavior that tries to impose a mechanism of social control on the government and Israeli society based on the theoretical work of Donald Black.

37. See Nettler, 1982: 201.

38. "Confessions" became more central when women were the victims. In some cases (for example, the killings by Lehi of Chaya Zeidenberg and Vera Duksova, both in 1948), women were forced to sign documents that described the alleged crimes for which they were being killed.

39. See Ploscowe, 1935; and Hurst, 1983.

40. See Eisenstein, 1951. I am deeply grateful to Prof. Brachyahu Lifshitz for his help and counsel about this.

41. Regarding the attempt to use Halakha to justify the assassination of de Haan, see Nakdimon and Mayzlish, 1985: 194–95; Meshi-Zahav and Meshi-Zahav, 1985: 242–43.

42. See Simmel, 1971: 143–80.

43. In the terminology of Schur, 1980, this is a process of "deviantization."

44. See Weisburd, 1981, 1989; and Segal, 1987.

45. See Karmen, 1983.

46. Rosberg and Nottingham, 1966: 303.

47. Arnon-Ohanna, 1982: 139–40; Eshed, 1988: 55–56; *Davar*, November 12, 1938.

48. *Ha'aretz*, March 3, 1986: 1. For data about the Intifada, see Shalev, 1991; Schiff and Ya'ari, 1990; Shaked, Broide, and Regev, 1990; Amnesty International Report, Nov. 1989; B'Tselem, 1994.

49. See Gaucher, 1968: 3–27.

50. Ibid.: 155–73; see also Ford, 1985: 259–60.

51. See Gaucher, 1968: 140–52; and Ford, 1985: 268.

52. Gaucher, 1968: 238–39.

53. Ibid.: 238–39, 260–64.

54. See Clutterbuck, 1977: 62–65; Corfe, 1984; and Alexander and O'Day, 1984: 21–22.

55. See Ford, 1985: 310. The quote is from Dobson and Payne, 1977: 187–91.

56. Clark, 1986: 132; see also pp. 136 and 138.

57. See Douglas, 1966; and Scott, 1972.

References

Abel, Richard L. (ed.) (1982). *The Politics of Informal Justice*. 2 vols. New York: Academic Press.

Alexander, Yonah, and Alan O'Day (eds.) (1984). *Terrorism in Ireland*. London: Croom Helm.

Arnon-Ohanna, Yuval (1978). *Fellahin in the Arab Revolt in Palestine 1936–1939*. Tel Aviv: Student Publishing House, Tel Aviv University [Hebrew].

———— (1982). *Fallachs in the Arab Revolt in Eretz Israel 1936–1939*. Tel Aviv: Tel Aviv University, Papirus [Hebrew].

Bar-Elli, Gilead, and David Heyd (1986). "Can Revenge Be Just or Otherwise Not Justified?" *Theoria* 21 (1–2): 68–86.

Ben-Yehuda, Nachman (1985). *Deviance and Moral Boundaries*. Chicago: University of Chicago Press.

———— (1990a). *The Politics and Morality of Deviance*. Albany: State University of New York Press.

———— (1990b). "Positive and Negative Deviance: More Fuel for a Controversy." *Deviant Behavior* 11: 221–43.

———— (1990c). "Political Assassinations as Rhetorical Devices: Events and Interpretations." *Journal of Terrorism and Political Violence* 2 (3): 324–50.

———— (1990d). "Gathering Dark Secrets, Hidden and Dirty Information: Some Methodological Notes on Studying Political Assassinations." *Qualitative Sociology* 13 (4): 345–72.

———— (1993). *Political Assassinations by Jews: A Rhetorical Device for Justice*. Albany: State University of New York Press.

———— (1996). "Saturday Night, November 4, 1995, Kings of Israel Plaza, Tel Aviv: Political Assassination in the Land of Israel." *Alpayim*, no. 12: 181–210 [Hebrew].

Berger, Peter L., and Thomas M. Luckmann (1966). *The Social Construction of Reality*. Baltimore: Penguin Books.

Best, Joel (ed.) (1995). *Images of Issues: Typifying Contemporary Social Problems*. 2d ed. New York: Aldine de Gruyter.

Black, Donald (1983). "Crime as Social Control." *American Sociological Review* 43: 34–45.

———— (ed.) (1984a). *Toward a General Theory of Social Control*. 2 vols. New York: Academic Press.

———— (1984b). "Crime as Social Control." In *Toward a General Theory of Social Control*. Vol. 2. New York: Academic Press, pp. 1–27.

Bohem, Christopher (1984). *Blood Revenge*. Philadelphia: University of Pennsylvania Press (1987 ed.).

B'Tselem, the Israeli Information Center for Human Rights in the Occupied Territories (1994). *Collaborators in the Occupied Territories: Human Rights Abuses and Violations*. Jerusalem, January.

Clark, Robert P. (1986). "Patterns of ETA Violence 1968–1980." In Peter H. Merkl (ed.), *Political Violence and Terror: Motifs and Motivation*. Berkeley: University of California Press, pp. 123–41.

Clarke, James W. (1982). *American Assassins: The Darker Side of Politics*. Princeton, N.J.: Princeton University Press.

Clutterbuck, Richard (1973). *Protest and the Urban Guerrilla*. New York: Abelard-Schuman.

——— (1977). *Guerrillas and Terrorists*. London: Faber and Faber.

Cohen, Ronald (ed.) (1986). *Justice: Views from the Social Sciences*. New York: Plenum Press.

Cohen, Stanley (1986). "Bandits, Rebels or Criminals: African History and Western Criminology (Review Article)." *Africa* 56 (4): 468–83.

Corfe, Tom (1984). "Political Assassination in the Irish Tradition." In Yonah Alexander and Alan O'Day (eds.), *Terrorism in Ireland*. London: Croom Helm, pp. 106–20.

Crotty, William J. (ed.) (1971). *Assassinations and the Political Order*. New York: Harper and Row.

Crummey, Donald (ed.) (1986). *Banditry, Rebellion and Social Protest in Africa*. London: James Currey.

Daly, Marti, and Margo Wilson (1988). *Homicide*. New York: Aldine de Gruyter.

Dobson, C., and Ronald Payne (1977). *The Carlos Complex: A Study in Terror*. London: Coronet Books/Hodder and Stoughton.

Douglas, Mary (1966). *Purity and Danger*. London: Routledge and Kegan Paul.

Durkheim, E. (1933, 1964). *The Division of Labor in Society*. New York: Free Press.

Eisenstein, Yehuda-David (1951). *Ozar Israel: An Encyclopedia of All Matters Concerning Jews and Judaism*. Vol. 6. New York: Pardes Publishing, 229–31 [Hebrew].

Eshed, Haggai (1988). *One Man "Mossad": Reuven Shiloah: Father of Israeli Intelligence*. Jerusalem: Edanim Publishers/Yediot Aharonot Edition [Hebrew].

Feierabend, Ivo K., Rosalind L. Feierabend, Betty A. Nesvold, and Franz M. Jaggar (1971). "Political Violence and Assassination: A Cross-National Assessment." In William J. Crotty (ed.), *Assassinations and the Political Order*. New York: Harper and Row, pp. 54–140.

Feierabend, Ivo K., and Rosalind L. Feieraband (1976). "Cross-National Comparative Study of Assassination." In Doris Y. Wilkinson (ed.), *Social Structure and Assassination Behavior*. Cambridge, Mass.: Schenkman, pp. 151–213.

Ford, Franklin L. (1985). *Political Murder from Tyrannicide to Terrorism*. Cambridge, Mass.: Harvard University Press.

Gaucher, Roland (1968). *The Terrorists from Tsarist Russia to the O.A.S.* London: Secker and Warburg.

Ginat, Joseph (1984). "The Role of Mediator: With Special Reference to Blood Disputes." In S. G. Shoham, *Israel Studies in Criminology*. Vol. 7. New York: Sheridan House, pp. 98–131.

Goode, Erich (1989). "The American Drug Panic of the 1980s: Social Construction or Objective Threat?" *Violence, Aggression and Terrorism* 3 (4): 327–48.

Goode, Erich, and Nachman Ben-Yehuda (1994). *Moral Panics: The Social Construction of Deviance*. Oxford: Blackwell.

Gurr, Ted Robert (1988). "Empirical Research on Political Terrorism: The State of the Art and How it Might Be Improved." In Robert G. Slater and Michael Stohl (eds.), *Current Perspectives on International Terrorism*. London: Macmillan, pp. 115–54.

Havens, Murray C., Carl Leiden, and Karl M. Schmitt (1970). *The Politics of Assassination*. Englewood Cliffs, N.J.: Prentice Hall.

Hobsbawm, E. J. (1959). *Primitive Rebels*. Manchester: Manchester University Press.

Hurst, James Willard (1983). "Treason." In Sanford H. Kadish (ed.), *Encyclopedia of Crime and Justice*. New York: Free Press, pp. 1559–62.

Hurwood, Bernhardt J. (1970). *Society and the Assassin*. New York: Parents' Magazine Press.

Hyams, Edward (1974). *Terrorists and Terrorism*. New York: St. Martin's Press.

Ivianski, Ze'ev (1977). "Individual Terror: Concept and Typology." *Journal of Contemporary History* 12: 43–63.

——— (1981). "Individual Terror." In David Kna'ni (ed.), *Encyclopedia of Social Sciences*. Vol. 6. Tel Aviv, Al HaMishmar [Hebrew], pp. 409–14.

Jacoby, Susan (1983). *Wild Justice: The Evolution of Revenge*. New York: Harper and Row.

Karmen, Andrew A. (1983). "Vigilantism." In Sanford H. Kadish (ed.), *Encyclopedia of Crime and Justice*. New York: Free Press, pp. 1616–18.

Kirkham, James F., Sheldon G. Levy, and William J. Crotty (eds.) (1970). *Assassination and Political Violence*. New York: Praeger.

Kooistra, Paul (1989). *Criminals as Heroes: Structure, Power and Identity*. Bowling Green, Ohio: Bowling Green State University Popular Press.

Lentz, Harris M. (1988). *Assassinations and Executions*. Jefferson, N.C.: McFarland.

Lerner, Max (1930). "Assassination." In Edwin Seligman (ed.), *Encyclopedia of the Social Sciences*. Vol. 2. New York: Macmillan, pp. 271–75.

Lester, David (1986). *The Murderer and His Murder*. New York: AMS Press.

Marongiu, Pietro, and Graeme Newman (1987). *Vengeance: The Fight Against Injustice*. Totowa, N.J.: Rowman and Littlefield.

Meshi-Zahav, Zvi, and Yehuda Meshi-Zahav (1985). *De Haan: The First Zionist Murder in Eretz Israel*. Jerusalem: Institute of Ultra-Orthodox Judaism [Hebrew].

Nakdimon, Shlomo, and Shlomo Mayzlish (1985). *De Haan: The First Political Assassination in Palestine*. Tel Aviv: Modan [Hebrew].

Nettler, Gwynn (1982). *Killing One Another: Criminal Careers*. Vol. 2. Cincinnati, Ohio: Anderson.

Padover, Saul K. (1943). "Patterns of Assassination in Occupied Territory." *Public Opinion Quarterly* 7: 680–93.

Ploscowe, Morris (1935). "Treason." In Edwin R. A. Seligman and Alvin Johnson (eds.), *Encyclopedia of the Social Sciences*. New York: MacMillan, pp. 93–96.

Rafter, Nicole Hahn (1990). "The Social Construction of Crime and Crime Control." *Journal of Research in Crime and Delinquency* 27 (4): 376–89.

Rapoport, David C. (1971). *Assassination and Terrorism*. Toronto: Canadian Publishing Corporation.

Rieder, Jonathan (1984). "The Social Organization of Vengeance." In Donald Black (ed.), *Toward a General Theory of Social Control*. New York: Academic Press, pp. 131–62.

Rosberg, Carl, and John Nottingham (1966). *The Myth of "Mau Mau": Nationalism in Kenya*. New York: Praeger.

Schiff, Zeev, and Ehud Ya'ari (1990). *Intifada: The Palestinian Uprising, Israel's Third Front*. New York: Simon and Schuster.

Schur, Edwin M. (1980). *The Politics of Deviance*. Englewood Cliffs, N.J.: Prentice Hall.

Scott, Robert A. (1972). "A Proposed Framework for Analyzing Deviance as a Property of Social Order." In R. A. Scott and J. D. Douglas (eds.), *Theoretical Perspectives on Deviance*. New York: Basic Books, pp. 9–36.

Segal, Haggai (1987). *Dear Brothers*. Jerusalem: Keter [Hebrew].

Shaked, Roni (1988). "This Is How We Liquidated Bernadotte." *Yediot Aharonot*, September 11, 1988, a special Rosh Hashana supplement, pp. 2–5 [Hebrew].

Shaked, Roni, Haim Broda, and David Regev (1990). "Yesterday the 200th Victim from the Beginning of the Intifada, Was Murdered by Reulei Panim." *Yediot Aharonot*, March 22 [Hebrew].

Shalev, Aryeh (1991). *The Intifada: Causes and Effects*. Jerusalem Post and Jaffee Center for Strategic Studies, Tel Aviv, Tel Aviv University.

Simmel, Georg (1971). *On Individuality and Social Form*. Edited and with an introduction by Donald Levine. Chicago: University of Chicago Press.

Snitch, Thomas H. (1982). "Terrorism and Political Assassinations: A Transnational Assessment, 1968–1980." *The Annals of the American Academy of Political and Social Science*, 463 (September): 54–68.

Turk, Austin (1983). "Assassination." In Sanford H. Kadish (ed.), *Encyclopedia of Crime and Justice*. New York: Free Press, pp. 82–88.

Wagner-Pacifici, Robin Erica (1986). *The Moro Morality Play: Terrorism as Social Drama*. Chicago: University of Chicago Press.

Wardlaw, Grant (1982). *Political Terrorism*. New York: Cambridge University Press.

Weisburd, David (1981). "Vigilantism as Rational Social Control: The Case of Gush Emunim Settlers." In M. J. Aronoff (ed.), *Cross-Currents in Israeli Culture and Politics*. New Brunswick, N.J.: Transaction Books, pp. 69–87.

—— (1989). *Jewish Settler Violence: Deviance as Social Reaction*. University Park: Pennsylvania State University Press.

Wilkinson, Doris Y. (ed.) (1976). *Social Structure and Assassination Behavior*. Cambridge, Mass.: Schenkman.

Wilson, Stephen (1988). *Feuding, Conflict and Banditry in Nineteenth-Century Corsica*. New York: Cambridge University Press.

Wolff, Kurt H. (1950). *The Sociology of Georg Simmel*. Translated, edited, and with an introduction by Kurt H. Wolff. Glencoe, Ill.: Free Press.

CHAPTER 3

Israel's Radical Right and the Countdown to the Rabin Assassination

EHUD SPRINZAK

Rabin's assassination did not take place in a vacuum. Although he acted alone, the slaying by Yigal Amir was the culmination of a process of delegitimation of the Israeli government by Israel's ultranationalist right. The devastating blow of the 1993 Oslo Peace Accords, in which the government agreed to the principle of territorial compromise, Israel's recognition of the Palestine Liberation Organizaton (PLO), the eruption of Muslim terrorism, and the continued implementation of Palestinian autonomy on the West Bank that had been occupied by Israel in 1967 had led to unprecedented radicalization of the extreme right and the creation of the circumstantial conditions for the murder. This chapter represents an effort to reconstruct the psycho-political trajectory of the Israeli extreme right, which paved the way for Yigal Amir and strengthened his determination to act.

After Oslo: The Struggles of Gush Emunim and the Yesha Council

The Oslo agreements, made public in September 1993 and welcomed by a majority of Israelis, stunned Gush Emunim, the leading settler movement, and the heads of the Council of Yesha (an acronym for Judea, Samaria and Gaza—the occupied territories). As experienced in setbacks as they had become over the years, none of them had expected Yitzhak Rabin, Israel's Mr. Security, to recognize the PLO and approve a far-reaching autonomy plan. The settlers' dedication to their cause led them to believe that Israelis would never accept Yasser Arafat's "terrorist organization" and would take to the streets to stop the government. The positive response of most Israelis to the agreement and their fascination with the Rabin-Arafat handshake on the White House lawn doubled the shock of the settlers.

Approval of the Oslo agreements by most of the nation seems to explain the mild response of the Yesha Council to the new reality and its initial hesitancy to launch an opposition. Although a virulent antigovernment demonstration, held on September 7 in Jerusalem, attracted nearly 200,000 angry Israelis, this impressive showing had no meaningful follow-up. A series of demonstrations in front of the Knesset protesting official ratification of the agreements looked more like a big picnic than an emphatic response to a looming disaster.

The sluggish settler struggle caught fire in response to an unwelcome but expected stimulus—Islamic terrorism. At the end of October 1993, the grace period for Oslo that had lasted nearly two months was brought to an abrupt end. Several squads of Muslim terrorists—most associated with Hamas and the Islamic Jihad—attacked and killed a number of settlers, soldiers, and Israeli civilians. This violence ignited the settler community at once. Triggering an immediate radicalization of the Yesha Council heads, the outbreak of Muslim terrorism led to a "Jewish intifada": a mini-insurrection of settlers consisting of a series of attacks on Arab transportation, the stoning and destruction of hundreds of cars, tire burning, road blocks, property damage, and even killing.

The event that touched off the Jewish intifada was the ruthless killing of Haim Mizrahi, a Beit El settler burned alive by his Palestinian attackers. In the context of pent-up frustration, settler fury over this awful slaying brought about an especially aggressive response. Hundreds of Jews ravaged Arab villages, destroying property and attacking individual Palestinians. After learning that the Mizrahi murder was carried out by a group belonging to Yasser Arafat's Fatah organization, Yesha heads claimed the government was directly responsible for the murder. Frightened by the prospect of new terrorism, they made a public commitment to fight Palestinian militants with or without governmental approval. A few days after the bloody reaction to the Beit El murder, hundreds of settlers took to the roads during morning rush hour and brought all Arab traffic to a standstill. After a promise from the military commander in the area that the army would take aggressive action against the terrorists, the settlers agreed to evacuate—but not before declaring their intention to repeat the action in the future. Members of Yesha's moderate rabbinical council subsequently ruled that shooting Palestinian attackers and their collaborators was legitimate. And religious followers of these rabbis were told that no legal barriers should stop them from pursuing their interests.[1]

The settler radicalization, culminating in the Yesha Council's decision to use all nonviolent means at its disposal to bring the government down, was further intensified by a new series of assassinations. A lethal Arab ambush near Hebron led to the killing of Ephraim Ayubi, Rabbi Haim Drukman's driver. Drukman, a revered rabbinical authority and Gush Emunim founder, somehow survived the attack. The terror wave peaked in January 1994, with the murder in Kiryat Arba of Mordechai Lapid and his son Shalom, a yeshiva student. Lapid, a long time "Refusenik" from the Soviet Union who had finally been allowed to leave for Israel in the early 1970s, was an exemplary figure within the settler movement. A member of the original Elon Moreh group, husband of popular political militant Miriam Lapid, and father of eleven children, Lapid was a settler legend. The government was virtually powerless in controlling the emotional eruption of the settler community—especially the enraged residents of Hebron and Kiryat Arba.

The Hamas terror campaign, which resumed in October and November, created deep fears among the settlers. The prospect of an impending Palestinian autonomy and Palestinian police force convinced the Jewish residents of Judea and Samaria—who believed that all Palestinians were terrorists—that terrorism would now be officially recognized by the Rabin government. This led to a hysterical public relations campaign based on the slogan "Don't Give Them Guns." The people of Israel were warned—with ominous posters plastered all over the country—that thousands of guns, freely handed to the Palestinian police, constituted the liberation and arming of thousands of terrorists. Settler and radical right leaders threatened that if they were stopped by armed Palestinian policemen they would shoot to kill. A plan to create a vigilante settler militia, HaShomer (the watchman), was also unveiled. (Israelis with long memories recalled that the name of the first self-defense organization of the Jewish community in Palestine, an underground organization formed in 1907, was also HaShomer.)

The most significant effect of the campaign of terror on the settler community was the introduction by extremist settler organizations of the language of delegitimation in reference to the Rabin government. Apart from Rabbi Meir Kahane's followers, who have always favored the use of Jewish counterterrorism against the Arabs, two groups began gaining momentum at the expense of the more restrained Yesha Council: Mateh Ma'amatz (effort center) and Elyakim Ha'etzni's Center for Struggle to

Halt the Autonomy Plan. Mateh Ma'amatz, a once-defunct Gush Emunim action group, was revived under Yitzhak Novik, a devotee of extremist settler leader Rabbi Moshe Levinger. Inspired by the government's "betrayal" of Eretz Israel and its inability to defeat Palestinian terrorism, Mateh Ma'amatz activists began to recruit yeshiva students for rioting. Ma'amatz activists were responsible for posters depicting Yitzhak Rabin's face in Yasser Arafat's *kefiya* headdress and labeling the prime minister "traitor." Soon the titles "assassin" and "murderer" were added to the posters and emblazoned on huge banners.

The wave of terror was especially helpful to Elyakim Ha'etzni, a Kiryat Arba attorney known for his radicalism and vitriolic language. Ha'eztni's traditional catastrophic warnings against a coming settler disaster, which had fallen on deaf ears, became more influential in January 1994. More frustrated settlers began to listen to Ha'etzni's appeals and to heed his call to launch an opposition campaign capable of bringing down the government.

> Rise up and act! We have done nothing. Protests, demonstrations, tent cities, even setting up road blocks are insufficient against a government engaged in national treason. In France, defeated in 1940, when Marshal Pétain gave in to Hitler and made an alliance with him—just as Lieutenant General Rabin did by shaking Yasser Arafat's dirty hand—de Gaulle did not demonstrate in protest. Although the regime was born in a democratic way. . . . He deserted, rebelled against a Nazi army of collaboration. . . .
>
> This is why I am saying loud and clear: an IDF [Israeli Defense Forces] soldier, though Jewish, who would pull us, our wives, our children, and grandchildren from our houses and make us refugees—will, in our view, be conducting a pogrom. We shall look upon him as a violent thug behaving like a Cossack. It is no secret that all through Israel's glorious history, there were dark and shameful chapters in which Jews beat, tortured, turned in, and even put to death their brothers, and leaders have led their followers to disaster.[2]

Although the more pragmatic Yesha Council did not lose its organizational grip over the settler struggle against the Oslo agreements, it was Mateh Ma'amatz and the Center for Struggle to Halt the Autonomy Plan that gradually began to dictate the rhetoric of the campaign. Ha'etzni's anti-Rabin posters, increasingly seen in right-wing demonstrations, were even more vitriolic than his articles in *Nekuda*, the settlers' journal. The most nefarious of these posters depicted Rabin as an unsavory Arab, smiling at Yasser Arafat and washing his hands in blood. The caption associated the prime minister with Palestinian terrorism and assigned him direct responsibility for Jews killed by Hamas violence. And Ha'etzni, though the key figure in the Center for Struggle and the one directly responsible for the style of the campaign, was not alone. Several distinguished right-wingers declared their support for the organization, not the least of whom was Colonel (res.) Shlomo Baum, an Israeli war hero of the 1950s. Little effort was made by the Yesha Council to contain the virulence of Ha'etzni's propaganda. Thousands of copies of the posters were distributed to participants in Yesha antigovernment rallies.

The Hebron Massacre in Perspective

The Hebron massacre, the most extreme reaction to Arab terrorism, took place at 5:10 in the morning on Friday, February 25, 1994. About 500 Muslims were kneeling in Ramadan prayer in the Isaac Hall of the Tomb of the Patriarchs in Israeli-occupied Hebron. A captain in the Israeli Defense Forces, armed with an automatic Galil rifle, broke into the hall and sprayed the worshipers with bullets. Fully engaged in their prayers, unarmed and unprepared, the praying Muslims never had a chance. In less than 3 minutes, the officer unloaded four magazines containing 111 bullets. Twenty-nine Muslims were killed at once; more than 100 were wounded. A clog in the captain's gun ended the killing spree before the fifth magazine could be loaded and allowed several unhurt worshipers to throw a fire extinguisher at the killer, bring him down, and beat him to death. In the hysteria, panic, and outrage that spread through the occupied territories as the Hebron tragedy became known, additional violence took place. Palestinians and Israeli soldiers clashed throughout the West Bank and Gaza leaving nine more Palestinians dead and nearly 200 wounded.

The shock of the Hebron massacre multiplied when the killer's identity was discovered. He turned out to be Dr. Baruch Goldstein, the emergency physician for Jewish settlers in Hebron and the adjacent town of Kiryat Arba, and a devout Orthodox Jew. Goldstein, 38, father of four, was one of the most respected residents of Kiryat Arba. An able doctor and former town council member, Goldstein was responsible for treating many Jewish victims of Palestinian terrorism. He also at times cared for wounded Arabs; at least one Palestinian resident of Hebron said that Goldstein had saved his life. Goldstein, according to several reports, woke up early on the morning of February 25. Dressing in his army uniform as if he were on reserve duty, he attended an early Jewish prayer service at the Abraham Hall of the Tomb of the Patriarchs, a shrine sacred to both Muslims and Jews. Sometime after 4: 45 A.M., upon the conclusion of his prayers, Goldstein stepped into the

Isaac Hall and hid behind a large pillar. According to eye witnesses, he did not immediately shoot but waited for the traditional Muslim *sojud*, a prayer in which the worshipers kneel in the direction of Mecca.

Goldstein's massacre was immediately described as the unpredictable act of a madman. The prime minister, Yitzhak Rabin, advanced this deranged lone-killer theory, maintaining that Goldstein was insane. The killer could not, according to the prime minster, be just a normal Jew. Speaking before a packed Knesset hall, Rabin said that he was personally ashamed of the massacre and that in his worst nightmares he could not dream of an Israeli conducting such a heinous crime. Not surprisingly, the prime minister's crazy-loner theory was supported by the leading settler organization in the occupied territories, the Yesha Council. The heads of the council were quick to point out that Baruch Goldstein represented no one but himself and that the settlers were as shocked by the massacre as anybody else. Accusing Rabin of tolerating Arab terrorism, these right-wing Jews argued that it was the blunders of the government that drove Goldstein to commit this atrocity.

The problem with the crazy-loner theory was that it was not shared by many of Goldstein's close friends in Kiryat Arba. While denying any previous knowledge of the attack plan, they justified it as a response to Palestinian terrorism. According to this reasoning, the Palestinians had to be taught that Jewish blood is not cheap, and Goldstein's was the only way of getting that message across. But the massacre was not just an act of political-military revenge. It was, according to these colleagues—members or supporters of the radical fundamentalist Kach movement—a religious act and a sacred mission. In killing these Muslim enemies of the Jewish people, Goldstein was engaged in *kidush hashem*, sanctification of God's name. By avenging the blood of settlers recently murdered by Palestinian terrorists, Goldstein did what God wanted him to do: he glorified God's name. And the act carried another purpose. In addition to the warning of terror it sent to the Arabs, Goldstein had a message for Rabin and his ministers: to put an end to the peace process with the Palestinians. The fundamentalist and messianic doctor had no doubt that God wanted the government of Israel to abandon the sacrilegious sale of Eretz Israel (the biblical Land of Israel). A number of Baruch Goldstein's friends made it known that in their eyes he was a holy man: Goldstein had engaged in a supreme act of *mesirut nefesh* (total devotion), which they themselves should also have done had they had the doctor's courage and sacred sense of mission. One could even detect a sense of guilt about Goldstein's extraordinary personal sacrifice.

There is no question that Baruch Goldstein conducted the crime on his own and that nobody knew about the plan or assisted in either its preparation or its execution. It is equally clear that the act was purposeful and premeditated. The Hebron massacre was conducted within an elaborate ideological and political framework that provided justification for anti-Arab terrorism. Although we will never fully understand the ultimate emotional trigger that ignited this suicidal massacre, it is patently clear that the Kiryat Arba physician planned the attack well in advance, wanted to kill as many Muslims as possible, was certain that God approved of the killing, and hoped and believed that the massacre would halt the peace process. If we add to these facts Goldstein's long and close association with Kach, the radical fundamentalist movement established by the late Rabbi Meir Kahane, the Hebron disaster loses its one-time, isolated status. It acquires, instead, a political meaning: it becomes a collective act by proxy, a colossal demonstration of political violence expressing crisis in an entire fundamentalist milieu. Given the enormous potential damage that the Israeli-Palestinian peace process holds for Zionist religious fundamentalists, it is not an exaggeration to describe the Hebron massacre as an extreme reaction of these messianic Jews to the political threat posed to their theological convictions and collective existence.

The Hebron massacre had a most dramatic and radicalizing effect on Arab and Jewish extremists. For the Arabs, it appears certain that the massacre triggered a massive Hamas retaliation. There are many indications that Iz-a-Din al-Qassam squads, the military arm of Hamas, as well as the Islamic Jihad, were determined to engage in strategic anti-Israeli terrorism before the Hebron tragedy. Yahya Ayash, Iz-a-Din al-Qassam's mastermind, the "engineer," was apparently eager to strike. But Goldstein's atrocity instantly upgraded Hamas retaliation. All inhibitions regarding the killing of innocent Israeli civilians within the Green Line, the post–June 1967 border, were now removed. Two Hamas car bombs in the cities of Afula and Hadera killed and wounded a large number of Israeli civilians. There was more to come.[3]

The Hebron massacre also had a profound impact on Jewish extremists. Though unprepared and shocked, Israel's pragmatic extreme right blamed the authorities for Goldstein's act. Rabin's government, not the deranged doctor, was responsible for the terrible tragedy. By recognizing the PLO "terror organization" and reducing its own antiterrorist efforts, the government was instrumental in bringing about a national disaster of unimaginable proportions. The Hebron massacre was increasingly and fatalistically seen by a large number of settlers as just the preface to a larger storm. Blood and catastrophe were hanging in the air and the time for moderation was gone.

The Crisis of Tel Rumeida and Rabbinical Rulings for Soldiers

The Israeli government's immediate reaction to the February 28 atrocity in Hebron was to outlaw Kach and Kahane Chai. The Kahanist groups, which continued to preach anti-Arab violence and praised Baruch Goldstein as a martyr, were declared illegal terrorist organizations. Their offices were sealed and their propaganda materials confiscated. About ten leaders of these organizations were put in administrative detention, an emergency procedure used by the military commander of the area in high-risk circumstances.

Although the leaders of the Yesha Council, who never subscribed to Kahanist ideology, disapproved of the draconian measures taken against Kach and Kahane Chai, they did not make a big deal out of it. Most understood that Goldstein's ideological supporters had to be punished. Government officials were privately told by Yesha activists that the banning of the Kahanist organizations was long overdue.[4] Of much greater concern to the settler establishment was a by-product of the massacre—the increasing likelihood that Hebron's Jewish community would be evacuated.

Before the February massacre, there were no evacuation plans for the small Jewish community of Hebron. Although Prime Minister Rabin knew that this radical enclave, consisting of 500 Jews living in the midst of 130,000 Palestinians, was the most volatile settlement in the West Bank, he did not have contingency plans for their removal. The Oslo agreement with the PLO stipulated that settlement evacuation would be discussed only in the final stage of the Israeli-Palestinian negotiations and after implementation of Palestinian autonomy in Gaza and the West Bank. Neither the PLO nor the Israeli government had legal grounds for demanding an immediate evacuation. But the massacre at the Tomb of the Patriarchs, which led to the indefinite suspension of the peace process, created a new reality. It validated the call of many Israeli doves, who considered the settlers anti-Oslo provocateurs, for an immediate evacuation. Evacuation advocates maintained that the removal of Hebron's Jewish community was no longer a Palestinian desire but an Israeli interest. Referring to the massacre, left-wing members of Rabin's cabinet warned of worse confrontations in the future. They maintained that the continued presence of Jewish provocateurs among Hebron's Palestinians was a recipe for future massacres and a time bomb on the road to peace. Only decisive government action could, in their view, stop settler provocations and send a reassuring message to peaceful Palestinians and Jews.

In mid-March the government began to seriously consider evacuating the seven Jewish families living in Tel Rumeida. This small hill in central Hebron had been settled since the mid-1980s by a small number of very radical Jewish families. If Jewish Hebron spelled trouble for Arab-Israeli relations, Tel Rumeida was the eye of the storm. Some of the most extremist settlers, such as Kach's head, Baruch Marzel, chose to live there, isolated from the rest of Hebron's Jews and surrounded by 30,000 Palestinians. Tel Rumeida expressed the ultimate ultranationalist defiance. It epitomized the claim of the Jewish right to settle all of Eretz Israel. Constantly guarded by an entire army company lest they be butchered by their neighbors, Tel-Rumeida's Jewish residents kept up a constant provocation of their Palestinian neighbors.

The news of a possible evacuation stunned the settler leaders. Evacuating Hebron or even small Tel Rumeida would not be interpreted as a benevolent act but as a huge blow to the very heart of the Jewish venture in Judea and Samaria. Hebron, the City of the Patriarchs, second in holiness only to Jerusalem, was the first settlement site chosen by Jews after the Six Day War. Hebron's ancient Jewish community had been destroyed in 1929 in a brutal Arab pogrom. When the government of Israel decided in 1968 to evacuate Hebron's illicit settlement, it was only able to do so by establishing Kiryat Arba, a Jewish city adjacent to Hebron. But by 1979 the settlers were back in the city itself, under the leadership of Rabbi Moshe Levinger. Taking advantage of the weakness of Menachem Begin, who was outraged by the terrorist murder of a local yeshiva student, they forced resettlement of old Jewish property in the middle of the city. There was plenty of blood spilled in this struggle to settle and remain in Hebron, including intense PLO terrorism and the birth and operation of the Jewish underground.[5] So the possible removal of the Jewish enclave on Tel Rumeida was seen by the settlers as the beginning of the end. If the Rabin-Peres government, already responsible for the Oslo "treason," could evacuate Tel Rumeida, it could evacuate all the settlements in Judea and Samaria.

The looming "disaster" in Tel Rumeida produced one of the most effective mobilization efforts in settler history. Though not officially informed about the planned evacuation, the settlers prepared for the worst. Israel's parliamentary opposition was put on alert. Contingency plans were made to bring tens of thousands of ultranationalist activists to Hebron, to stop the removal by planting their own bodies on the holy ground. Heads of right-wing organizations, including many support groups formed within the Green Line, were instructed to prepare for an unprecedented ordeal. Numerous lobbyists pleaded with Rabin to spare Tel Rumeida, arguing that the danger of another massacre was minimal. Others warned the prime minister of a desperate settler struggle he could not win. Israel's General Security Services (GSS), already under investigation for failing to antici- pate the Hebron massacre, had become increasingly concerned about Jew- ish bloodshed.

The most dramatic response to the Tel Rumeida evacuation plan was made by several prominent rabbis—Shlomo Goren, Abraham Shapiro, Shaul Yisraeli, and Moshe Tzvi Neria. The four rabbis issued several Ha- lakhic rulings categorically prohibiting evacuation of Jewish settlements within Eretz Israel. Rabbi Goren, Israel's former chief rabbi and a highly regarded Halakhic authority, was the first to rule against settlement re- moval. He did it in a detailed reply to a question addressed to him in No- vember 1993 by the rabbinical council of Yesha.[6] In an expanded version of that judgment, written in the aftermath of the Hebron massacre, Goren wrote:

> The criminal initiative to evacuate Hebron should be met with *messirut hanefesh* [utmost devotion]. The ruling on such a heinous crime, like the ruling on saving life, is *yehareg uval ya'avor* [be killed but do not trespass]. If the gov- ernment succeeds in its plan, God forbid, the evacuation of Hebron must be responded to by *kria* [ripping one's clothing—a sign of death in the fami- ly]. . . . According to the Halakha, the meaning of the destruction of Hebron, God forbid . . . is like the killing of people, which requires *kria* for the dead. . . . This is why we must give our life in the struggle against this vicious plan of the government of Israel, which relies on the Arabs for its majority, and be pre- pared to die rather then allow the destruction of Hebron.[7]

Although Rabbi Goren's ruling, which preceded the Tel Rumeida crisis, produced only a minor controversy, the ruling of Shapiro, Yisraeli, and Neria reverberated throughout the country. The three rabbis were by far the most influential and authoritative in the Zionist religious camp. The first two were the heads of Yeshivat Mercaz Harav—Gush Emunim's founding yeshiva—and Neria, the oldest of the three, was the historical fa- ther of all Bnei-Akiva yeshivas. The shocking nature of the latter ruling was that it was addressed to the nation's soldiers. All Israeli soldiers were publicly told that evacuation orders were illegal. They were instructed by the three rabbis to disobey any order to evacuate Jewish settlers from Jewish land.[8]

The most damaging aspect of the rabbis' ruling was not, however, the potential refusal of a few religious soldiers to participate in Tel Rumeida's evacuation, but its symbolic effect. This was not just a case of asserting the preeminence of a religious-Halakhic text over the Knesset and its laws. The new and shocking development was that highly regarded spiritual authorities no longer respected the sanctity of the Israeli army. Long recognized as the nation's only guarantee of survival, the IDF has never been seen as merely an instrumental institution for compulsory army duty. Service in the Israeli army had become a moral calling and a virtue. The very rabbis who called for disobedience were themselves part of the post-1967 religious enhancement of this norm. Few Israelis missed the profound implications of the rabbinical ruling, and the issue refused to leave the headlines.

Although the rabbinical ruling failed to get endorsements from nonreligious Jews, it was approved by the majority of Israel's Orthodox rabbis. Rabbi Eliezer Waldman, head of Kiryat Arba's *hesder* yeshiva—one that combines religious studies and army service—saluted the ruling and promised to abide by it: "This government was born in sin. It relies on the votes of the PLO and has no right to go against any Jewish settlement." Rabbi Dov Lior, Waldman's colleague in the yeshiva leadership and Kiryat Arba's chief rabbi, was even more adamant. Besides fully endorsing the decree of the three rabbis, he privately issued a special ruling that Jews should be ready to give their lives for Hebron.[9] One interpretation of Lior's judgment was that suicide was permissible in the event of forced evacuation.

Ultimately, neither Hebron nor Tel Rumeida was evacuated. Based on careful analyses submitted to him, which predicted a high likelihood of violent confrontation with the settlers and possible Jewish fatalities, Rabin decided to let the settlers stay.[10] The message was delivered to Israel's Chief Rabbinate on April 4, 1994. The messenger was Mota Gur, deputy defense minister and close to the settlers. Walking a fine line between their official duty as state rabbis and their respect for Shapiro, Israeli, and Neria, Israel's chief rabbis produced this statement:

> The Council of the Chief Rabbinate acknowledges with great satisfaction the announcement of Deputy Defense Minister Mota Gur that the government of Israel has no intention of evacuating either Jewish settlers or Jewish settlements. . . . It is therefore clear that the question of military orders to evacuate

settlers or settlements—which are against the Halakha—is not on the agenda and the army must be kept out of the political debate.[11]

The relief expressed by the council as well as by several other rabbinical bodies was greatly diluted by a new blow to the settlers. The Gaza-Jericho plan, part one of the Oslo Accords, which had been suspended since the Hebron massacre, was finally implemented in April. Yasser Arafat was allowed to land in Gaza, and the Palestinian autonomy became a fait accompli. The extremist rabbinical ruling, which under other circumstances might have been reversed, remained in full force. It became, in fact, a symbol of rabbinical defiance. A larger number of Orthodox rabbis, hesitant until then, expressed their readiness to support it. On May 3, 1994, a large rabbinical gathering, convened under the title the Eretz Israel Rabbinical Union, fully endorsed the judgment that soldiers must disobey orders. Rabbi Nahum Rabinovitz, head of the *hesder* yeshiva of Ma'ale Adumim, called upon his colleagues to take Torah scrolls into the streets of Jerusalem and stay there "until our outcry is heard in Heaven and our message penetrates secular hearts too." Representing more than 1,000 rabbis from all over the country, the new body issued an unequivocal warning to the government:

> The so-called peace agreement, made by a government supported by a tiny majority dependent on the Arab vote, is a complete contradiction to peace. The implementation of the agreement may lead, God forbid, to great danger to human life. This is why anyone who can stop this "agreement" and does not do so breaks the rule "you shall not stand idle when your brother is in danger."[12]

The intense struggle against the legitimacy of his government did not leave Yitzhak Rabin unaffected. Rabin, a secular sabra to the bone, never liked the settlers and their messianic rhetoric. During his first term as prime minister (1974–77), he was the target of a large number of Gush Emunim protests. After 1975, Rabin had also learned to appreciate the dangerous maneuverability of the settlers as well as their determination. Convinced that these fanatics were ready to do anything to fulfill their dream of a Greater Israel, he concluded that he could neither trust them nor take their words at face value. In 1994 and following the intensification of the settler struggle against his peace policies, Rabin lost his patience. Unable to understand the settlers' sense of despair over the potential collapse of their Judea and Samaria dream, he saw only their efforts to delegitimate his government. Unlike President Ezer Weizmann, who had psychologically disarmed many of these angry people by paying occasional visits to their West

Bank settlements after terror attacks, Rabin remained aloof and cold. He had no sympathy for those who vilified him and wished to bring down his government. Repeatedly humiliating them with gestures and name-calling—he called them *kugelagers* (a mechanical part of the car wheel that squeaks noisily) and "propellers" (loud devices that circulate hot air)—Rabin was telling the settlers that regardless of their opposition and pain he was determined to move ahead with the peace process. It was difficult to say who was the winner of this tragic psychological warfare—Rabin the bitter and insecure prime minister, at whose house protestors screamed "traitor" and "assassin," or the settlers, who felt humiliated and marginalized by their government. What had become increasingly clear was that the settlers' political struggle against Yitzhak Rabin had assumed a highly personal character. They hated him; he despised them.

Din Rodef and Din Moser

The rabbis' confrontation with Yitzhak Rabin, already intense, reached new heights in February 1995. Following an unprecedented series of Hamas and Islamic Jihad suicide bombings inside Israel, which took the lives of 87 Israelis, wounded 202, and traumatized the entire nation, the heads of Yesha's rabbinical council decided to explore the possibility of putting the government on trial based on *din rodef* and *din moser*. A *moser* and a *rodef*, according to the Halakha, are among the worst kinds of Jews. They betray the community through acts that could result in the loss of innocent Jewish life. A *moser* is a Jew suspected of providing gentiles with information about Jews or with illegally giving them Jewish property. Since the Halakha refers to Eretz Israel as the sacred property of the Jewish people, Jews are obliged to kill a *moser*. A *rodef* is a person about to commit or facilitate the murder of a Jew. The purpose of his immediate execution is to save Jewish life. This rule does not apply to a killer caught after the murder, who must go on trial. *Din rodef* is the only case in which the Halakha allows the killing of a Jew without trial.

The fact that the escalation of Muslim terrorism and the indiscriminate targeting of Israeli civilians were largely a response to Goldstein's massacre was hardly noticed by the ultranationalist rabbis or anybody else among Israel's extreme right. Instead, the right blamed two individuals—Yitzhak Rabin and Shimon Peres—for the lives of innocent victims. By ordering Israeli soldiers out of Gaza and Jericho, by allowing the formation of a large armed Palestinian police, and by relaxing the anti-Palestinian struggle of the nation's security forces, Oslo's two architects made it possible for Hamas and the Islamic Jihad to kill Jews. Their hands were seen as "drenched in Jewish blood." The rabbis explored the validity of *din moser* and *din rodef* for Rabin and Peres in a long question addressed to 40 Halakhic authorities:

> What is the rule about this bad government? Can they be regarded as accomplices to acts of murder committed by terrorists, since in their plans they are responsible for the reinforcement and arming of these terrorists. . . . Should they be tried according to the Halakha? And if proven guilty as accomplices to murder, what should their sentence be? If they are, indeed . . . punishable in court, is it the obligation of every individual to bring them to trial in a court of justice, or, for lack of an alternative, in an ordinary secular court? Is it not the obligation of community leaders to warn the head of the government and his ministers that if they keep pursuing the agreement, after the terrible experience of stage one [Oslo I] in all of Judea and Samaria, they will be subject . . . to the Halakhic ruling of *din moser*, as those who surrender Jewish life and property to gentiles?
>
> It is no longer possible to silence the question that bursts from the broken hearts of many Jews in this country and abroad. . . . We know that the very interest in this issue may stimulate, God forbid, intense controversy in the nation. Aware of the actual conditions on the ground, we are worried that the situation will get worse, that these questions will be asked by the majority of the people, and that many of the victims [of terrorism] may be filled with sentiments of revenge.[13]

Although the letter of the rabbis was formulated as a question addressed to other, more prominent, rabbis, it was itself a highly incriminating document. The questions about *din rodef* and *din moser* were not presented even-handedly. The long letter was full of harsh statements about the government and suppositions about its iniquitous activities. The causal relation between the government's peace process and Muslim terrorism was stated as a given, and all Palestinians were collectively referred to as terrorists. No distinction was made, for example, between the peaceful PLO and the Hamas terrorists. There was, moreover, no reference to the possible impact of the Hebron massacre on the eruption of Muslim terrorism. The reader was led to unequivocal conclusions about the criminal responsibility of Yitzhak Rabin and Shimon Peres for the suicide bombings. An objective reader might easily conclude that the three rabbis who drafted the letter, Dov Lior, Eliezer Melamed, and Daniel Shilo, had themselves reached the conclusion that Shimon Peres and Yitzhak Rabin qualified for *din moser* and *din rodef*.

Especially noticeable in this context was the harsh language increasingly used against Israeli leaders by North American Orthodox rabbis. In a stormy meeting with Shmuel Hollander, Israel's Orthodox cabinet secretary who visited New York over the high holy days, the rabbis compared Yasser Arafat to Adolf Hitler. They told the stunned official that his boss was a *moser* and a *rodef*.[14] Rabbi Abraham Hecht, the prominent head of New York's large Sha'arei Zion synagogue, did not hesitate to say in public what many of his colleagues had been saying privately. In an October 9 interview, Hecht maintained: "According to Jewish Halakha, Rabin deserves to die. He who intentionally transfers living people, money, or property to strangers commits, according to the Halakha, a crime punishable by death. Maimonides maintained that he who kills such person is doing the right thing."[15] In a television interview about this uncommonly harsh statement, Hecht smiled and said it was a *mitzvah* (Jewish commandment) to kill Rabin and that he was sorry he was personally unable to fulfill it.

Following the assassination of Prime Minister Rabin and the growing interest in the rabbinical authorities who may have legitimized Yigal Amir's act, there were additional indications that many discussions of *din moser* and *din rodef* preceded the murder. Rabbi Yoel Bin-Nun, a Gush Emunim founder and long-time critic of the extremist wing of the movement, openly charged several rabbis with authorizing the killing. In a meeting with Israel's chief rabbis, Bin-Nun mentioned the names of Kiryat Arba's Dov Lior and Ma'ale Adumim's Nahum Rabinovitz. Bin-Nun maintained further that a young rabbi from Gush Etzion, Shmuel Dvir, who had made death threats against Rabin in the previous months, had told others that he knew of a *rodef* ruling by seven prominent rabbis.[16] Although none of Bin-Nun's charges could be fully substantiated and he later apologized in public, his allegations exposed the culture of Halakhic defiance that preceded the assassination, including the widespread discussion of *moser* and *rodef*. It is unlikely that any of the aforementioned rabbis issued a death sentence for Rabin and Peres, but a number of them allowed their students to believe that Rabin and Peres had more than qualified for the infamous titles. With perhaps the exception of Rabbi Shlomo Aviner, who forbade his students to use slanderous language against the heads of state,[17] rabbis such as Lior and Rabinovitz had increasingly joined the smear campaign. A retrospective examination suggests that it was just a question of time before a hot-headed disciple would jump to his own conclusion.

The culture of Halakhic character assassination was accurately expressed in the ultra-Orthodox journal *HaShavua*, which devoted many pages to anti-Rabin incitement and occasionally used the terms "traitor," "madman," and "non-Jew":

> There are today [settler] groups that favor violence of the first order. They even demand permission to assassinate the heads of the government, especially Prime Minister Yitzhak Rabin, against whom there is *din rodef*. . . . The heads of the nationalist ultra-Orthodox assert that an extremely hard line against the government—subject to *din rodef*—must be adopted. All those with whom we spoke tried to maintain that the discussion is totally theoretical and that there is no intention to kill Rabin and Peres. . . .
>
> The new situation presents the ultra-Orthodox public with alternatives it has never before faced. One option is to forcefully challenge the group that took over governance of the state. . . . There is no reason for us to allow the vicious maniacs who run this government to take Jews as sheep to slaughter. "Rabin is a traitor," says Rabbi Gadi Ben-Zimra, "and I have no problem with saying this. It's clear that the government is betraying all values . . . and endangering the state."[18]

Baruch HaGever: The Maturation of the Kahanist Counterculture

Purim in 1995 was an occasion for a special ceremony among the radical right, the anniversary of the Hebron massacre and the death of Dr. Baruch Goldstein. Most Israelis, deeply repelled by the 1994 massacre, knew vaguely about Goldstein's supporters and the special tombstone at his grave in central Kiryat Arba. What they did not know, however, was that an entire Baruch Goldstein cult had been formed and that Goldstein's memory had become the rallying point for the disbanded Kahane movement. A surprisingly large number of people had come to consider Baruch Goldstein a holy man and an exemplary figure.

In spite of the fears of a major Arab or Jewish provocation, the Goldstein memorial services went smoothly. The entire Palestinian area was put under strict curfew and Kiryat Arba itself was sealed off. Only a small number of local Jews were allowed to participate. Organized by "friends of the family"—Kach and Kahane activists who could not appear under movement banners—the memorial service was subdued and controlled. Participants prayed for Goldstein and contributed money to religious institutions named after him. They also bought a large quantity of Goldstein memorabilia.[19]

Of much greater significance in the commemoration and preservation of the Goldstein legacy was, however, a 550-page edited volume published in March 1995. The full title of the book was *Baruch HaGever* [Baruch, the Man]: *A Memorial Volume for Dr. Baruch Goldstein, the Saint, May God Avenge His Blood*. The volume, edited by Michael Ben Horin, a Golan settler and former president of the "Free State of Judea," had been prepared in total secrecy. Although Ben Horin's editorial board failed to convince several prominent Goldstein supporters—such as Dov Lior, Kiryat Arba's chief rabbi, and Rabbi Israel Ariel of Jerusalem's Temple Institute—to contribute to the volume for fear of public condemnation, it was an unusual collection of essays, testimonies, and letters of support. Never before had any Israeli extreme right organization produced such an impressive compendium. The fact that of all right-wing organizations it was the small and defunct Kach and Kahane Chai that were able to put together *Baruch HaGever* was a testimony to the maturation of Israel's small Kahanist counterculture. The volume's contributors had two things in common: at some period in their lives most had been disciples of Rabbi Meir Kahane, and they all admired Baruch Goldstein.

The major theme of the book was conceived by Rabbi Yitzhak Ginzburg, head of the radical Tomb of Joseph Yeshiva in Nablus. Ginzburg, a Lubavitcher Hasidic rabbi who wrote the lead essay, had never been a follower of Rabbi Meir Kahane. An extremist thinker in his own right who had specialized in the study of Kabbala, Ginzburg made headlines in 1988 by providing Halakhic support for several of his students who had unilaterally shot Arab civilians. Making it clear that there is a vast difference between the killing of civilian Arabs and Jews, the radical rabbi did not conceal his opinion that under the prevailing security conditions in Judea and Samaria it was fully legitimate to kill noncombatant Palestinians.[20] As for the Hebron atrocity and Baruch Goldstein, the rabbi urged his students and readers to be "broad-minded" and consider the positive aspects of the massacre, not just the negative ones stressed by the nation's media and most rabbis.

Ginzburg identifies in Goldstein's atrocity five virtuous aspects: "sanctification of the name of God," "saving life" (of Jews), "revenge" (against Hebron's Palestinians), "cleansing evil," and "struggle for Eretz Israel."[21] Goldstein was not, according to this presentation, a reckless criminal. He was a pious man of deep religious convictions who wanted to save Jews. Sacrificing his own life for this purpose, he committed the supreme act of *kidush hashem* (sanctification of the name of God). The Hebron massacre was committed, according to Ginzburg, in the context of increasing information about an upcoming Arab pogrom. It was conducted against a hostile population that had provided enthusiastic support for every act of Palestinian terrorism. The massacre may have seemed wrong, but given the urgent need to save Jewish life, it was utterly virtuous. There is, Halakhicly, no question that saving Jewish life justifies everything else, including the killing of Arab civilians:

> About the value of Israel's life, it simply seems that the life of Israel is worth more than the life of the gentile, and even if the gentile does not intend to hurt Israel it is permissible to hurt him in order to save Israel. . . .
>
> In a situation in which there is danger—even remote—that the gentile will operate (even if indirectly) to hurt Israel, there is no need to care about him and "thou shalt kill the best of the gentiles." . . . We are consequently taught that the war referred to is not necessarily a real battle, but even a situation of national conflict justifies such killing. Those who may later help another [killer], when forced to by the ruler, deserve to be killed.[22]

Most of the essays in *Baruch HaGever* addressed the Jewish-Muslim conflict with a Goldstein-like interpretation of what should be done in time of crisis. There was, however, one noticeable exception, an essay written by Benjamin Zeev Kahane, the son of the slain rabbi and young leader of Kahane Chai. The importance of Kahane's contribution lay not in his words about the Arabs but in what he had to say about the Jews. Kahane argued that had the Jews shown resolve toward the Palestinians—expelling them by force and abandoning the fiction of "Jewish democracy"—there would have been no Arab question and no Goldstein tragedy. The problem, according to the younger Kahane, is that a fierce cultural war is being waged between real and Hellenized Jews, with the secular Hellenized on the winning side. While young Kahane does not call for a violent Jewish struggle against the "Hellenized," the historical example he uses is telling. The analogy goes back to the Hasmonean period and the precedents of "pious" Jews who slaughtered Hellenized Jews in the name of God. One has only to note that *Baruch HaGever* was avidly read by Yigal Amir—it was one of three books found in his room—to understand that young Kahane had identified in his essay the delicate passage between targeting Arabs, which was the "virtue" of Goldstein, and targeting Jews, so tragically expressed by Amir.

> *The problem is not the Arabs—the problem is the Jews.* The truth, the way we look at it, is that there has never been an Arab problem. We could have solved that problem in 48 hours, *if only we wanted to.* The real war is not with the Arabs but with the *Hellenized Jews.* All the blood shed by Arab terrorism is "as if" shed by

the Arabs; the people really responsible for the bloodshed are Jews scared by the gentiles and attached to distorted Western ideas.

Today's cultural war is more intense than the Hasmonean one. Hellenization has deeply penetrated our lives, and its ideas have influenced even the "nationalist" and religious public. The moment of truth has arrived. One option is to follow the path of Judaism, the entire Jewish idea, to reject the fear of the gentile, Western democracy, and the idea of coexistence with the Arabs. This way is the condition for the existence of a Jewish state. The other option is acceptance of the yoke of democracy and giving up the dream of a Jewish state. There is no "third way."[23]

The publication of *Baruch HaGever* had a meaning larger than the book itself. It was a sign of the maturation of the Kahanist counterculture and its small periphery. This counterculture, probably no larger than a few dozen activists and several hundred supporters, was politically insignificant. It constituted, however, an aggressive radical vanguard, increasingly allowed to participate and express itself in the large antigovernment operations of the Israeli opposition. The Kahanist counterculture brought the legitimacy crisis between the settlers and the Labor government to a peak. Comprising the outlawed Kach and Kahane Chai as well as extremist yeshivas (Ginzburg's Tomb of Yosef Yeshiva and a small *kolel* in Kiryat Arba), the Kahanist counterculture publicly expressed its desire to engage in anti-Arab terrorism and to try Rabin and Peres for treason.

The outlawing of Kach and Kahane Chai and the inability of their members to openly fly their banners led to the rise of Eyal—an acronym for "Israeli Fighting Organization"—a new Kahanist group. Eyal was formed two years earlier by Avishai Raviv, a Tel Aviv University student. First making a name for himself by demanding the resignation of the Arab head of Tel Aviv University's Student Association on the grounds that an Arab cannot be trusted, Raviv was eventually expelled from the university. He moved to Kiryat Arba, where he and a small number of activists started to attract media attention by using provocative anti-Arab rhetoric and staging aggressive ceremonies against Jewish traitors. Eyal claimed to be more militant and radical than the original Kahane movements. In addition to admiring the slain Rabbi Kahane, Eyal activists expressed loyalty to the legacy of the anti-British undergrounds in Palestine, and particularly to Abraham Stern—one of the leading Jewish underground fighters. New recruits for the organization were expected to swear allegiance on Stern's grave. The oath included a solemn pledge to fight the nation's enemies, including the enemies within. Raviv proposed contingency plans for expelling Hebron's

Arabs in the event the government of Israel pulled out, and even staged special horror shows for Israel's TV networks. Masking their faces, armed Eyal activists moved in the Arab Casbah of Hebron and practiced terrorist acts against the local population in front of the cameras.[24] Raviv and his vocal friends joined the other Goldstein admirers in becoming the major promoters of the character assassination of the nation's top leaders. Responsible for the mass production of vicious anti-Rabin posters, they were also involved in the printing of Rabin's picture in Nazi uniform.[25]

During the interrogation and subsequent trial of Yigal Amir, it turned out that Raviv had cooperated with the GSS and was their informer. This fact cast suspicion on Raviv as an *agent provocateur* of the Security Services within the extreme right, and even served as a basis for the conspiracy theory that accused the GSS of having prior knowledge and even actual involvement in the assassination. The published parts of the sentence in the Amir trial refuted these allegations, but the exact nature of Raviv's relations with the GSS remained somewhat vague.

Pre-Assassination: The Rabbinical Struggle Against Oslo II, the Rise of Zo Artzenu and the Pulsa di Nura

The process of delegitimation of the Rabin government by the radical right reached a new peak in the summer of 1995. At issue was the implementation of Oslo II, the second stage of the agreement between Israel and the PLO. Stipulating that Palestinian autonomy should be expanded to seven major West Bank cities and several hundred villages, Oslo II significantly reduced Jewish control over Judea and Samaria. It also provided for the introduction of thousands of armed Palestinian policemen to the area. The Israeli right was increasingly frustrated; the Gaza-Jericho autonomy, contrary to the expectations of the right, seemed to be working well, and Arafat's police had not become a terrorist gang. Against this background, most settler demonstrations, geared to attract public attention and intimidate the government, were less and less effective. Calls by right-wing leaders such as M.K. Hanan Porat for early elections fell on deaf ears.

A dramatic response to the new challenge was launched again by the spiritual authorities of the settlers. After a lengthy consultation, which included interviews with senior military officers, a distinguished rabbinical body ruled that it was illegal to evacuate military bases in Judea and Samaria and that soldiers should disobey such orders. The ruling was an aggressive extension of the previous decree, made over a year earlier, instructing soldiers to disobey settlement removal orders. The difference was that the rabbis had expanded their judgments to purely military matters. Everybody recognized the huge difference between civilian settlements and military compounds. No civilian rabbi in Israel had ever ruled, or claimed to be competent to rule, on technical matters involving the location of military bases. The rabbinical statement, which had behind it fifteen prominent rabbis, including Rabbis Shapiro, Neria, Ya'acov Ariel, and others, read:

> We hereby assert that there is a Torah prohibition against the evacuation of IDF bases and their transfer to the gentiles. . . . A permanent military camp is a Jewish settlement in the full sense of the term. Its uprooting and abandonment into the hands of the gentiles is subject to the same rule as the uprooting of an Eretz Israel settlement, which is prohibited by law. It is therefore clear that no Jew is allowed to take part in any act that assists the evacuation of a settlement, camp, or military compound. . . .
>
> Never before has the army put its soldiers in a position where they had to act against their conscience. We call upon the government and the army to refrain from putting soldiers into a situation where they must choose between army orders and loyalty to their convictions.[26]

The new rabbinical ruling created a national commotion even louder than the one fifteen months earlier. Israel's president, Ezer Weizmann, who had been particularly attentive to the settlers' agony, was furious. Weizmann, a respected former general, refused to admit to the presidential manor a delegation of rabbis that came to explain. He demanded categorically that the new ruling be called off. The attorney general declared his intention to try the rabbis for incitement. Hebrew University professor Aviezer Ravitzky, a leading Orthodox academic, stated that the ruling implied the symbolic collapse of "the Israeli social contract." Writing in *Yediot Aharonot*, Israel's largest daily, Ravitzky charged the rabbis with expressing "an extremist political position characteristic of a minority group, not the opinion of Israel's religion." Ravitsky doubted that most *hesder* yeshiva soldiers would follow the reckless judgment, but he warned against the danger of insubordination.[27]

While loud voices of anger were expressed by several generals, a number of yeshiva students said they would not obey the rabbis. Prime Minister Rabin made it clear that soldiers who followed the rabbis' order would be instantly court martialed. Infuriated, Rabin told journalists:

It is unheard of that the democratically elected government will be coerced by rabbis, using the Halakha to allow soldiers to disobey orders. There has never been anything like this in Israel's history. It is one of the worst things possible that a small number of rabbis, who do not represent the majority of Israeli rabbis, can make such a decision. It is unthinkable that we turn Israel into a banana republic. The entire Knesset, not just the government, ought to reject this matter.[28]

The public uproar over the new rabbinical ruling did not move any of the major signatories to apologize or retract his statement. Nor did it diminish the commitment of Israel's ultranationalists to use the streets to bring down the "illegal government." It led, on the contrary, to further radicalization. The polarization of Israeli Jews in the summer of 1995 was as wide as ever.

The growing frustration over the inability of the rabbis or the Yesha Council to derail the peace process led to the meteoric rise of a new radical-right movement—Zo Artzenu (this is our land). Zo Artzenu was formed by two relatively unknown settlers, Moshe Feiglin and Shmuel Saket, residents of Ginot Shomron, an affluent bedroom community close to the Green Line. They were soon joined by Rabbi Benny Elon, former head of the defunct Emunim Movement. Zo Artzenu's contribution to the anti-peace struggle involved new measures of aggressive civil disobedience and campaign rhetoric. Between July and October 1995, the activists of the new movement engaged in illicit settlement, road-blocking of the nation's major highways, and aggressive protests in front of government offices. Zo Artzenu drew attention to several other protest groups such as "Women in Green," already active in places like the affluent town of Efrat.[29] In the summer of 1995, the activists of the new organization set the agenda of the radical right and dictated the style of its struggle.

By the summer of 1995, the level of settler frustration had reached new heights. Outraged, bitter, and eager to improve their lot, the established settler leaders did not have new ideas for waging struggle. The peace process seemed unstoppable, and many activists became increasingly fatalistic. The time was ripe for Feiglin and Sacket to test Zo Artzenu's ideas with "Operation Duplicate II." Begun on August 8, this strategy involved the establishment of 30 new strongholds as twin settlements in the West Bank. Thousands of eager activists were ready to start extralegal settlement and refuse the army's evacuation orders. Hundreds were arrested and sent to prison. Settler-soldier confrontations were heavily reported in the media, and a formidable protest movement was quickly developing.[30]

Boosted by their growing coverage in the Israeli media, the heads of Zo Artzenu decided to bring their campaign across the Green Line. The idea was to disrupt life and public order in Israel proper, telling the government that unless it suspended the peace process, its own operation would be stopped in the streets. "Operation Road Block," conducted by several thousand Zo Artzenu activists, was a military-style mission. Spread out in nearly 80 road junctions across the country and coordinated by Rabbi Benny Elon hovering overhead in a chartered helicopter, these activists succeeded in disrupting transportation for several hours. Nearly 3,000 policemen were needed to clear the roads and highways. The clearing was not completed before 130 activists had been arrested, including Moshe Feiglin, the movement head.

While fulfilling their expectation of gaining publicity, Zo Artzenu heads failed in their main objective—making their struggle popular inside Israel. Stuck for hours on the roads, most Israeli drivers resented the disorder. Instead of becoming sympathetic to the antipeace struggle, they became increasingly hostile. "Operation Road Block" proved to be counterproductive and made Zo Artzenu an unpopular organization countrywide. Later efforts to repeat the disruption on September 13 and 29, the second anniversary of Oslo I and the signing day of Oslo II, were even less effective. Fewer volunteers were ready to participate in the unpopular activities within the Green Line, and the operation did not achieve any of its objectives. Another provocative venture, a spectacular plan to have hundreds of thousands of Israelis turn off the lights all over the country, failed miserably. No serious disruption was reported by Israel's Electric Company and the event made little impact. Asked about the failure, Feiglin responded, "We didn't fail, because we had nothing to lose."[31]

The intense attention given to Zo Artzenu and its increasing role in shaping the agenda of the radical right were not solely a result of the organization's disruptive tactics. Of special attraction for the media were the new faces and unfamiliar voices. The most active members of Zo Artzenu were Americans who immigrated to Israel. In their interviews with the media, they stressed commitment to the American tradition of civil disobedience. Most Israelis learned for the first time about the civil rights movement, Martin Luther King, Jr., and the struggle against the Vietnam War. Dominated by liberal and left-wing journalists, Israel's media loved the new images, which were a far cry from the conservative and messianic rhetoric of Gush Emunim. A Zo Artzenu activist, David Romanoff, told this to a reporter:

The organization doesn't have a history and we don't suffer from deep-seated Israeli inhibitions and commitments. This is what we absorbed in American universities demonstrating against the Vietnam War. I was deeply impressed by Martin Luther King's argument that there is a superior moral law above state law. I remember going to Columbia University in support of Jewish students working to free Prisoners of Zion [in the Soviet Union]. At the time I saw students striking against the Vietnam War. Our methods of civil disobedience or refusing to obey the law were very effective there.[32]

Heavily reported in the foreign press, Zo Artzenu's rhetoric was particularly effective with an American audience. The young movement succeeded in establishing nearly 40 American support groups, with concentrations in Seattle, Miami, and New York. Much of the funding for the big operations came from the United States. Also attractive to Americans was the conscious effort to justify the struggle against the Israeli government in the language of American democracy. Moshe Feiglin, born to Australian parents but married to an American, commented on the new phenomenon:

This is an American approach to freedom that does not exist in this country, and I live among Americans who know the real meaning of individual freedom. Freedom does not mean that the government, which won the elections, is free to do whatever it pleases. This is how things are done in Israel, which is not a democracy but a "dictatorcy." When someone who barely wins a majority acts to take away the most precious objects of the Jewish majority in the country and speaks in the name of democracy, he cannot expect his actions to pass without resistance. The reason the opposition comes mostly from American immigrants is because they understand the meaning of democracy.[33]

Zo Artzenu failed in its efforts to use the streets to bring down the Israeli government. It was very successful, however, in intensifying the atmosphere of delegitimation surrounding the government. The movement's operations served as rallying events for the entire hard core of the radical right, whose numbers reached the hundreds. In addition to thousands of yeshiva students bused over from their seminaries, one could meet there former members of the now-illegal Kach and Kahane Chai as well as a few Eyal activists. Present also were students of the extremist Tomb of Joseph yeshiva in Nablus, Hebron and Kiryat Arba radicals, a large number of veteran Gush Emunim types, and radical students and activists from within the Green Line such as Yigal Amir. All of them mingled, argued, vented frustrations, and shared struggle experiences. Old and new posters and slogans, "Rabin and Peres are Traitors," or "Assassins," or "Collaborators of

Terrorism," were the order of the day. Not a few of the activists started to speak and chant freely about the need to execute the "traitors."

On October 6, 1995, just two days after Yom Kippur, an odd group of extremists gathered in front of the prime minister's Jerusalem residence. The purpose of the meeting, convened by Avigdor Eskin, a former Kach activist, was to conduct the traditional *Pulsa di Nura* rite against Yitzhak Rabin. *Pulsa di Nura* ("blaze of fire" in Aramaic) is the most severe death curse that can be invoked against a Jewish sinner. The invocation of this mystical penalty is rare and done, if at all, by Kabbalistic rabbis. The curse rite is so rare and mysterious that it is not even written down. The rules of its execution are said to be passed orally from father to son and are not a simple matter. Ten rabbis and community heads must convene in a synagogue, fast for three days, and then say the curse at midnight. The curse is considered dangerous because, if made against an innocent person, it ricochets against the cursers. The curse text, uttered after a long ceremony focused on a mystical dialogue with the angels of destruction, reads: "Angels of destruction will strike him. He is damned wherever he goes. His soul will instantly leave his body . . . and he will not survive the month. Dark will be his path and God's angel will pursue him. A disaster he has never experienced will beset him, and all curses known in the Torah will apply to him."[34]

It is not known whether all the formal requirements of the *Pulsa di Nura* were met by the group convened in front of Rabin's residence. But the fact that Israeli citizens, although very few and very extreme, took part in its invocation and preparation during Yom Kippur was telling. It indicates that the verbal violence directed at Rabin in the fall of 1995 had become serious enough to include death wishes. It showed, furthermore, that given the risks involved in a fake *Pulsa di Nura*, the rabbis felt very confident.

Another indication that the conflict between Mr. Rabin and his political opponents was getting out of control was made a week later, at Netanya's Wingate Sport Institute. While visiting with a gathering of Israeli citizens of English-speaking origins, Rabin met an aggressive group of hecklers. In contrast to past experiences with this crowd, which had never overstepped the bounds of verbal violence, the Wingate confrontation looked very much like a physical assault on the prime minster. Rabin was not shielded by his guards as one of the hecklers physically approached him.[35] It was then apparent how easy it could be to walk up to the prime minister, security detail or not.

Yigal Amir: Profile of a Jewish Zealot

The assassination of Prime Minister Rabin stunned the nation. Naturally the peace camp, whose activists had to despise the rhetorical violence of the Israeli right, was shocked. But shocked also were those on the extreme right, including most of those who had either used that rhetoric or allowed it to be used in their rallies and demonstrations. There are many indications that the vast majority of organizations and individuals who spoke the language of delegitimation and engaged in character assassination had not really wished to see Rabin dead. The possibility of a Jew killing the nation's top leader, who was also hero of the 1967 war in which Israel greatly expanded its borders, was inconceivable to them. Even Kahane supporters and the few messianic types close to that extremism—who may have wanted to see Rabin dead—were probably not mentally prepared to murder him.[36]

But there were also some who recognized that only a dramatic act would stop the withdrawal, and one of them decided to undertake such an act. Yigal Amir was one of these—a true believer convinced that the killing of the prime minister was an order from God. Rabin's assassin was a loner who felt uncomfortable as a registered member of any ideological movement or cell. But he participated in many of the activities of the anti-Oslo extraparliamentary opposition and ran with the hard core of the extremist messianic right. Amir's personal convictions, reinforced by his radical friends, told him that only an extraordinary act could save the people of Israel from the gathering storm. This is how he explained the assassination to his investigators:

> Without believing in God—a belief in the afterlife—I would never have had the strength to do it. In the last three years I came to realize that Rabin is not the leader who can lead the people. . . . He didn't care about Jews, he lied, he had a lust for power. He brainwashed the people and the media. He came up with ideas like a Palestinian state. Together with Yasser Arafat, the murderer, he was awarded the Nobel Peace Prize, but he failed to address his people's problems. He divided the people. He marginalized the settlers and didn't care about them. I had to save the people because they failed to understand the true situation, and this is why I acted. He repeatedly used the term "victims of peace." Soldiers were killed in Lebanon, and the government didn't respond because there was a political [peace] process. . . .
>
> If not for a Halakhic ruling of *din rodef* made against Rabin by a few rabbis I knew about, it would have been very difficult for me to murder. Such a murder must have backing. If I had not had backing and the support of many people, I wouldn't have done it.[37]

Amir, a slight, dark-skinned, dark-haired son of Yemenites, was born in Herzliya in 1970 to a lower-middle-class family. Amir's mother, Geula, mother of eight and the dominant figure in her family, was a nursery school teacher in Herzliya's Neve Amal neighborhood. She was known for her extremist views, reflected by a pilgrimage she made to Baruch Goldstein's grave in Kiryat Arba. Amir's father, Shlomo, a devout Orthodox Jew, specialized in calligraphic transcription of Jewish holy books. Most of the family's modest income came from Geula's private nursery, located in the family backyard.[38]

Yigal's first years of schooling were in an ultra-Orthodox elementary school belonging to Agudat Israel. His secondary education was in HaYeshuv HeHadash, an ultra-Orthodox yeshiva in Tel Aviv. Unlike most of his peers in this yeshiva, Amir wanted to do military service. After graduation, he parted company with his classmates and entered Kerem DeYavneh, a large and highly respected *hesder* yeshiva known for the relative moderation of its instructors and graduates. Nothing in this early training carried portents of exceptional future radicalism.

In the army during the intifada, Amir served in the occupied territories where, according to his army buddies, he took pride in torturing local Palestinians.[39] After his service, unlike most extreme right-wingers who moved to settlements in the occupied territories or continued their studies in an advanced yeshiva, Amir returned to Herzliya. He registered for law school at Bar-Ilan University, but before starting school he was chosen to join a group of former *hesder* soldiers who went to Riga, Lithuania, to teach Hebrew to young Jews.[40]

While at Bar-Ilan, Israel's only religious university, Yigal Amir's political views became greatly radicalized. He began his studies after the September 1993 Oslo agreement, and he seems to have ignited at once. Though enrolled in two prestigious university programs—law and computers—the young man devoted more time to his studies at the university *kolel*, an institute for the rigorous study of Halakha. But Amir's free time was increasingly spent in right-wing political action. He became the driving force behind the student protest activities at Bar-Ilan University and was also responsible for arranging discussion groups about the future of Eretz Israel.[41]

It was around that time that Amir began to organize student support groups for several Yesha settlements. Starting in Netzarim, the isolated Gaza Strip village, Amir soon shifted his efforts to Hebron. The government threat to evacuate Tel Rumeida had a profound effect on him. Determined to fight both the Israeli government and the Palestinian population, Amir began running solidarity weekends in Hebron. Dozens of Bar-Ilan students, sometimes hundreds, would go for the weekend to express their commitment to the holy city. They held Shabbat services together, prayed, sang, and mingled with the local radicals.[42] Amir told investigators that his goal had been to recruit students willing to defend the settlements by force if the government decided to evacuate them.

Amir's obsession with the radical right put him in touch with many leading groups and activists. He showed up for most Zo Artzenu actions, took part in the large rallies, and was visible in several settler confrontations with the army. At the university, Amir became friendly with Avishai Raviv, Eyal's leader and a well-known provocateur.[43] After the Rabin assassination, when Raviv was identified as an informer for the Security Services, Amir said that friends had warned him about Raviv and that he had been cautious with him. In one exchange with Benny Katzover, a veteran radical leader of Gush Emunim, Amir had spoken bitterly and critically of the lack of determination among the settlers. He told Katzover that the only way to bring down the government was by force.

In spite of his increasing radical work, Amir still did not become an official member of any protest group. He acted on his own or in concert with a small group of friends, mostly Bar-Ilan students, who heard him speak repeatedly of *din rodef* and the obligation to kill Rabin and Peres. No one, including Avishai Raviv, the Security Services informer, took him seriously. Raviv's failure to report Amir's threats later gave rise to the baseless conspiracy theory alleging that Secret Service people were in on the assassination because "they knew but did nothing." Yigal Amir's closest friend, who shared all his political convictions, was his brother Haggai. Haggai Amir, tried as an accomplice to the murder, was an amateur gun aficionado, crazy about special weapons. In a raid of the Amir house after the assassination, the police discovered a small but sophisticated arms cache consisting of hand grenades, bullets, and explosives. Haggai had manufactured the hollow-point bullets used in the assassination.[44] A third person close to the Amir brothers and their activity was Dror Adani, a Beit Haggai settler with family in Herzliya. Adani had met Yigal Amir in the *hesder* yeshiva and the two served together in the army.[45] There are indications that in addition to their discussion of the need to assassinate Rabin, about which only Yigal was totally serious, the group had other violent plans. These included reprisal raids on West Bank Arabs and an attack on Palestinian terrorists freed by Israel as part of the peace process. The Amir brothers entertained several spectacular ideas about how to kill Rabin and discussed such alternatives as a car bomb or injecting nitroglycerine into the water system of Rabin's home.[46]

Two other Bar-Ilan students, Hila Frank and Margalit Har-Shefi, also belonged to Amir's close circle. They participated in many Bar-Ilan demonstrations and attended several Hebron solidarity weekends. Yigal Amir seems to have had serious talks with Har-Shefi in which he tried to interest her in an antigovernment underground. Learning of his desire to kill the prime minister, an idea she rejected, Har-Shefi told the young man she would only join if no violence were involved.[47] But under Amir's influence, Har-Shefi asked the rabbi of her Beth El settlement, Shlomo Aviner, if Rabin qualified as a *rodef.*

Yigal Amir admired Baruch Goldstein, who had also acted on his own. He is said to have decided at Goldstein's funeral that he also had to engage in an exemplary act. *Baruch HaGever* was one of the few books found in Amir's library.[48] During the interrogation, Amir said, "*Din moser* and *din rodef* are a Halakhic ruling. Once something is a ruling, there is no longer a moral issue. If I were now involved in the biblical conquest of the land, and, as it says in Joshua, I would have to kill babies and children, I would do so regardless of the issues of morality. Once something is a ruling, I don't have a problem with it."[49]

It is almost certain that Yigal Amir had no unequivocal rabbinical sanction to kill Rabin. Rabin's assassin told his investigators that he discussed the issues of *din rodef* and *din moser* with several rabbis, but none was willing to give him a green light. When asked his opinion about these or other rabbis he admired, Amir said he was disappointed with the rabbis because they were all "soft and political." Rather than ruling on this matter according to the Halakha, Amir said, the rabbis introduced irrelevant political considerations. Amir also told his interrogators that there was no prominent rabbi he admired in this generation. The decision to kill Rabin was his alone. Amir believed he was fully informed of the relevant Halakhic law and had sufficient knowledge of the misery of the Israeli people to act on his own.[50]

The Halakhic instrument that ultimately convinced Amir he should kill Rabin was the ancient Jewish doctrine of zealotry. This doctrine maintains that under very extreme circumstances a God-loving Jew can kill another person without first asking permission. The tradition goes back to Phinehas, son of Eleazar, who killed another Jew during the exodus from Egypt. The victim, Zimri son of Salu, was among many Israelites who defied God's orders and made love to Midianite girls in the desert. In killing

Zimri, young Phinehas committed an unauthorized murder of a fellow Jew and had to be severely punished. And yet not only was his act forgiven by God, "for he was zealous for my sake among them," but a plague that had already killed 20,000 Jews was instantly lifted and all male descendants of Phinehas were made priests of Israel.[51] The prophet Elijah is also described in the Bible as a zealot who killed 400 priests of Baal, a Canaanite god, in his wrath.

The Jewish doctrine of zealotry has never been fully institutionalized, nor could it ever be. This is why the the zealot and zealotry have always remained exceptional and extraordinary concepts. According to Rabbi Shaul Yisraeli, an act qualifies as zealotry if it is conducted in a dire emergency, if it is clear that the act is guided by total awe of God, if the actor is ready to risk his life in the name of God, and if there is no shred of personal gain.[52]

Yigal Amir convinced himself that killing Rabin was in the best tradition of Jewish zealotry. He was sure that Rabin had to be killed in order to save the land and the nation. He was certain that this was God's will, which other believers acknowledged but were hesitant to carry out.[53] Although it is evident that he did not wish to die, Amir was ready to give his life if self-sacrifice were the only way to serve God's will. He certainly understood that he would spend his life in prison. After admitting to his interrogators that no specific rabbi authorized his act, Amir told them about the biblical precedents of Phinehas and Jael (who killed the Philistine warlord Sisera). He also told them that before he committed the murder he had reread the biblical chapter of Balak, which tells the story of Phinehas and the slaying of Zimri.[54]

According to the psychological evaluators, Amir has the complex personality of a highly intelligent young man who sought love and admiration at any price. He had a desire to prove to himself, his mother, his friends, and others that he could go further than anybody else. Amir noted that he was afraid someone else would kill Rabin before he did, thereby stealing his chance for fame: "I wanted a thinking person to do it. I was afraid an Arab might kill him. I wanted Heaven to see that a Jew had done it."[55] He discussed at length with his interrogators his training, self-discipline, and faith in the Torah.

Amir zeroed in on Yitzhak Rabin after the first Oslo agreement and would not let go of the idea that Rabin was "evil." After identifying the goal, he took steps to accomplish it in stages. The ability to kill Rabin was "a self-courage test." The State Commission of Inquiry was told by Amir, "I never chased Rabin. I didn't believe I would ever do it. I always thought I was just talking, that I would never have the strength to do it, even though I knew it had to be done. I said, 'Rabin should be killed' and I would smile. Nobody believed that a legitimate fellow, very nice, very logical, funny guy, would kill Rabin. Even I, myself, didn't know I would kill Rabin." Rabin's assassination may have been, from this perspective, the act of a megalomaniac seeking to demonstrate his strength of will in public.[56]

Dr. Uriel Weil, a clinical psychologist who also examined Amir, identified an additional dimension to Rabin's killing—his depressive personality, which had been sensitized by his dogmatic ideology. Amir "had within him depressive elements prior to his act. Emotional drives, including rage and frustration, may have burst out despite his effort to fully control his emotions and act only according to pure reason."[57] Amir's girlfriend, Nava Holtzman, a pretty, religious woman, had left him after five months—in January 1995—to marry one of his good friends. Amir, who attended the wedding, is said to have gone into deep depression over this.[58] Yigal's father, Shlomo Amir, said after the murder that had his son married Nava he would never have committed the crime. Geula Amir, Yigal's mother, also spoke about her son's deep depression after the split. Amir's brother, Haggai, also did not believe that his brother, under normal circumstances, would have been capable of murder. He confirmed the reports that Yigal had become deeply depressed after breaking up with his girlfriend. After the breakup he began to talk about sacrificing himself.

Amir testified in court that before leaving for the assassination he had prayed he would manage to kill Rabin without hurting himself. He did not want to be a dead hero. He was very quick to give the policemen his identity card, lest there be a name mistake. Amir seems to have wished all those who believed him incapable of murdering the prime minister—friends, family, the girls who did not return his affection—to know that he did it, that he was the best.[59]

Amir's depression deepened as the peace process advanced and the right-wing protests failed to halt them. He began to feel a growing obligation and a heavenly calling to commit the extreme act. The unique mixture of mysticism and religious nationalism was reaching an explosion. A reading of the testimony of Amir's friends suggests that there were many warning signs that Amir was serious about his conviction that Rabin should die. Yigal took his brother, Haggai, to Rabin's house numerous times. The two discussed many ways of killing the prime minister. Amir told his investigators that on at least two previous occasions he was armed and ready to kill Rabin. But on both occasions he had had a "sign from heaven" not to act. On one such occasion Rabin did not show up; on another, he was heavily protected by security. On the night of November 4,

Amir received the "go" sign. He easily negotiated the Kings of Israel parking lot and waited patiently for 40 minutes. According to Amir's testimony, God made it clear that He wanted Rabin dead.[60]

Notes

1. Rabbi Shlomo Aviner, "Morality and the War Against Terrorism," *Yesha Rabbis' Communiqué*, no. 9, May 1993 [Hebrew].

2. Ha'etzni, "Civil Disobedience Now," *Nekuda*, 1994, pp. 25–27 [Hebrew].

3. Aviva Shabi and Ronni Shaked, *Hamas* (Jerusalem: Keter, 1994), pp. 318–27 [Hebrew].

4. Interview with settler leader Aharon Domb (Dompa), November 9, 1994.

5. Ehud Sprinzak, *The Ascendance of Israel's Radical Right* (New York: Oxford University Press, 1991), pp. 89–99.

6. Nadav Shragai, *Ha'aretz*, December 1, 1993 [Hebrew].

7. Ibid., March 7, 1994 [Hebrew].

8. Shlomo Dror, *Ha'aretz*, March 30, 1994 [Hebrew].

9. Gideon Alon, *Ha'aretz*, April 1, 1994 [Hebrew].

10. I was personally involved in writing one of these memorandums.

11. Avirama Golan, *Ha'aretz*, April 5, 1994 [Hebrew].

12. Nadav Shragai, *Ha'aretz*, May 5, 1994 [Hebrew].

13. Rabbi Dov Lior, Rabbi Daniel Shilo, and Rabbi Eliezer Melamed, "What Is the Rule About This Bad Government?" in Dana Arieli-Horowitz (ed.), *Religion and State in Israel, 1994–1995* (Jerusalem: Center for Jewish Pluralism, 1996), pp. 120–23.

14. Shimon Shiffer, *Yediot Aharonot*, September 11, 1995 [Hebrew].

15. Shlomo Shamir and Reli Sa'ar, *Ha'aretz*, November 9, 1995 [Hebrew].

16. Tzi Zinger, *Yediot Aharonot*, November 13, 1995.

17. See comments in Aviner, "Morality and the War Against Terrorism."

18. Shachar Ilan, "HaShavua: Rabin and Peres: Israel's Evil People: Judenrat Men and Capos," *Ha'aretz*, November 12, 1995 [Hebrew].

19. I attended the Goldstein memorial services.

20. Sprinzak, *The Ascendance of Israel's Radical Right*, p. 165.

21. Rabbi Yitzhak Ginzburg, "Baruch HaGever," in Michael Ben Horin (ed.), *Baruch HaGever* (Jerusalem: Special Publication, 1995), p. 20 [Hebrew].

22. Ibid., pp. 27, 28.

23. Benjamin Zeev Kahane, "A Cultural War," in Horin (ed.), *Baruch HaGever*, p. 256 [Hebrew].

24. *Ha'aretz*, April 13, 1995; November 19, 1995 [Hebrew].

25. *Ha'aretz*, November 20, 1995 [Hebrew].

26. *Yediot Aharonot*, July 13, 1995 [Hebrew].

27. Ibid. See the chapter by Ravitsky in this book.

28. Ibid.

29. Daliah Karpel, "One Must Scream Gevald," *Ha'aretz*, Supplement, January 17, 1995 [Hebrew].

30. Nadav Shragai, *Ha'aretz*, July 31, 1995 [Hebrew].

31. Dani Sade et al., "Zo Artzenu Fails Again," *Yediot Aharonot*, September 19, 1995 [Hebrew].

32. Lili Galili, "No Need to Give Up the Barbecue," *Ha'aretz*, February 6, 1994 [Hebrew].

33. Ravit Naor, "Moshe Feiglin, Zo Artzenu Chairman . . ." *Ma'ariv*, Supplement, August 18, 1995 [Hebrew].

34. Dov Elboim, "The Killing Curse," *Yediot Aharonot*, November 13, 1995 [Hebrew].

35. Arieli-Horowitz, *Religion and State in Israel*, p. 287.

36. This judgment is based on several interviews I conducted with Kahane supporters after the assassination.

37. *Report: State Commission of Inquiry into the Matter of the Murder of the Late Prime Minister Yitzhak Rabin* (Jerusalem: State Publishing House, 1996), p. 89 [Hebrew].

38. David Lavie, *Ma'ariv*, November 6, 1995 [Hebrew].

39. Yael Gvirtz, "Death's Vile Servant," *Yediot Aharonot*, Supplement, March 29, 1996 [Hebrew].

40. *Report*, p. 88.

41. Ariela Ringler-Hoffman, "A Murderer's Breeding Ground," *Yediot Aharonot*, Supplement, November 10, 1995 [Hebrew].

42. Yaron Kaner, "Eyal Seminar in Hebron, the Organizer: Yigal Amir," *Yediot Aharonot: Seven Days*, November 10, 1995 [Hebrew].

43. *Ha'aretz*, November 19, 1995 [Hebrew].

44. Buki Naeh, *Yediot Aharonot*, November 7, 1995 [Hebrew].

45. *Ha'aretz*, November 10, 1995 [Hebrew].

46. *Ha'aretz*, December 12, 1995 [Hebrew].

47. Zvi Harel, *Ha'aretz*, December 12, 1995 [Hebrew].

48. Yoram Yarkoni, *Yediot Aharonot*, December 11, 1995 [Hebrew].

49. Gvirtz, "Death's Vile Servant."

50. This information is contained in the undisclosed and confidential report on Amir's investigation. I was allowed to see the documents on the condition that I reveal no specifics.

51. Numbers: 25.

52. Shaul Israeli, *Amud Hayemini*, chap. 15.

53. Ibid.

54. See note 52.

55. Gvirtz, "Death's Vile Servant."

56. Ibid.

57. Zvi Harel, *Ha'aretz*, February 2, 1996 [Hebrew].

58. Avihai Becker and David Lavie, "Profile of a Jewish Assassin," *Ma'ariv*, Supplement, November 10, 1995 [Hebrew].

59. Gvirtz, "Death's Vile Servant."

60. Becker and Lavie, "Profile of a Jewish Assassin."

CHAPTER 4

Self-Destructive Processes in Israeli Politics

ISRAEL ORBACH

The assassination of Prime Minister Yitzhak Rabin was not only the murder of the head of the state of Israel, but also a shot in the head of the Israeli people. It was also a culmination of many self-destructive processes bordering on suicidal behavior.

There are methodological and epistemological problems with applying processes and principles from the intrapsychic domain to the interpersonal and social psychological domains. Intrapsychic processes are based mostly on the symbolization of the inner and external worlds by means of self-representation and object representation based on subjective perceptions and feelings. Social processes are based on inter- and intragroup influence, identification with the group, the impact of leadership, and other relationships. There is some parallel between the two domains, but they are certainly not identical. Any inference from one area of psychology to the other should be done with caution. This is especially true when we examine pathological developments.

Although aware of this epistemological problem, I nevertheless believe that examining social phenomena with concepts borrowed from the intrapsychic sphere may help us gain insight into problematic social processes.

Suicide is a complicated phenomenon based on many dynamic processes, all of which gradually contribute to the subjective experience of facing a dead end. Step by step, the scope of possibilities for choices and actions narrows to the point that there is no alternative for action except suicide. This is, of course, a subjective state.

I shall borrow some concepts and processes from theory and clinical knowledge that explain the narrowing of avenues of possible action to a dead end and eventual suicide. I shall then try to apply them to the historical, social, and political reality in Israel, trying to shed light on the enigma of how a Jewish head of state was murdered by one of his own people. The concepts that I shall use for this purpose are "murder in 180°," "a trauma from the past that compulsively intertwines in present-day life," "difficulties in problem-solving," "illogical and distorted thought processes," "coping with unresolvable problems," and the "loss of the life fantasy."

Some Dynamic Processes of Suicide

The orthodox psychoanalytic view of suicide was formulated by Freud and Stekel (Freud, 1955): no one kills himself except as he wishes the death of another person. From this perspective, suicide is seen as hostility unconsciously directed toward an ambivalently viewed person, one who is both loved and hated at the same time, who has been introjected into one's own unconscious mind. Shneidman (1980) has termed this process murder in 180°. In this process, it is as if one part of the ego sets itself over and against the other part, judges it critically, and attacks it. One part of the personality "treats" another part of it as if it were an external, hated object and executes it (Litman, 1967). In other terms, we are talking here about introjected aggression, which implies turning the anger and violence aimed originally at another ambivalently viewed person toward oneself. Self-punitive actions are accompanied by emotional catharsis and self-purification. This phenomenon is especially evident in acts of self-mutilation. Individuals who are afraid of expressing and experiencing anger and aggression discharge their locked-up anger through physical self-injury, thereby gaining emotional relief (Walsh and Rosen, 1988). The view that internalized aggression is involved in suicide and suicidal behavior has received support from many empirical and observational studies (e.g., Biaggo and Godwin, 1987; Maiuro, O'Sullivan, and Vitaliano, 1989; Tatman, Greene, and Karr, 1993).

Suicide cannot be explained on the basis of present acute pressures or crises. Almost every suicide is fed by a major past trauma that is compulsively relived in the present and demands relief, a correction of the past, and healing (Fish-Murray, 1993; Solomon, Mikulincer, and Flum, 1988). The victim attempts to rectify the passive stance he or she took at the time of the tragedy by taking decisive action (Van der Kolk, 1987). The trauma dominates the mental life of the victim long after it occurs, and the human mind tends to compulsively repeat and restore it in an attempt to master it

(Freud, 1955). Traumatic memories cannot be avoided; they come back in the form of nightmares, emotional restlessness, and various other symptoms. The traumatized victim experiences the emotional intensity of the original trauma in any stress in his or her present life, but does not always consciously remember the trauma itself. Any resemblance to the original in the present situation can evoke similar feelings.

Trauma victims have lost the sense that they can actively control their own lives. The mind and the body are on constant alert for the return of the past trauma in the present. The strong sense of helplessness is intrusively reexperienced. Sounds, smells, and situations easily revive the traumatic memory and the overwhelming feelings associated with it. People who have been traumatized as children suffer from what Van der Kolk (1987) termed a "disorder of hope." Other people may be either idealized or hated by the victim. Both extremes lead to new disappointment and reenact the sense of victimization.

Trauma victims have difficulty controlling feelings of anxiety and aggression. Many concentration camp survivors have a hate addiction. Traumatized youngsters have trouble modulating aggression. They tend to act destructively against others or themselves. Aggression can replace fears and helplessness with feelings of omnipotence (Van der Kolk, 1987).

Because of its unusual nature, the trauma cannot be placed in an appropriate schema and cannot be assimilated by the mind. The event is so different from the usual events that no existing schema of the mind is able to absorb, categorize, and assimilate it. When a past, unsettled trauma continues to upset the subjective experience of well-being, the suffering individual may eventually commit suicide in a desperate attempt to escape the pain.

Difficulties in problem-solving, coping, and distorted thinking also have important roles in self-destructive behavior. The cognitive functioning of the suicidal person is characterized by rigidity and polarization—the tendency to construe situations in extreme terms with no intermediate shades of gray (Hughes and Neimeyer, 1993). Such cognitive functioning results in poor problem-solving abilities. Studies have consistently shown that suicidal individuals perform more poorly than others on a variety of problem-solving tasks (Hughes and Neimeyer, 1990; Levenson and Neuringer, 1971; Neuringer, 1964; Orbach, Bar-Joseph, and Dror, 1990; Patsiokas, Clum, and Luscomb, 1979; Rotheram-Borus et al. 1990; Schotte and Clum, 1987). They tend to be more sensitive to the problematic and negative aspects of a difficult situation than to the alternatives of possible new and creative solutions (Waye and Runco, 1994).

Shneidman (1980) has suggested that the suicidal individual suffers from a cognitive constriction that he describes as seeing the world through a tunnel—with a narrowing range of perceptions, opinions, and options. The person is not only opinionated and prejudiced but also suffers from a kind of "tunnel vision." Ordinary thoughts, loves, and responsibilities are suddenly unavailable to the conscious mind. It is not that a person simply "forgets" who he is or who the people around him are; it is far worse—his identity, his ties to people and values, are blocked out and disappear. The suicidal person turns his back on his own past and permits his present and past to become unreal; thus they cannot serve to save him. In this state of tunnel vision and narrowed outlook, the mind is focused almost entirely on the unbearable emotion and, especially, on one specific way to escape from it.

An important characteristic of constriction is a tendency for "either/or" thinking, in which the world is divided into two, and only two, parts—good or bad, love or hate, a desired life or a "necessary" death. Such dichotomous thinking in the suicidal person is characterized by words like "always," "never," "forever," "either/or," and especially the word "only." When the mind constricts, the anguished person sees only the mechanism for stopping the anguish—and that leads to the triggering process (Shneidman, 1980).

Suicidal people also suffer from distortion in thought processes. Such distortions feed the negative subjective experience and pain. They tend to use idiosyncratic reasoning and logic. Their faulty reasoning not only abrogates the rules of logic but also destroys the logician who uses them (Shneidman, 1985). Suicidal people make wrong syllogistic deductions and draw conclusions based on mistaken premises or unclear and confused concepts. Shneidman supplies one example of a semantic fallacy characteristic of suicidal individuals: "Nothing is better than hard work. A small amount of effort is better than nothing. Therefore, a small effort is better than hard work" (Shneidman, 1985).

Circular thinking by which new information is adjusted to the individual's basic negative premises is another variety of self-destructive thinking characteristic of suicidal individuals. This leads inevitably to negative conclusions, self-devaluation, and hopelessness, which may ultimately terminate in suicidal behavior.

Matte-Blanco (1975) has pointed out other maladaptive forms of thinking that I believe are relevant to this discussion. Aberrant generalizations and distinctions may lead to severe distortions in thinking. Categorization based on overgeneralization may cause a person to bring totally different concepts or objects together into a meta-category. Thus, an inanimate object, a person, a part of a body, and an abstract concept may be grouped together under the meta-category of "things that a person can think about." Hence, generalization becomes unlimited and includes items and objects that have nothing in common. In the next step of faulty generalization, objects that are similar to each other in some ways become identical and can be substituted for each other. Thus the mind of the suicidal person can group together a person he or she hates with another person on the basis of irrelevant resemblance and then treat the second person as an enemy, adding further inner anguish.

Not only do suicidal individuals suffer from difficulties in problem-solving enhanced by rigidity and faulty thinking that make it difficult to cope, but at times they are faced with and forced to address unresolvable problems (Orbach, 1986). Perceiving problems as unresolvable can be characterized as a state of mind that reflects the person's subjective experience of being trapped and incapacitated. Four characteristics define an unresolvable problem: (a) the problem is beyond a person's ability to resolve; (b) there are limited external alternatives for resolution; (c) every resolution creates a new problem; and (d) an external problem over which the suicidal individual has no control is construed as a personal problem.

The phenomenological nature of the unresolvable problem can be demonstrated in specific family situations: excessive parental demands for an adolescent to excel beyond his or her capability; a mother's obsession with her child's homework as a way of coping with the father's absence from the home; a father's rejection of his daughter as a way of expressing hidden anger toward his wife for giving birth to a girl instead of a boy; and conflicting demands on the part of the parents for an adolescent to mature and at the same time remain dependent.

It has been suggested that being pressured to resolve an unresolvable problem brings about feelings of hopelessness, helplessness, depression, and suicidal acting out (Orbach, 1986).

The loss of one's "life fantasy" is another major dynamic in suicidal behavior (Smith, 1983). The life fantasy can be conceived as one's philosophy of life, or what is most important in life that makes it worth living. Smith (1983) has described the life fantasy as involving the individual's self-views, views of others, and beliefs about how to obtain nurturance and maintain self-esteem. The loss of someone dear, the loss of a job, or a divorce can signify or in itself become the crushing blow to a person's special life-guiding fantasy. For many suicidal people, there does not appear to be a single major event that conveys the futility of realizing the life hope. Rather, it is the accumulation of disappointments that leads to the breakdown of major character defenses that brings them precariously close to suicidal behavior. Seemingly small disappointments or rejections can be the "last straw" that precipitates the suicidal act.

Self-Destruction in Israeli Society

Shlomo Aharonson, a prominent political scientist in Israel, suggested on a TV talk show following Rabin's assassination that the combination of nationalism, religion, and the introjected experience of the Holocaust were a deadly combination that led to his murder. I would like to develop this idea from the perspective of self-destructive processes in Israeli society.

The Holocaust is the biggest trauma of the Jewish people. It is deeply introjected and is reflected in the everyday life of people. Only now are we beginning to digest the meaning of this trauma. First and foremost, this is a shocking trauma of loss by a cruelty unmatched in history. The other impact of this trauma is the sense of total helplessness and humiliation that the Jewish people experienced at the hands of the Nazi murderers.

After the birth of the state of Israel, the young generation was obsessed with the suicidal helplessness and passivity exhibited by their fellow Jews, the victims in the concentration camps. How, young Israelis asked, could they, the European Jews, succumb as lambs to slaughter? How could they not resist; why didn't they fight to death, rather than die a humiliating and cruel death? Why didn't they protect their children? These questions bothered the proud and courageous Israeli youngsters more than anything else. They knew what loss and sacrifice meant. Losing their best friends and family on the battlefields was perceived as a necessity in order to accomplish the goals and values embedded in the utopian Jewish state. They could not accept the surrender to passivity, humiliation, and helplessness.

I believe that the fear of helplessness and the hatred of the Nazis have gone through several metamorphoses and emerged compulsively onto the scene of Rabin's murder. The trauma of helplessness was the main dynamic and motivational force behind Kahanism. Meir Kahane founded in America and later in Israel a small but extreme right-wing movement impregnated with fascism. Kahane was obsessed and haunted by the trauma of the Holocaust. He reconstructed and dramatized the Holocaust and the Nazis in the everyday life of Jews in America. In this dramatization he took the role of the avenging victim, searching compulsively for the brutal enemy.

He found Nazis in every corner. He chose some group of Americans as the main protagonists in his reconstruction of the Holocaust, identifying every robbery and every anti-Semitic expression with the Nazi ideology. He was driven to relive the Holocaust's dark days, wishing to recover from the frightening incapacitation as the victor. "Never again" was the leading slogan in his violent activities.

Kahane left the United States with an unfulfilled wish. The Jewish Defense League was not a success. Kahane changed the arena and reconstructed the drama and the protagonists in Israel. This time the Nazis were the Israeli Arabs and the Palestinians. But Kahane was gunned down by his enemies, the blacks in the United States and the Palestinians, still shouting—"never again."

The impinging spirit of the Holocaust did not die with Kahane. Some Israelis continue to identify all Palestinians—not only the murderous terrorists of Hamas and Islamic Jihad—with the new Nazis. Their nightmare was and still is that a new Holocaust is approaching.

It was not surprising to see and hear in the violent demonstrations against Rabin so many signs and slogans that refer to the Holocaust. Members of the right-wing movements felt constrained by Israeli democracy. Democracy came to be a severe obstacle in their crusade against animosity acted out by Hamas and other Palestinians. Democracy and the "nightmare" of peace came to be viewed as the road to a new Holocaust. In a chain of false and distorted syllogisms and thought processes, the Holocaust drama was recreated, but this time all the heroes were Jews. No difference was seen between Arafat, the leader of the Palestinians, and Hamas, the extremists. Their view was, "They are all out to get us, they are all Nazis." And if there was any similarity between Rabin and Arafat by virtue of their common goal—labeled "the nightmare of peace"—then Arafat and Rabin were perceived as identical twins. Rabin was Arafat was a Nazi and should be destroyed. The Holocaust was reenacted, but this time as a victory: the Nazi—personified by Rabin—was annihilated and the victims of the trauma earned a corrective experience. We could not avenge the Nazis, we could not wipe out the Palestinians, but we could kill our own leader. It is easier to introject the pent-up hatred and turn it against ourselves than to direct it externally. Here is the murder in 180°, the self-destructive act.

Not only did the right-wing extremist completely identify Rabin with Arafat and both of them with the Nazis, and not only did he see a new Holocaust approaching, but he also experienced a threat to his "life fantasy." The great messianic dream of the unison of the Greater Israel, the nation, and the Bible was slipping away with the materialization of the Oslo agreements, of achieving this holy goal. In the eyes of these extremists, the Six Day War of 1967, with its swift victory, brought Israelis close to the fulfillment of a life fantasy by expanding the borders of Israel and restoring the holy cities of Jerusalem, Bethlehem, Hebron, Jericho, Nablus, and other sites of ancient Israel. The victory was a Godly miracle, helping Israel accomplish its utmost purpose and mission. The Oslo agreement, led by Rabin, under which some of those holy places have been returned to the Palestinians to form their autonomous political entity, was perceived to be in total contradiction to the ambitious life fantasy of some Israelis. In an "all or nothing" attitude, these groups felt that their dreams were ending. To them, life became meaningless as their life fantasy vanished. Indeed, when the murderer set out on his deadly mission, he was ready to die; he believed that he would be killed in the process. His life or Rabin's life or anybody else's life meant nothing to him.

The rigid ideology and inflexibility in the face of a changing political era also intertwine in the self-destructive processes. An orthodox ideology does not allow any new perspectives or compromises in the complicated political, social, and spiritual dilemmas of the reality of Israel. This ideology was demonstrated in a soul-searching meeting of rabbis heading nationalistic yeshiva colleges in Israel, following the murder of Rabin, who concluded: "We have not failed at all and there is no fault whatsoever in our education. We cannot give up one inch of land, one drop of Jewish blood." This view exemplified a distorted thought process and gross inner contradictions. In the present political reality of the Middle East, one simply cannot have all the land and all the Jewish people without losing a single drop of blood. For more than 50 years Israelis have shed blood while fighting over a piece of land, not even all of it. Although *Hazal*, the sages of old, proclaimed time and again that the Torah can be interpreted in at least 70 ways, thereby emphasizing the flexibility in the teachings of the Bible, and although most of the great rabbis and scholars throughout history have valued life and humanity over a Greater Israel, nothing can move the extremists from their position. *Hazal* have named God by many names, one of which is Shalom—peace, the love of peace—but to no avail. According to this extremist group, one should commit suicide rather than compromise the life fantasy.

The last concept relevant to this analysis of self-destructive processes in Israeli society and its political entanglement is the unresolvable problem. The life fantasy of the Greater Israel is simply unattainable in the Israeli reality. The differences of the people of Israel with regard to the peace process seem unreconcilable. Even if a compromise could be reached, the Palestinians are as extremely divided among themselves as the Israelis. Moreover, the world's great powers have vested interests in the Middle East and are not going to leave the scene to the Israelis and Arabs alone. In addition, Iraq, Sudan, Libya, Iran, and Syria are not sitting by idly. From this perspective, the political dilemmas in the Middle East seem to constitute an unresolvable problem. Such a complicated situation requires ingenuity and creativity, not stubbornness and rigidity. A rigid attitude in the face of such a complicated situation is self-destructive in and of itself.

The self-destructive processes did not change after the murder of Rabin. Attitudes and intense feelings did not change much. The divisions, splits, and conflicts are unresolved. Of course, the murderer, whose intent was to bring an ultimate solution and avenge the Holocaust, did not achieve his purpose. I believe that the self-destructive processes in Israeli society are not unique to Israel. Rather, they reflect what happens in any traumatized and stress-driven group of people or nations.

The lesson that we can learn from the Israeli experience is that individual traumas, like societal traumas, must be dealt with directly. The two most important principles in individual treatment of any mental or life problem are caring and limit-setting. These energize the individual toward inner harmony in the face of conflicts, splits, and self-hate. A traumatized nation does not need a psychotherapist but a strong, loving leader who can also set limits. Only a leader whose ultimate goal is to integrate diverse and opposing groups with love and limits for all can unite a divided and self-destructive society. Political wisdom, awareness of complexities that require flexibility, and compromise can be a remedy for societal suicide.

References

Biaggo, M. K., and W. H. Godwin (1987). "The Relation of Depression to Anger and Hostility Constructs." *Psychological Reports* 91: 87–90.

Fish-Murray, C. C. (1993). "Childhood Trauma and Subsequent Suicidal Behavior." In A. A. Leenaars (ed.), *Suicidology: Essays in Honor of Edwin Schneidman*. Northvale, N.J.: Jason Aronson.

Freud, S. (1955). "Beyond the Pleasure Principle and Other Works." In J. Strachey (ed. and trans.), *The Standard Edition of the Complete Psychological Works of Sigmund Freud*. London: Hogarth Press.

Hughes, L. S., and R. A. Neimeyer (1990). "A Cognitive Model of Suicidal Behavior." In D. Lester (ed.), *Current Concepts of Suicide*. Philadelphia: Charles Press, pp. 1–27.

———— (1993). "Cognitive Predictors of Suicide Risk Among Hospitalized Psychiatric Patients: A Prospective Study." *Death Studies* 12: 103–24.

Levenson, M., and C. Neuringer (1971). "Intrapunitiveness in Suicidal Adolescents." *Journal of Projective Techniques and Personality Assessment* 34: 407–11.

Litman, R. E. (1967). "Sigmund Freud on Suicide." In E. S. Shneidman (ed.), *Essays in Self-Destruction*. New York: Aronson, pp. 324–44.

Maiuro, R. D., Michael M. C. O'Sullivan, and P. P. Vitaliano (1989). "Anger, Hostility and Depression in Assaultives vs. Suicide Attempting Males." *Journal of Clinical Psychology* 45: 531–41.

Matte-Blanco, I. (1975). *The Unconscious as Infinite Sets*. London: Duckworth.

Neuringer, C. (1964). "Rigid Thinking in Suicidal Individuals." *Journal of Consulting and Clinical Psychology* 28: 54–58.

Orbach, I. (1986). "The Insolvable Problem as a Determinant in the Dynamic of Suicidal Behavior in Children." *American Journal of Psychotherapy* 40: 511–20.

———— (1988). *Children Who Don't Want to Live*. San Francisco: Jossey-Bass.

Orbach, I., H. Bar-Joseph, and N. Dror (1990). "Styles of Problem Solving in Suicidal Individuals." *Suicide and Life-Threatening Behavior* 20: 57–64.

Patsiokas, A., G. Clum, and R. Luscomb (1979). "Cognitive Characteristics of Suicide Attempters." *Journal of Consulting and Clinical Psychology* 47: 478–484.

Rotheram-Borus, M. J., P. D. Trautman, S. C. Dopkins, and P. E. Shrout (1990). "Cognitive Style and Pleasant Activities Among Female Adolescent Suicide Attempters." *Journal of Consulting and Clinical Psychology* 58: 554–61.

Schotte, E. D., and A. G. Clum (1987). "Problem-Solving Skills in Suicidal Psychiatric Patients." *Journal of Consulting and Clinical Psychology* 55: 49–54.

Shneidman, E. S. (1980). *Voices of Death*. New York: Harper and Row.

———— (1985). *Definition of Suicide*. New York: Wiley.

Smith, K. (1983). "Suicide Assessment: An Ego Vulnerability Approach." *Bulletin of the Menninger Clinic* 49: 489–99.

Solomon, Z., M. Mikulincer, and H. Flum (1988). "Negative Life Events, Coping Responses, and Combat-Related Psychopathology: A Prospective Study." *Journal of Abnormal Psychology* 97: 302–7.

Tatman, S. M., A. L. Greene, and L. C. Karr (1993). "Use of the Suicide Probability Scale (SPS) with Adolescents." *Suicide and Life-Threatening Behavior* 23: 188–203.

Van der Kolk, B. A. (1987). *Psychological Trauma*. Washington, D.C.: American Psychiatric Press.

Walsh, B. W., and P. M. Rosen (1988). *Self-Mutilation: Theory, Research and Treatment*. New York: Guilford Press.

Waye, M., and M. Runco (1994). "Suicide Ideation and Creative Problem Solving." *Suicide and Life-Threatening Behavior* 24: 38–47.

PART II

The Public Reaction

CHAPTER 5

"Let Us Search Our Path": Religious Zionism After the Assassination

AVIEZER RAVITZKY

There was one who killed him with a gun,
And many who killed him with their words,
and even more who killed him in their hearts.
—Rabbi Zvi Tau

On the twelfth day in the month of Heshvan in the year 5756, the prime minister of Israel was killed by a Jew—a yeshiva graduate, soldier in the Israeli army, law student, and political activist—the heart and soul of Israeli society. In the first weeks after the assassination, Israeli society was thunderstruck and gripped by anxiety. For the first time the blow had come from within; the enemy appeared not at the gate, but inside the home.[1] The forms of public reaction and expressions of collective mourning were therefore fierce and polarized, and embodied a series of paradoxes.[2]

Anxieties and Contradictions

The first strain or paradox related to the religious background of the assassin and the religious motive that drove him. On the one hand, powerful antireligious sentiment prevailed in Israel at the time—open hostility toward establishment Judaism and its symbols, more vehement than anything I can recall. Many Israelis expressed the view that it was not a particular ideology or theology that inspired the bloodshed, but an entire culture—faith, literature, collective memory—that spread the poison and hence bore responsibility. In a telling incident about a week after the assassination, an educator from the central region of the country told me of the helplessness she felt when her pupils spurned their (secular) Bible teacher and the text he taught, identifying them with the deed of assassination. On the other hand, many people at the time also experienced clear feelings of "religiosity," manifested in a search for religious symbols and new-old rituals: the candles and melodies, the seven- and 30-day mourning ceremonies, the prayer over the dead (*kaddish*), pilgrimage to relevant sites, and, in the words of the emcee at the memorial event in the Tel Aviv plaza, a sense that the site was a huge synagogue and that the singers were cantors.

The second paradox during this period related to the emphasis placed on the sense of community in Israel in an effort to redefine a particularistic national identity while clinging to the universalist world. Before Yitzhak Rabin was killed, only the Greater Land of Israel was cast in blue and white (the colors of the flag), while the peace process was cast in gray for pessimism or red for alarm. Immediately following the assassination, however, peace also began to appear in blue and white—on bumper stickers, posters, and ads, and also in deeper expressions of the social and cultural ethos: Even the Land of Israel and the People of Israel—for twenty years the "property" of only one camp and its symbols—were restored as symbols of Israel's secular left in this hour of crisis. Together with the nationalist and "tribal" emphasis, however, a strong need also arose to grasp the outside world. And who coined the new Israeli slogan "Shalom, Haver" (Good-bye, friend) if not the president of the United States, symbol in all his pomp and circumstance of a supertribal universalism? And how our hearts swelled to see the leaders of the world gather in Jerusalem to pay last respects to our fallen head of state—with eulogies that overshadowed those given by our own leaders—elevating the funeral from a national to a supranational ceremony.

The third strain was evident in the reaction of the youth; the same young people who are generally so individualistic ("just leave me alone"), perhaps even egocentric, became collectivistic for a moment. Young people could be seen clinging to each other until the wee hours of the morning at the Tel Aviv city plaza, the Jerusalem grave site, opposite the widow's home—just so they would not be alone with their fear for a moment. It was hard at the time to discern the profile of individuals—separate boys and girls; one saw only young people massing everywhere, swallowed up into the collective experience of mourning and protest.

The fourth paradox was manifested in the relations between various segments of the population: polarization and hostility, and simultaneously an unprecedented dynamic of dialogue. Never before had there been so many encounter groups—religious and secular, right and left, settlers and kibbutzniks, and a few Jewish and Arab groups as well. The dialogue seemed to reflect the fear of the abyss—the threat of polarization and its terrifying outcome. Several years ago, some friends tried to organize a meeting between the leadership of Peace Now and Gush Emunim, but it never came off. The representatives of these two groups refused to grant "legitimacy" to each other by meeting together. After the assassination, however, they suddenly held a series of long and trenchant meetings, without the need of mediators. Out of the sense of danger—the fear that we had reached the brink—emerged the dialogue.

The last paradox I cite relates to the norm of tolerance. In the first weeks after the assassination, the social conflicts and modes of expression were marked by moderation and self-restraint in both content and style, like a desperate attempt to defuse a bomb. It was not surprising that the number of car accidents in Israel decreased dramatically during that difficult period. And yet there were also harsh incidents of intolerance at the time, bordering on the curtailment of freedom of speech (one man was detained for questioning after telling a tasteless joke while waiting in line at an ATM). An open desire for brotherhood and friendship seemed to hover in the air, but this was linked to the latent desire that the entire country speak in one language and use the same words.

Identity and the Sublime

All these contradictions and fears were a sharp reflection of a social process that had evolved throughout the years and reached a climax. For a long time all Israelis have known or believed that one large segment of the society is doomed to have its dreams and hopes shattered—a group whose sons and daughters would feel battered and defeated and, what is worse, by their brothers, sisters, and compatriots. If progress is made in the peace process (and territorial concessions increase), one segment of Israeli society will feel itself betrayed. If the process stumbles and falls, others will feel betrayed. But one fact seems inevitable: over the course of time, two very different Zionist dreams have evolved, and the two cannot both be fully realized. Thus both camps are poised and alert, facing each other across the divide, pending the outcome. This highly charged and contentious situation has for some time threatened national solidarity and the social fabric. "Do not build your dream on the ruins of our dream," appealed Rabbi Yoel Bin-Nun to the Israeli left when the Oslo Accords were signed.[3] But the same fervor was heard from the other side on days when Israeli settlements expand in densely populated Arab cities across the Green Line. The conflict is not about pragmatic aspirations or political interests, but about lofty hopes and faith on both sides, and even different perceptions of personal identity.

I deny that there is a sharp social division between the religious right and secular left. Indeed, about half the secular Jewish population feel reservations about the peace process, while a significant minority of religious Jews support it. But for purposes of sharpening the issues, I shall initially look at the two polarized camps.

For the religious right in Israel, territorial concessions in the heart of Judea and Samaria reflect not only a collapse of their political point of view, but also a loss of completeness and totality. Why did most Orthodox rabbis and leaders at the beginning of the century object to the Zionist revival? It was not just because of Zionist secularism or its activist desire to have a historic breakthrough before the coming of the Messiah. They also objected to the revival because of the feeling that Zionism would betray completeness, preclude total realization of the integral traditional dream.[4] According to the vision of completeness (as developed over generations in Jewish tradition), someday the entire people will return to live in the entire Land of Israel—a land that is good, prosperous, and spacious—and all its sons and daughters will cling to God's perfect Law; and when this people makes peace with its neighbors, it will be a covenant of complete peace based on brotherhood, friendship, and swords beaten into plowshares, as in the prophecy of Micha and Isaiah. But suddenly the Zionists arrived and sought partial fulfillment, an abridged version of the dream: part of the people, part of the land, parts of the prophetic tradition and the biblical peace, and certainly only part of the Law. It is not surprising that the religious sensibility responded almost instinctively by saying: If for 1,900 years we believed and expected the Messiah, we shall continue to pray another 200 years, as long as we neither harm nor betray the complete vision.

But following the impressive historical accomplishments of Zionism—the Balfour Declaration, creation of the state of Israel, the Six Day War, and mass immigration from the former Soviet Union—many religious Jews began to seek realization of the lofty vision within the Zionist enterprise.[5] In other words, they adapted the classic messianic dream to the concrete shape of the Zionist state—"identifying absolutely with the truth that the state of Israel is a divine state!"[6] Thus a new expectation gradually emerged that Zionism and then Israel would fulfill the complete hope and realize the messianic vision. Thus, in the eyes of this public, all of the recent events, from Camp David and Yamit to Oslo I, Oslo II, and the erratic withdrawal from territories, constituted a direct violation of this exaltation. From the point of view of many believers, a rift appeared not just in the completeness of the Promised Land, but also in the completeness of the biblical prophetic peace that brooks no suspiciousness or self-interest, but only love and harmony.

The change in the political perspective of Rabbi Yoel Bin-Nun epitomizes this dynamic. In a sense, he exchanged one camp for another, not because he moved from a perspective of the sublime to one of pragmatism, but because he moved from the sublime to the sublime. As Bin-Nun wrote approximately a month after the assassination, reality reveals that the Lord chooses to bring redemption by way of the peace process. Those who opposed any territorial withdrawal did everything in their power to prevent the process, but "Go forth and see the ledger kept by the world, how every step that appears to us obstructive and thwarting was transformed into an impetus": We chose the Likud and they retreated from Sinai; we went to war against Lebanon and gravely harmed the fighting spirit of the people; we built settlements and thereby created an intifada on one side and a Palestinian willingness for peace on the other; the assassin sought to murder peace, but he catalyzed for the first time a solid Jewish majority in favor of the peace accords (as was evident from the polls at the time). That is to say: "The peace process is the coming stage in the redemption of Israel. The fact that the 'leftists and seculars' correctly identified Divine Will and the plan of redemption is infuriating and painful, but it cannot stop a believing Jew from recognizing that this is indeed Divine Will. . . . The same *shofar* [ram's horn] that heralded the miracle of 1948 and the miracle of the Six Days, now heralds, yes, now, the miracle of peace."[7] Which is to say that politics is umbilically connected to theology—and that they strengthen each other.

Yet on the opposite side, among veteran Israeli doves, many also took a stand of exaltation toward events—perhaps not religious and messianic, but exaltation nonetheless. I am not referring here to the usual rhetoric that juxtaposes the New Middle East and the Greater Land of Israel as two incompatible utopias, but to a deeper level. If matters do work out, believe many supporters of the peace process, the future historian of Zionism will cite three formative events in the twentieth century: the Balfour Declaration (1917), the Proclamation of Independence (1948), and the peace agreements (1979, 1993, and to come). The Balfour Declaration symbolizes the acknowledgment by the Western world of the right of the Jewish people to a national home of their own. The Proclamation of Independence symbolizes the willingness of the Jewish people to dare create this home.

The peace process is intended to close the circle, symbolizing the reconciliation of the enemy-neighbor-Palestinian to this revival. This, too, contains a lofty historical perspective and not just a reference to political events—that is, a vision of exaltation. In addition, the peace process restored to the moderate left in Israel the feeling that the national enterprise was fundamentally a just cause, as they had once believed. In their eyes, it restored the image of being human and seeking good, an image that had faded or entirely disappeared since the 1970s. Thus with the political deed and historical perspective also comes a sense of purification and moral rectification. This, too, has recently taken its fervent place against the rival from the right.

The perception of personal identity has also played a significant role in shaping the dreams of both camps. Religious Zionists grew up in Israel in the 1950s and 1960s feeling culturally marginal relative to either the secular "builders" or the ultra-Orthodox "faithful." On one side, the seculars are the generals, diplomats, pioneers, and builders. It is they who are the "steam" pumping at the head, while the religious Zionists are left behind in the dining car, busy being kashruth monitors.[8] On the other side, the ultra-Orthodox are the consistent and "authentic" Jews. It is they who devote their lives to their faith, not compromising with the outside, secular, or modern world, while religious Zionists bend and adapt. Despite declarations to the contrary by educators and leaders at the time, this was the image that many carried within in the 1950s and 1960s.

And then in the 1970s, a new reality took shape, followed by creation of a new option that enabled those on the margins to enter the mainstream. This option was borne aloft by members of Gush Emunim (the bloc of the faithful) and their settlement activity. The seculars will be sent to the dining car as the religious forged ahead to lead the Zionist cause. As for the ultra-Orthodox, they will be left to their resigned ways a passive existence in closed neighborhoods, while religious Zionists alone will fervently fulfill the commandment of settling the Land, equal to all the other commandments combined. They, not the ultra-Orthodox, will demonstrate consistency and unbending devotion, going off with seven children to live in a leaky trailer in Samaria. This was the new ray of light for young religious nationalists. And it was used to the hilt, not just on an ideological level, but also on sociological and psychological levels, until the peace accords and territorial concessions arrived to jeopardize their enterprise and key role on all three levels. These then threatened a crisis to the very identity of this camp.

But identity issues were also at the heart of the opposing camp. The peace process had begun to restore the positive self-perception of secular Israelis. It reshaped the Israeli discourse of values, democracy, rights, and the sanctity of life, and a new kind of civil religion began to coalesce that even included Arab citizens. At the same time, it made possible a rapprochement between the Israeli left and The People/The Land, after these concepts had served as the symbols and ethos of the right for years. Even the buds of secular interest in the Jewish bookshelf began to surface. The Shenhar Commission, asked to examine Jewish education in the nonreligious school system, called upon the nonreligious public to take responsibility for the Jewish education of their children (1994).[9] This heralded a secular breach of the unwritten agreement that imparted to religious Jews an exclusive mandate for keeping the historical memory and dealing with Jewish sources. Rabin's assassination gave additional access to this positive identity, one endowed with new-old national colors and imbued for a while with a religious and collectivist spirit.

In this confrontation between the sublime and the sublime, between identity and identity, the decisive victory of one always appears to be the defeat, or even trampling, of the other. Many saw this as inevitable and feared it:[10] It threatened not only to permanently scar the collective, but even to undermine the unwritten Israeli covenant by which soldiers from the left served lengthy stints in Lebanon, even though they disapproved on principle, while soldiers from the right evacuated Yamit and its satellites, though doing so contradicted their views. It is not surprising that when Yesh Gvul called upon soldiers to refuse en masse to serve in the territories, most leaders of the Israeli left and Peace Now spoke out against it; and when a group of rabbis called upon soldiers to refuse orders to evacuate settlements, they were attacked by most right-wing religious and political leaders. In all these cases, the collective ethos and national myth—together with apprehensions about the future—overcame the forces that sought to undermine the social contract, and reaffirmed it. Even those who did not see up close the pain of the other understood that they could not go far without each other. They too wanted to maintain the rules of the game and a minimal fellowship.

Thus the assassin raised his hand against a society already under threat and raked all its raw nerves simultaneously. There is nothing more total than death, and nothing more wicked and threatening than bloodshed—all the more so when it is the blood of the elected leader, who represents with his body the structure itself, the national pathos, and systems of rule; and even more so when this man embodies for many not just political power, but military strength and victory. The assassin thus assaulted the entire system and its symbols, as if seeking by his deed to undermine all power and consensus, all boundaries and law. Hence, "The assassination of Rabin was perceived as the loss of a father . . . the loss of a man turned into a collective father as his personal biography was merged into the history of the state."[11] As I argue below, many of the social phenomena that followed the assassination—lowering of the political volume, curbing ideology, avoiding decisions, supporting "pragmatic" leadership, legitimizing the ruling power, repressing the assassination, and fostering dialogue—are directly related to this process.

Let Us Search Our Path

In the first days after the assassination, the religious Zionist public was in shock. This population was faced with a double conflict. In addition to the general postassassination trauma, there was the private trauma: not only did the assassin emerge from among them, but he justified his deed by religious motives, and some said that he received permission or encouragement for it from rabbinical authorities (even though the assassin himself testified that he was "beyond" the need for Halakhic permission and operated on his own).[12]

Several days after the assassination, Rabbi Aharon Lichtenstein, head of the *hesder* yeshiva (which combines religious studies with military service) at Allon Shevut, delivered a stern sermon to hundreds of his students entitled "Let Us Search Our Path and Examine It." A passage from that sermon:

> This man was nurtured in our best institutions. Ten days ago we would have pointed to him as a symbol of success, a story we would all be proud of—"See the produce that we have raised."[13] Now voices can be heard in our camp that say, "We raised him? Perish the thought! This is a weed, a wild flower, one that grew at the side of the road, ostracized and shunned. We raised him?!" Gentlemen, it cannot be that one who is willing to take credit for someone when the sun shines suddenly disassociates from him when the rain begins to fall. If ten days ago we would have held up the young man with pride—"See the produce that we have raised"—we must learn to say the same thing today. . . . There is some level of cover-up that allowed and even nourished this produce. If only we could say that what happened took place not entirely "owing to" the path traveled by the young man or "because of" the education he received, but rather "despite" it all. We must ask ourselves "Indeed?!"[14]

As a result, the rabbi demanded that the religious-nationalist sector and its educators do a thorough soul-searching, draw educational conclusions, take moral responsibility for the rotten fruit that grew there, and purify the camp. Indeed, Rabbi Lichtenstein is a spiritual leader of the moderate camp of religious Zionists. For years he has taken a compromising political stand and a rigorous moral stand. But words no less harsh were uttered by Rabbi Zvi Tau, then spiritual guide of the Merkaz HaRav Yeshiva in Jerusalem, the flagship of redemptive, settlement-oriented religious Zionism. Rabbi Tau's soul-searching focused on the question of the appropriate role for the state of Israel and its government and the sin of deriding and inciting against the national leader, since, from his point of view, the state of Israel is the redeemed House of the Lord and to be honored like royalty. But Rabbi Tau also demanded that he and his listeners assume collective moral responsibility. He even hinted at the traditional concept of the zealot—one who operates outside halakhic constraint but believes he is carrying out the wish of his rabbis[15] or the will of some community:

> I told one rabbi that we are all in need of repentance. He was amazed: Did all the teachers sin, raise a weapon to kill? No, certainly the teachers did not kill . . . [but] when among the great ones there is no respect, [decent] attitude, faith in the uniqueness of Israel, or honor to the kingdom of Israel and its way to redemption, [then] matters end up in murder among the most corrupt pupil . . . sometimes an individual acts knowing that he is fulfilling the expectations of a public that he seeks to belong to. There were also rabbis who did not mince words. Why not clean our house? . . . When you have contempt for the [national] leader, you scorn not [just] him. You are maligning royalty, the leadership, the totality of our togetherness.[16]

Rabbi Tau did not refrain from drawing an analogy between the assassination of Yitzhak Rabin and the ancient assassination of Gedalya Ben Ahikam, a deed that expunged the last vestige of Jewish autonomy in the Land of Israel during biblical days and that has been remembered by generations as a catastrophe, marked by a day of fasting and repentance:

> On this day, the Fast of Gedalya, a Jew killed a Jew, killed a leader, did it "for the sake of the Lord," because Ishmael Ben Netanya [who killed Gedalya] was a "right-wing extremist" from the seed of David, the seed of royalty, who wanted to restore the kingdom of the House of David. While Gedalya Ben Ahikam was a "defeatist," who left the walled city to meet Nebuchadnezzar because he believed in the words of the prophet Jeremiah who advised him to surrender to the King of Babylon. . . . One may wonder: If one person kills, must all Israel do repentance for it? What does it have to do with us? [It can be said:] "He [who killed Rabin] was not from the settlements, he was from

Herzliya. . . ." But to this very day we sit and mourn and fast over what happened then [when Gedalya was killed].

The assassination of Rabin was thus depicted by Rabbi Tau as a historic tragedy with symbolic dimensions beyond its time and place.[17] Some were even more blunt. Across the sea, Rabbi Aharon Soloveichik, the religious authority of the centrist (or modern) Orthodox camp in the United States, went further than everyone else in his reaction to the assassination: "This is the greatest crisis in 2,000 years of Jewish history!" said the rabbi. "I also failed in not sufficiently protesting those who sought license for murder. [Therefore,] We cannot say that 'Our hands did not shed the blood.'"[18] Rabbi Aharon Soloveichik has been one of the sternest critics of the Oslo Accords and had led a delegation of American rabbis who met with Yitzhak Rabin to protest the withdrawal from territory and its attendant dangers.[19] Despite this—or perhaps because of it—he viewed the act of assassination through almost mythic lenses.

But other voices were heard as well. I am not referring to the scoundrels who expressed support for the assassination, but to those who condemned the act, who might have been horrified by it, but who completely rejected the notion of collective responsibility, and, in contrast with Rabbi Soloveichik, declared, "Our hands did not shed this blood!" This includes those who castigated the act but found mitigating circumstances, presenting it as the sorry result of the Oslo Accords. These words were uttered tentatively right after the assassination, but they later became the dominant voice in the camp.

Each of these distinct voices was clearly heard in a soul-searching conference held by the religious Zionist movement four days after the assassination (November 8, 1995) in Jerusalem. This event was unusual in that all factions, right and left, came together and used some rather blunt and bitter language.[20] On the one hand were heard the protest and pain of Rabbis Yehuda Amital and Yoel Bin-Nun, who did not refrain from sharp internal criticism: "I heard the assassin speak in court," said Rabbi Amital, "and there was nothing new in his words. Every word he uttered had been said more than once this past year in the circles of religious Zionism." In the opinion of this rabbi, the disaster came about because of using Halakha for political matters, educating for simplistic thinking, and delegitimizing the ruling order and other viewpoints. "Cursed be the murderers, cursed be those who send them, if there are such," were the severe words of Rabbi Bin-Nun, demanding the resignation of every person in spiritual authority who had loosed his tongue in the previous year, opening the door to violent deeds. "Every person who said *rodef* [a Jew who leads to the death of other Jews, and thus should be killed] . . . not fools, not weeds, not the marginalized, but Torah authorities." These words cast the entire country into a turmoil.[21]

But from the opposite camp came a demand to share the responsibility, refrain from self-flagellation, and "understand the depth of the soul's abyss that calls out." These words were spoken by Knesset member Hanan Porat from the National Religious Party after condemning the act of murder as terrible and despicable:

> I want to outline for you the profile of the murderer, the persecutor, the persecuted, this poor, desperate individual. . . . When at night, in sleepless nights, I pass the graves of Rachel and Bethlehem . . . and hear "the voice of Rachel weeping for her children, refusing to be comforted for her children who are not [here]" and the word of God calling out, "And the children shall return to their own borders" [Jeremiah 31: 14–16]. . . . I understand the depth of the soul's abyss that calls out, "What are you doing? What are you doing?" . . . And when you add to this all sorts of Halakhic innuendo bent out of shape and Kabbalist secrets greatly distorted, this is how matters can end up.

From the point of view of Porath and many others, the Rabin government was leading to the abyss those who were faithful to the Land of Israel, who found themselves attacked by their government and that holiest to them threatened. Nevertheless, no one should fall into this abyss as the assassin did: "He who sets his hand upon the upon the prime minister of Israel murders the people of Israel."

Much harsher words were said at the conference by Rabbi Menachem Felix, head of the Neve Dekalim yeshiva. Rabbi Felix denied the legitimate right of the Rabin government to lead the people and realize its political goals. Although "the murder is a murder, and it is mad and abominable," he also noted that, as a result, the entire nation had taken the prime minister to its heart. Until the assassination, however, it was "a government that ruled by grace of the enemies of Israel," referring to the Arab members of the Knesset. "Although this government was in charge de facto . . . it was PLO supporters who gave this government a majority and ruling power. But was it a legitimate kingdom of Israel? In my view, no." Furthermore, he said, it was the Rabin government that jeopardized the People and the Land by its destructive act of giving away portions of the Land of Israel to a foreign power. Thus, added Rabbi Felix, even if the religious community erred by not taking strong measures against "mad extremes," this should be seen in the perspective of the deeds of the government: "I do not place myself upon the chair of the accused. I do not feel guilty." This speaker was not alone, and after the criticism leveled from outside, his approach increasingly resonated in the community.[22] In the words of Rabbi Felix, "I do not think that our camp is impure, that we must cleanse it."

It is no coincidence that Rabbi Lichtenstein, delivering a sermon to his yeshiva students several days later, closed with the words, "May we know how to purify our hearts, may we know how to purify our camp, and through a spiritual Torah effort, we shall aspire as best we can to purify and sanctify our city."[23] And thus the question arises, Do these two speakers still belong to the same camp? Do they share the same concept of purity?

Attack and Defense

So far, I have focused on the initial, unmediated reactions of some important leaders of religious Zionism to the Rabin assassination. But the tempest did not end there, and the mood gradually shifted. I would like to distinguish between three different phases in the response of the public and its leaders. As noted, the first reaction was mainly one of internal criticism and protest, with a demand to clean house (the above citations were several among many).[24] In the second phase, however, the voice of defensiveness and denial gained in volume. The harsher the attacks from the outside, the more the religious Zionist camp barricaded itself, quelling the voices of internal criticism. While in the third stage the trauma had been internalized and, like the trauma of land concessions, has created a surprising ideological and theological silence barely precedented in the community for dozens of years.

The religious background of the assassin and the reasons he gave for his deed evoked strong antireligious sentiment among the Israeli public. This criticism naturally focused on the religious Zionist movement in whose institutions the assassin studied. For a while it seemed as if all the undertakings of this movement—a source of pride for so long—were at risk. Member of the Knesset (M.K.) Ori Orr (Labor), chairman of the Knesset Committee for Foreign Affairs and Security, called upon the government to close down the *hesder* yeshivas. M.K. Moshe Katzav (Likud) called into question the need for government religious schools. In a meeting of the Council for Higher Education, direct criticism was heaped upon Bar-Ilan University. And needless to say, particularly sharp barbs were aimed at the religious settlements. Taken together, these four items comprise the cultural syntheses and institutions that shape the self-image of religious Zionism: government religious education (religion and modernity), the *hesder* yeshivas (Torah and the military), a religious university (Torah and science), settlements (Torah and labor/nationalism). An entire culture, not just a specific ideology, faced criticism and found itself in jeopardy. Two personal anecdotes illustrate the atmosphere that prevailed at the time. A member of Netivot Shalom, the left-wing religious movement, related to me with tears in his eyes that his sons were fearful and ashamed of going out in public while wearing a knit skullcap, a symbol of the religious Zionist movement. Another friend, a psychologist by profession, related that an ultra-Orthodox couple came to consult with him about their son's schooling problems. When the mother raised the possibility of their son transferring out of the ultra-Orthodox yeshiva and into a government religious school, the father angrily replied, "Do you want him to grow up to be a murderer?"

It is not surprising that the national religious community, which feels pressure from several directions, has become defensive. The soul-searching was rapidly replaced by denial and fortification against the outside world.[25] Some even launched a counterattack. Thus evolved the second, better-known phase in the reaction of the religious Zionist community toward the assassination of the prime minister.

Note that ultra-Orthodox spokespersons and writers were also sharply critical of religious Zionist culture, but they blamed the assassination on modern secular culture—a power-hungry culture that sanctions permissiveness and licentiousness and the exposure of religious nationalist youth to this culture. If the religious element were to blame, why has there never been bloodshed in the ultra-Orthodox community? And why did it not appear in Jewish communities in the diaspora? Some attacks were directed against the theological ground of messianic religious Zionism. Rabbi Israel Eichler, the polished spokesman of the radical ultra-Orthodox camp, drew a direct link between the assassination and the perspective of the state as redemption. In Eichler's dialectical claim, one who attributes religious messianic meaning to the secular state of Israel and its government is liable— according to this internal logic—to shed the blood of a political leader who is "in charge of" the messianic implementation but betrays his function. Raising the government and expectations from it to the realm of the sacred opens the gates to grave injury at a time of crisis (the hour of "profanization"). This is not true for ultra-Orthodox Jews, who expect nothing of value from the secular government and hence are not disappointed with it on the normative level:

> The most basic distortion in perspective is bestowing a religious dimension upon the secular state of Israel. This is the element that opens the door to a messianic, Shabbatean madness. If the state is [believed to be] the dawn of redemption, withdrawal of sovereignty from territories in the Land of Israel is [considered] a regression from redemption. And he who destroys "the Third Commonwealth" will be portrayed as a *moser* [a Jew who betrays the Jewish community to the gentiles], with all the distorted casuistry. When the state is holy and the government the Holy of Holies, the prime minister is the priest of this idolatry. Along comes someone who believes in that idolatry, and kills the high priest because he injured the "sanctity" of sovereignty of this idol worship. . . . Halakhicly speaking [however], there is no difference between the Israeli secular government and the British or American secular government. Thus, this [raising of a secular state to the sublime] is a foreign culture not recognized in a Jewish perspective.[26]

This is, of course, the reverse position of that presented by Rabbi Zvi Tau and his colleagues at the Merkaz HaRav yeshiva. As noted, the latter identified the cause of assassination as public contempt for the Kingdom of Israel and the leaders of the state in redemption ("Its significance is not that they do not like the government of Israel; they do not like the Lord of the universe!").[27] Eichler, by contrast, identified the root of the assassination in the religious meaning bestowed upon secular sovereignty and the sanctified role granted to the secular state and its leaders.[28]

Thus the attacks on religious Zionists that came primarily from the nonreligious, but also from the ultra-Orthodox, silenced the internal moral criticism of the community. Several days after the assassination, a religious person from the town of Petah Tiqva called me up in pained turmoil. He insisted that I come to his congregation to speak about the assassination, the victim, and especially about ourselves and our soul-searching. "I'm right-wing in my views," he said, "but we must have a profound examination of how we reached this point and where to go from here. Things must not return to how they were." When I arrived at his congregation about a month after the assassination, the man requested, almost begged, that I talk about a "less volatile" subject than the soul-searching of religious Zionism. I was not sure if he himself had calmed down in the interim, but he was clearly worried about the anger of his friends.

Theological Silence

Yet the trauma of the assassination has not passed; it has only been internalized and repressed. From the viewpoint of many supporters of the Greater Land of Israel movement, it has joined an even greater trauma—ongoing withdrawal from portions of the Land of Israel—and the two traumas together yield a surprising silence on the ideological and theological plane. Whether consciously or not, a deep change has taken place in the religious discourse. Rabbis and spiritual leaders who for 30 years claimed to interpret the movement of Divine Will in history seem to have taken a vow of silence in this sensitive area. Those who always knew how current events served the larger plan of redemptionare now almost speechless about it,[29] and write and publish even less. The debate about the Land of Israel, which had previously focused primarily on concepts of faith and redemption, now focuses almost entirely on matters of security and politics. Half the land of Judea and Samaria is designated for withdrawal, but no response is forthcoming on the theological plane. The leaders of Gush Emunim appear today to be pragmatic, and one has to make an effort to distinguish the dialogue of rabbis from that of politicians and generals.

Even *Nekuda*, the journal of the Jewish settlements in Judea, Samaria, and Gaza, has undergone a profound transformation (confirmed by the editor). And the *Gilyon Rabanei Yesha*, representing the settlement rabbis, has not appeared for a few years (owing to lack of time, explains the editor).[30] And perhaps one anecdote will be illustrative. During Passover 1997, the annual national conference of the Bnei Akiva youth movement was held. Unlike in previous years, the only questions discussed in the keynote panel were burning social issues, while the workshop "The Beginning of Our Emerging Redemption"—which in the past would have garnered most of the attention—had very few participants. Sometimes the reactions of youth are a sensitive seismograph to change.

But youth are not the only ones aware of the change; so are rabbis and spiritual leaders, some of whom have voiced their protest:

> On the face of it, it's hard to see our "flowering redemption." . . . It's easy to assume that the only language we can use today to save the Land of Israel, or whatever can be saved of it, is language on a level that everyone understands. Some reminder about the Land is heard, of course, but primarily talk about security, fears, and apprehensions. Where will this soldier be positioned, what are the dangers lurking on the roads, what risks will there be tomorrow for the settlements or elsewhere? We'll [mistakenly] use the language spoken by the

individual because security is a concept that affects the individual, and the entire point of peace is to bring security . . . as if the nation of Israel does not know or understand another language. Perhaps we shall also speak about holy places. The Land of Israel is sacred land and there are holy sites in Hebron, too, such as the Tomb of the Patriarchs and the Tomb of Othniel Ben Knaz.[31]

These ironic words, spoken by none other than Rabbi Moshe Bleicher, head of the Shavei Hebron yeshiva, are fascinating because they were uttered just as, a few hundred meters from the yeshiva, the Israeli army had begun to withdraw from large areas of Hebron in early 1997. The yeshiva students, gathered in the study hall, heard their rabbi open, of course, with a direct reaction to the immediate event: "We are poised at a moment when the government of Israel in the Land of Israel has made a terrible, shocking decision under pressure from the nations of the world and the uprising of the wickedness of Ishmael who insolently aspires to inherit the oasis of the Lord." However, Rabbi Bleicher moved quickly into a more reflective consideration of the spiritual meaning of the period of national revival and the destiny of the Jewish people in its land. Indeed, there was one recurring motif in his talk: We must not reduce ourselves to the mundane political issues of our national existence, even to the sacred land of Hebron and Jerusalem, or the army and state: "The people demands from us more authentic concerns, not about the physical side of the land, but about itself, its essence, its direction. And the direction will not become clear without understanding the Israeli life force, the divine presence that returns and resides within the nation."

In other words, Rabbi Bleicher called for raising the political-security-territorial analysis to a level of spiritual-theological-historiographic discourse in the spirit of Rabbi Abraham Isaac Kook and his disciples. Only this examination can give organic meaning to mundane discourse and ultimately conquer the heart of the nation. Needless to say, even the "peace process" reflects for the speaker a sinking into a hedonist and banal realm, a desire "to live life in a nice way." Similarly, the focus on the security and survival argument: "The main innovation of our period is not . . . that several million Jews exist [here], nor that they live in and build up the Land of Israel. . . . The innovation is the existence of a national living entity, a concrete divine presence, alive and active, which is revealed in all these details."

Rabbi Bleicher is not alone on this front. In recent years, however, it was this approach that led the camp and illuminated its path, while today it calls out its protest from the sidelines (or from above). Indeed, immediately after the assassination it was Bleicher who gave one of the most creative sermons in the religious sector about the assassination and the meaning of the national mourning.[32] In it, Bleicher did not hesitate to discuss the tragedy using traditional images from catastrophic messianism, in particular the legendary figure of the Messiah son of Joseph.[33] In Jewish sources, the Messiah son of Joseph symbolizes the last historical battle before the dawn of redemption. Although this advances the nation toward political salvation, it also embodies the element of crisis and downfall. This Messiah is thus fated to be a casualty of war and thereby pave the way for the utopian appearance of the final spiritual redeemer—the Messiah son of David. Naturally it is not Rabin the man who is the Messiah son of Joseph, but the political-military process that he symbolized: "The personality of Yitzhak Rabin, may his memory be a blessing, expressed an entire era . . . an entire process . . . reflecting the daring and courage . . . the inner strength through all the wars . . . that accompanies the building of the nation in its land . . . and hence the great mourning."[34] And he called for taking the next step toward organic spiritual redemption, bringing the Messiah son of David.

Bleicher thus made a conscious effort after the assassination to encourage theological and historiographic perspective on the event (two sentences were also devoted to the moral dimension). But he too seems to have known that community reaction did not move in that direction. As he noted more than a year after the redeployment in Hebron, "There seems to be no point in speaking as if the people of Israel does not know or understand." Yet one might ask if perhaps there is another religious language, a third one, neither messianic nor pragmatic but ethical and Halakhic, that could be understood?

A Political Center

While theological silence was enveloping the religious Zionist community, ideological decibels were lowering in Israeli society at large. This could be seen in the search for pragmatic, "centrist" leaders who do not represent a solid faith and hence do not resolve the tension between the dream of a Greater Israel and the dream of a New Middle East, let alone the debate between sublimeness and sublimeness, identity and identity. The role played here by the assassination is unclear, but it clearly had some impact. As noted above, the assassin raked all the exposed nerves of society at once. He assaulted the entire system and its symbols—the moral ethos, national pathos, social consensus, elected government, military might—as if seeking to undermine every system and covenant, every boundary and law. He also made salient all the social rifts and fissures between the right and left, the religious and the secular, and to a great extent also between ethnic groups. It is no wonder that many began to fear fervor and ideological confrontation; that people began to think that it is ideas that kill, not scoundrels, and thus sought leaders who represent power rather than the pathos of faith.

Settlement leader Israel Harel observed that in one matter the assassin was an abject failure: Through his deed, a broad political center was created, one that shuns every form of radicalism and extremism, which brought about a significant reversal in the Israeli discourse.[35] The winner of the next election, in 1996, was the politician who persuaded the public that voting for him would not lead to abrupt change in either direction: Benjamin Netanyahu was successfully portrayed as one who would abide by the peace process but lead us there slowly; would give away less and ensure a "secure peace." Before the 1996 elections, the two large parties colluded in repressing and ignoring the assassination, in the belief that the public did not want a threatening polarization or the painful memory drummed into their heads. A fear for the stability of Israeli democracy was also expressed by the elites. Some even called for "lowering the octaves." An antidemocratic periphery exists in Israel, and when a society loses the ability to defend itself in the wake of repeated traumas, its survival is in jeopardy."[36] Hence a conscious effort was made to reconfirm the legitimacy of the elected government.

The assassination also fully exposed the gap between subcultures in Israel, especially between religious and secular language.[37] One rabbi was accused of incitement to murder and perhaps was interrogated by the police because he opined that anyone who gives away territories from the Land of Israel is considered "as if he has become liable for his life." The accusers did not understand that in the language of Jewish sources this is hyperbole and nothing more (as in the language of the Mishna: "He who was going along the way and repeating [his Torah tradition], but interrupts his repetition to say, 'how beautiful is this tree, how lovely this plowed field,' the Scripture reckons to him as if he has become liable for his life").[38] Even Rabbi Ya'akov Ariel, the chief rabbi of Ramat Gan, who gave a Halakhic answer that clearly nullified any possibility of applying *din rodef*—the punishment of death for a *rodef*—against the prime minister,[39] was initially asked to resign from his post because of a misunderstanding about what he wrote in the language of Jewish sources. On the other hand, the secular public was terrified by its first exposure to concepts like *rodef*, *moser*, and *pulsa di nura* (a mystical curse invoked against a Jewish sinner), not to mention first learning that their relevance for political life was discussed in rabbinic correspondence.[40] However, it appears that because of this very alienation—due to the poverty of common language as well as the dreadful tumor that emerged from Jewish religion—secular people called off the old deal that bestowed upon the religious an exclusive mandate for Jewish sources and the historical memory. I believe that the explanation for the recent renewed interest in the Jewish bookshelf among the secular intelligentsia cannot ignore this factor.

I have dealt here with reactions and fears, shouting and silence, theology and politics. But beyond all these, the heart of the matter should not be forgotten: the murder, the bloodshed, the evil, the sin, the mark of Cain. "Lay not the guilt of innocent blood in the midst of thy people Israel."[41]

Notes

The phrase in the title, "Let us search our path," comes from Lamentations 3: 40. Under this same title, two men provided incisive reactions to the assassination from both sides of the ideological divide in religious Zionism—Rabbi Aharon Lichtenstein and Rabbi Zvi Tau. The quotation from Rabbi Tau comes from a conversation with members of the settlement Keshet, who asked for his comments after the assassination. The discussion appeared in the local publication under the title, "Following the Assassination of Prime Minister Yitzhak Rabin, may he rest in peace"; the sentence ends with "and even after his murder, there are those who drink a toast" (p. 1).

1. Yaron Ezrachi, "Israeli Democracy Looks at Itself," *Ha'aretz* Supplement by the Jerusalem Van Leer Institute, April 1996, p. 3 [Hebrew].

2. I address this issue briefly in "Israeli Dialogue After the Assassination," *Ha'aretz* Supplement, April 1996, pp. 5–6.

3. Quoted from memory of statements made on a public debate on Israeli television.

4. Because elsewhere I have dealt at length with this question, I shall be very brief here. On the complete dream, see Ravitzky, *Messianism, Zionism, and Jewish Religious Radicalism* (Chicago: University of Chicago Press, 1996), pp. 1–6. On the complete peace, see Ravitzky, "Peace, " in A. A. Cohen and Paul Mendes-Flohr (eds.), *Contemporary Jewish Religious Thought* (New York: Charles Scribner's Sons, 1987), pp. 685–702 (reprinted in my book, *History and Faith*, [Amsterdam: J. C. Gieben, 1996], pp. 22–45); Ravitzky, "You Must Not Remain Indifferent" (Jerusalem, 1990–91); and Ravitzky, "You Cannot Ignore This" (Jerusalem: Oz VeShalom/Netivot Shalom, 1987–88), pp. 1–7.

5. The memory of the Holocaust also played an important role in the redemp-

tive perception of the state. Only efforts to bring the messiah could "balance out" the heinous destruction and give it meaning.

6. Rabbi Hayim Druckman, "Our Rabbi," in *Rabenu* [Zvi Yehuda Kook] (Jerusalem: no pub., 1981–82), p. 47 [Hebrew]. Compare with Rabbi Zvi Yehuda Kook, *To the Ways of the Public* (Jerusalem: Mosad Harav Kook, 1986–87), p. 246 [Hebrew]; idem, *The Paths of Israel* (Jerusalem: Mosad Harav Kook, 1967), Part B, pp. 157–58 [Hebrew].

7. Rabbi Yoel Bin-Nun, "The Broken Heart of Religious Zionism," *Yediot Aharonot* (December 15, 1996) [Hebrew].

8. This image is taken from a statement made by Amos Oz in a conversation with settlers (1983). Also see his book *In the Land of Israel in Fall 1982* (Tel Aviv, 1985), pp. 83–122 [Hebrew].

9. Shenhar Commission, *Nation and World: Jewish Culture in a Changing World* (Jerusalem, 1993–94), pp. 8–9 [Hebrew].

10. Ehud Sprinzak, *Political Violence in Israel* (Jerusalem: Jerusalem Institute for Israel *Studies:* Research Series, no. 60, 1995), pp. 141–51 [Hebrew].

11. S. N. Eisenstadt, "Collective Consciousness, Public Discourse and Democracy," *Ha'aretz* Supplement by the Jerusalem Van Leer Institute, April 1996, p. 5 [Hebrew].

12. For an angry article about this, see Rabbi Avraham Shapira (former chief rabbi of Israel), "The Chutzpa of the Assassin," *HaTzofeh*, November 17, 1996 [Hebrew].

13. *Midrash Tannaim* 22: 21; *Yerushalmi, Ketubot* 4: 3; *Bavli, Ketubot* 45: A.

14. Rabbi Aharon Lichtenstein, "Let us Search our Path and Examine It," *Allon Shevut Graduates*, Allon Shevut 1995–96, p. 17.

15. Menachem Friedman, *Society and Religion* (Jerusalem: Yad Ben Zvi, 1978): 19–20. [Hebrew]; idem, "Religious Zealotry in Israeli Society," in *On Ethnic and Religious Diversity in Israel* (Ramat Gan: Bar Ilan University Press, 1975), pp. 99–111; C. S. Liebman, "Extremism as a Religious Norm," *Journal for the Scientific Study of Religion* 20 (1983): 75ff [Hebrew].

16. Tau, "Following the Assassination of Prime Minister Yitzhak Rabin, may he rest in peace" (see unnumbered note above), p. 2.

17. Rabbi Tau repeated this analogy in lectures after the assassination. Besides reports by members of Keshet, there are internal publications of his lectures in Elon Moreh and Atzmona (Heshvan 1995–96), in which he repeats and emphasizes this motif.

18. This appeared after the assassination in the Anglo-Jewish newspaper *The Forward* from November 17, 1996. At my request, Professor Hayyim Soloveichik, the Rabbi's nephew, confirmed the accuracy of the report with his uncle.

19. His position on the Oslo Accords contrasts with the moderate positions and policies of his brother, Rabbi Yosef Dov Soloveichik, who passed away several years ago.

20. The proceedings of the conference were printed in *Nekuda*, 190 (1995–96): 58–64. They were also reprinted in the anthology *Religion and State in Israel 1994–1995* (Jerusalem: Hemdat, 1996), pp. 148–55 [Hebrew].

21. An open attack appeared in *Gilyon Rabanei Yesha* against "the wicked invective" and "he who slanders." See "Announcement of the Committee of Judea and Samaria Rabbis," *Gilyon Rabanei Yesha* 29 (Kislev 1996–97): 1; Rabbi Eliezer Melamed, "There is Smoke Without Fire," ibid. [both in Hebrew].

22. The very act of participating in this broad-based conference, convened as a public soul-searching, indicates some moderation and outreach to the opponent. The extreme elements presumably did not attend.

23. Lichtenstein, "Let Us Search Our Path and Examine It," p. 27.

24. See, for example, Rabbi Eli Sadan, head of the pre-IDF program in the settlement of 'Eli: *Letter to My Brothers and Friends, the Youth of Bnei Akiva*, circulated in thousands of copies; Rabbi Yehuda Amital, "Soul-Searching," *Alon Shevut Graduates*, 1995–96, pp. 11–14; Rabbi David Ben Meir, *In the Name of All Israel*, internal publication, Jerusalem, 1995–96; Rabbi David Hartman, "Through Traditional Eyes," *Ha'aretz*, January 17, 1997; the sources cited in the article by Arye Na'or, "Examining the Reactions of the Religious-Nationalist Camp to the Assassination of Rabin," *Ha'aretz* Supplement by the Jerusalem Van Leer Institute, p. 3. See also excerpts from the response of Rabbi Ovadia Yosef, "Comments Following the Assassination," *Ma'agalim*, no. 2 (1995–96) [all the above in Hebrew].

25. In a discussion at the Israel Democracy Institute held on the first anniversary of the assassination, the possibility of a process of defensiveness and denial was also raised by Professors Moshe Lissak and Mordechai Kremnitzer.

26. Israel Eichler, "Watch Your Words," *HaMahane HaHaredi*, no. 754 (Heshvan 5756 [1995–96]), pp. 171–72; see also *Religion and State in Israel 1994–1995*, pp. 171–72.

27. Tau, "Following the Assassination of Prime Minister Yitzhak Rabin," p. 5.

28. Compare Yeshayahu Leibowitz, "After Qibya," in *Judaism, the Jewish People and the State of Israel* (Jerusalem: Schocken, 1975–76), pp. 233–34 [Hebrew]: "It is incumbent upon us to ask ourselves: From where do these youth come who feel no compunctions or moral constraints about carrying out this atrocity [the murder of Arabs]? . . . This is one result of using the religious category of *the sacred* for social, national, and political matters. . . . The concept of sanctity . . . [is] transferred to the profane. . . . On matters of the sacred—and perhaps just for them—an individual can act *without restraint*" (emphasis in the original).

29. See Ravitzky, *Messianism, Zionism, and Jewish Religious Radicalism*, pp. 125–36; idem., "Messianic Myth and Historical Drama," in *Mytos VeZikaron*, David Ohana and Robert Wistrich, eds. (Jerusalem: The Van Leer Jerusalem Institute, 1996), pp. 100–103 [Hebrew].

30. Based on personal conversations in 1997 with Uri Elitzur (former editor of *Nekuda*) and Rabbi Eliezer Melamed (editor of *Gilyon Rabanei Yesha*).

31. Rabbi Moshe Bleicher, "We're Not Fighting over Hebron, but over the State of Israel and Its Soul," *Nekuda*, no. 202 (1996–97): 16–19 [Hebrew].

32. Rabbi Moshe Bleicher, "The Course of Our Era" Kiryat Arba, 1995–96 [Hebrew].

33. The paradoxical motif of the Messiah son of Joseph, the redeemer who dies, also served Rabbi Abraham Isaac Kook in his eulogy of Herzl, "The leader [who]

fell victim to grief and trouble." See, "Mourning in Jerusalem," *Writings of Rabbi Abraham Isaac Kook*, Jerusalem, 1983–84 [Hebrew].

34. Bleicher, "In the Course of our Era," pp. 11–12.

35. From a discussion held at the Israel Democracy Institute, Jerusalem, September 18, 1997.

36. Ibid., where Emmanuel Sivan represented this point of view.

37. See my article, "Religious and Secular in Israel: A Cultural War?," in Michael Brown and Bernard Lightman (eds.), *Creating the Jewish Future* (Walnut Creek/ London/New Delhi: Altamira Press, 1999), pp. 80–100.

38. Mishna, *Avot* 3: 9.

39. Rabbi Ya'akov Ariel, *"Rodef* Fences," *HaTzofeh*, November 13, 1996 [Hebrew]. This was first published two years earlier.

40. See the letter of the Rabbis Dov Lior, Daniel Shilo, and Eliezer Melamed to 40 other rabbis, reprinted in the anthology *Religion and State in Israel*, pp. 120–23. See also the words of Rabbi Aharon Soloveichik cited in note 18.

41. Deuteronomy 21: 8.

CHAPTER 6

An Illusion of Belonging: Reactions of the Arab Population to Rabin's Assassination

MAJID AL-HAJ

For the Arab population in Israel, which constitutes 16 percent out of almost 6 million citizens, two reference groups are significant in shaping its national and civic identity. With regard to its civic identity, the reference group is the Jewish majority in Israel. Thus, the Arab population's struggle for rights and equality is based on its comparison with the Jewish citizens of Israel. This is what defines the gap and the level of discrimination. Arab citizens also measure their economic and social achievements against those of their Jewish neighbors, considered by many Israeli Arabs to be agents of modernization and Westernization.

Over time, the Arabs in Israel underwent a profound process of becoming both bilingual and bicultural. This process was essentially forced upon them, because the state controls the Arab education system and as a result of the Arab population's economic dependence on the dominant Jewish center. Gradually, however, the Arabs rationalized the process, and their impact on various areas of life increased. Paradoxically, this process is also a means by which the Arab population has integrated itself into Israeli society and improved its social and economic standing. However, there is clear evidence that the class gap has even widened between the dominant Jewish majority and the Arab national minority (Carmi and Rosenfeld, 1992).

In terms of national identity, Arabs in Israel view the Palestinians and the Arab world as their reference group. Their attitude toward resolving the Israeli-Palestinian-Arab conflict is influenced by the attitudes of the Palestinian leadership. Even their opinion of world leaders—Arabs, in particular—is derived from the positions these leaders take about the Palestinian issue. For a long time, developments in the Israeli-Palestinian conflict played a critical role in the political behavior of Israeli Arabs, including their voting patterns in Knesset elections.

The national identification of the Arabs in Israel is a product of the fact that this population belongs nationally and culturally to the Arab world and the Palestinian people. However, this national identification has also been affected by the fact that defining Israel as a Jewish-Zionist state leaves no room for Arab citizens to take part in the process of "nation-building" or even to participate legitimately in the political culture shaped by the Jewish majority (Rouhana and Ghanem, 1998). Thus, ever since the founding of the state, the Arabs in Israel were expected to be "loyal" citizens, but the issue of their identification with the state remained ambiguous and secondary for both Jews and Arabs. The simultaneous existence of reference groups that are not just different but even oppose each other prevents natural development of the national and civic components and perpetuates a state of tension between these two elements in the identity of Israeli Arabs. Exacerbating the tension is the fact that Arab citizens find themselves at a double periphery: they are marginalized by both reference groups—Israeli society and the Palestinian national movement.

This situation was evident in the response of the Palestinian population in Israel to the intifada, the Arab uprising (1987–93). On the one hand, the Arabs in Israel identified with the Palestinian national uprising and supported the goals set by the Palestinian leadership, including liberation from Israeli occupation and establishment of a Palestinian state alongside the state of Israel. Israeli Arabs also expressed their moral and material support for their Palestinian brethren in the occupied territories. Even though these manifestations of support were within the law, they were considered by a large part of the Jewish leadership and population to reflect "anti-Israeli" behavior and "support for the enemy." As a result, in the 1990s the Arab citizens were further marginalized in Israeli society, which negatively affected the legitimacy of their struggle in the civic sphere.

But even in their support for the intifada, Arabs in Israel were influenced by the civic-Israeli component. Every measure taken by the Arab leadership in Israel was within the "rules of the game" of Israeli society, which are governed by the Jewish majority. In various events, such as commemoration of Land Day (March 30, 1976, when a number of Arab demonstrators were killed by the Israeli army) or during general strikes, the Arab mayors ensured adherence to law and order, and the security forces generally had little to do. Before each such event, the Arab leaders stressed that the Arabs are citizens of Israel, and that despite their support for the Palestinian struggle they have a different orientation toward the future than their Palestinian compatriots in the occupied territories. Hence, the Palestinians in Israel did not participate in the intifada. They also took no part in the political decisions of the Palestinian national movement. They maintained the status of an auxiliary, not an active, partner, and their role at the fringes of the Palestinian national movement became more and more evident (Al-Haj, 1993).

The state of "double periphery" in which the Israeli Arab population found itself increased their sense of frustration and, to some extent, also their sense of powerlessness. And yet the Arab population is young (more than 70 percent under the age of 30) and has undergone a profound process of modernization and politicization, as well as changes in patterns of leadership—from local, traditional to countrywide, young, educated leaders.

The change of government in 1992 that brought a Labor-Meretz coalition into power and efforts toward peace instilled hope in the Arab population of improving its civic status and making progress toward peace. Even though the Arab members of the Knesset had little influence, their support was a crucial element in the government's parliamentary majority, and this put them at the margins of the decision-making process. Although Arab Knesset members did not fully participate in the cabinet because they were not considered part of the coalition, they functioned as a so-called "obstructing bloc," which in some cases became an "obstructed bloc." This fact enabled the Israeli right to claim that the government did not represent the majority of the Jewish population, and to argue that a decision to withdraw from the occupied territories should not be based on Arab votes.

Arab expectations of the peace process have always been high. An examination of their attitudes toward the process and establishment of a Palestinian state revealed that Arab citizens believe all sides will benefit from this development: the Palestinians in the occupied territories, the Palestinian citizens of Israel, and the Jewish majority in Israel. The basic perspective of the Arabs is that their economic situation and especially their status in Israeli society will improve as a result of reconciliation between their state and their people (Al-Haj, Katz, and Shye, 1993). In the opinion of the Arabs, perception of them as a security risk and hostile minority may dissipate, while the legitimacy of their demands for civic equality may be enhanced in consequence of the peace agreement.

Thus the Oslo agreements between the PLO and Israel, and the subsequent Palestinian-Israeli peace process, won massive support among Israeli Arabs, despite some intellectuals' criticism. However, the peace process had a complex and multidimensional impact on the Arab population in Israel.

On the one hand, the process dulled but did not eliminate the tension between the civic-Israeli and the national-Palestinian-Arab components deeply intertwined in the identity of the Arab citizen. As the peace process progressed, a feeling that "the conflict is over" prevailed among the Arab population of Israel. In light of the hurdles still to be overcome, this was an optimistic response. However most Israeli Arabs tended to believe this, both because they perceive the process to be vital to all parties and also because they are eager to apply their energy and attention to civic matters related to their rights and daily lives.

On the other hand, the peace process only sharpened the status of the Arab population as a "double periphery" within both Israeli and Palestinian society. The peace process did not change the fact that Arab citizens are peripheral to Israeli society in many spheres—economic, social, and political. The process did not make them part of the national consensus in Israel, and it certainly did not change the political culture of Israeli society of which they are not considered a legitimate part.

What is more, the peace process has still not brought—and is not expected to bring, at least in the early stages—the emergence of a common civic culture of Jews and Arabs. On the contrary, what is evident so far is the intensified struggle of the Jewish majority for the Jewish-Zionist identity of the state. For the Israelis, the primary motivation for peace was the need to separate Palestinians from Israelis in order to preserve the Jewish-Zionist character of Israel and prevent it from becoming a binational state. This argument was shared by Jewish leaders from the right and the left. Thus, one can envision that the Jewish-Zionist identity of the state of Israel will be reinforced by the peace process.

Because the resolution of external conflicts only sharpens internal friction, the peace process laid bare major fault lines within Jewish society—a religious-secular cleavage, ethnic rifts, and the issues raised by immigration. Thus, the Jewish-Arab division was further pushed into the shadows. From the point of view of Israeli society, civic equality is not a significant issue. It is not on the public agenda and, for most Israeli Jews, has no importance in the national order of priorities.

This situation only heightens the frustration of Arab citizens of Israel. For the Arab population, the peace process moved the civic issue to top priority and sharpened the struggle over the status and rights of the Arab minority in Israel. As a result, the Arab population in Israel is demanding rectification of its civic status. From this point of view, the emphasis of Israeli Arabs on civic membership and participation in the Israeli discourse and society has gathered momentum. This is the paradoxical result of the double periphery in which the Palestinian Arabs in Israel find themselves: aspiring to advance their status within Israeli society and, simultaneously, to advance the peace process and strengthen their ties with the Palestinian people and the Arab world.

Reactions to the Assassination of Rabin

The assassination of Rabin had a crucial impact on the geopolitics of the region, the Israeli public, and the Arab population of Israel. The response of the Arab population to the assassination reflects several concurrent factors that derive from the political orientation described above, the attitude toward Rabin the person, and the desire to demonstrate a sense of belonging to Israeli society. The remainder of the chapter presents a short summary of the reactions and mood, and then an attempt to understand the significance of these reactions.

The Arab population expressed anger and pain about the assassination of Rabin, who was called a "victim of peace" (Muhammad Khalilia, "Mourning in the Arab Sector," *Davar Rishon*, November 6, 1995). All the political parties and movements published mourning notices in the newspapers and sent condolences to the president of Israel, the government, the chair of the Knesset, and the family. The Arab municipalities published mourning notices and hung them at the entrance to the municipality buildings and on the main streets. Schools began with an hour-long discussion in the homeroom about the assassination and the need for tolerance and pluralism. The National Committee of Arab Mayors convened a special meeting and dispatched a large delegation of mayors and Knesset members to represent the Arab population at the funeral. The Druze and Circassian mayors also convened a special meeting in Daliat al-Karmil after which the participants went to Jerusalem to participate in the funeral (ibid.). Arab leaders from the entire political spectrum expressed sorrow and shock, condemned the act, and lauded the contribution of Yitzhak Rabin to peace and equality. The following is a selection of reactions, some of which appeared in the newspapers and some from interviews conducted for this chapter.

In an October 1996 interview, Member of the Knesset (M.K.) Hashim Mahamid then of the Democratic Front for Peace and Equality said: "The entire world was surprised by the assassination of Rabin, and so were the Palestinian Arabs in Israel. Many Arabs participated in Rabin's funeral and everyone without exception was in shock. This is a result of the political change that took place under Rabin—although it was slow and insufficient—regarding the Israeli-Arab conflict and the relationship between Jews and Arabs in Israel. I will never forget Rabin's reaction, several days before his assassination, to the right-wing protest against the government's reliance on Arabs as an 'obstructing bloc.' Rabin had said, 'Now I realize that Jewish racism exists,' adding, 'The Arabs in Israel are legitimate citizens of the state and have the full right of partnership on every issue.' Thus, the Arab citizens saw the change in Rabin as hope for advancing the issues of peace and equality."

Hussein Suleiman, then spokesman for the National Committee of Arab Mayors: "The Arab masses were deeply shocked by Rabin's assassination. He was mourned in every Arab home, despite his previous attitudes about the Arab sector and the intifada. What caused the deep sorrow among the Arabs about his assassination was the fact that Rabin, for the first time, formally recognized the PLO headed by Yasser Arafat, and the Arabs were convinced that Rabin was the one who would fight for and believe in peace" (interview, October 1996).

Sheikh Abdullah Nimr Darwish, one of the leaders of the Israeli Islamic Movement, spoke in a similar vein: "Rabin was the bulldozer who paved the way to peace. Every other leader who comes after him will travel this paved road and complete the journey" (*Ma BaPetah*, the Petah Tiqva weekly, November 10, 1995).

The mayor of the Bedouin village Arab al-Shabili emphasized: "He who was murdered was not only a friend, but a father, a son of the village who grew up among us and was one of us" (*Kol Ha'Emeq VeHaGalil*, November 10, 1995).

Ibrahim Nimr Hussein, former head of the National Committee of Arab Mayors: "We weep of course at the death of Mr. Rabin. We the Arabs of this country appreciated the contribution he made and his support for peace. Rabin led a courageous effort; for the first time in its history, he placed this region on a road that was full of hope for a more secure and fertile future" (*Kol HaTzafon*, November 17, 1995).

M.K. Taleb a-Sannaa (Arab Democratic Party): "The shots fired at the prime minister were intended to harm the peace. . . . Although they reached the prime minister and ended his life at a rally in support of peace and against violence, they will not harm the peace in the hearts of millions who live in the region and the forces for peace" (*al-Sinnara*, November 7, 1996).

The response of the Arab population came both from the leadership and the public at large, adults and youth. Many Arab schools throughout Israel held special classes in memory of Rabin, and several held art exhibits in which children presented their work about the assassination.

Several merchants in the Arab city of Nazareth set up memorials for Rabin in the local market. Jews who passed were surprised and sat down beside the memorials together with the Arab merchants (*al-Sinnara*, November 14, 1996). In the Arab town of Baqa al-Gharbiyya, a memorial service was held in memory of Rabin, in which public officials and mayors from the Arab sector participated (*Ma'ariv*, November 12, 1995).

In various Arab localities, the population stood in silence during the siren that was sounded at the funeral of the prime minister. This was perhaps the first time that Arab citizens stood at attention during a siren as a sign of national mourning in Israel, sounded annually for one minute on Holocaust Day and Memorial Day for Fallen Soldiers (Fawzi abu-Toameh, "The Arab Citizens of the State Stood in Silence . . . ," *Emtza Hadera*, November 10, 1995). One resident of Nazareth noted, "I didn't believe that Arabs from Nazareth would stand silent in memory of the prime minister Yitzhak Rabin, because Rabin once meant to us the person who broke the bones of our fellow Palestinians" (*Yediot Aharonot*, November 7, 1995).

In dozens of Arab localities, mourning and memorial services were convened in memory of the late prime minister at the initiative of municipalities and organizations. Communing with the memory of Rabin also took in the Arab parties that constituted the "obstructing bloc," who declared their support for Shimon Peres and called upon him to continue the policies of peace and equality begun by Rabin (*Davar Rishon*, November 12, 1995).

The reaction of the Arab population in Haifa, a mixed Jewish-Arab city, had special significance. The political and religious leadership was unified in its expression of pain, anger, and sorrow about the assassination of the prime minister (*Kolbo*, November 10, 1995).

The Arab residents of Jaffa also expressed deep sorrow. In the words of Suleiman Mashrawi: "'I wept like a child; I decided to fast for three days.' On the second day, Mashrawi took his car to Rabin Plaza, draped a black ribbon on it, and hung a sign on which he wrote: 'I'm a resident of Jaffa; Jews and Arabs mourn the death of Prime Minister Yitzhak Rabin, whose body was murdered, but not his ideas. His legacy is peace between the Jewish and Arab peoples'" (*Zeman Tel-Aviv* weekly, November 10, 1995).

Makram Khouri, a well-known Arab artist who had succeeded in the Jewish sector as well, noted: "I admit that at the beginning of the intifada when he was defense minister in the National Unity Government, I thought and felt differently about him. After the change and the milestone in Israeli politics about peace, Yitzhak Rabin became my prime minister as well" (*Ma'ariv*, November 10, 1995).

The reactions of Arab citizens of Israel indicate that the image of Rabin engraved in their memories is complex. The Arabs remember Rabin as a tough military man who was prime minister during the events of Land Day. They also associate Rabin with the Palestinian intifada as the defense minister in the National Unity Government who called upon soldiers to "break bones" in order to end the intifada (*Davar Rishon*, November 13, 1995). However, the peace rally and the assassination that followed seem to have made it possible for Arabs to participate in the secular-Israeli ceremonies, to sing the "Song of Peace" instead of the national anthem, and to participate in the civil discourse.

It should be noted that beyond the expressions of shock, sorrow, and sympathy, the assassination gave the Arab population an opportunity to protest its status and the attitude of the Jewish majority toward it.

Sheikh Kamal Khatib, a leader of the Islamic Movement: "Clearly the assassination of Rabin plunged the region into a new reality, a mystery whose end we don't know, and I ask myself and note: The hands that murdered innocent workers and then murdered those worshiping in the Tomb of Abraham [in Hebron] are the same hands that spilled Jewish blood, especially that of the prime minister, and this is because these extremists did not get the punishment they deserved" (*al-Sinnara*, November 7, 1995).

Camelya Arraf-Bader, journalist: "As long as occupation, oppression, and violence were directed to the Other outside the gate, it was all right. But once violence reached the threshold of one's home, the inhabitants were shocked. Especially when it was a direct hit on the head." (Camelya Arraf-Bader, *Davar Rishon*, November 10, 1995).

M.K. Hashim Mahamid: "We all warned the political leadership and academics that racism and fascism may begin against the Arabs, but it will undoubtedly reach the Jews as well. However those in power ignored our words. And even after Rabin was assassinated, most Jews said, 'a Jew killing a Jew!?' as if a Jew killing an Arab was understandable, but not another Jew! We warned again and again that continuing the occupation, support of the settlements, and oppressing the rights of another nation will undoubtedly give birth to racists and murderers such as these" (interview, October 1996).

These reactions reflect the mood among the Arab population of Israel following the assassination of Rabin. The claim of the Palestinians in Israel has always been that violence against Palestinians on each side of the Green Line will eventually spill over onto the Jews. This claim is based on the perception that the attitude of the Jewish majority toward the Arabs both reflects and fosters an undemocratic political culture.

Shattering the Myth

The assassination of Rabin shattered a myth among both Jews and Arabs concerning Israeli political culture. In the Jewish sector, it was believed that political assassination was the lot of Arabs only. This perception in one form or another was also pervasive among Israeli Arabs. A large portion of the Arab public believed that whatever happened, the political debate between Jews would remain verbal and not degenerate into physical violence. The Arabs believed that the Jews were united and that the debate among them was superficial, reflecting the division of labor among various political streams who, in the final analysis, maintain the national consensus.

Thus, the assassination of Rabin shattered a long-standing illusion. It proved that the Jewish people are not outside history and certainly not above history, but an integral part of human history with chapters that are both enlightened and dark. This fact was sobering not only to Jews but also to Arabs, including the Arab citizens of Israel, who, as noted, view the Jews as one of their reference groups.

Camelya Arraf-Bader expressed it well: "Political assassinations have taken place in history from the days of ancient Rome to today. . . . In our region, Abdullah and Sadat were assassinated, but everyone was sure that 'it won't happen to us,' because this happens only among the Arabs, not among 'the chosen people.' Indeed, how did it happen among this nation? Maybe by virtue of regarding itself as the chosen people. But now it turns out that the Jewish people does not dwell on Olympic heights" (*Davar Rishon*, November 10, 1995).

Disappointment at Being Ignored

Since the founding of Israel, there were very few events in which the Arabs in Israel felt or wanted to feel a shared destiny with the Jews. This is a result of the deep cleavage between the two peoples in the shadow of the ongoing political conflict, and because the state of Israel was founded by Jews and for Jews, and not as a binational state or a state for all its citizens.

During the Gulf War in 1991, many Arab citizens felt for the first time a common destiny with the Jewish citizens of Israel. This happened despite the difference in attitudes between Jews and Arabs toward the war itself and the action against Iraq. However, the defense measures against the missile attacks, the sealed rooms, gas masks, waiting for the sirens, and the fear of chemical attack all created a sense of partnership.

The assassination of Rabin was the second event in which Arabs wished to demonstrate partnership and belonging to Israeli society. The reactions of the leadership and the public at large cited previously were an expression of this feeling. The Arab population expected its reaction to be appreciated by the Jewish majority. However, the gap was again revealed between expectations and reality. The Hebrew-speaking mass media ignored or marginalized the response of the Arab population. The Rabin assassination was grasped as an internal event that belonged to the Jewish-Jewish discourse and did not include the Jewish-Arab or even the civic-Israeli discourse. The media paid no attention to Arabs who went to Rabin's grave on Mount Herzl or to Rabin Plaza (*Hadashot Haifa VeHaTzafon*, November 16, 1995).

In a special issue of *Ma'ariv* devoted to Rabin's funeral (November 7, 1995), the Arab citizens of Israel were almost completely ignored. The only mention of Arabs was the picture of a Druze dignitary standing beside the coffin with the caption, "Brothers to the Sorrow." This issue carried reports of many children in schools, but not one Arab school was included. There was extensive coverage of statements by Jewish leaders and leaders from Arab countries, but nothing about the participation of Arab leaders in Israel.

This fact evokes both anger and disappointment among the Arab public. The spokesperson of the National Committee of Arab Mayors spoke bitterly of this: "The media completely ignored the reactions and sorrow of Arab citizens over the assassination of Rabin. Ignoring their presence has been a deliberate policy in the past and today, and it evokes frustration and bitterness" (interview, October 1996).

M.K. Hashim Mahamid: "The Hebrew media—newspapers, radio, and TV—completely ignored it, just as they consistently and systematically ignore the reaction of the Arab population to events. The spontaneous reaction to the crime of Rabin's assassination, and condemnation by the Arab population of the bus bombings and other violent incidents that claimed innocent lives, were not given the least bit of attention by the Hebrew media. This is because, in my opinion, the Zionist mentality does not view us as part of the state and therefore does not see the need for us to express our opinion" (interview, October 1996).

The writer Misbah Halabi protested the disregard for the reaction of the Arab population: "The media did not pay sufficient attention to the warm attitude of the late prime minister to the Arabs and Druze in the country, or to their warm attitude toward him" (*Hadashot Haifa VeHaTzafon*, November 16, 1995).

Conclusion

The reaction of the Arab-Palestinian population in Israel to Rabin's assassination was complex and multidimensional. Despite the image engraved in Arab memories of Rabin as a tough military man, both during the events of Land Day in 1976 and at the beginning of the Palestinian intifada in the occupied territories, Rabin's efforts in the last years of his life on behalf of peace and equality created a sympathetic image of a man of peace who struggles and pays with his life on behalf of his principles. Thus, Arab citizens wished to demonstrate a sense of belonging to Israeli society and emphasized the civic sphere.

The secular-civic character of the peace rally in which Rabin was assassinated gave the Arab population an opportunity to participate in the Israeli civic discourse. This discourse is virtually absent within the political culture of Israeli society, of which Arab citizens are not considered a legitimate part. The need for a demonstration of civic belonging has increased in light of the distress of the Arab population at being a "double periphery" at both the civic and the national levels, and because the Arab population has made the civic issue its top priority following the peace process.

However the reaction of the Arab population was pushed to the margins in the Hebrew media and also among the Jewish public at large. The Jewish majority related to the assassination of Rabin as an internal Jewish affair; the call for soul-searching remained within the Jewish-Jewish sphere, and the discourse that developed around the assassination was a Jewish nationalist-religious ideological discourse, not a civic discourse.

As a result, the feeling of belonging and partnership shown by Arab citizens quickly turned into disappointment and added to the existing frustration and alienation. The Arab leadership used the assassination to protest the attitude of the Jewish majority toward the Arab population and acts of discrimination. Two points stood out: the shattered myth about Jewish-

Jewish relations and the double standard of the Jewish majority when violence is directed against Arabs.

The conclusion is that Israeli political culture is a closed, ethnocentric culture that leaves Arab citizens outside its borders. This is a result of Israel's defining itself as a Jewish-Zionist state, which, together with the absence of a multicultural conception of Israel, eliminates the civic realm as a legitimate sphere and disallows development of a common civic culture. The fact that one of the key motives for support of the peace process by the Zionist left in Israel was the principle of separation and ensuring the Jewish-Zionist character of Israel demonstrates not only that the ethnic identity of Israel has not weakened, but also that it can be expected to intensify as a result of the peace process. Under these circumstances, the sense of belonging felt by the Arab population in Israel continues to be a one-sided illusion of a national minority that wishes to integrate into a state that is still trapped between its democratic and its Jewish-ethno-national identity.

References

Al-Haj, Majid (1993). "The Impact of the Intifada on the Arabs in Israel: The Case of a Double Periphery." In Akiba Cohen and Gadi Wolfsfeld (eds.), *Framing the Intifada: People and Media* (Norwood: Ablex), pp. 64–75.

Al-Haj, Majid, Elihu Katz, and Samuel Shye (1993). "Arab and Jewish Attitudes Towards a Palestinian State." *Journal of Conflict Resolution* 37 (4): 619–32.

Carmi, Shulamit, and Henry Rosenfeld (1992). "Israeli Political Economy and the Widening Gap Between Its Two National Groups." *Asian and African Studies* 26: 15–61.

Rouhana, Nadim, and Asa'd Ghanem (1998). "The Crisis of Minorities in Ethnic States: The Case of the Palestinian Citizens in Israel." *International Journal of Middle Eastern Studies* 30: 321–46.

CHAPTER 7

The Media and the Rabin Myth:
Reconstruction of the Israeli Collective Identity

YORAM PERI

A few days before his assassination, during the Israeli Oscar award ceremony, Rabin had said, "For us, life is bigger than the movies." He had no idea how portentous his words. In the reaction of Israeli society to the assassination, the media assumed a singular role. Although the media were viewed as the central arena for deliberating the national identity, no such discourse actually took place. Dominant groups in society used that critical event not only to reintegrate society but also to reinvent it (Anderson, 1983). They did so by broadening the hegemonic coalition and by distancing the others, using the media to deconstruct Rabin's biography and martyrdom, to reconstitute the mainstream secular Zionist story.

The unit of time under study was the week starting with the day of the killing. Had a shorter time period been chosen—for example, from the assassination to the end of the funeral, sundown on Tuesday, November 7—the relevant unit of analysis would have been the "media event," such as a coronation, or an assassination, such as that of John F. Kennedy (Dayan and Katz, 1992) or Indira Gandhi (Minwalla, 1990). A week was chosen not just because of its association with the Jewish custom of shiva—the seven-day period of mourning—but primarily because this was the duration of the official national period of mourning, the period in which the crisis ended and the social system returned to equilibrium (see Schramm, 1965: 7).

The media planned special programming to coincide with the seven-day shiva. This is the liminal period in which the event—the assassination and what it evokes—"occupies society's center" (Dayan and Katz, 1992: 89). Indeed, the week culminated in a mass rally that paralleled the one that had served as the setting for the assassination, in the very same town square, whose name had been changed from Kings of Israel Plaza to Rabin Plaza. It was at this rally that the widow of the assassinated prime minister crowned his successor, Shimon Peres. At the end of the week-long ritual of national mourning the media returned to their routine schedule of programs.

The Media and Political Ritual

The assassination of Rabin plunged Israelis into bewilderment, shock, and deep anxiety. For many, the anger and bereavement were intense and personally felt: the mourning was not an expression of tertiary loss (of someone remote), but of primary loss (of a member of one's family or someone in a primary relationship). On the collective level, the assassination created a liminal moment, a situation of intense communal emotion, heightened social relations, *communitas*, a reflexive condition in which society "looks at itself and asks not just what it is, but what it should be" (see Turner, 1969, 1974).

Indeed, from the moment that word of the assassination became public, Israeli society behaved the way a modern society behaves in a liminal moment. Although there were no acts of sedition, incitement, or outbursts of aggression, behavior was characterized primarily by an interruption in the daily routine and high emotional intensity. The public drew together for a secular ritual of national mourning in which the media played a key role. In modern society, in which the media bestow meaning and are a primary source of social cohesion (Jensen, 1991: 2), the ritual itself dons the garb of a media event. It becomes a secular ritual that television not only covers, but also shapes and creates (Chaney, 1983), a political ritual fraught with secular symbolism that casts light on the core values of society and the components of the collective memory (Lukes, 1975: 12).

In fact, in the spirit of Rabin's remark about the movies and "real life" in Israel, it is not hard to create this symbolism. Instead of the invisible hand of a highly imaginative director, reality itself provided an ample supply of details: the site of the murder—a dim area at the foot of the stairs to the stage; the context—a mass rally intended to condemn political violence; the "Song of Peace" at the end, its printed words stuffed deep inside the jacket pocket of the murder victim and stained with his blood during the assault; the fact that the Bible reading of the week was the Sacrifice of Yitzhak (Isaac); the day on which tradition holds that Rachel the biblical matriarch died; and finally, the funeral in Jerusalem with Senator Ted Kennedy casting earth from the grave of his assassinated brother John Kennedy upon the fresh tomb.

The media, especially the two television channels, were the main factors shaping and constructing the political ritual (Gusfield and Michalowicz, 1984), and they did so according to the acknowledged model of a media event. Entry into the liminal period was marked first by upsetting the regular schedule of programs and creating an intense level of media transmission. The new programming was characterized by live or "direct" broadcasts and round-the-clock coverage. Even channels were unified— nine radio stations consolidated into one—and an attempt was made to consolidate the two television channels, which succeeded only for coverage of the funeral. Commercials were, of course, suspended on both radio and television.

Not only was the schedule of programs disrupted, but distinctions between television genres became vague, with narrative forms intermingling. Instead of the standard division into drama, news, documentation, fiction, and entertainment, the ongoing broadcast on each channel was blended into one program that combined these genres: "The conferral of media event status consists in pulling it away from the news and translating it into a fictional register" (Dayan and Katz, 1992: 114). The text that was created thus blurred the distinction between news and fiction.

Even the traditional role of the newscasters was altered. From an ostensibly neutral and objective stance, reporting events "from a distance," newscasters became identified with, involved in, and expressive of the political center (Levi, 1981). These were no longer skeptical, critical, ironic, and occasionally cynical independent journalists, but partners to the cultural and political elite in playing the game, spelling out its views, and serving as a kind of preacher or town crier for the government. This was reflected in the style of Hayim Yavin—"Mr. Israel Television"—on Channel One. Yavin, who had once been reprimanded for implying a political view by raising his eyebrow to an interviewee, spoke after the assassination in the tones of a preacher suffused with deep faith. The delivery changed, assuming a dimension of holiness, of deep drama, while underscoring symbols and their ongoing interpretation.

Similar phenomena were evident in the newspapers during this period. The routine newspaper style was supplanted by a poetic, lofty rhetoric. Journalists lost their standing as observers or disinterested parties. They knowingly and openly assumed an active role in distributing and replicating values. This was reflected not just in the writing, but also in the decisions of the editors. More than a million stickers were enclosed in the week-end editions of *Yediot Aharonot* and *Ma'ariv*, Israel's two tabloid newspapers, one saying "No more violence," accompanied by a photograph of Rabin and the *Ma'ariv* logo, and the other with the words "Shalom, Haver" (Good-bye, friend) (see Chapter 11 by Linda-Renée Bloch).

Also disrupted was the direction of messages in both the electronic and printed media. Most messages flow from the media to the audience, but after the assassination the flow increased in the opposite direction, from the audience to the media. The number of listeners who called television stations with their opinions about and responses to the coverage increased severalfold; calls and letters from readers to the newspapers increased as well. The media themselves allowed the general public—as opposed to those in positions of authority—to express their views much more than usual.

Messages during this period also became less of a monologue and more of a dialogue. And the audience did not just express opinions about the situation, but also influenced program content. For example, members of the Broadcasting Authority decided, upon directives from the Ministerial Committee for Ceremonies and Symbols, to continue mourning programming for 48 hours from the end of the funeral. When regular programming was partially resumed on the third evening, however, the media were deluged by viewer calls demanding that the special programs be continued. Channel Two received a similar response from its viewers. Listeners also largely dictated the character of the programs on the popular IDF Radio. "We operated according to the 'publicometer'—telephone calls from listeners," said Moshe Shlonsky, director of the IDF Radio station.[1]

But the entire week of mourning was more than just a media event, even though it occurred in the context of a crisis similar to the assassination of Kennedy or Indira Gandhi. Media events revolve primarily around one location where the event takes place, with most participants in the political ritual sitting at home and watching it with their families and friends, as if it were theater: "Media events have shifted the locus of ceremoniality from the piazza and the stadium to the living room" (Dayan and Katz, 1992: 211). Even if viewers dress up for the event and insist that they are taking part in a celebration, it is still primarily passive participation (Minwalla, 1990).

What took place the second week of November 1995 was quite different. First, it took place not only on the air, but simultaneously in the presence of a large public. About a quarter of a million people participated in the mass rally in Kings of Israel Plaza on the night of the assassination, and some 35 percent of all television owners in Israel watched it from their homes. On the very night of the assassination, no fewer than 93 percent of the population had already heard about it—about 60 percent from the television and some 20 percent from the radio (Teleseker Survey, Tel Aviv, December 1995). Approximately half (42 percent) immediately called their friends and relatives to tell them what had happened (*Yediot Aharonot* survey, November 9, 1995). From that moment, pilgrimages began to the Rabin home in Jerusalem and later to their private home in Tel Aviv, to the plaza where Rabin was shot, a day later to the expanse in front of the Knesset where his body lay in state, and finally to Mount Herzl where he was buried. From the time of the assassination until the end of the burial, approximately 80 percent of the 1.5 million households in Israel viewed at least part of the special broadcast on television.

Over the course of the week, between a quarter and a third of all Israelis took part in outdoor events at the three pilgrimage sites.[2] Several hundred thousand congregated at the Rabin family private residence, the home of the victim, and the political-civic site of the plaza. According to estimates, close to a million people passed the coffin lying in state at the Knesset, and about half a million took part in the funeral cortege or visited the grave on Mount Herzl. More than a hundred thousand letters poured into the Office of the Prime Minister and his home; these included texts, poems, pictures, drawings, and gifts. Hundreds of condolence albums were also sent with expressions of sympathy from thousands of people. These actions do not fit easily into a description of an event that moves from a piazza or stadium to the living room, characteristic of media events. It was more like an "epidemic of *communitas*," the need of people to be together, to talk to each other, to feel close to each other.

Moreover, behavior in a media event is determined in advance; it is known and expected. The assassination of Rabin, however, evoked a wave of spontaneous and unplanned public behavior. The most dramatic expression of this was the congregating of tens of thousands of youth in the Kings of Israel Plaza at all hours of the day and night throughout the week. Their sitting in small circles in the light of the memorial candles, the melancholy songs they sang, and the atmosphere suffused with religiosity surprised and greatly moved the Israeli public. This spontaneous behavior in the plaza, and to a lesser extent at other pilgrimage sites, brought out the television cameras, although this was not planned. And the boundaries between reality on the streets and television reality intermingled. The congregating of people in the plaza and in the expanse in front of the Knesset drew the cameras, which caused even more people to congregate there. Reality influenced television behavior, which in turn shaped reality, in a cycle. Thus the border dissipated between symbolic behavior on the street and television ritual at home, and the thin tissue dissolved that had separated "true" and "apparent" reality.

The literature that deals with political ritual notes several roles that the media perform in dramatic events such as the assassination of a head of state (Greenberg and Parker, 1965). Together with the politicians, the media participate in shaping the pattern of national mourning, are a key factor in constructing the event, and bestow upon it symbolic meaning—that is, they carry out what might be termed the engineering of symbols. The media enable the participation of everybody in the ritual, create social networks, and participate in shaping the social structure. They facilitate the expression of grief and enable catharsis over the experience of loss (Schlesinger, 1987).

Political ritual has important functions in reasserting the political order that was damaged by the assassination. The murder of the supreme political authority generates a series of onerous political problems that affect the very roots of government, the democratic political culture and the normative system (Elderman and Simon, 1971; Marvick and Marvick, 1971). It is necessary to reestablish command quickly by selecting the heir and conferring legitimacy immediately upon his or her rule. There is a need for the audience to swear allegiance, to reformulate its contract with the heir, and to undertake to do battle with the forces that caused the assassination and shook up the political system. The heir uses the ritual to consolidate power by pledging to continue along the path of the predecessor and to restore life to its normal course. Legitimacy is premised upon social reintegration, and it is the media that build the social networks and reshape the social order, just as they reinforce the core values set by the political center.

But in Israeli society at the time of the assassination, the media performed these roles—which media have performed in similar circumstances, such as the Kennedy assassination—as well as an additional one: the articulation of the collective identity (Barbero, 1993). Because the assassination took place in the context of an identity crisis, it could have developed into a "critical discourse event" (Herzog and Shamir, 1994), a significant social event in which a public debate ensues about issues fundamental to society, with various interpretive groups competing to bestow symbolic meaning on them.[3] The national media, press and electronic alike, gave the impression that such deliberation did take place, and ample articles were devoted to an analysis of the causes and consequences of the murder. However, although the national media could have provided the major arena for such competing analyses, there was no such debate. On the contrary, the dominant elite groups seized control of the media and sounded their voices; all other voices were ignored, silenced, or excluded. The exclusion of these interpretations of the collective identity made the one presented by the elite unacceptable to the rest of society, thus deepening the social division and segmentation rather than integrating the mourning.

The Struggle for Collective Identity

At the time of the assassination, Israeli society was deeply divided. The debate over the peace agreements with the Palestinians and the Arab states was not just waged over the future of the territories that were occupied in 1967. A much deeper struggle to define its collective identity has preoccupied Israeli society. Thus, the question of peace borders involves more than just geographic, strategic, or political issues; it entails a redefinition of the social borders with the "other" (LaPierre, 1984) — the relationship between the Jewish people and the nations of the region and the world — and the particularistic character of its national culture (Schlesinger, 1987: 285).

It was in this context that Rabin was assassinated, as testified by the assassin himself. Yigal Amir could not bear to have Rabin, representative of one school of thought about collective identity, be in a position of such great influence, and because Amir had no way to curb this influence, he sought to exclude Rabin from the social negotiation. "I wanted to get rid of him," he said, "it didn't have to be murder. I wanted to neutralize him. Had he been injured and left the game, that would have been good enough. He didn't necessarily have to die."[4]

The assassination of Rabin — who as prime minister represented political stability and as minister of defense was Israel's symbol of security — produced a palpable sense of insecurity, a fear of social disintegration, and apprehension of what the future holds in store: subversion of the public order, the crumbling of the normative system, civil war, even war with foreign powers. If Mr. Security could be murdered, anything could happen. "A danger of clashes and loss of control threatens to split Israel from within," wrote a level-headed political analyst the day after the assassination (Dan Margalit, *Ha'aretz*, November 6, 1995). It is no wonder that a poet used even more dramatic language: The assassination, she wrote, was "something supernatural that toppled everything we believed in. Our entire world has been transfigured" (Dalia Rabikovitch, *Yediot Aharonot*, November 6, 1995).

The media, which during times of crisis usually help restore social integration, reshape the social structure, and recreate the national consensus—the renewed social contract—performed a much more valuable function in Israel because of the deep cleavage in society. The media responded to the assassination in ways that took advantage of the event to help define and crystallize the collective identity. They promoted the political ritual surrounding Rabin, building the myth of the man who became a symbol in his death. This the media accomplished by addressing a critical point in the collective identity—construction of the collective memory: "Collective identity relates to a collective memory through which the contemporary group recognizes itself through a common past, remembrance, commemoration, interpretation, and reinterpretation" (LaPierre, 1984: 196). In modern society, the media join the intellectuals in their traditional task: "the selective interpretation of history" (203–4).

Indeed, over the course of the week, the media were intensely preoccupied with the personality of Rabin, deconstructing his biography and constructing it anew, with the finished product elevated from a personal to a collective biography. In fact, the media used elements of Rabin's biography to shape a collective memory in order to construct a collective identity for Israeli society. The man Yitzhak Rabin metamorphoses into a symbolic representation of all Israeli society. "He was us," wrote Yonatan Geffen (*Ma'ariv*, November 6, 1995). "We wept for our father figure, and more so for ourselves. For Yitzhak Rabin; and more so, for our own image," were the words of Ofer Shelah (*Ma'ariv*, November 11, 1995).

This is the significance of constructing the Rabin myth in the week following his assassination. It was not to carry on the cultural tradition of "speak[ing] of the righteous only after their death," but much more. This was a case of constructing a collective memory, "a reshaping of the practices through which people construct themselves as cultural authorities" (Zelizer, 1992: 4; see also Chapter 12 in this volume).[5] What identity did the media assign to Rabin, which they intended to become the identity of Israeli society as a whole? What are its characteristics? Its components? What are the events that shaped it and how was it structured?

Personal Biography and Reconstructing Collective Identity

In an effort to answer these questions, I reviewed all articles written about Yitzhak Rabin in the five national daily Hebrew newspapers during the period of the event. These included all biographical items that mentioned Rabin in the two most influential newspapers, *Ha'aretz* and *Davar Rishon*; the two popular newspapers, *Yediot Aharonot* and *Ma'ariv*; and the business daily, *Globes*, which also carries general news.

I examined 348 articles of various length in all sections of the newspapers—news, features, and commentary. As the main forum for public discourse, the daily newspapers, whose combined circulation soared during the week of the assassination to almost 1 million copies in print, reached almost 80 percent of Israeli households.[6]

A content analysis was performed on all the texts. Items were graded on three variables: (1) mention of traits characteristic of Rabin or events of his life used to reflect traits characteristic of him (e.g., "He was a hero and loved Israel"—Shalom Rosenfeld, *Ma'ariv*, November 10, 1995); (2) the comparative importance of various traits: importance was determined both by the number of appearances of each trait and the weight ascribed to it by the writer (e.g., "Rabin was the most outstanding example of . . ." editorial, *Ha'aretz*, November 5, 1995); and (3) any explicit or implicit statement that a trait both relates to Rabin the individual and reflects the collective personality of Israeli society (e.g., Yitzhak Rabin "symbolized the new Israeli," Orit Harel, *Ma'ariv*, November 10, 1995; or "the Palmachnik who is my private father, who is Rabin, who is the collective [father], my protector," Talma Admon, *Ma'ariv*, November 10, 1995).

Also analyzed were the linguistic techniques and methods writers used to reconstruct the collective biography. It was not always easy to establish causal connections between the traits and events related to Rabin the man and those related to the Israeli collective as a whole. Techniques commonly used to draw this connection were, for example, metaphor, metonymy, and analogies. ("Yitzhak Rabin was the first Jewish flower to bloom in the earth of the homeland from out of the ashes of exile and the Holocaust," Gabriel Ben-Simchon, *Davar Rishon*, November 19, 1995). The solidarity theme also appeared frequently through use of the "royal we"—not in the sense of 'I the king', but meaning 'You + I', to create a sense of involvement, a merging of the writer and the audience of readers into one cultural community, as in Meir Shalev's words: "And the pining . . . for a generation of young people that is disappearing before our very eyes," or "We'll continue along his restrained but determined path" (*Yediot Aharonot*, November 6, 1995).

What then is the reconstructed image of Rabin as it emerged in the media? Six traits were used most often to depict Rabin and seemed to be considered most important by the writers. Additional traits appeared in the texts, but much less frequently than these (from several to twenty mentions). The first two traits appeared approximately 140 times, the third and fourth appeared approximately 100 times each, and the last two traits appeared several dozen times each. The traits in order of relative importance: (1) Israeli sabra; (2) peacemaker; (3) Zionist; (4) Americophile; (5) antipolitician; (6) empathetic figure.

To provide perspective for the content analysis of the articles published during the week of the assassination, I also examined a group of articles published in the previous three years, since Rabin became prime minister in 1992. Sampling news, features, and commentary from the same periodicals used in the postassassination research—the five Hebrew dailies—I chose these articles for their resemblance to those published after the assassination: they were longer; more comprehensive, descriptive, or critical and focused on Rabin's character, personality, methods of work, or behavior. However, since there were only sixteen items and they were published over a three-year period, they could not be used as a basis for comparative content analysis with the corpus of 348 articles, and hence my reading of them was rather interpretive.

The term "sabra," like "the Palmach generation" or "the generation of 1948," is a broad, inclusive concept. In the newspapers, it was used in general terms, to mean one or more components of the sabra archetype—warrior, unpolished but authentic, straight-talking, a do-er, devoted to his comrades and willing to sacrifice himself for the good of the whole, and so forth: "The symbol of the new Jew, comely, with cowlick" (David Grossman, *Ma'ariv*, November 6, 1995). "His image epitomizes the sabra spirit of the pre- and early-state period—straight-talking and to the point" (Hila Komem, *Davar*, November 6, 1995). The components of this image are discussed at length in research about the myth of the sabra. In describing the sabra, much use is made of the symbols of the period, images and metaphors taken from songs of the War of Independence and especially the world of the Palmach. This was "a generation different and more wonderful than all the others—the Palmach generation. A generation that was the antithesis to the freeloader spirit, the antithesis to shirking one's duty, the antithesis to messianism, the antithesis to pomp and ceremony, the antithesis to extremism, the antithesis to demagoguery. It was a generation that spurned praise, but yes, a silver platter and yes, what comradeship" (Meir Shalev, *Yediot Aharonot*, December 6, 1995).

Naturally, nothing negative or critical was linked to the concept of sabra or Palmachnik. In the past, the "redheadedness" of the sabra or Palmachnik was a hook on which writers could hang negative qualities—simpleness, hot-headedness, aggressiveness, or lack of sophistication. Yoel Marcus (*Ha'aretz*) juxtaposed the negative redheadedness with the positive "analytical mind" of Rabin. After the assassination, however, being a "redhead" had only one meaning—all positive, or disappeared altogether: "A proud, sweet sabra with blonde curls and freckles on his nose. . . . We wanted to be like him" (Gabriel Ben-Simchon, *Davar Rishon*, November 12, 1995). The lack of polish of the sabra was even transformed into a commendable quality: "Rabin had an unpolished style, but there are two kinds of lack of polish: that of Weizmann, who stands beside Rabin's grave and says, 'We drank, we ate'. . . [referring to the president's poor eulogy, which was very much criticized] [and] Rabin's lack of polish [which] was a kind of honesty . . . never crude" (Sami Michael, *Davar Rishon*, December 5, 1995).

The death of Rabin turned him into a "peacemaker," the symbol of Israeli society's longing for peace. This element in his personality emerged before the assassination, of course, and winning the Nobel Peace Prize in 1995 reinforced it. However, before the assassination Rabin was still being criticized for his hesitancy about the peace process, for the halting pace of progress (e.g., not evacuating Hebron, and the tough policies toward Palestinians in the territories). The assassination at the conclusion of a peace rally and in the context of opposition to his peace policies bolstered the transformation of his image in the Arab world. During the week of mourning, no media stories described the warrior-like, violent, and tough side of Rabin (whose public speech had included phrases such as "break their bones" and "tighten the siege of Beirut"). Even his military background, an aspect impossible to ignore, was used to emphasize his character as a man of peace. "Soldier for peace," "warrior for peace," and similar expressions appeared frequently. According to a typical profile: "The old soldier who led the state of Israel to victory in the Six Day War will now fight for peace" (Yael Gvirtz and Anat Meidan, *Yediot Aharonot*, November 5, 1995).

The longing for peace of the Israeli peace camp is regarded among many of the nationalist camp, especially the fundamentalists, not as a noble

expression of lofty goals, but as a product of weakness and short-sighted-
ness, a reflection of materialistic, hedonistic, American values, a lack of national pride and historical consciousness, and even—among the extremists—as treason. Peace, formerly perceived by the left as instrumental, a
deal, the product of weariness and an unwillingness to carry on the fight,
was elevated through the restructured image of Rabin to the level of a value
that holds its own against the values represented by the other cultural
streams.

The third concept frequently used by writers in describing Rabin was
Zionism. In an editorial in *Ha'aretz* the day after the assassination, Rabin
was described as "a man who more than any other reflected the rebirth of
Israel." Zionism, as manifested in the descriptions of Rabin, was elevated
to supreme heights. In the words of Yaron London, Zionism is no less than
"the most daring and most successful social and national revolution in
modern times" (*Yediot Aharonot*, November 6, 1995). Zionism embodies
not just the simple, limited meaning—advocating the right of the Jewish
people to gather in its historic homeland and enjoy national independence;
its broader meaning is love of homeland, statehood, nation-building and
state-building, the public over the private weal, and collective values over
individual rights. This was Rabin according to the new portrait, and this
was and should be Israeli society: "The only value remaining [in our era] is
that of personal fulfillment and financial success. Rabin represents the
complete opposite of this. He, who could have done things on his own behalf, never gave it a moment's thought" (Gabi Bashan, *Ma'ariv*, November
9, 1995).

The diplomatic chapter in the life of Rabin—serving as ambassador to
Washington, during which he developed a special tie to the American nation—is a critical element in his personal biography and its collective
meaning. The term "diplomat" does not refer to the values, content, or
status of this profession. On the contrary, Rabin was described as an
undiplomatic diplomat. The heart of the matter was the partner, the
United States: "Rabin conducted an ongoing love affair with America . . .
which returned the compliment" (Akiva Eldar, *Ha'aretz*, November 8,
1995). Stories emphasized the fact that Rabin was Israel's most prominent
ambassador to the United States "and focused on fostering the strategic alliance between the two countries" (Moshe Zack, *Ma'ariv*, November 6,
1995).

Although Rabin based the foreign and defense policies of Israel on its
links to the United States as an ultimate national resource, the description

of his attitude toward the United States goes beyond international relations and strategic considerations. Rabin is described as an authority on American society and politics, an unabashed advocate of American values and the American way of life, and the importer of the American dream to Israel. Before the elections, Rabin was criticized more than once for his quasi-American, presidential style of governing (Yoel Marcus, *Ha'aretz*, February 19, 1993), for his exaggerated American orientation in both foreign affairs and defense (Uzi Benziman, *Ha'aretz*, March 12, 1993), and primarily for his republican values, which replaced the social-democratic underpinning of the labor movement. After his death, Rabin is portrayed as having imported to Israel an uncommonly positive product: "American culture that won his heart . . . the Protestant ethos, values, and beliefs . . . etc." (Gabi Bashan, *Davar Rishon*, November 9, 1995).

The deconstructed description of Rabin's personality is particularly dramatic in representing him as something other than a politician. Though Rabin was involved in political affairs while still in uniform during the War of Independence and held political jobs for 26 years after finishing his army career, he was perceived as the antithesis of a politician. "Rabin has never been a politician . . . not a functionary, he was an outsider to the party ambience," according to Yael Gvirtz and Anat Meidan (*Yediot Aharonot*, November 5, 1995). In an era in which public criticism of politics is harsh and being a politician implies something negative, those who can avoid this label enjoy a marked advantage. In the United States, the outsider—one who does not come up through the Washington corridors of power but emerges from "authentic" society—has an edge in running for president. But it is a little hard to define a politician who spent a quarter-century in Washington as an outsider. Perhaps this was an image that the politician Rabin created for himself? Rubik Rozental in *Davar Rishon* (November 6, 1995) suggests that in contrast with other politicians, "Rabin never created for himself an image, but always remained himself."

Of particular irony was the reconstructed image of Rabin as an empathetic figure—a devoted family man, someone who liked people, was surrounded by friends, was amiable, sociable, and sensitive to and concerned about others. This assortment of qualities was emphasized in particular throughout the event, and yet it contradicts how Rabin was described throughout his public career—as closed, introverted, lacking close friends, one whose body language and handshake expressed a painful shyness and discomfort with others. He was accused of never greeting the woman who served him tea every morning in Labor Party headquarters, as someone surrounded and influenced by a closed circle of patricians and the wealthy. But the portrait drawn of him after his death was diametrically opposed to this: "[He was] the opposite of a snob, never arrogant, he treated with equal respect and seriousness simple people and those with power and position" (Hila Komem, *Davar Rishon*, November 6, 1995). He who had been described by the newspapers as "autistic," whose hand gesture of impatience for and dismissal of others, even ministers in the cabinet, was remarked about (Daniel Ben-Simon, *Davar*, October 17, 1994), was portrayed after the assassination as "sensitive and attentive, one who loved to converse and listened without interrupting" (ibid).

The issue is not which of these portrayals is "accurate," but the fact that after his death the media described him very differently from how they had in the past. The reason appears obvious. The picture drawn of Rabin in the newspapers before the assassination was much more complex than that drawn afterward. In almost all the articles before his death, negative descriptions appear beside positive one, and sometimes often. The change had less to do with a change of opinion over his policies, which is less relevant for our discussion, but with the image, character, and components of his personality, and their symbolic significance. In fact, some of the positive statements made the week after the assassination had never before appeared, though their opposite had been. It is not so surprising, then, that after the assassination Rabin was transformed into the collective figure desired by the writers, since after all, in the words of Yonatan Geffen, "He was us" (*Ma'ariv*, November 6, 1995).

The Relative Edge of the Hegemonic Interpretive Community

Who participated in the building of this version of the biography, a version that sought to give a particular character to the collective identity by linking it to the collective memory? Scrutiny of the writers whose articles, statements, and quotes crammed the Hebrew press during this critical discourse event reveals that they represented three elite groups: politicians, the media, and the cultural elite. I found no real difference between opinion pieces by authors or politicians and reportage by professional journalists. Likewise, and no significant difference in their ranking of traits and events. The similarity among the three was so striking because all were members of one interpretive community.

Zelizer (1992) notes that the concept "interpretive community" was taken up by fields beyond media research, where it is not a socioeconomic

group but a group distinguished by how it structures cultural forms and social reality. Thus, interpretive communities are culture groups in a broader
sense than media audiences are.

In the week of Rabin's assassination, major social and cultural groups
were absent or disappeared from the public discourse. Most noticeably absent were the Arab community, the Russian immigrants, the "other Israel"
(referring to the residents of development towns of primarily Mizrahi origin), and, of course, the ultra-Orthodox and nationalist Zionists. Each of
these interpretive communities has a different perception of reality; and
they are engaged in a struggle with each other, and particularly with the hegemonic group, over defining the collective identity of Israeli society. Their
under-representation on television caused the leaders of the Arab population to protest to the Broadcasting Authority during the week of mourning
that they were being excluded from the programs.

The dominance of the hegemonic interpretive community over the national newspaper and electronic media editorial desks, the proximity of this
group to the cultural-entertainment elite in Tel Aviv, and the ideological-
political affinity of the media elite to the political elite was clearly reflected in
the reaction to the assassination. Hence, it was not surprising to find a link
between those who participated in shaping the collective profile—that is, the
collective identity of Israel—and the specific characteristics of this identity. In
fact, the image created during the reconstruction of the collective identity is
that of the hegemonic interpretive community. In a liminal moment, Turner
notes, a society looks upon itself and asks not just who it is, but primarily who
it wants to, or feels it should, become (Turner, 1977). The restructured image
of Rabin is what this community wanted to become.

When Shils and Young studied the significance of the coronation ceremony in Britain, they regarded it as a symbol of the values that unify British
society, the suppliers of consensus despite political differences (Shils and
Young, 1953). Birnbaum took issue with this claim, well before Gramsci's
concept of hegemony became popular. In "Monarchs and Sociologists,"
Birnbaum argues that he is not at all sure that different classes interpreted
the ceremony in the same way; on the contrary, he says, the ceremony expresses the values of the upper and middle classes, glossing over the social
gap and conflict (Birnbaum, 1955). In this spirit, Lukes also analyzed political rituals in Britain, noting that these rituals "help to define as authoritative certain ways of seeing society" (Lukes, 1975: 306). It is an authoritative
interpretation intended to serve the needs and interests of the ruling groups
and to maintain their dominance.

In the Israeli context, the hegemonic interpretation of the collective identity by the neo-Zionist-Ashkenazi-Labor elite, which had been unchallenged since the formative years of Israeli society, faced a serious challenge in the 1990s. The assassination was an extreme symbolic act of someone who wanted to undermine the authoritative position of that elite as the sole legitimate interpreter of the collective identity. The ascension of what was perceived to be a real threat, and the crisis brought on by the assassination, caused the hegemonic elite to respond with all its power. A situation in which everything is fluid and in flux, which can be shaped and kneaded before it hardens, is an opportunity that must not be missed. Gramsci (1971) refers to a crisis as the moment of the blink in which frameworks are reorganized; what gels at this moment is solidified in the collective memory. Into these circumstances in which most members of the collective yearn for a different life, for a more desirable situation, the hegemon comes and offers its own model.

The Rabin myth constituted and disseminated by the media, in addition to the political ritual celebrated that week, was the most significant practice used by these hegemonic groups to consolidate their position and world view. To broaden their base of support, they initiated ties with the younger generation. The identification of the "candle children" with the late prime minister caused an overnight change in the old-timers' attitudes toward the individualistic, pleasure-oriented culture of the younger generation. They were praised by spokespeople of the elite for their dedication to the peace process, the ultimate goal of the Zionist movement. When the television management was asked if the live broadcast from Rabin Plaza did not attract more youngsters to the spot, thus distorting reality rather than reporting it, the answer was, "This is where the important story is taking place."[7]

The feeling that the entire population of Israel reacted similarly to the political murder and shared the martyr's values and attributes was created by the shutting out of all the other voices and interpretive communities from the national media. When, during the week-long mourning period, some reporters presented the views of Israelis who thought differently about the assassination and its causes, these were censored by the editors. They felt "the lesson of the tragic event was that we were too lenient about incitement. After the horrific event, we had to be more strict about it."[8]

The official state institutions reacted similarly. The attorney general issued new directives about freedom of expression, arguing that verbal incitement could harm the public order. The police hauled in some individuals who were disrespectful of Rabin's memory, and several offenders who had been accused of incitement in the previous two years but had never been tried suddenly received trial dates. These actions aroused the ire of some civil rights organizations, and indeed the stricter policies were lifted after several weeks. The attorney general, for example, restated his position as "an ethical directive, not a binding legal order." But that was too late. At "the moment of blink," with various interpretive groups competing to bestow symbolic meaning on them, the critical discourse did not take place.

It took no less than five weeks for the first reservations to be heard on the national media. When Yoel Marcus, though a member of the hegemonic group and a senior journalist at *Ha'aretz*, expressed his reservations about the new, rose-colored image of Yitzhak Rabin, Rabin's widow reacted harshly, announcing that she would cancel her subscription to the newspaper. Another month was needed before representatives of the other interpretive communities were able to protest in the general press what had happened. The first, Yitzhak Laor, made his statement in reference to a memorial album for Rabin. Entitled "Group Picture with Mirror," Laor's article criticized the literary wheeler-dealers, always close to the ruling powers, who demean themselves by exalting Rabin and serve the goal of national unity by "a Rabin festival . . . as if there is no other way for culture other than togetherness and kitsch, identity and unity, as if plurality that does not merge cannot exist" (*Ha'aretz*, January 26, 1996). The other writer, a prominent member of the settlers' movement and editor for many years of their journal, *Nekuda*, forcefully attacked the Israeli media for "taking sides in the debate"—presenting the views of only one political camp and not allowing other views to reach the public.[9]

No other groups attempted to challenge the collective portrait of Israeli society as shaped by the cultural-political-media elite, or the monopoly they claimed in fashioning this portrait. Dissenters expressed their wrath at the media and the hegemonic group only in their internal media: Russian-language newspapers, synagogue newsletters, notices pasted up in ultra-Orthodox neighborhoods, and other community media. There the post-Zionist Russian immigrants could criticize the political as "a personality cult like the one we knew in the USSR," and the ultranationalists argued that "Rabin has brought it [his death] upon himself because he betrayed the Jewish people.[10]

Many more months had to pass before Israelis realized, after the Ministry of Education published the report of an investigative committee, that the teens who sat in Rabin Plaza singing and crying were only one faction of their age group, while others, and not insignificant numbers, were critical of Rabin's policies, indifferent to the assassination, or even supportive of the killing. [11]

The suppression of public discourse after the assassination did not mold the Israeli collective memory or foster the reinvention of the Israeli collectivity. The other narratives, aspirations, images, and social forces were simply concealed, but they broke through six months later in the May general elections, unveiling the tormented and shattered Israeli identity. In the Knesset, a "coalition of minorities"—parties that represented the Russian, the nationalist, the religious, and the ultra-Orthodox communities—made unprecedented achievements. Prime Minister Shimon Peres, Rabin's partner and heir, had to hand his seat over to Benjamin Netanyahu, the leader of the Likud Party and the clerical-nationalist camp. No wonder the election results were described by the defeated camp as "the second assassination of Rabin."

Notes

1. Interview with Moshe Shlonsky, director of IDF Radio, December 17, 1995. I obtained information about Channel One in an interview with Director-General Ya'ir Stern on the same date. I also conducted interviews with producers and program writers for radio and television and with editors of the daily newspapers.

2. This is a police estimate. Although only an estimate, the magnitude speaks for itself.

3. In this context, see the views of Philip Smith (1994), which are consonant with the neofunctionalist approach of J. C. Alexander.

4. Interview by the police interrogators, December 25, 1995, the Police Archive. Yigal Amir claimed that his mission was to redeem the nation from Yitzhak Rabin. In Hebrew, "Yigal" derives from the root "ga'al," which means "redeem" and "Amir" contains the word "ami," which means "my nation." The leftover "Yi" and "R" in his name are a reference to Yitzhak Rabin.

5. For the distinctions between "speech community," "discourse community," and "community of memory," see Zelizer, 1992: 89.

6. In the first few days, there were more news stories, but the proportion of features increased during the period of mourning. The length of the articles varied widely, from short items to detailed profiles of 3,500 words. Other Hebrew periodicals were also examined, such as the weeklies *BaMahaneh* (published by the IDF), *LaIsha* (a women's magazine), and less-regular periodicals that appeared after the assassination. However, because these magazines are directed to specific readers and not to the general public, the results are not included in this chapter.

7. Interview with Moshe Shlonsky, December 17, 1995.

8. Interview with Moshe Shlonsky, December 17, 1995.

9. Israel Harel in an interview on the television program "Shetah Hefker," December 27, 1995.

10. In November 1996, the first anniversary of the assassination, such expressions were very common in the alternative community media. They became even more so in the following years.

11. A letter from the director-general of the Ministry of Education, October 8, 1996. See also Chapter 9 in this volume.

References

Anderson, Benedict (1983). *Imagined Communities*. London: Verso.

Barbero, J. Martin (1993). *Communication, Culture and Hegemony: From the Media to the Mediation*. Trans. Elizabeth Fox and Ronald White. London: Sage.

Birnbaum, N. (1955). "Monarchs and Sociologists: A Reply to Professor Shils and Mr. Young." *Sociological Review*, no. 3: 5–23.

Chaney, David (1983). "A Symbolic Mirror of Ourselves: Civic Ritual in Mass Society." *Media, Culture and Society*, no. 5: 119–35.

Crotty, William J. (ed.) (1971). *Assassinations and the Political Order*. New York: Harper and Row.

Dayan, Daniel, and Elihu Katz (1992). *Media Event*. Cambridge, Mass.: Harvard University Press.

Elderman, Murray, and Rita J. Simon (1971). "Presidential Assassinations: Their Meaning and Impact on American Society." In W. J. Crotty (ed.), *Assassinations and the Political Order*. New York: Harper and Row, pp. 455–88.

Gramsci, Antonio (1971). *Selections from the Prison Book*. New York: International Publishers.

Greenberg, Bradley S., and Edwin B. Parker (eds.) 1965. *The Kennedy Assassination and the American Public*. Stanford, Calif.: Stanford University Press.

Gurevitch, Michael et al. (eds.) 1982. *Culture, Society and the Media*. London: Methuen.

Gusfield, Joseph R., and Jerzy Michalowicz (1984). "Secular Symbolism: Studies of Ritual, Ceremony, and the Symbolic Order in Modern Life." *Annual Review of Sociology* 10: 417–35.

Hall, Stuart (1977). "Culture, the Media and the 'Ideological Effect,'" In J. Curran et al. (eds.), *Mass Communication and Society*. London: Edward Arnold.

——— (1982). "The Rediscovery of 'Ideology': Return of the Repressed in Media Studies." in M. Gurevitch et al. (eds.), *Culture, Society and the Media*. London: Methuen.

Hall, Stuart et al. (1980). *Culture, Media, Language*. London: Hutchinson.

Herzog, Hanna, and Ronen Shamir (1994). "Media Discourse on Jewish/Arab Relations." *Israel Social Science Research* 9 (1–2): 55–88.

Jensen, Klaus Bruhn (1991). "The Qualitative Turn." In Klaus B. Jensen and Nicholas W. Janowski (eds.), *A Handbook of Qualitative Methodology for Mass Communication Research*. London: Routledge.

Johansson, Olof (1995). "Swedish Reaction to the Assassination of the Swedish Prime Minister Olof Palme." *Scandinavian Political Studies* 18, no 4: 265–83.

LaPierre, G. (1984). "L'identité Collective, Object Paradoxal: d'Ou Nous Vient-il?" *Recherches Sociologiques* 15 (2–3): 155–64.

Levi, Mark R. (1981). "Disdaining the News." *Journal of Communication* 31 (3): 24–31.

Lukes, Steven (1975). "Political Ritual and Social Integration." *Sociology* 9, (2): 289–308.

Marvick, Dwaine, and Elizabeth W. Marvick (1971). "The Political Consequences of Assassination." In W. J. Crotty (ed.), *Assassinations and the Political Order*. New York: Harper and Row, pp. 489–544.

Minwalla, S. (1990). "TheAssassination of Indira Gandhi." Annenberg School of Communication, University of Southern California, unpublished ms. Quoted in Daniel Dayan and Elihu Katz (eds.), *Media Event*. Cambridge, Mass.: Harvard University Press.

Schramm, Wilbur (1965). "Communication in Crisis." In Bradley S. Greenberg and Edwin B. Parker (eds.), *The Kennedy Assassination and the American Public*. Stanford, Calif.: Stanford University Press, pp. 1–25.

Schlesinger, Philip (1987). "On National Identity: Some Conceptions and Misconceptions Criticized." *Social Science Information* 26 (2): 219–64.

Shils, Edward, and Michael Young (1953). "The Meaning of Coronation." *Sociological Review* 1: 63–81.

Smith, Philip (1994). "The Semiotic Foundations of Media Narrative." *Journal of Narrative and Life History* 4 (1–2): 88–118.

Turner, Victor W. (1969). *The Ritual Process*. Chicago: Aldine.

———— (1974). Dramas, Fields and Metaphors: Symbolic Action in Human Society. Ithaca, N.Y.: Cornell University Press.

———— (1977). "Process, System and Symbol." *Daedalus*, no. 106: 61–80.

Verba, Sidney (1965). "The Kennedy Assassination and the Nature of the Political Commitment." In Bradley S. Greenberg and Edwin B. Parker (eds.), *The Kennedy Assassination and the American Public*. Stanford, Calif.: Stanford University Press, pp. 348–60.

Wolfsfeld, Gadi (1996). "Framing Political Events." Unpublished ms.

Zelizer, Barbie (1992). *Covering the Body: The Kennedy Assassination, the Media, and the Shaping of Collective Memory*. Chicago: University of Chicago Press.

PART III

The Grief and the Mourning

The Many Voices of Israeli Youth: Multiple Interpretations of Rabin's Assassination

TAMAR RAPOPORT

From Rock Concerts to the Assassination of Rabin

In July 1995 during school vacation, three teenagers were crushed to death at an annual rock festival in Arad as a result of overcrowding at the entrance to one of the popular events. The Israeli public was shocked, a commission of inquiry was convened, and everyone was placed on the defendant's stand, above all the teens themselves. The image of youth was at a nadir, and the teenagers were left feeling guilty and frightened. The volume was turned up on the discourse about Israeli youth, who entered the public consciousness for a fleeting moment. A collective soul-searching, conducted primarily through the media, repeatedly raised issues about the younger generations of the past, present, and future: Had young people gone downhill? What was their character? Where are they headed?

The discourse about youth ebbed quickly after this festival and was then renewed after the assassination of Rabin on November 4, 1995. Between the Arad festival and what happened at Kings of Israel Plaza, a dramatic transformation took place in the collective image of Israeli youth: the screwed-up generation (a term coined by Israeli pop singer Aviv Geffen) turned into a generation of excellence. Teens who had been labeled baboons, hedonists, narcissists, unbridled, and confused were suddenly seen as sensitive, creative, and responsible to a fault. These same teenagers who were accused of excessive individualism, blind pursuit of decadence, behaving like sheep, and vacuousness were suddenly flesh of our flesh, one of us, involved, moral, responsive, true partners, authentic, and the essence of Israeliness.

This revolution in the collective image and status of Israeli youth sharpens the picture of the ambivalence of Israeli adults, like that of adults the world over, toward the younger generation (Alon, 1986). Moreover, it again reveals the sensitivity of Israeli society to its sons and daughters, and the almost compulsive preoccupation with the qualities of the younger generation—their motivation, values, life style, and daily behavior. The sense of dependence on the next generation for carrying on the social revolution—especially their willingness to take part in the national struggle through army service—leads adults to relentlessly scrutinize their behavior for signs of loyalty to the Israeli collective (Rapoport, Lomsky Feder, et al., 1995).

The public discourse that heaped praise on Israel's "wonderful teenagers" for their response to the assassination of Rabin was itself an adult endeavor. Missing almost entirely was one voice—that of the youth themselves: the voice that describes their experience of mourning, their feelings and deeds in the context of this dramatic event. This research, then, asked the young to speak for themselves—to describe how they experienced the mourning (their feelings and activities during that period); to explain their grasp of the assassination (its causes and implications on a personal, social, and national level); and to describe how they perceived Israeli society before and after the assassination and their role in it.

A Chronology of Mourning

It was a long night after the announcement of Rabin's assassination. TV and radio broadcasts from the plaza where the killing took place went on and on, and the process of transforming the plaza into a memorial site was already in motion. The few teenagers who spent the night there were joined in the morning by many friends. TV gave them increasing coverage, and as the plaza became a focus of media attention during the mourning period, the cameras and teenagers there seemed to merge.

The pattern of spontaneous mourning created by teenagers in the plaza was replicated beside the Knesset, where the coffin lay in state, near the grave at Mount Herzl, and beside Rabin's homes in Jerusalem and Tel Aviv. The culture of Israeli mourning was given a new look that Israeli society had almost never before witnessed, a look largely created by young people. This culture of mourning was marked by strong ritualization and a small number of motifs: quiet crying, memorial candles, flowers, people sitting in small circles on the ground, repetitive singing of songs, graffiti on the walls. Although these signs of national mourning had already appeared at the sites of terrorist attacks, repeating them in symbolic spaces during the week of mourning for Rabin helped shape a new form of collective mourning.

On the day after the assassination, masses of young people from all over Israel streamed to the Knesset in Jerusalem. As they and thousands of other citizens waited long hours to walk past the coffin, the teenagers remained in the spotlight. The cameras turned them into the "heroes of the mourning." The funeral took place two days after the assassination, and after that mass pilgrimages to the grave began. Again, the large number of teenagers and their intense grieving were featured prominently. At the end of the designated week of mourning, a memorial rally was held in the newly named Rabin Plaza, where Tel Aviv mayor Ronni Milo declared: "These last few days, we have been witness to a poignant spectacle that we had never seen before, and we are still moved to see. Youth came and sat and came back here day after day, expressing their grief and ours; and for the sake of all these children, we want tomorrow morning to see a better country."

The innovative pattern of mourning created by the teenagers and the powerful emotions they revealed surprised Israeli society. The feeling was that young people were setting the pace of the mourning, shaping its patterns, providing it with a collective dimension. In their grief, adult Israelis seemed to look to the younger generation for comfort. Very soon, a phenomenon took shape that reverberated in the Israeli public discourse — "the reaction of young people to Rabin's assassination." Thus, Rabin's death and young people became intertwined in the historical memory and the Israeli collective consciousness.

Public discourse perceived all Israeli teenagers to be cut of the same cloth regarding the assassination — united in their reaction and experience of mourning. The feeling was that all teens were grieving and mourning the death of Rabin. But were they?

Even academic analyses of the mourning behavior spoke generally of "the reaction of youth." One of the primary explanations offered by educators was that the teenagers' reaction reflected their difficulty in forming an identity in an age that lacked values and direction, characteristic of modern or postmodern, post-Zionist Israeli society. In their view, this difficulty was channeled into a search for a ritualistic experience that allowed for teenage outbursts of emotional energy. This explanation placed the responsibility on adults — parents and teachers — for abandoning youth, not giving them meaningful values, and not taking them seriously. Accordingly, it obligated adults themselves to do some soul-searching and figurative self-laceration.

Other explanations from dynamic and developmental psychology were derived from models of psychological trauma and mourning about the loss of a father or grandfather (Erlich, 1996). In Erlich's explanation, Rabin as the grandfather figure stood outside the sphere of the oedipal conflict represented by the father. The grandfather figure is one that children and teenagers can love because it responds to the childhood wish of "the ideal other . . . with which they can merge." Lieblich rejects the analysis of mourning for a family figure and explains that because Rabin symbolized peace the assassination created a fear among young people that the peace they were dreaming of was lost (see Meidan, October 18, 1996). Other psychological explanations emphasized the tendency of adolescents to deal with separation and death as part of the development of the ego and as something that gives meaning to their lives.

The shortcomings of the post-assassination psychological analyses are that they are theoretical, relying heavily on the testimony of young people in clinical situations. The cultural availability and attractiveness of psychological explanations during national crisis are not unique to the Rabin assassination and were dominant at the time of the Gulf War, for example. The fact that psychological discourse has become so popular makes it more accessible and appealing at such times (El-Or, Halbertal, and Rapoport, 1997).

Most of these explanations, however, ignore the key roles played by the cultural-political orientation, generational consciousness, and experience of adolescence in shaping the interpretation of the assassination for young people. Moreover, because explanations focused on processes of identity-formation and the psychological needs and tendencies of young people, they minimized the importance of historical, social, and political contexts in shaping the differential experience of adolescence and creating their generational consciousness (Alon, 1986; Mannheim, 1952). In other words, explanations of this kind ignore the fact that adolescents are part of the larger society and that their experience is formed and shaped in various sociocultural and political contexts. Youth are exposed to a historical, cultural, and nationalistic context of Israeli society, to ethnopolitical groups with whom they grow up, and to socialization frameworks (school, family, youth movements, peer groups). These groups and agencies are not homogeneous; many, in fact, are in continual conflict; thus it would be surprising, to say the least, to conclude that the reaction of all teenagers would be "cut of the same cloth."

In this chapter, I explore reactions to the assassination of various groups who make up the fabric of Israeli youth. And as part of that examination I seek to reveal the kulturkampf and the young people's negotiation for identities through their various interpretations of the assassination of Yitzhak Rabin.

Methodology: The Voices of the Youth

The voices of young people reveal the social-cultural-political identity of those who participated in mourning activities, as well as the identity of those who absented themselves from or were left out of the discourse about Rabin's assassination. Analyzing teenagers' interpretations of the assassination, of Rabin himself, and of society and politics in Israel, as well as their stories, experiences, and activities during the week of mourning makes it possible to draw a preliminary cultural, social, and political map of "Israeli youth" today, and to learn about the groups that constitute it. Because I conducted this research only among nonreligious Jewish teenagers, it does not cover the entire range of interpretations of the assassination or their distribution in the population, but only highlights the main patterns of identity among nonreligious Israeli youth today.

This analysis is based on 8 facilitated group interviews (64 youths altogether, half of them boys) and 19 in-depth individual interviews of Jewish boys and girls age 15–18 from varied social, cultural, and ethnic backgrounds who study in secular schools.[1] The format of the group and individual interviews was similar: respondents were asked to talk about their feelings and actions following the assassination in rough chronological order (especially during the first week). This formulation allowed them to talk spontaneously about their attitudes toward Rabin and his politics, as well as to express their social and political views and give their explanation for the assassination, and to talk about their own experiences of adolescence. The interviews took place two to three months after the assassination (in January and February 1996). Thus the story of every respondent was already affected by the intense public discourse on the event and by discussions at their schools.

The interviews were conducted by three different interviewers. First, analysis of all the interviews was carried out by each interviewer independently. Second, the three interviewers discussed all of the interviews, identifying the main themes and the "interpretive schemes" that characterized the voice of different groups of youth that interpreted the assassination. By interpretive schemes, we mean the networks of meaning and interpretation that represent ways to understand an event (Geertz, 1973). The assumption is that interpretive schemes are shaped within a context, and that the interpretations given by young people to the assassination are fed by the complex web of ethnopolitical meanings in Israeli society.

The interpretive schemes for understanding the assassination and mourning were derived from an analysis of four subjects addressed by all the respondents: (1) the message—their spontaneous reaction upon hearing the news of the assassination; (2) who was killed—the meaning they attributed to Rabin as a man and leader; (3) what was killed—the meaning they attributed to the assassination and its implications; and (4) the pattern of mourning—their behavior and feelings during the days of mourning.

The Message: From "They Tore Out a Part of My Heart" to "Yippee"

Information about the attack on Rabin and his death came as a blow to most of the respondents who were engaged in routine Saturday-night activities: Alina and Sarit (names of all respondents are fictitious), like many others, were watching TV. David saw the assassin on TV with the rest of his family "and then we realized that [the murderer] was our neighbor and his mother was my nursery school teacher." As soon as they heard the news of the attack, he and his brother took the car "without thinking twice" to the home of the parents of Yigal Amir, and on the way they heard the announcement of Rabin's death. Gitit heard the news on the radio as she was buying ice cream with a friend. Nurit had just returned home from the rally and was talking on the phone with her youth movement counselor, telling her how much fun it had been. Yifat and Ro'i were preparing for bed at their boarding school while their friends were watching TV in the lounge. The news of the death of Rabin spread like wildfire that night, skipping over only those few who had already gone to sleep.

All the respondents reported being shocked by the news. Some of those who opposed Rabin's political views were indifferent or happy about his death, but even they were shocked to hear of an assassination of a Jew by a Jew. All described their feelings in dramatic terms of shock, stress, confusion, fear: "[I] can't believe it," "it can't be," "I didn't know how to respond," "I didn't absorb it." Sarit in Jerusalem, who said she agreed with Rabin's politics, gave a characteristic description of the inability and unwillingness to absorb the news:

And then I saw them bring him to the hospital . . . but I didn't take it so hard because I thought, okay, they shot him in the arm or the leg and that's it and he'll be in the hospital. And then suddenly I saw and heard Hayim Yavin [a newscaster] say that the prime minister died, Yitzhak Rabin died, and it . . . I was left like that, with my mouth open, facing the TV all night and I didn't know what to say, how to react, and what to think.

Similar descriptions were given by others who believed in Rabin and his politics. Their feelings were captured by Oded's words: "[I felt] as if a part of my heart was torn out."

These dramatic reactions were not universal. Viki, for example, reacted indifferently to the shooting: "I heard they shot the prime minister and it didn't interest me very much; let's put it this way . . . I wasn't happy and wasn't sad, I said it happened and he's wounded and that's that." Avri reported: "They said he was killed and it wasn't so nice"; Amihai carried on with what he was doing: "I didn't have any special reaction, I just kept working, I wasn't sorry about it or anything."

Although most reacted with shock and fear upon hearing the news of Rabin's death, some jumped for joy and shouted "yippee." Reactions of joy, expressed in their rooms or hallways, were reported primarily by some of the students from Hadas (the fictitious name of a boarding school in Jerusalem for youth from collective farm communities and "disadvantaged areas"). Odelia, like several others, tried to convey the feeling that the dominant reaction there was one of joy:

I didn't like him or his political views very much, and I didn't agree with the Oslo agreement and giving back territories, so when I heard that they shot the prime minister . . . I didn't relate to it. I said that it happened, he was hurt, and that's it, and then when I heard he died, I was still like that. . . . A lot of people here started to laugh and be happy, really most of them.

To the question "How did you react when you heard Rabin was shot?" Orna replied, "Everyone in the room yelled 'yay' when we heard, and someone said 'let's hope he dies.' Then later we heard that it was true and we were in shock." And Ruth was happy about both the attack on Rabin and his death: "Truthfully in the beginning when they said, 'Rabin was hurt' I was happy and I ran around yelling 'yippee, yippee,' and I danced with my friends and we took pictures, and then later I said, great, he's dead."

Who Was Killed? From Intimate Friend to Anonymous Politician

The respondents' varied views of Rabin were reflected in their descriptions of the meaning he held for them. The range of answers to the question "What did he mean to you?" was broad: He was "like any person who was killed"; "a Jew who was killed"; "prime minister" or "a leader"; "our leader" or "my leader." At one extreme, the word "my" expresses an intimate connection to the victim, a feeling of personal closeness and familiarity; at the other extreme, "like anybody" expresses the feeling that he was anonymous. Those who used this language avoided identifying Rabin in personal terms.

MY LEADER WAS MURDERED

Those who referred to Rabin as "my leader" or "my prime minister" were expressing a feeling of personal loss: "They took Rabin from me, and what will happen now and what will we do," or "They took from me my leader, who I counted on to take care of things for us." In this context, comments about Rabin included: "the ideal leader of Israel"; "the only politician that I believed in," "I trusted him," "a quiet, calm man," "he projected warmth and confidence," "sweet," "shy," "well-intentioned," "speaks logically," "he knew how to calm people," and "forgiving." An attitude like this characterized those who identified with Rabin and his politics, and usually also their families. In other words, these young people felt almost a personal familiarity with him that was inseparable from their feeling of closeness to his social and political world view.

The deep sense of kinship with Rabin went beyond political agreement with him. Those for whom Rabin was a leader seemed to be saying that they had lost someone close to them, and that their connection to him was almost personal and physical. He was not just another of the "imaginary community" of peace supporters, but a real member of a concrete community in which everyone knows everyone personally. This claim is corroborated by descriptions of almost intimate familiarity with Rabin: Gitit knew Rabin's granddaughter, who had studied in her school, Alina and Ilana from Jerusalem said that they saw him every morning on their way to school, that their fence bordered where the prime minister lived.

One of Oded's relatives was a member of the commission of inquiry to investigate the circumstances of the assassination. Nurit related that her grandfather was a neighbor of Rabin's, and Meital had a friend whose family is close to the Rabin family. Others met Rabin during visits he made to their school, on the first day of school that year in Or Yehuda, or in a condolence call he paid to the René Cassin School in Jerusalem, which lost a great many graduates in military action. And there were some who met Rabin only in their imaginations, like David, who said that he dreamt about him and predicted the assassination, and Tali, who wrote in her school newspaper that she had conducted an imaginary interview with him before he was killed. Teenagers from different backgrounds felt that they had known him personally, not just those who lived near him or whose parents were part of his social network. He was their leader, they supported his politics, and he radiated to them peace and confidence.

THE PRIME MINISTER WAS MURDERED

Those who equated Rabin with his role and the service he performed for the nation were saddened by the loss of the leader, noting, "This was not just anybody, a great man died." Their words do not convey a sense of emotional closeness with him, or personal familiarity. Teenagers who felt this way included those who disagreed, wholly or partially, with his politics before the assassination, who also said: "I didn't like his politics," "I didn't agree with him," "I didn't trust him"; and those in the middle, who said: "I just felt myself in the middle and a little like that even today . . . an attitude that goes back and forth." Among those who disagreed with Rabin's politics, we found young people who, at least temporarily, modified their opinions about him and his politics in the wake of the intense public discourse after the assassination. And there were some, like Alina, who continued to find themselves in the middle: "I keep going back and forth about Rabin's politics . . . a kind of cycle of confusion that you can't get out of. . . . I don't have strong views about whether his politics was right or not."

Sarit also vacillated. She defined her father as a right-winger ("He really didn't like him [Rabin]"), her mother as liberal, and her sister as tending to the left. She grew up in a very political home and heard many reactions of happiness to the assassination. As a youth counselor in the Scouts, she devoted her life to the movement. She participated in all the mourning rituals, sometimes more than once. In very emotional words she interweaves expressions of intimacy toward Rabin, who she believes did a great deal for the country, with feelings of ambivalence:

I'm torn. . . . I didn't agree with his politics when he first started, I'm very much in the middle. . . . I thought [before the assassination] that I didn't give a damn about the nation, but this guy really cared about the country, so how can I not like the politics of someone who cares so much about this country?. . . After he died I began to appreciate him differently. But still I didn't exactly like his politics. . . . All in all, I didn't know him, so I can't hate him. . . . What's the big deal. . . . He was murdered so okay, it's sad because he was after all a person, and after all it's sad that somebody is murdered, and a prime minister no less.

The young Russian immigrants who came to Israel from the former USSR at the beginning of the 1990s related to the assassination of Rabin primarily, though not only, in political terms, expressing no sense of intimacy toward him. Because Israeli society and politics were so new for them, they still looked on as outsiders. Thus they equated the assassination of Rabin with the assassination of leaders of the Soviet Union. Yehuda, who spoke of Rabin not as "my prime minister" but as "the prime minister of my country" noted, "For me, the death of a leader of the country is not new, because we had that before, in Russia . . . but there it was different, it was a natural death."

Misha, for example, thought that Rabin was "an okay prime minister" and agreed in general with his politics. But when he saw the reenactment of the assassination on TV, his whole body trembled: "Because it wasn't just a regular crime. . . . In Russia, I lived in an atmosphere of crime, I'm used to violence, but the scene where he shoots him in the back shocked me, it's both the fact of the murder, which is a terrible thing, but even more it's the murder of the person because he was the prime minister."

IT WAS JUST SOMEBODY WHO WAS MURDERED

A completely different interpretive scheme characterized those who related to Rabin anonymously, epitomized by expressions such as, "[Rabin is] like any other person murdered" and "My brother's best friend was recently murdered." Shula, a new immigrant, compared the death of Rabin to getting killed in a car accident: "I was sorry to hear about it because of the person who was killed, it's like hearing on the news about a murder or a car accident, and it's too bad." Ina placed the murder in some distant country: "It's exactly like hearing about the assassination of someone important in France, only here it's bigger because there isn't TV, for example, or because of the problems of security and all that."

Those who espoused this interpretation, especially some of the new immigrants and teens in the Hadas school, drew an analogy between the assassination of Rabin and any other murder. Their use of the words "just like" or "always" reduced the importance of Rabin as a leader and someone with special qualities. In other words, their language minimized or diminished the figure, divesting Rabin of both his political and his personal robes. These youths spared few words about Rabin and hurried on to the next subject.

THE PERSON MURDERED DESERVED TO BE KILLED

Some identified the assassination of Rabin with the murder of other "victims of peace" (an expression coined by Rabin himself), those murdered in terrorist attacks. Ruth from Hadas held this view, and she was not the only one:

> For me, the fact that he was murdered is no different than any other Jew being murdered. How he died was painful to me, but I didn't see it like the prime minister and a leader and all that, for me it was like the story of Nahshon Wachsman [an Israeli soldier held hostage and killed by a Palestinian group], for example. . . . It hurt me the same. . . . Lots of Jews died because of this peace who weren't prime ministers, so what's the difference between them and the prime minister? . . . I always said Peres or someone should be shot to show them that if they want to give back territories, lots of Jews will die, and they don't give a damn and keep going, so they should be shot.

Ruth's interpretive strategy relates to the negative implications of Rabin's policy, which in the final analysis brought about his assassination. Her words can be interpreted by the logic of "an eye for an eye," which justifies blood revenge as a legitimate sociocultural custom. This logic, which holds the victim responsible for the murder, releases the murderer from culpability and transforms him into a hero. The rationalization given by Ruth for killing a leader who strays from the correct path rests on the perception of murder as a rational strategy to halt a political process seen as dangerous to the nation. Accordingly, she explains Yigal Amir's action as sacrifice on behalf of the nation:

> Despite all the attempts to condemn him and the assassination he did, Yigal Amir is someone who was trying to help. He's someone with his whole life ahead of him. . . . After all, a law student can have a family and be happy and be a wealthy man in this country, and why should he ruin his life? He sacrificed something of himself on behalf of this nation. . . . He wanted to do something good for the nation and to help everybody.

Quite unlike the visible public mood following the asassination and fostered by the media, this interpretation, as shown in a survey commissioned by a newspaper upon the discovery of a Yigal Amir "fan club," was held by 10 percent of the students in secular schools in Jerusalem (Wurgaft, 1996).

Even those, like Ruth, who maintained that this was "just another murder" and viewed Rabin as yet another victim of the false peace that endangers the Jewish nation, with Yigal Amir as redeemer, condemned murder per se because "nobody can take someone's life." Rhetorical use of the universal moral principle "Thou shalt not murder" gave those who justified the assassination by trivializing and minimizing it a feeling of universal morality. Those with this interpretation signaled that they were not deviating from the bounds of morality of the Israeli Jewish collective. The prohibition against murder and the justification of blood revenge sounded parallel in the rhetoric of these respondents. They floated between these two contradictory moral views, a belief in the sanctity of Jewish blood sometimes stronger than the universal precept against murder.

What Was Killed?: From "Everything" to "It Was Just Another Murder"

The feeling that "the assassination symbolizes the situation our country is in" was shared by all the respondents, though they differed in the personal and national meaning they ascribed to it. All acknowledged that the assassination was a turning point in Israel's history, a highly significant event in shaping its future character.

EVERYTHING WAS MURDERED

"Rabin was murdered and everything was murdered with him," "Peace was murdered, democracy was murdered, everything was murdered," said those who related personally to Rabin. These young people used particularly dramatic expressions to capture the enormity of the tragedy: "The worst thing that ever happened," "We're finished, there's no more state of Israel." For Efrat—active in the Scouts, Peace Now, and Meretz Youth (a left-wing political party)—this was a sudden "national tragedy," and she added: "The assassination is like a mark of Cain, a disgrace that will always remain."

What was killed that transformed the mourning into such a total experience? When Nitzan (from Hadas) was asked what he would title a book about the assassination of Rabin, he replied, "the assassination of democracy and the man of peace who died." The loss of hope for peace took center stage for those who felt that "everything was murdered."

But more than anything, the assassination engendered a sense that the distinctive nature of the nation and the state—the national character—had been lost. Efrat: "I feel that this nation is going downhill, like losing all its national character, everything that the Jewish people who is a chosen people is based on, because this is the first time that a Jew stood up and killed another Jew out of, like, the intention to kill because of political views. I don't know, this [Jewish chosenness] always seemed to be what distinguished us from others."

The disappointment about a Jew killing a Jew was shocking to all the respondents, without exception, and reflects perhaps more than anything else the experience of a national trauma. Alina puts this together with the fear of the collapse of the cosmic, political, and national order: "In Israel, that such a thing could happen? Even though the religious and the secular are . . . completely . . . isolated and two entirely separate blocs, they're also together. We're all Jewish, we're all brothers, and somehow there has to be agreement about the sanctity of life, about the supremacy of the prime minister when he's the prime minister. When I heard this thing, everything fell apart. Everything."

For both secular and religious youth the perception of national uniqueness and cultural superiority is constructed by comparison with the "other" (Smith, 1989; Rapoport, Penso, and Garb, 1998). Hence they felt betrayed by the assassination, suggesting that Israel was just like any other nation. Oded wanted to believe the Jewish Israeli ethos, of the "chosen people," but was disappointed:

> They always said, and it was a feeling, that Judaism is a kind of nation and people, that Israeli Jews are in fact something special, kinda like when you walk in the street and somebody falls, so 20 people will help each other out. . . . Go to London and people will pass you by even if you cry for help. . . . But after what happened, I reached the conclusion that we're not so very special. Like it happened then to Kennedy, kinda like we're not such a chosen people and . . . an unusual people, we're like everybody.

As a result of the assassination, Yehuda, who moved to Israel for Zionist reasons, lost his faith in the uniqueness and superiority of Israeli society over Soviet society. The assassination caused him an identity crisis:

> I was very proud of the fact that not only was our nation special, but also our country. . . .Yes, it may happen in the United States, but I don't care what

happens there, they're allowed, they're not special, but we are special and it can't happen to us. . . . And now look, how are we different than other nations and other countries? . . . Everything that was holy and clean for me began to get dirty, something broke, was shattered. . . . Because that's my dream. . . . How can it be? . . . It's like something broke in the ideals that I built because I didn't believe that a Jew can murder another Jew. . . . [And the assassination] broke the whole ideal and the appearance and image of the state that I want to live in and the nation that I am part of.

The impression could be created, he continued, that "I am talking about my ideals being broken and don't care about the other things. No, I do care and I stood there for four hours [in line to see the coffin], and I paid my last respects to the prime minister of my country." At the same time, he was angry that Israeli society returned to normal so quickly after the terrorist bombings, which brought up the bad feeling that "Rabin's blood was redder."

"ONLY" RABIN WAS MURDERED

Those who opposed Rabin's politics and what he represented interpreted his assassination as just one murder among many in Israeli society: "It's too bad when anybody dies" or "It's no different than the death of anybody else." From the context in which statements like these were made in the interviews, it is clear that they only seemed universalist; the intention of those who said them was that it is too bad when anybody dies, except Rabin.

This interpretive strategy combined the understanding of who was murdered and what was murdered, and separated the causes of the murder from Rabin and his political stand. Thus for Avri: "It's always unpleasant when people are killed and every murder you hear about is shocking. . . . The assassination didn't affect me, it was an unpleasant feeling and that's it. . . . The assassination does not change anything politically, that's it, it's a terrible thing that happened and all that, but it's not connected to politics."

The interpretation that disconnects politics from the assassination strips it of collective implications and limits the mourning to the narrow circle of "family" members. It trivializes and normalizes the assassination.

The young people who attributed enormous significance to the victim and the assassination felt a sense of total loss. They used an interpretive strategy at the heart of which was glorification of Rabin and his beliefs, and they fused the man, the country, politics, and peace. In contrast, the young people who opposed this reaction trivialized the assassination and the victim. This trivialization seemed to ascribe to the assassination a universal—not personal or national—significance and hence negated its importance. The one who identified Rabin with the victims of terrorism went one step further in diminishing his significance as a leader. The underlying logic was that the assassin did the right thing because he killed the person responsible for the murder of innocent Jews.

The Pattern of Mourning: From Mourning as Work to Perfunctory Mourning

Wider differences between the various interpretive schemes emerged in response to questions such as "What did you do during the mourning period?," "How did you feel?," and "When did you return to your routine?" These answers reveal two main patterns of mourning: maximal and minimal.

MOURNING WITH FEELING

Respondents who identified deeply with Rabin and his politics transformed their mourning into almost a ritual that involved intense activity and a deep emotional investment. They were constantly occupied with activities related to the mourning, and even initiated mourning events such as memorial and commemoration ceremonies. During the week of mourning, their world was turned upside down: mourning became the routine and the routine became mourning (see Turner, 1974). Those who transformed mourning into ritual did all or many of the following: they participated in a memorial service at school or in their youth movement (one or more), organized a mourning ceremony, paid respects at the coffin lying in state (alone, with friends, or in an organized group), wrote for their newspapers (school or youth movement), visited memorial sites (Rabin's homes in Jerusalem or Tel Aviv), visited the grave, watched TV programs about the event, and attended the rally at the end of the mourning week. Many who lived in the Tel Aviv area—but not only those young people—visited the plaza and initiated mourning activities there.

Those for whom the experience of mourning was total found it difficult or refused to return to the normal routine during the seven days of mourning. Said Nurit, "I wasn't tired of it, I wanted to continue it as much as possible, and I constantly watched TV and taped it and constantly read newspapers." She also clipped newspaper articles "so I won't forget and can pass it on to my children." These young people also negotiated with their parents (and especially their teachers), who tried to return them to the daily routine. Michal from the René Cassin School: "We told the teachers that we can't [return to normal]. Something terrible happened, a civil war, no way, because we can't go back to normal. The whole country is coming apart and they say go back to normal, 'snap out of it, folks.'" The unwillingness to return to normal was not an expression of rebellion against their elders, because the adults generally did not insist on a quick return to the routine.

This, then, was a group of young people whose devotion to the mourning reached a high pitch and absorbed them completely. Prominent among them were counselors in different youth movements, such as Sarit, who visited the coffin four times in one day, and Efrat, who defined herself as an "extreme left-winger."

Efrat rejected an opportunity on the day of the funeral to enter Mount Herzl because she did not feel herself worthy yet. Only after participating in every possible activity of mourning did she allow herself a visit to Rabin's grave. Through her mourning, Efrat reduced the guilt she felt about Rabin's having "died without knowing that I was behind him and without my having done enough before the assassination." Feelings of guilt and regret like these were not exclusive to Efrat, and they mobilized intense mourning activity among even those who did not agree with Rabin's politics.

MOURNING WITHOUT FEELING

Even those who minimized the importance of the assassination and the victim participated in the mourning and memorialization activities by watching TV or taking part in school-sponsored activities. Many visited memorial sites in an organized or spontaneous way, observing the mourning from a distance or peeking at it from up close. Amihai: "I went to the funeral, but not on purpose. We were in town, me and my friend, and we had nothing to do, it was boring so we went to the funeral. We were standing near Binyanei Ha'Uma ['building of the nation'] and the cortege drove by and we stood and watched. We didn't actually wait for the coffin but we watched to see the reactions of the other people there."

The difference between Amihai and those "devoted" to the mourning was not merely in the frequency of their visits to mourning sites, but their willingness to invest emotionally in mourning. During the first days, with the coffin lying in state and then the funeral, it was hard to remain entirely detached and indifferent, unaffected by this wave inundating Israeli society. For young people, it seems to have been even harder. The desire to join the wave, if only at the margins, touched almost all the respondents. The media and schools contributed to it by directly or indirectly encouraging mourning and visits to the mourning sites. The fear that a civil war would break out also brought young people into public spaces, watching up close for signs of unity and disunity.

What seemed to be a reaction of the entire nation attracted people for a fleeting moment to the mourning sites, including those who perceived the public reaction to be excessive. Those who saw the mourning as upsetting their daily schedule and wanted to return to normal as soon as possible tended to minimize the grieving. David regrets having watched the mourning of his friends from a distance because "I saw that everyone was there and I wasn't." Ina, a Russian immigrant, was also sorry, but for other reasons. She found herself on the outside and was envious of those who felt the need to grieve: "I had great respect for those who sat in the plaza, I envied them. I also want very much to do things for the state, only I don't feel an emotional need to do it and that bothers me." Captive to the hegemonic discourse, Ina, too, believed that every veteran and native Israeli was plunged into heavy mourning.

Four Voices of Israeli Youth

Our analysis revealed four different interpretive schemes, each characteristic of one ethnopolitical group or subculture among Israeli youth. My discussion is based on types of interpretations, and no claim is made about prevalence among the population of Jewish youth in Israel. Three of the groups can be placed on a continuum. At one end is the group with the "inside voice" and at the opposite end the group with the "other voice." Between these two groups is "the wavering voice." The fourth group, which I call "the outside voice," is not on the continuum.

THE OUTSIDE VOICE: I'M NEITHER HERE NOR THERE

The group with the outside voice are young immigrants from the former Soviet Union. By virtue of their marginal position, they do not share the Israeli collective memory. They view Israeli politics and decipher their new cultural and social reality from inside and outside at one and the same time. Because of their position as newcomers, some have no clear opinions about the leaders of the Israeli body politic. Most are immersed in a process of learning the political, democratic, and social order in Israel, which they do not take for granted. Like those in the other groups, these young people—especially those who came to Israel out of Zionist ideology—expressed sorrow about losing their naive belief in the "chosen people."

In their attempt to comprehend the assassination and the behavior of Israelis, they drew upon interpretive schemes familiar from their country of birth, particularly those that link the individual and the state and those having to do with citizens' relations to authority and leadership. More than those in other groups, all the young people in this group emphasized the state's total responsibility for their personal security. Yehuda, who said the assassination reflected Israel's "failure as a state and a society," rebelled against the muzzling of "illegitimate" voices after the slaying and compared it to what he left behind: "They started to incite against and silence people and it was impossible to say what you think, and I felt that I had not immigrated, that it was exactly the same government that was there. . . . I hoped that when I immigrated I would find a truly free people here who can speak out. . . . And this [attempt to silence] pained me no less than the assassination of the prime minister." Of those who went to sit in the plaza, Yehuda said: "It reminded me of the youth movement there, when they go to places and don't understand what's going on and who anyone was and what he did, but they take flags and flowers and I don't know what else, and it has to do with policies—okay not Communism—but the government."

Yehuda, who said he immigrated "with ideals," felt that the assassination reinforced his identity as an immigrant from Russia. Other Russian immigrants remained entirely removed from the society and hence the mourning. Some, like Ina, felt they could not share the grief of the others: "Unfortunately, I don't feel like Israelis who say how wonderful he was and what a pity."

Ina suggested a sociological explanation for the behavior of the Russian immigrants in Amihai's story, who opened bottles of vodka to celebrate the event. "In my opinion," said Ina, "it was to declare their foreignness and lack of nationalism . . . to demonstrate how much it didn't affect us, how much we didn't care about it." Shlomit adopted withdrawal and apathy as her strategy: "I don't know what happened at all. . . . I knew that the prime minister's name was Rabin, but I didn't know what the extremists thought and why they killed him."

The outside voice has special importance. Because it is relatively free of "taking things for granted," it can help decode and dismantle common assumptions. Although the young people who came from Russia felt themselves "not really inside," each one chose a different strategy for coping with the sense of foreignness.

THE INSIDE AND THE WAVERING VOICES: DECISIVENESS VERSUS DILEMMA

Unlike the voice from outside, the voice from the inside stands out, belonging to teenagers with a left-wing political orientation who identified with Rabin's peace policies. They experienced a heavy feeling of personal and national loss and devoted themselves to mourning on several levels: at school and with the youth movement, their friends, and their families. In all these socialization frameworks, adults and young people with similar views participated in the mourning together.

The wavering voice belonged to those who vacillated between identifying with the inside voice and criticizing it. They floated between political views on the right and left. The political dilemma was agonizing and confusing: "I'm torn," said Sarit; "I'm confused," said David. These young people opposed Rabin's views before the assassination, but the killing and the discourse that followed aroused in them strong ambivalence about the politics that he represented. They claimed that the image of Rabin in the public and school discourse after his death led them to view him in a new light. They wondered how they could not have supported someone who had done so much for the country for so many years. Their stories clarified that they lived in a setting marked by opposing political views among agents of socialization (e.g., father and mother) and the frameworks of socialization (e.g., neighborhood, family, and friends). These were primarily youth who grew up in settings (family and neighborhood) that supported the right, while they associated in school with left-wing students. For seven days, youth from the right, left, and center were immersed in mourning, but the waverers were more eager than the others to get back to normal life.

Both the young people who spoke as insiders and those who were in the wavering group had high social awareness. They noted that after the assassination they felt even more willing to participate in the social and political realm. Many who were involved in traditional activities on behalf of Israeli society (counseling in a youth movement, political activity, volunteering, etc.) believed that young people could have an impact. An inseparable part of their experience of adolescence was an expectation of themselves to be involved in civil-political activity.

The demand for commitment and the expectation that young people will become involved in the national-collective sphere has always been part of the Zionist discourse (Rapoport, Penso, and Garb, 1994). On the back of the June 1996 report cards from Ben-Gurion Junior High School in Herzliya appears the following quotation: "The image of the human being in Israel means first of all the image of the youth in Israel, your creative ability, pioneering initiative, loyalty to the mission placed upon you by the history of our generation" (David Ben-Gurion, June 1954). These words bring together the ethos of the centrality of youth in society and its historical role of carrying out the Zionist revolution. The assassination enabled those young people for whom this discourse was available and known to connect with it and "show the adults that we care."

Involvement, commitment, and caring were an inseparable part of the experience of adolescence for those who generated the mourning activities. In this respect, these values can be seen as cultural capital at their disposal (Bourdieu, 1995). The capital of caring and involvement is more available to those who use them regularly and have "ownership" of them. Rabin's assassination brought to the fore the importance of commitment and increased the motivation of these teenagers to accumulate more of this capital.

Orientation to the collectivity does not contradict the postnationalist culture of youth (as it is often called). According to Michal, awareness and involvement in society and politics are part and parcel of the daily life of young people:

> Why do I have to open the newspaper and read that Miberg [a journalist who criticized the behavior of youth in the Zemah rock festival] thinks that I'm superficial and that we "young people" are worrying him. I want to inform Miberg that there are some teenagers who go to Zemah and have fun because this is our time to have fun, but then some of us come home, go to the youth movement, open the TV, watch the news, and know what's going on. So even if politics doesn't become part of our social life on Friday nights, it doesn't mean that it doesn't enter the lives of young people on other days. For some reason, when people get old, they develop this hobby of defining youth and telling them how fucked up you are. I feel like pressing a button, jumping 40 years ahead, and showing them that when we grow up, we're going to take care of this country, and we'll do it well too. (Michal Ashkenazi, age 16, quoted in *Ma'ariv* newspaper, June 14, 1996).

Michal was protesting Miberg's collective portrait of Israeli teenagers as "vacuous, degenerate, and disgusting youth." "We are involved," she counters, "but involved differently than adults." "Don't try to force us to be serious all the time," adds Yonit Cohen, age 15; "When necessary we also know how to take seriously important things and to carry on," and if "teenagers want a little peace and quiet from politics, let them have it" (Katriel, 1991). Michal and Yonit were defending youth against those in the Israeli discourse—heard loudly from the religious Zionist camp (Rapoport, Penso, and Halbertal, 1996)—who argue that a "fun" youth culture is not compatible with national seriousness and commitment. The important sociological message they were sending is that the generation of excellence is simultaneously a screwed-up generation and that the problem of adults is that they periodically insist on emphasizing a different facet of this generation: after the tragedy at the Arad festival, the younger generation was screwed up; after the assassination of Rabin, it was excellent; after the Zemah Festival, it was screwed up again.

But why does society periodically get stuck on one image? Clinging to a one-dimensional conception enables adults to apply stricter social control mechanisms over youth. A more complex image creates vagueness and limits adults' ability to convey clear messages about what is expected of young people and what the rewards and punishments are.

During the period of mourning, adults showered rewards on the youth who mourned because they were demonstrating commitment. These "candle children" took advantage of the opportunity to invade the public space, to make their presence felt, and to demand center stage, if only for a brief period. Together with the feeling of power, generational awareness was strengthened (Mannheim, 1952), and the sense of youthfulness of the mourning teenagers grew stronger, as described by Efrat:

> We said that from here we can either go down or up, now it all depends on us, and we have got to do something, because if as young people we only kept our mouths shut, shut, shut all the time, now is the time to talk. Because better late than never. . . . I have the power to change things. . . . Presumably there are masses of teenagers in Israel, and that already gives us power. We have so much power that we are not doing anything with, and it just gets me angry. I don't know, the time has come to change something, to start moving something.

The formation of generational awareness during the period of mourning was reinforced by a situation of double liminality: the liminal social status that characterizes youth in a "transition period" (Turner, 1974: 94–97) and the liminal situation of mourning in which society was absorbed. The liminal situation charged with potential for revolt was suffused with emotionality: "I love Rabin and also Rakefet" [a girl's name] scrawled a young boy on one of the walls in Rabin Plaza, blurring the distinction be- tween the personal and the political.

The liminal situation in which a *communitas* can grow sharpens the consciousness and sense of partnership and togetherness. The blurred boundaries of age, characteristic of periods of mourning, reinforce the generational awareness of young people. When an entire society is in limbo, outside the normal order of things, intergenerational relations also take on a new cast. The shared experience of an intense, historic crisis was translated by youth into generational awareness, reinforcing both inter- and intragenerational relations. Paradoxically, the generational awareness and the feeling of empowerment among the young people in the limelight during the period of mourning simultaneously heightened both their distance from and their closeness to adults.

Israeli adults expect young people to be committed but not blindly obedient, caring but not "wimps," happy but not hedonists. According to Alboim-Dror (1996), these contradictory expectations have characterized the attitude of adults to the younger generation since the first waves of Jewish immigration to Palestine. The mourning in the plaza enabled youth to fulfill this expectation and to please the adults. Rabin Plaza was a perfect example of a cultural-social-political arena in which youth synthesized a secular teenage culture with the demand for national commitment placed on them by the Zionist discourse. The pattern of mourning opened a space for individual expressions of mourning, and these were observed, encouraged, and even joined by the adults with great pleasure and excitement. Nevertheless, the individualism of youth was controlled and circumscribed: although adults gave the young people freedom, allowing them to break out of accepted cultural idioms, they still expected them to adopt the Zionist-national discourse and express loyalty to the collective (Alon 1986: 289). From this point of view, one can speak of the generation of "individualistic conformity" or of "conformist individualism."

Teenagers in the public space used creative means to fashion a collective culture of mourning. The years of adolescence are a natural period for creativity and innovation (Esman, 1990). The openness to new situations, spaces, and conduct—which typifies young people (Erikson, 1968)— fostered particularly powerful forms of mourning. This was acknowledged by those who saw them as original, creative, or trite, as well as by those who stressed the import of ritual symbols from distant worlds (Buddhism and Christianity), those who saw signs of a "secular martyrology" or "religion of rock 'n roll," and those who detected in these same activities a taste of Jewish tradition (Eisenstadt, 1996) or original Israeli culture (Malkinson and Witztum, 1996).

THE OTHER VOICE: "TEENS IN THE PLAZA WERE ONLY LOOKING FOR ATTENTION"

The "other voice" belongs to those who identified originally with the Israeli nationalist right wing and the ideology of "peace with security." In this study, these voices were heard primarily from respondents in the Hadas school. It is important to note that not everyone who identified with the right responded this way. Those of the "other voice" were happy about the slaying, and some even reacted with joy upon hearing about it. Some sought to depict Rabin's assassination as just another death, thereby emptying it of deeper meaning. Others justified the assassination indirectly, on the basis of revenge. Those who so interpreted the assassination did not experience the loss or immerse themselves in mourning. Nevertheless, some joined the rest of the nation in visiting the memorial sites in response to the wave of mourning that swept Israeli society. Some later felt regret about this reaction, alleging that the mourning, theirs or that of their friends, was hypocritical. The intense lesson they heard from their teachers about the essence of democracy, the significance of the killing, and the greatness of Rabin the man and leader (a lesson given to many Israeli youth) clashed with their basic world view. Like those with the "inside voice," they expressed a resolute political opinion, but unlike them, those of the "other voice" had minimal political and social knowledge. For example, they had no idea what "the 1967 borders" referred to or when the state of Israel was created.

The dominance of the social discourse after the mourning blurred, camouflaged, and drowned out this voice from public awareness. The young people in this group were aware that their reaction to the mourning was considered by most to be illegitimate and unacceptable. Therefore, their awareness of and attention to the "inside voice" was unavoidable, even if not necessarily conscious; they "conversed" with those who spoke with an "inside voice."

Young people with the "other voice" sought to minimize the intense mourning of the "plaza youth" and its resonance: "The media made a circus out of it," said Yoav. Others criticized the "show" put on by teenagers in the plaza, who they said were looking for attention and exaggerating the mourning. Rotem accused them of hypocrisy, quoting Leah Rabin's emotional accusation: "Where were you then, when you were needed?": "In my opinion, they're showing their pain too much, looking for attention. If they really cared, they would go comfort Leah Rabin. . . . Their solidarity won't hold up over time, because when people stood opposite Rabin's house every Friday and yelled 'murderer,' these guys didn't come and cry, believe me they didn't."

Ruth expressed real contempt for the youth in the plaza, accusing them of being led by the noses by the adults and their friends. Like others with the "other voice," she felt cut off from the "candle children": "Even if there are teenagers who support Rabin, it's disgusting that they sit in the plaza for a week and cry. . . . They're doing what their parents think. . . . If I had talked to them, I would have told them that they're just getting carried away, one after the other, and it's social pressure, they should stop getting carried away, stop putting on shows, and get up."

In short, "you went overboard" said those with the "other voice" to those with the "inside voice," accusing them of being disingenuous. What they were actually angry about is how comfortable the plaza teens felt in the public space and how naturally they exposed their emotions there. They perceived these youth as spoiled, looking for attention, able to afford to waste time and emotions and not return to normal life.

The difference in reaction to Rabin's assassination between groups with various voices and the "candle children" reflects their fundamentally different experiences of adolescence. Teenagers construct their experience of adolescence while comparing it historically to the ideal of youth in the past, especially regarding matters of commitment, voluntarism, and motivation to do something for the country.

Teens with the "other voice" in the group claimed that activity for the public weal was no longer characteristic of them or Israeli youth in general: "It's not what it once was," said Amit, "Today there's a very small group who say they'll volunteer for the Magen David [Red Cross] and all that stupid stuff." They also don't believe in the ability of youth to affect society and politics in Israel. Yoram from Beit Shemesh also believed that the generation had changed: "We're a screwed-up generation, we're not like the generation that came before us. Once there were good kids and today it's not like that. . . . We have no future as a generation, other than each one of us individually." The esprit de corps that had characterized the generations of the past had been replaced by individualism. Both Ami and Yoram remarked that the generations were deteriorating and that it was impossible to create a positive generational awareness.

They Didn't Tell Everyone's Story

"They didn't tell everyone's story." Historian Rachel Alboim-Dror makes this claim in her article about the cultures of youth during the first waves of Jewish immigration to Palestine (1996). This article restores the voice of "other" youth and suggests its structural generational characteristics, as well as its struggle with hegemony. One learns from her work that ignoring youth groups and cultures who did not fit the hegemonic Zionist ethos was not new; it happened during the prestate period as well. Thus, most people never heard "the voices that deviated from the main story and did not conform to the Zionist ethos-in-formation that gave meaning and value to symbols and also served as a means of control and domination" (Alboim-Dror, 1996: 2). Thus the history of ignoring and silencing this voice is long, and its politics has deep roots.

Prof. Alboim-Dror and I did not coordinate our research, but we both sought "to encourage those silenced to speak," as she wrote, and examine critically the canonical research about youth—she of historians and I of sociologists. Our point of view ascribes importance to revealing the multiple voices and understanding how each creates the space for Israeli adolescence.

The use of phenomenological research enables us to listen multiple voices and to understand the key interpretive groups who weave the fabric of youth in Israel. This differs from positivist-quantitative studies of Israeli youth, important as they are, which often focus on the components of national identity and their political-democratic orientation. The goal of such studies is to examine the link between young people and the Israeli collective, and to gauge the strength of youth solidarity and their commitment to the collective and its values (Ichilov, 1988 and 1995; Herman, 1980; Meisels, Gal, and Fishoff, 1989; and Binyamini, 1990). These studies use the level of correlation between political attitudes and identity components to distinguish between youth who represent the two ideological poles. They do not, however, reveal the connections among these types or their evolution within the contexts in which the generational consciousness and experience of adolescence are formed.

The research presented here also differs from the dominant structural-functional model used to study Israeli young people, which is constrained by the ethos of Israeli youth (Rapoport, Lomsky Feder, et al., 1995). That model seeks to construct an "ideal type" of youth and youth organization (Eisenstadt, 1956; Kahane, 1975), and in parallel to study the nature and development of those defined as youth-at-risk, who are considered difficult to integrate into main Israeli society (Adler, 1986). These teenagers, who are defined as "other," are targeted for rehabilitation to turn them into normative Israelis (Penso, 1996). This approach is based on the assumption that teens defined as "established" should and do serve as positive role models for the others. This approach, which reflects dominant discourse contexts in sociological research and Israeli society about "center and periphery," also helps create these contexts (see the excellent study by Griffin [1993] concerning the academic discourse about youth in England).

Unlike the hierarchical assumptions underlying the model of center, periphery, and cultural-social integration, the phenomenological model allows for discussion about the universe of meaning of young people in subcultures or different groups. Such a model makes it possible to map the field of meanings and examine the interrelationships between groups. This examination delineates an intricate system of chains of meaning, all of which draw upon the complex web of Israeli identities in the late 1990s.

The differences between interpretive groups revealed in this research are not between those committed to national Zionism and Judaism, peace, the unity of the Jewish people, and support for democracy and those who are not. The analysis here suggests that teenagers in all four groups support these values, although the meaning they ascribe to them differs. Key to the distinct meanings are the different political and national viewpoints they hold.

The differences between the groups, especially between young people who made their voices heard from the inside and those with the "other voice," is not only right- and left-wing politics and the interpretation of nationalism, but also a world view and style of life. The universe of meanings of teens in these two groups is distinct in terms of their grasp of adolescence, generational consciousness, and the way they are expected to take advantage of time and space resources. During the period of mourning, teenagers who were part of these two subcultures were cut off from each other. The youth on the "inside," closed within their own world, were convinced that their feelings of mourning were common to all. They felt comfortable in the public-secular space and among adults who watched and joined them. Because the adults who mourned were their "natural allies" at the time, these teenagers were not called upon to define themselves or compare themselves with the other youth groups.

In contrast, the young people with the other voice had no choice but to relate to the inside voice that captured center stage and resonated in the public space. The voice of the Zionist ethos of youth on the inside did not represent them, however, and they refused to be empathetic to it and understand it. Their reaction indicates that Rabin and mourning for Rabin did not belong to them. They did not try to appropriate the public space, they did not feel ownership of it, and very soon they avoided it. They cynically criticized youth on the inside for their mourning behavior, conformity to media consumerism, excessive weeping for a stranger, wasting time, and externalizing feelings toward "someone who's not even a member of the family."

These reactions can be interpreted as anger, alienation, and frustration rooted in the desire to "be like them" without being able to make it happen. However, they can also be explained as opposition to the dominant, hegemonic voice and subversion of those who speak in it. Thus, the reactions of the young people who raised the other voice can be seen as an attempt to establish another kind of Israeliness and to strengthen a separate group identity as young Israelis: "There's more than one political party and also more than one kind of teenager; it's a different kind of education and everyone is looking for his own opinion," said Ruth, explaining the division of youth along political-educational lines. She fumed about the "brainwashing" of the left-wing media that led people to behave hypocritically, and insisted on defending her own political view even though it was not popular. "In a demonstration before he was killed," she added, "when everyone was shouting that we have to put a bullet through his head, I yelled too, so why should I cry now?"

I believe that too little was done to understand the universe of meaning of youth with the other voice. At the time, research had not developed a language to understand them. To unravel these meanings, the local culture in which youth evolve needs to be better understood. When this happens, we will also better understand the complex meaning of Israeli adolescence.

Today, as in the past, the cultural, social, and political space of young people in Israel is not monolithic. It is occupied by various identities with complex and changing interrelationships in the context of power relations and negotiation. Those who are missing and those who are kept out are no less important than the canonical culture (see also Alboim-Dror, 1996;

Giroux, 1996). Both forgetting and memory, like definitions of the mainstream and the marginal, together construct the collective identity and shape the national culture. The importance of wresting these voices from the silence, voices that have been defined as secondary, marginal, or less valuable, derives not just from the need to correct and diversify the memory, but also from the need to give a more complete explication of the concept of "Israeli youth."

Note

1. Group interviews: three with members of the Scouts Youth movement in the center of Israel (from Or-Yehuda, Ramle, and Re'ut); two with youth who study in elite schools in Jerusalem; and three with youth in the Hadas Boarding School (fictitious name) in Jerusalem for youth from "disadvantaged areas" in Israel—development towns in the South, some areas on the outskirts of Jerusalem and Tel Aviv, and *moshavim* (collective farm communities) in the Jordan Valley. An additional group interview was held with teenagers who immigrated from the former Soviet Union and study in a special class for immigrants in a Jerusalem high school. Individual interviews: twelve in-depth interviews with youth from Herzliya (most from established families) and Jerusalem (most from families of Mizrahi ethnic origin—coming from Muslim countries); and seven interviews with immigrant teens from the former Soviet Union now living in Jerusalem. The average interview duration was an hour and a half.

References

Adler, Chaim (1986). "Youth-at-Risk: Who, Why, and Is There No Choice?" In Tamar Rapoport (ed.), *Between Two Worlds*. Jerusalem: Academon, pp. 327–40 [Hebrew].

Alboim-Dror, Rachel (1996). "He Came and Went, from Within Us He Came, the New Hebrew: On the Culture of Youth During the First Waves of Immigration." *Alpayim* 12: 104–35 [Hebrew].

Alon, Muni (1986). *The Eternal Chance: Youth and Social Change*. Tel Aviv: Sifriyat HaPoalim [Hebrew].

Binyamini, Kalman (1990). *Political and Civic Attitudes of Jewish Youth in Israel*. Research report, Faculty of Social Sciences, Department of Psychology, Hebrew University, Jerusalem, pp. 1–14 [Hebrew].

Bourdieu, Pierre (1995). *The Logic of Practice*. Oxford: Polity Press.

Eisenstadt, S. N. (1956). *From Generation to Generation*. New York: Free Press.

———— (1996). "Concluding Remarks: Collective Consciousness, Public Discourse and Democracy." Lecture at the Jerusalem Van Leer Institute published in *Ha'aretz*, special supplement, "The Day After: Analysis of Society's Reactions and Israeli Politics After the Assassination of Rabin," April 1996 [Hebrew].

El-Or, Tamar, Tova Halbertal, and Tamar Rapoport (1997). "Apples from the Desert: Literature Teaches Reading Through and Beyond Local Culture." Unpublished manuscript.

Erikson, Erik H. (1968). *Identity: Youth and Crisis*. New York: W. W. Norton.

Erlich, Shmuel (1996). "Reaction of Adolescents to Rabin's Assassination: Is It Really Patricide?" Lecture at a conference sponsored by Keshev, "Youth After the Assassination of Rabin: Coping with Trauma," January 22, 1996, Jerusalem Van Leer Institute, Jerusalem [Hebrew].

Esman, Aaron H. (1990). *Adolescence and Culture*. New York: Columbia University Press.

Geertz, Clifford (1973). *The Interpretation of Cultures*. New York: Basic Books.

Giroux, Henry (1996). "Pedagogy of Limits and the Politics of Modernism/Postmodernism." In Ilan Gur-Zev (ed.), *Education in the Age of Postmodernist Discourse*. Jerusalem: Magnes, pp. 43–64 [Hebrew].

Griffin, Christin (1993). *Representations of Youth*. Cambridge: Polity Press.

Herman, Simon (1980). *Jewish Identity*. Jerusalem: HaSifriya HaTziyonit [Hebrew].

Ichilov, Orit (1988)., "Educating for Citizenship and Democracy: Policy and Contents." *Educational Planning Policy 1988–89*, Jerusalem, Ministry of Education and Culture, pp. 283–315 [Hebrew].

——— (1995). "The Educational System and the Shaping of Orientations for Citizenship and Democracy Among Youth in Israel." In Hanoch Flum (ed.), *Adolescents in Israel: Personal, Familial and Social Aspects*. Even Yehuda: Rechess, pp. 225–41 [Hebrew].

Kahane, Reuven (1975). "Informal Youth Organizations: A General Model." *Sociological Inquiry* 45: 17–28.

Katriel, Tamar (1991). *Communal Webs: Communication and Culture in Contemporary Israel*. Albany: State University of New York Press, pp. 35–49.

Malkinson, Ruth, and Eliezer Witztum (1996). "From 'the Silver Platter' to 'Who Will Remember the Rememberers?': Psychological Aspects of Mourning in Historical and Literary Analyses." *Alpayim* 12: 211–39 [Hebrew].

Mannheim, Karl (1972 [1952]). "The Problem of Generation." In K. Mannheim (ed.) *Essays on the Sociology of Knowledge*. London: Routledge and Kegan Paul.

Meidan, Anat (1996). "Children Are Crying for Rabin." *Yediot Aharonot*, Friday Supplement, October 18, 1996 [Hebrew].

Meisels, Ofra, Reuven Gal, and Eli Fishoff (1989). *World Views and Attitudes of High School Students Toward Subjects of the Army and Security*. Zikhron Ya'akov: Israel Institute for Military Studies [Hebrew].

Penso, Anat (1996). "From 'Youth-at-Risk' to 'Israeli Woman': The Educational-Rehabilitational Process in a Boarding School." M.A. thesis, Hebrew University of Jerusalem [Hebrew].

Rapoport, Tamar, Anat Penso, and Yoni Garb (1994). "Contribution to the Collective by Religious-Zionist Adolescent Girls." *British Journal of Sociology of Education* 15 (3): 375–89.

——— (1998). "The National Identity of Young Religious-Zionist Women." Unpublished manuscript.

Rapoport, Tamar, Anat Penso, and Tova Halbertal (1996). "Girls' Experiences of Artistic Ambition: The Voices of a Religious Zionist and a Kibbutznik." *Journal of Contemporary Ethnography* 24 (4), pp. 438–61.

Rapoport, Tamar, Edna Lomsky Feder, Nura Resh, Yechezkel Dar, and Haim Adler (1995). "Youth and Adolescence in Israeli Society." In Hanoch Flum (ed.), *Adolescents in Israel: Personal, Familial and Social Aspects*. Even Yehuda: Rechess [Hebrew].

Regev, Motti (1995). *Rock: Music and Culture*. Tel-Aviv: Dvir [Hebrew].

Smith, A. (1989). "National Identity and Myths of Descent." *Research in Social Movements, Conflict and Change* 7: 95–130.

Turner, Victor (1974). *The Ritual Process: Structure and Anti-Structure*. Chicago: Aldine.

Wurgaft, Nurit (1996). "8.8% of the Secular High School Students in the City Support Yigal Amir." *Ha'aretz—Kol Ha'Ir*, August 16, 1996 [Hebrew].

CHAPTER 9

Rabin's Burial Ground:
Revisiting the Zionist Myth

HAIM HAZAN

Sometime after Prime Minister Rabin's assassination, graffiti appeared on a pedestrian bridge near Bar-Ilan University, proclaiming: "Israel erased Rabin" (Yisrael mahaka et Rabin). There was a poetic touch to this wording in Hebrew, recalling Labor Party's 1992 campaign slogan: "Israel is waiting for Rabin" (Yisrael mehaka leRabin). And this slogan was a paraphrase of the popular song from the Six Day War, "Nasser is waiting for Rabin" (Nasser mehake le-Rabin). The double poetic twist in this metamorphosis of a cultural narrative is telling. A halo-less army general is hesitantly and desperately installed as would-be hero—chief of staff—at a time of public panic and mistrust of politicians. Six days in June 1967 transform him into a world-admired national hero, a status used to ensconce him in the national pantheon.[1] That was the first poetic twist in Rabin's cultural career. The second, however, is a complex one since it holds in store two possible endings to Rabin's narrative: one expressed by the graffiti on the bridge and the other, its rival, by the immediate public reaction to the assassination. Both endings seem to reflect mutually exclusive schemes for the writing of the Israeli collective memory and how that affects the prospects for nation-building and national identity.

It is not the purpose of this chapter to evaluate the "real" political consequences or cultural implications of the assassination. Rather it is to examine the national mourning that swept the country as a nonspontaneous reaction to the contingencies implicit in the graffiti solution of eliminating Rabin from the story of Israeli history. I therefore argue that Rabin's posthumous apotheosis could be construed as a collectively constructed attempt to reinstate the injured body social through an internally coherent complex of interwoven symbolic practices.[2] However, this argument also hides its own twist. Reinstatement of the body social is possible only by resorting to components of the ending meted out to Rabin and to the Israeli collective narrative by the assassin. Thus, reconstitution of that body was not a reflection and reproduction of a premurder state, but a rearrangement and editing of Rabin's cultural biography. This symbolic rewriting was systematically engraved on designated sites and in ad hoc rituals.[3] It presented a modified-alternative social body whose mourning temporarily rerouted the premurder course of current Israeli history to a different path, one that bypasses the assassin's version of Rabin's symbolic historiography. Indeed, my interpretation of the funerary and bereavement procedures draws on understanding them as cultural products of the rendezvous between history and myth.[4] Here I argue that the assassination plaza in Tel Aviv was a metaphorical arena for a battle between two concepts embedded in the fusion of myth and history, and that the dilemma faced by the mourners was how to inscribe their version of the relations between the two onto Rabin's public monument despite the realization that both narratives stem from the same origin. In other words, the dilemma was how to reconcile the apparent contradictions in the Zionist ethos as thrown into relief by the act of the assassination. It is my contention that if the off-the-cuff depictions of the assassin as a "religious fanatic," "fundamentalist," "lunatic," or "stray weed"—all of these terms appeared in the national press at the time—had been accepted by the mourners, the need to grapple with the first principles of Zionism would not have arisen. However, what was evident subsequent to the assassination was an outright rebuttal (albeit not by the right wing of the political spectrum) of idiosyncratic, pathological, or nonconsensual images of the murderer and his breeding ground. Conversely, the assassin's biography (which included state religious education, combat army service, and the promotion of immigration) wove him into the very fabric of the Zionist enterprise and shaped the reaction to the assassination as a structurally antithetical format to the assumed and overt message of the deed.

The following is an analysis of the sequence of media-reported public performances in the wake of the assassination. It is by no means a step-by-step description of the events that followed Rabin's death. Such a sequential yarn would be impossible, since events were registered concurrently and through multimedia channels. Rather it is a media-informed, broadly sketched rendition of the cultural narrative constructed during the first few days after the assassination. This account documents the procedures by which Rabin's social body was constituted, and it follows an exposition of the dilemma of myth versus history underpinning that reaction.[5]

A Split Myth

Scholars have long realized that throughout the historical evolution of the Zionist ethos two intermingling cultural codes have unfolded: the universally humanistic and the nationally specific. This duality in the Zionist ethos is explicated by Sternhell (1995) and reflected in Israeli political and literary culture (Gertz, 1995). It has been established that the interplay between the two alters its form and emphasis in different periods of Zionist history.[6] Furthermore, recent works note the self-deception built into the explicit ideological platform that carries and inculcates that ethos—that is, the pervasive infrastructure of Jewish nationalism concealed in the guise of declared socialist principles (Sternhell, 1995). Thus the process of Israeli nation-building could be considered a double-edged sword of cultural discourses that seem to be diametrically opposed.

The symbolic devices constructed to sustain that duplicity are varied and diffuse. They embrace public insignia of collective memory such as monuments to the fallen (see, e.g., Almog, 1992), the curriculum taught in government schools (Resnik, 1993), the rulings of the Israeli High Court of Justice (Shamir, 1994), and most important, the omnipresence of the military and its spirit of cultural militarism (Kimmerling, 1985; Ben-Eliezer, 1995; Kimmerling, 1993). These trappings of collective identity constitute the language of the imagined community of Israeli nationals and hence laid the foundation for some of the most prominent myths that furnish it.[7] Even though the cultural impact of many of these myths has been eroded, at times even "shattered," in recent years their presence in the making of "the Israeli" (Katriel, 1991) is still very much apparent, if only for lack of new codes to supersede the old.

No homogeneous picture of cultural hegemony in current Israeli society has been depicted. Nevertheless, some scholars maintain that despite far-reaching differences and exceptions at the political and cultural margins, the common denominator of the Zionist imperative manifested in Israeli "civil religion" still reflects a broadly shared, consensual raison d'etre for a wide range of interlocutors engaging in the same discourse (Liebman and Don-Yehia, 1983).

That discourse is the symbolic site where shared myths form the course of historical events. In terms of its social practice and performative codes, that site was territorially indivisible for many years. Political disagreement over the future of occupied land was kept at bay, leaving the fundamentals of the post–Six Day War "civil religion" unshaken and untested, until the peace accord with the Palestinians.[8] This agreement called into question the validity of practices rather than beliefs, of contexts rather than texts, and of history rather than myth. Not only did the common discourse split, but it was dually and separately located either inside the "green line" (the post–Six Day War border) or outside it. However, until Rabin's death the two discourses still emanated from the same ambivalent mythical source that had maintained and constituted the Zionist ethos since its inception. As will be shown, media representations of the public's response to the assassination signified a critical awareness that the tacitly acceptable, self-contradictory myth could turn into a self-subversive one, and hence a choice about its fate had to be made and implemented.

Clearly, media-reported public reaction was not consciously informed by deliberations about such abstract matters. Despite a media barrage of debates and reflections on the cultural and political ramifications of the assassination, grassroots response seems to have been unaffected by this discourse and formed its own social dynamics for handling the event, since the dramatic circumstances created problems prompted by the exigencies of the moment. Thus, the public was bedeviled by the unprecedented nature of the calamity and the urgency of making sense of it in terms of ad hoc funerary and mourning practices. The first concern, therefore, was how to bury Rabin. The management of that problem reveals the bedrock of fundamental issues of myth and history.

How to Bury a Murdered Prime Minister

Israel had formulated a ceremonial routine for the lying in state and burial of its departed leaders. However, those codes of practice assumed a natural death. No provisions existed for burial after a violent, premature termination of office. The annals of late Israeli presidents and prime ministers—indeed of all Israeli political figures—include death by natural causes only and, in most cases, after retirement. The procedures that follow such deaths are designed to maintain a sense of symbolic and political continuity.[9] The immediate predicament generated by the assassination was how to preserve cultural permanence in the midst of cultural breakdown. More specifically: how to prepare for burial of a body politic composed of the mythical elements of the imagined community it represents, at a time when the unity of that myth is in a shambles.[10] As will be shown, Rabin's public image was a proverbial representation of the spirit of canonized Zionism, and yet the murderer's credo was integral to that very codex. The cultural task of differentiating between the two without dismantling them altogether proved to be problematic—and arduous if not impossible for the mourners.

The solution to that dilemma was in the reediting of Rabin's biography to project a new version of cultural hero. That symbolic creation enlisted only those elements of Rabin's life story that were not commensurate with the assassin's ideological stance. Hence any reminiscence of Jewish nationalism was systematically expurgated from the mythical rebuilding of Rabin's "legacy."[11] The national hero that emerged out of the shattered Zionist ethos thus possessed civil, humanistic, and universal traits rather than culturally specific traits upholding fundamentalist values. Before I describe the process by which that configuration of Rabin's heroism was symbolically encoded, two elements necessary for its understanding must be clarified.

First, there were the events surrounding the temporary disappearance of the body from the public eye. Amid the confusion into which the media were plunged at the moment of the assassination and immediately after, the prime minister's own person temporarily vanished. The grand finale of the peace rally, with both Rabin and Peres joining in the exhilarated chanting of the "Song of Peace," projected the two leaders as part of an indivisible collective body overarching and effacing personal and political differences.[12] The social body is by nature nonbiological and hence could be symbolically immortal (Becker, 1973; Lifton, 1983). It should be noted that the lyrics of the song call for silencing the dead, who cannot be returned to life, and bringing instead a future of peace. This plea to overlook the past and not dwell on the cult of the fallen soldier (Mosse, 1990) was regarded as heretical at the time of the song's first performance (after the Six Day War). In fact, public protest caused the song to be banned for a period from the state-controlled media. That repudiation of death sung by Rabin only a few moments before his own demise contributed a great deal to the inclusion of that song in the canon of his posthumous myth.

Rabin's body was rushed to the hospital without any media monitoring. In fact, the body social as manifested and inscribed in the mass demonstration never reverted to the private one. It was "snatched" to the hospital not to reappear in any physical form. With no transitory passage of dying, Rabin's body skipped the customary funerary biological transformation from the biological to the social. It preempted biological terminality by entering symbolic immortality while still barely alive. It could be argued that this uninterrupted transition from predeath to posthumous social body facilitated the continuity of Rabin's body politic. In a sense, there was no need to dispose of a missing or decomposed biological body by way of a private funeral, hence avoiding the dual burial of the private and social bodies. The duality described by Kantorowicz (1957) — the decomposed corpse and the eternal effigy — was hence also avoided.

A second situation emerging from the assassination and enabling the work of myth-making was the public preoccupation with the status of words. Almost as soon as news of the assassination reached the media, attention was poignantly directed to the role of words in paving the way to the plausibility of the event. Be it politically or culturally motivated, the role of incitement in legitimizing the assassination was hyped by all the media. While socialist Zionism was known to separate words from deeds, discounting the former and emphasizing the latter, the opposite occurred after the assassination — speech and action were deemed one.[13] The public controversy over the relationship between the two precipitated an atmosphere in which members of the public had to be extremely cautious about making any casual utterance, lest it be construed as seditious. Outright accusations were leveled at right-wing leaders for making incendiary remarks before the murder that were responsible for it; and the refusal of Rabin's widow to accept condolences from some public figures, and her charge that they instigated and legitimized the assassination by their words, left a resounding impact on the media. The assassin himself kept citing phrases and slogans from the ideology of the right, which they brandished at their mass demonstrations. Of particular importance in that context was the TV broadcast of a memorial evening organized by some of Israel's most prominent performing artists, on which right-wing leaders were directly implicated in the murder.

The cultural premium placed on the significance of the word rendered mythical any use of speech or writing. Myth is a narrative generated by utterance, and the terms set after the assassination laid the foundation for formulating new myths by way of words.[14] The fusion between narrative and performance, speech and act, is one feature of the mythical state, where historical time is suspended and superseded by "totemic time" — total identification with a core cultural trope.[15] The supposed sacredness of such experience spells its liminal qualities — that is, an atemporal status of between-and-betwixt roles, hierarchies, and differences.[16] This temporary obliteration of diversity and rank turns the enactment of a myth into an apparent state of egalitarianism whence the individual is submerged into an undifferentiated collective entity.[17] This allows for an unreserved commitment to mass participation in the public worship of mythical objects. Such participation, being by nature a public performance, requires the co-presence of fellow worshipers, a presence that must be anchored in designated sites. The sites of the cult of mythologizing Rabin were, not coincidentally, three locations where the dead man's newly constructed biography could be engraved. In effect, three sanctified focal points of mass pilgrimage were selected to generate and sustain the emerging myth.[18] The following text describes how these three sites merge into one metaphorical burial ground situated in the State of Israel rather than the Land of Israel, where the body social interred is that of the ageless sabra, the perennial hero of the Six Day War, rather than a messianic representative of Jewish eternity (*netzah yisrael*).[19]

A myth can function as a social charter, legitimizing and reaffirming key beliefs and values regarding the origins of a people and its place within the universe (Cohen, 1969). Hence an attempt to modify an existing myth ought to address the cosmological issues embedded in it. As indicated at the outset of our discussion, the Zionist myth contains a constant interplay between two contradictory symbolic idioms—the exclusively cultural and the universally human. Myths are known to harbor contradictory constituents, and in that respect the Zionist myth is no exception.[20] However, when myth is challenged by history, as in the case of Rabin's assassination, inherent ambivalence can be revealed, and thus recreating the myth means editing its cultural text. The Zionist mythical text as a social charter for the settlement of Jews in the Land of Israel contains an unequivocal reference to the line of descent from the "legitimate" settlers of that land—that is, the Israelites. Thus the unison of blood and land constitutes the mythical at the very core of the Zionist enterprise. It is that unison that the alternative myth of the mourners was set to dismantle. That was accomplished by transforming the culturally specific descent line of a consanguineous tribal nature into a sense of belonging to the modern global village of civil society and world culture.[21] In this respect the international media, into which Israeli broadcasting readily integrated itself, served as an appropriate site for staging that mutation in the mythical codes.[22]

The sites for globalization of the Zionist myth are three: Rabin's family home, replacing the Judaic lineage kinship system; the Tel Aviv plaza where the murder was committed, substituting for the idea of the Greater Israel; and the grave at Mount Herzl, superseding the ancestral-apocalyptic celestial "New" Jerusalem with the pantheon of nation-builders in earthly Jerusalem.[23] These three sites for the public performance of burial rites drew hundreds of thousands of worshipers in a threefold pilgrimage. Notwithstanding certain variations in the distribution of the crowds attending the three respective sites, the overall circuit of visits encompassed a large portion of the population regardless of age, ethnic origin, gender, or faith. The family home and the plaza were frequented mainly by youngsters, however, a fact that will be shown to be of paramount significance.

The Symbolic Burial Ground

The cultural work of rewriting Rabin's biography commenced almost at the moment of the murder. It took the media, in particular the TV authorities, only a couple of hours after the initial shock to produce and broadcast extensive archive footage of Rabin's political career, of which two epochs were distinctly highlighted: the War of Independence and the current era of peacemaking. The interrelatedness was particularly evident in the presentation of the young Rabin as the complementary side of his older counterpart, hence closing a life cycle of war and peace. That was indeed the foundation for the emergence of Rabin's image as a sacrificial son-cum-patriarch, whose nation-building enterprise is encapsulated within the entire course of his life (the association with the sacrificial binding of the ancestor Yitzhak is self-evident). The mixture of the youthful commander and the elderly statesman was a theme running through the media presentation of Rabin's biography. It is important to note that Rabin's role as chief of staff during the Six Day War in 1967 was played down. Before Rabin's death, several efforts were made to undermine his contribution to the two wars. Rancor related to his alleged nervous breakdown during the 1967 war was regarded as legitimate, carried some weight in public opinion, and was exploited by the right wing in the 1992 election campaign. The other attempt, which was related to the War of Independence, did not seem to capture the media gaze and caused few ripples.[24] The explanation for this difference might rest with the cultural representation projected by the two images. Rabin of the War of Independence became an icon for all time—the mythical sabra who embodied the "silver platter" (a metaphor used by poet Natan Alterman that has become one of Israel's cultural idioms in the symbolic language of commemorating the fallen) upon which the Jewish state was given to the nation. By the Six Day War, however, Rabin had become a replaceable hero whose attributes were embedded in the military machine of which he was a part. Thus the two pioneering images—sabra and peacemaker—converged into a character of unique features and indispensable presence in the life of the nation. His role in the Israeli imagined community was that of an eternally youthful forefather; thus Rabin's demise could be likened to a father's abandonment of his children.

Indeed, the key metaphor for the whole gamut of mourning practices was the father-child relationship. Expressions such as "we have lost our father," "we are now orphans," "why have you gone from us father," etc., were rife. That motif set the scene for the media's replacement of ancestral lineage with sabra-lineal descent. That cultural redesigning was achieved by interlocking two protagonists: the mourning youth and the mourning family. Radio and TV swiftly moved from one site to another to create, in effect, three burial grounds where the young were omnipresent. The media focused insistently on the practices and utterances of young attendants. Notwithstanding the visible presence of other generations, interviewers and cameras sought and caught the behavior of youngsters, including toddlers and school children, adolescents, and persons in their early twenties. Older mourners were given scant screen space unless in the company of the young.

To understand what that youthful configuration means, it is necessary to analyze the symbolic language of mourning that was heard and seen in the media. The vocabulary of that language consisted of a few major cues that together constituted a grammar of public mourning hitherto unknown in Israel. Even though no new symbol was invented for the occasion, the new context endowed familiar codes with different meanings arranged to form an internally coherent and novel cultural pattern.

1. *Rabin's family*. The chief protagonists in the emerging cult of the new lineage were members of Rabin's family, particularly the young. Whereas the widow was already a well-known public figure, the children and grandchildren had remained relatively anonymous until the assassination. Media discovery of the second and third generations was sparked by the granddaughter's eulogy at the funeral. This was presented as the heart-rending emotional peak of the funeral, overshadowing all the tributes paid by the illustrious galaxy of world leaders attending the burial. Interestingly, runner-up status for the most moving eulogy went to King Hussein's emotive speech, in which he employed terms of putative kinship, calling the widow "my sister" and Rabin "a brother." In that ranking of familiarization, Bill Clinton's phrase "Shalom, Haver" (Good-bye, friend) also scored high and has become a buzzword emblazoned in graffiti and on bumper stickers and posters. Rabin has thus become not just the founding father of a lineage,

but also a metaphorical as well as real-life brother (his sister was extensively interviewed in the media), husband (the widow revealed details of their intimate joint life), flesh-and-blood father (both his children starred in numerous programs), and loving, caring, and warm grandfather (the two grandchildren made a few TV appearances on which they refused to discuss the political implications of the assassination and concentrated on remembering happy family moments in the company of their late grandfather).

All this is indicative of a cultural choice—preference for the option of a down-to-earth sense of loss with which mourners could identify personally, rather than a historically formidable, mythically elevated mode of mourning. This by no means contradicts the cultural production of Rabin as the archetype of the sabra. Conversely, these are two poles of the same symbol enforcing and reinforcing each other (Katriel, 1986). This dual meaning grounds the Israeli myth in the routinely familiar, the popular, and the commonsensical. It strengthens the tenuous link between the allegedly tarnished and alienating Zionist ethos in the everyday life of Israelis. Moreover, since that link was usurped by the settlement movement in the occupied territories, it enabled Israelis of a different ideological persuasion to set new terms for that connection. Such terms combined the mythical and the familiar so that their plausibility was not contingent upon apocalyptic visions and did not represent a nihilistic mood. The following four key metaphors attest to that contention.

2. *Songs.* The peace and death rally preceding the assassination ended with a sing-along of the "Song of Peace" with Rabin seen to be singing it. During the gathering, several artists performed on stage and expressed sympathy to the cause. The most notable of these was Aviv Geffen—an enormously popular, albeit controversial, rock star whose outrageous lyrics often provoked public outcry, from the prime minister's quarters as well. At the rally, Geffen sang a song of farewell to a dead friend, "To Cry for You." One immediate response to the assassination was the adoption of both songs as commemorative hymns. Other well-known songs were selectively added to the litany of mourning that comprised an almost canonized body of verse. All of the songs were elegiac odes intertextually connected by virtue of their cultural status as established lyrics expressing the contact between peace, death, and locality. (They were issued on a CD as part of the postassassination memorabilia.) The effect of that corpus was further dramatized by the revelation that the blood-drenched script of the "Song of Peace" was found in Rabin's pocket. The relevance of the local rather than the transcendental applies to the other three key metaphors.

3. *Flowers.* The culture of flowers is highly germane to understanding the Zionist ethos.[25] Bridled nature is one of the codes of the capacity and right of Zionism to claim the land and settle it, while at the same time protecting it from that very conquest.[26] Celebrations of flowers are conducted at special festivals where garlands crown children's heads. Protection of wild flowers is regarded as a highly important educational teaching, and the laying of wreaths is a ceremonial component of state funerals and commemorative events. Flowers, however, also carry the more general values of aesthetic beauty and the taming of nature. This combination of the local and the global may account for the proliferation of flower-laying as one of the predominant mourning rituals. Flowers are also an emblem of the hippie culture of rebellious adolescents. This symbolic quality encompassing global culture, local knowledge, and age-related tropes is also embedded in the practice of lighting candles.

4. *Candles.* It would be difficult to overstate the cultural significance of candle-lighting in Jewish tradition (Sered, 1991). From Sabbath candles to candles in saints' tombs, from commemoration candles to candles on the Menorah (a symbol of the ancient temple that appears at the center of the emblem of the state of Israel), candles are one of the most prominent artifacts of grand religion as well as domestic tradition. To confound that symbolic picture, the role of candles in pop-rock gatherings must be considered yet another source of cultural inspiration. The fact is that the three sites of pilgrimage became places of massive candle-lighting. Evidently the visibility and distinctiveness of this practice made for its media salience, but among equally dazzling images of flowers, youth, and graffiti, candles took the limelight. The interpretation of the motif of light within the context of youth culture gains further ground when juxtaposed with another youth-related practice—the painting of graffiti.

5. *Graffiti.* The fusion of fire and words has been a long-standing ceremonial code among Israeli youth movements (Katriel, 1991). Flaming scripts are used to display slogans of devotion to a variety of Zionist credos. Rabin's mourners separated the two and reserved the scripts for graffiti. Political protest graffiti sporadically appear on Israeli city walls, but graffiti writing has never gained the fierce and widespread momentum it claims in the modern urban world. In that respect, the use of graffiti to express views and feelings in the wake of the assassination can be regarded as a cultural novelty.

The center of graffiti writing was the plaza where the assassination took place. The imposing Tel Aviv Municipality building overlooking the plaza lent its enormous walls to the artists and displayed their work uncensored. It should be noted that a couple of months after the assassination a member of the city council (of leftist views) demanded in the name of aesthetics that the building walls be cleaned up. That demand met with broad opposition, which prevented the operation from taking place. The surge of graffiti writing was confined to the area of the plaza and the time of public mourning. With the exception of a few, mainly anti-Rabin, outbursts of wall spraying, the general level of graffiti reverted to its preassassination days.

It remains to be seen whether the indelible graffiti, together with the other cultural items, will enter the Israeli collective memory as reproducible national myths. However, the unique ad hoc pattern of mourning formed after the assassination calls for an explanation in its own right. It is claimed that whatever the long-term repercussions may be, the emergence of that bereavement culture was an experiment in rewriting the Zionist myth through the impact of the historical praxis meted out by the murder. The above observation reveals a code of practice that is neither haphazard nor planned. It possesses internal consistency and structural validity that could shed light on some of the interstices and scaffolding of the Israeli imagined community. The purpose of the following is to turn our gaze to these findings.

Conclusions

The shock waves caused by Rabin's death prompted a symbolic revisiting of some of the recesses of the Zionist code. Those who participated in the emerging cult of the dead unwittingly embarked upon an exploratory venture of reconstructing their own identity. That was done, or rather performed, by enacting a new but plausible set of practices that challenged the contours and content of the preassassination imagined community of Israeli nationalism. Obviously, the imagery of national identity was at stake long before the assassination. Fervent political debates and street riots demonstrated the profound divisions within the discourses defining the Jewish nation-state. However, the radical event of Rabin's death created a one-time opportunity to deal with national substance in the guise of apparently overarching national consensus. This unique opportunity cultivated the breeding ground for the performative statements made over the course of the public mourning.

Clearly there was an inadvertent act of cultural reversal, a resorting to dust-covered images of the old and trite trope of the sabra.[27] It is also clear that such reversal was a revival of values and themes long discounted and discredited in Israeli society but for the settlers' movement of Gush Emunim. The retrieval of the sabra symbol in the image of Rabin reclaimed the Zionist ethos from the apocalyptic messianic vision of the religious right.

This re-usurpation of the national credo entailed a cultural relocation of Zionism from the transcendental realm of Jewish ultimate nationalism, whose aspiration is the indivisible unity of land, people, and the holy scripture, to grounded bounds of state, citizenship, and manmade law. It was a collapse of an eternal celestial kingdom into the confines of time and place.[28] Rabin's image as the immortal youthful forefather of the new Israel, free of the burden of Jewish legacy and rooted in modern notions of the nation-state, reversed the fortunes of the fate of Zionism by providing both old and new options. These rediscovered opportunities were symbolically distilled in the fictive formation of the new lineage, whose double descent line gave its members a sense of belonging to both poles of the Zionist ethos—the culturally specific and the humanly universal.

The marriage between youth and adolescence on the one hand, and the media production of the youthful hero and his teenage descendants on the other, became a testing ground for restoration of a formative era in which culture is deemed to be molded and options are not yet closed. This stage of renewed liminality renders culture itself adolescent and unformed. The pilgrimage of the masses, particularly of the young, to the three sites of Rabin's cultural burial was a statement of symbolic choice among three Zionist paths: Jewish absolutism, local belonging, and globalization. In fact, it was a choice to accept three respective modes of temporality: mythical-eternal, modern progressive, and fragmentary postmodern. Furthermore, that choice embodied three alternative ideas of imagined communities: the messianic kingdom of heaven, the nation-state, and the global village.

It is evident that the latter two took precedence over the first. However it is equally clear that the performance at the mourning sites for the fallen hero reflected confusion and turmoil—a state not unfamiliar to adolescents. Their sense of cultural loss of direction was well expressed in some of the graffiti. Two examples will suffice: "Rabin, the bullets that hit you hit all of us," and the ultimate reprobation: "Yigal Amir [the assassin]—why have you done this to us?" In the midst of the shambles of the social body, another expression called for its reconstitution through an apotheosis of the dead leader, "Now there is a God in heaven." This new version of the first option of mythical thinking dislodged Judaism from the core of the Zionist ethos and replaced it with a metonymic representation—an element consistent with the internal language of Zionism. The attempt to deify Rabin therefore attests to the desire to recapture Zionism as an integral ethos.

Against this backdrop of forging an alternative Zionism, the deep structure of the graffiti is thrown into relief. The symbolic burial ground of Rabin is indeed a site for revisiting and contesting the principles of the current Israeli body social. The discourse between social bodies in Israeli culture took a new turn here, when the decomposed messianic organ was temporarily replaced by a contemporary transplant, whose totemic qualities are yet to be established.

Notes

1. After the Six Day War, a flood of victory books and albums inundated the market, and Rabin became a hero of popular culture, both locally and internationally.

2. The concept of the body social alludes to the symbolic position of the human body in cultural discourse as well as to metaphorical configurations of society in corporeal terms. For some recent recapitulation and discussion of the vast literature on the concept, see Shilling, 1993; Synnott, 1995.

3. The cult of civil religion in Israeli culture involves worship of and in allocated sites. See, for example, Liebman and Don-Yehia, 1983; Handelman and Katz, 1990; Azaryahu, 1995.

4. The intricate interrelationship between myth and history has been widely discussed both in general anthropological terms (e.g., Kapferer, 1988; Friedman, 1992) and with special regard to the Zionist ethos (e.g., Ben-Yehuda, 1995; Zerubavel, 1995; Gurevitch and Aran, 1994a).

5. This account is inspired by Handelman's treatment of public events (Handelman, 1990) and Dayan and Katz's approach to media events (1992).

6. Illuminating indicators of the interplay between the two constituents could be found in the choice of cultural discourse in children's games, educational rhetoric, and military rites (Katriel, 1991).

7. The concept "imagined community" was coined by Anderson (1983) to indicate the formation of national solidarity based on shared cultural identity.

8. On Israeli antioccupation protest movements, see Sasson-Levy, 1995.

9. The double burial of medieval kings was a practice designed to sustain continuity despite the death of a monarch. See the description by Kantorowicz (1957).

10. In this respect, Rabin's murder seems to be different from Kennedy's because the latter did not impinge on the composition of the body social.

11. On the ultranationalist underpinnings of Gush Emunim, see, for example, Avruch, 1979; Aronoff, 1984; Weisbrod, 1982.

12. The fierce hostility between the two leaders was poignantly expressed in Rabin's autobiography, *The Rabin Memoirs* (Berkeley: University of California Press, 1996).

13. The indivisible fusion of speech and action goes back to some of the fundamental idioms of Zionism. Katriel (1986) argues that "talking straight" in the "Dugri" culture was one of the principles of the prestate epoch.

14. Controversial though it may be, the concept of myth is rooted in the speech act.

15. Totemic time is an achronological state of sacredness governed by myth and cyclical rhythms. For an analysis of Israeli totemic time, see Paine, 1983.

16. Anthropological discourse employs the term "liminality" to indicate that social state. See Turner, 1969, for a discussion of the concept as part of rites of passage.

17. The role of commemoration in the formation of constitutive myths is discussed by Schwartz (1982) and Connerton (1989).

18. Mass pilgrimage is described as a journey toward the accomplishment of a collective myth. See, for example, Turner and Turner, 1978; Myerhoff, 1974.

19. A phrase taken from I Samuel 15: 29, "The eternal [glory] of Israel will not fail," meaning there is still hope for Israel.

20. For different approaches to the study of myth underlined by the principle of binary oppositions, see Barthes, 1972; Levi-Strauss, 1981; Ricoeur, 1991.

21. Research on the emergence of "civil society in the midst of Israeli military culture" is scant (see, for example, Keren, 1995).

22. On Israeli TV treatment of common collective narrative, see Liebes, 1992.

23. The Mount Herzl national cemetery in Jerusalem is the burial ground for Israeli nation-builders. All former heads of state are buried there, with the exception of Ben-Gurion, who was interred at his Negev kibbutz.

24. See, for example, U. Milstein, *Rabin's File: How the Myth Was Inflated* (Tel Aviv, 1995) [Hebrew].

25. On the symbolic significance of flowers, see Goody, 1994.

26. For a review of the cultural place of nature in the construction of Israeli national identity, see Arieli, 1994.

27. For a sociohistorical discussion of the changing image of the sabra from cultural hero to an object of pity and ridicule, see Roniger and Feige, 1992.

28. On the sacredness of "the place" in Judaism in relation to the secularity of "a place," see Gurevitch and Aran, 1994b.

References

Almog, O. (1992). "Monuments for the Fallen Soldiers in Israel: A Semiotic Analysis." *Megamot,* no. 34, pp. 179–210 [Hebrew].

Anderson, B. (1983). *Imagined Communities.* London: Verso.

Arieli, D. (1994). "Cultural Construction of Nature: The Case of the Society for the Protection of Nature." M.A. dissertation, Tel Aviv University [Hebrew].

Aronoff, M. S. (1984). "Gush Emunim: The Institutionalization of a Charismatic, Messianic Religious Political Revitalization Movement in Israel." In *Religion and Politics, Political Anthropology,* vol. 3. New Brunswick. N.J.: Transaction Books.

Avruch, K. A. (1979). "Gush Emunim: Politics, Religion and Ideology in Israel." *Middle East Review*, no. 11, pp. 26–31.

Azaryahu, M. (1995). *State Cults*. Beersheba: Ben-Gurion University of the Negev Press [Hebrew].

Barthes, R. (1972). *Mythologies*. New York: Hill and Wang.

Becker, E. (1973). *The Denial of Death*. New York: Free Press.

Ben-Eliezer, U. (1995). "A Nation-in-Arms: State, Nation and Militarism in Israel's First Years." *Comparative Studies in Society and History*, no. 37, pp. 264–85.

Ben-Yehuda, N. (1995). *The Massada Myth: Collective Memory and Mythmaking Israel*. Madison: University of Wisconsin Press.

Cohen, P. (1969). "Theories of Myth." *Man*, no. 4, pp. 337–51.

Connerton, P. (1989). *How Societies Remember*. Cambridge: Cambridge University Press.

Dayan, Daniel, and Elihu Katz (1992). *Media Event*. Cambridge, Mass: Harvard University Press.

Friedman, J. (1992). "Myth, History and Political Identity." *Cultural Anthropology* 7, pp. 194–210.

Gertz, N. (1995). *Captive of a Dream: National Myths in Israeli Culture*. Tel Aviv: Am-Oved [Hebrew].

Goody, J. (1994). *The Culture of Flowers*. Cambridge: Cambridge University Press.

Gurevitch, Z., and G. Aran (1994a). "The Land of Israel: Myth and Phenomenon." In *Reshaping the Past: Jewish History and the Historians, Studies in Contemporary Jewry X*. Jerusalem: Avraham Harman Institute of Contemporary Jewry, pp. 195–210.

———— (1994b). "Never in Place: Eliade and Judaic Sacred Space." *Arch. de Sc. Soc. des Rel.*, no. 87, pp. 135–52.

Handelman, D. (1990). *Models and Mirrors: Towards an Anthropology of Public Events*. Cambridge: Cambridge University Press.

Handelman, D., and E. Katz (1990). "State Ceremonies of Israel: Remembrance Day and Independence Day." In D. Handelman, *Models and Mirrors*. Cambridge: Cambridge University Press.

Kantorowicz, E. H. (1957). *The King's Two Bodies*. Princeton, N.J.: Princeton University Press.

Kapferer, B. (1988). *Legends of People, Myths of State*. Washington, D.C.: Smithsonian Institution Press.

Katriel, T. (1986). *Talking Straight: Dugri Speech in Israeli Sabra Culture*. Cambridge: Cambridge University Press.

———— (1991). *Communal Webs*. New York: State University of New York Press.

Keren, M. (1995). *Professionals Against Populism: The Peres Government and Democracy*. Albany: State University of New York Press.

Kimmerling, B. (1985). *The Interrupted System: Israeli Civilians in War and Routine Times*. New Brunswick, N.J.: Transaction Books.

———— (1993). "Patterns of Militarism in Israel." *Archives Européen de Sociologie*, no. 34, pp. 196–223.

Levi-Strauss, C. (1981). *The Naked Man: Introduction to the Science of Mythology*. London: Jonathan Cape.

Liebes, T. (1992). "Decoding Television News: The Political Discourse of Israeli Hawks and Doves." *Theory and Society*, no. 21, pp. 357–81.

Liebman, C. S., and E. Don-Yehia (1983). *Civil Religion in Israel: Traditional Judaism and Political Culture in the Jewish State*. Berkeley: University of California Press.

Lifton, R. (1983). *The Broken Connection*. New York: Basic Books.

Mosse, G. L. (1990). *Fallen Soldiers: Reshaping the Memory of the World Wars*. Oxford: Oxford University Press.

Myerhoff, B. (1974). *Peyote Hunt: The Sacred Journey of the Hulchol Indians*. Ithaca, N.Y.: Cornell University Press.

Paine, R. (1983). "Israel and Totemic Time." *RAIN 59*, pp. 19–22.

Resnik, J. (1993). "State National Ideology in Israel: National Images in the Educational System." M.A. dissertation, Tel Aviv University [Hebrew].

Ricoeur, P. (1991) [1986]. *From Text to Action: Essays in Hermeneutics II*. Evanston, Ill.: Northwestern University Press.

Roniger, L., and M. Feige. (1992). "From Pioneer to Freier: The Changing Models of Generalized Exchange in Israel." *Archives of European Sociology* 33: 280–307.

Sasson-Levy, O. (1995). *Radical Rhetoric, Conformist Practices: Theory and Praxis in an Israeli Protest Movement*. Jerusalem: Shaine Working Papers, no. 1 [Hebrew].

Schwartz, B. (1982). "The Social Context of Commemoration: A Study in Collective Memory." *Social Forces*, no. 61, pp. 374–402.

Sered, S. S. (1991). "Gender, Immanence and Transcendence: The Candle-Lighting Repertoire of Middle-Eastern Jews." *Metaphor and Symbolic Activity*, no. 6, pp. 293–304.

Shamir, R. (1994). "The Politics of Reasonableness." *Theory and Criticism*, no. 5, pp. 7–24 [Hebrew].

Shilling, C. (1993). *The Body and Social Theory*. London: Sage.

Sternhell, Z. (1995). *Nation-Building or a New Society?* Tel Aviv: Am-Oved [Hebrew].

Synnott, A. (1995). *The Body Social: Symbolism, Self and Society*. London: Routledge.

Turner, V. (1969). *The Ritual Process: Structure and Anti-Structure*. Chicago: Aldine.

Turner, V., and E. Turner (1978). *Image and Pilgrimage in Christian Culture*. New York: Columbia University Press.

Weisbrod, L. (1982). "Gush Emunim Ideology: From Religious Doctrine to Political Action." *Middle Eastern Studies*, no. 18, pp. 265–75.

Weiss, M. (1999). "War Bodies, Hedonist Bodies: The Dialectics of the Collective and the Individual in Israel." *American Ethnologist* 24 (4): 1–20.

Zerubavel, Y. (1995). *Recovered Roots: Collective Memory and the Making of Israeli National Tradition*. Chicago: University of Chicago Press.

CHAPTER 10

The Cultural and Social Construction of Mourning Patterns

ELIEZER WITZTUM AND

RUTH MALKINSON

One primary feature of Israeli society over the years is the practice of continuous mourning for those killed in its wars and terrorist attacks. Thus the nation became immersed in deep mourning on learning of the uncomprehended murder of Prime Minister Yitzhak Rabin. The phenomenon of national mourning was startling in its scope, intensity, and the dramatic participation of the "candle children" (youth who populated the mourning sites day and night holding lit candles)—at least as reflected in the lens of the massive media coverage of the event. The most intense stage of mourning was characterized by confusion and disorientation, a feeling on the part of many that reality had collapsed. This feeling was summed up by the director-general of the Office of the Prime Minister, Shimon Sheves, who stated, "I lost a country."

After the initial shock and bewilderment came attempts to understand what had happened. The "experts," who themselves were in a state of disorientation, placed the assassination into various contexts and provided numerous psychological, sociological, and historical explanations. The first and almost trivial explanation was a comparison with the assassination of John F. Kennedy, which appeared in the first week after the assassination. A leading sociologist, Prof. B. Shamir, analyzed Rabin's demise more parochially: "I hate to ruin the public feeling that has enveloped Israel since the killing of the prime minister, [but] the phenomenon we are witnessing is not particularly original. . . . The desire to visit the grave even at night, the deep sense of mourning, public crying [are all] rooted in a sense of loss of the father described in psychoanalytical theories, but this feeling is repeated." And although prime ministers Rabin and Begin may have symbolized different things in their lives, "for the public, they also symbolized something collective, and hence the desire to express solidarity."[1]

One psychologist discerned other consequences of the assassination in addition to the national mourning: "The killing shattered the basic relationship values between the individual and society and the individual and the other."[2] Another psychologist used the explanation of shock in a cognitive model: "This was a reaction of surprise; no one expected the murder of the prime minister. When an event or phenomenon is difficult for an individual to understand, his sense of shock or agitation becomes translated into a desire to be together, in the hope that the closeness of the group will help assuage this distress." According to that opinion, this solidarity also stems from a motif in Greek tragedy—"a man cut down in his prime"—while on the societal level "the assassination led to mobilization of the silent majority that ordinarily does not express its opinion." He also stressed the element of uncertainty and the fact that "there was a fundamental threat here to the orderly nature of the world," the immediate reaction to which was to close ranks: "It's a classic situation: In the absence of a leader, people want to stay close to each other. This phenomenon encompasses all population strata."[3]

Another explanation for this drawing together, the feeling of togetherness, was offered by a prominent anthropologist. In a TV interview, he said that following the assassination of the prime minister "a community of equals was created—*communitas*. In a community of equals, all barriers fall, all are equal—poor, rich, different ethnic origin, young, old. A situation like this has the potential for change, and it is not surprising that many young people are here [in the plaza where Rabin was killed]."[4]

Experts agreed that the reaction of youth was the most interesting. A communications expert emphasized the functioning of the media during times of crisis and described what was common to the assassinations of Kennedy and Rabin, noting the similarity in the symbolism of the blood, which testified to murder as early as the book of Genesis. Just as Jacob asks that Joseph's coat of many colors be brought to him as evidence of his death, so too "the blood-stained 'Song of Peace' found in Rabin's jacket (pocket) [became] a symbol, just as in the United States, the blood-stained clothing worn by Jacqueline Kennedy until her arrival in Washington the following day symbolized the assassination."[5]

Historians, too, tried to understand what had happened and drew comparisons with similar historical events. One historian referred to the mass mourning as "a secular cult in memory of a democratic leader." According to him the "symptoms" included aspects of a secular martyrology: memorial candles, enlarged pictures of the leader, hallowed sites, and graffiti. In addition to these external symptoms, he looked at the content: the figure of Rabin as "a man not free of criticism and opposition in his life . . . ceases to be what he was in reality and is transformed into an abstraction of himself."[6]

The killing of a leader, a native-born Israeli, a general and battle-tried soldier who beat his sword into a plowshare on behalf of an era of peace, a man whose biography is interwoven with the history of the country, led to Rabin's transformation into a symbol after his death, the figure of the sabra, the hero from the 1948 war of independence.

It is remarkable that these analysts used models and examples drawn from their particular fields of expertise; these were not cold academic exercises, detached in time and place, but in themselves attempts to cope with the shock of the assassination. The explanations of experts played an important role during the intense stage of mourning, providing a new cognitive construction of shattered assumptions and logical explanations to help understand the mourners' behavior, cope with the uncertainty, and deal with difficult and overwhelming feelings (Janoff-Bulman, 1989).

In this chapter we explain the theoretical background relating to coping with bereavement following a traumatic loss; we then describe the chain of events after Rabin's death and the mourning patterns that evolved at both the individual and the sociocultural levels and the interplay between the two. We apply concepts taken from the study of individuals during mourning and from the social-historical processes of constructing collective patterns of mourning, the culture of bereavement, and commemoration and memory in Israeli society.

Bereavement After a Traumatic Loss

To analyze the sequence of reactions that followed the death of Rabin, we turn to literature that deals with mourning and trauma to illuminate the cultural construction of national mourning in the initial phases after the assassination. We compare an individual's response to death and the process of personal mourning that follows with the response of Israeli society after the assassination. The more traumatic the circumstances of a death, the more intense the bereaved person's experience is known to be, and the more likely that he or she will have difficulties in the future, especially in coming to terms with the loss. The stages of bereavement can be regarded as time-related: immediately after the loss emotions are very intense: while their intensity decreases over time, awareness of the finality of the loss can increase in parallel (Malkinson and Witztum, 2000).

THE STAGES OF GRIEF

Although the grieving process is universal and stereotypical reactions have been identified, it is recognized as an idiosyncratic experience affected among other variables by its sociocultural context. The most observable components of the process include the following:

1. Shock and disbelief that death has occurred.

2. Denial of the death and of the pain and grief that follows its acknowledgment.

3. Disorientation (changes in eating and sleeping habits, social withdrawal).

4. Despair and feelings of anger and guilt over the death event.

5. Reorganization of the relationship with the deceased: from a reality-based relationship to one based on memories; also reorganization of one's own life to exclude the deceased.

6. Learning new behavioral patterns adapted to life with the pain and grief associated with absence of the person who died (Bowlby, 1980; Parkes, 1972).

It is our intention to use the model as a parallel process between individual bereavement and that of society as a framework within which we can understand national trauma and the social and cultural construction of bereavement and also examine the similarities and differences between the two processes (Malkinson and Witztum, 2000).

The Weeping Nation

The end of the first shock wave after the shiva (the seven ritual days of mourning) was marked by a mass rally at the site of the assassination in Kings of Israel Plaza and renaming it for Rabin. Thereafter people attempted to overcome their fears and uncertainties by trying to make order out of the events, trying to "understand" them through all sorts of models.

Rabin was becoming increasingly idealized, together with and as a reaction to a process of political soul-searching, including accusations and counter-accusations.

One week after the assassination, the following comment appeared in a newspaper: "The assassin's bullets that pierced the body of Yitzhak Rabin in the shadows of the stairway of the Tel Aviv municipality [building] transformed him from an important political leader into the hero of a major drama, a mythological figure, and launched him at the very moment of his departure from the world into the eternal heaven of legend" (Zertal, 1995). The elements of myth were always there: the perfect match between Rabin's personal biography and the history of Israel over the previous 70 years, his sabra qualities, his roles as soldier in the 1948 War and heroic chief of staff in the Six Day War.

But another trend also appeared in the media: political self-criticism and accusations that a political subculture rather than some madman was to blame for the assassination. Words in this vein filled the newspapers and electronic media, and the soul-searching continued. A national commission of inquiry was set up to continue the search for those guilty politically and operationally.

Two weeks after the assassination, the settling of political accounts became louder and finger-pointing became more direct. Right-wing groups accused of incitement defended themselves with statements such as "words are not what murdered [Rabin]"; and "Rabin was killed not because he insulted someone, but because he tried to redivide the Land of Israel" (Segev, 1995a). In the context of accusations and counteraccusations, even bizarre conspiracy theories emerged.

After the struggle over idealization, the process of commemoration began, with public debate over the social and cultural construction of the memory of Rabin and how to absorb it into the collective memory of Israeli society.

The 30 days after (Shloshim) the assassination were characterized by a kind of searching for the appropriate style of mourning. Newspaper articles pointed to the danger of banalization and cliches. In contrast to the lofty rhetoric of the media, Rabin's daughter in a weekly news magazine spoke simply about her father and described him as "a loving father with a movie camera," illuminating a hidden aspect of the prime minister. It was impossible not to be moved by the old home movie filmed by Rabin during a traditional family picnic.

There were dilemmas and debates by the media over the appropriate tone and manner to express grief on a national level. During this period, macabre jokes also began to circulate about the slaying. These were not generally directed against Rabin; they were about the assassination and those deemed guilty of the failure, such as the Security Services; the shape of the tombstone and what was to be written on it; or the reception given to Rabin in the afterlife. Some jokes ridiculed the overreaction of the police and Security Services after the assassination, when several people were arrested for making banal or vulgar remarks. Toward the end of the first month and immediately afterward, commemorative albums, books, video films, CDs, and TV programs began to appear, and roads, buildings, and other sites were renamed after Yitzhak Rabin. Some changed their names, such as a medical center and a famous high school. Although renaming Kings of Israel Plaza for Rabin was accepted and within the consensus, the wave of name-changing right after his death left people uncomfortable, and very soon the name-changing too became a subject of barbs and satire. The many hasty, and often tasteless, efforts at commemoration provoked public debate and caustic pieces in the newspapers about the nature of the mourning process. The growing controversy also led to a consideration of what public roles "national widows" are expected to fulfill.

There are different patterns of national widowhood. Jacqueline Kennedy did what America expected of her, and Americans revered her until she married Aristotle Onassis, when they spurned her as if she had betrayed the homeland. Coretta Scott King, the widow of Martin Luther King Jr., to this day continues the work of her husband. Some widows remove themselves from the limelight and rebuild their lives far from the media. In contrast, Rabin's widow was criticized "for her request for an office, secretary, and a car for at least as long as the burden continues: Her tragedy, of course, calls for a large degree of consideration. Thus she can also be forgiven for mistakes she made in the first days of mourning." (Segev, 1995b).

The public debate focused on the nature of a memorial worthy of Rabin and the role of his widow in this context. To avoid the controversy and the court battles, legal scholars proposed that an official institution be established through special legislation and named "Yitzhak Rabin Memorial." This proposition was finally approved formally by the government in 1996.

Three months after the assassination, memorial activities became intense, with a lavish production of albums, books, cassettes, and CDs. The culmination was the dedication of the Rabin Trauma Center, an impressive ceremony attended by King Hussein of Jordan, at the hospital where Rabin had passed away. The conflicting feelings about this commemorative event were expressed by a well-known journalist:

> You had to rub your eyes to believe the sight, as if it were a scene from one of Potter's TV plays: a State cocktail party in the trauma kingdom of the emergency room: petit-fours, marzipan, chefs in white hats, kings and czarinas and gourmets, all in exactly the same place that Rabin had been carried, shot and bleeding, and where his soul departed this earth. Here Rabin's car halted in the wail of sirens, related the doctor from a stage covered with flowers, and a choir of nurses from the emergency room got up and sang "A Song of Comradeship" [in memory of those who fell in war], whether in honor of the Trauma System named for Rabin or our own trauma. (Rosenbloom, 1996)

It can be noticed that the dual figures of Rabin portrayed in death cast great complexity on the process of memorialization. The late Rabin is memorialized differently from the prosaic, live Rabin: "just as the giant portraits of him drawn and photographed that accompany this huge enterprise of memorial rituals differ from the twitchy and bashful face that we so knew and liked" (ibid.).

For the purpose of analyzing the social and cultural construction of public mourning following the death of Rabin we will apply a few concepts drawn from research and observations that have emerged from the study of bereavement and trauma.

ACUTE INDIVIDUAL AND NATIONAL GRIEF

The symptoms of grief were most acute during the period of mourning immediately after the assassination. The sequence of societal reactions paralleled the first stages of the personal process of mourning. Society's initial intense reactions to Rabin's assassination (shock and agitation; attempts to cope; idealization and devaluation; accusations and counter-accusations) paralleled the first three stages of individual mourning, including denial and disorientation. Thus the similarities between the grief of the individual and that of the public suggest that wide segments of the population experienced the death of Rabin as a personal loss or trauma. Reactions of crying, confusion, and dysphoria were felt by Rabin's immediate circle of friends and family as well as by broad segments of the population.

There were even extreme examples of individuals who personally mourned by performing the ritual act of shiva (i.e. the seven days of mourning prescribed by Jewish law when an immediate family member dies). Empirical support comes from a survey about people's feelings of distress after the assassination (Kushnir and Malkinson, 1996). This survey sought to evaluate the impact of a traumatic national event on working people, their emotional and behavioral reactions at and outside their place of work. People reported dramatic emotional responses that negatively affected their mood, the mood of the children, and their concention at work.[7] Their bad mood reportedly continued for an average of 6.8 days. The respondents' behavioral reactions included visiting the plaza where Rabin was shot (41.6 percent), standing outside Rabin's home (12.1 percent), and visiting his grave (12.1 percent). Two-thirds watched the funeral ceremony on TV at home, not at work.

Some people may have responded so intensely because they were reminded of their own personal and family traumas of loss. Crying, confusion, and dysphoria were reported not only by Rabin's family and close friends but also by many individuals from different social strata. Visiting the place of assassination, standing outside Rabin's residence passing the coffin, and later visiting the grave are characteristic of a community in shock. A society that finds it hard to fully absorb what happened feels the need to gather near the place of the occurrence, in an effort to comprehend the tragic event.

LINKING AND SYMBOLIC OBJECTS IN INDIVIDUAL AND COLLECTIVE MOURNING

A significant parallel between individual and collective mourning relates to the creation of symbolic and ritualized links for constructing a process of separation from the person who died. One analysis of the behavior of mourners focuses on the role of "linking objects." This phrase was first coined by V. D. Volkan, a psychoanalyst and pioneer in the field of mourning (1972; 1983). According to Volkan, a linking object provides a continuing (imagined) relationship with the deceased. Linking objects may be real (a watch, a key, clothing) or symbolic (a melody or a song). Because a linking object belonged to or has some connection with the person who died, it becomes precious to the mourner. This concept sheds light on the significance of the rituals that were prominent during the mourning for Rabin.

Volkan suggested a model for explaining the relationship between the individual and the group mourning process (Volkan, 1988). On the group level, derivatives of linking objects are used in dramatic ways as focal points for public mourning. In collective mourning following the death of Rabin, people linked themselves to Rabin through specific actions, such as lighting memorial candles, writing poems, dedicating personal objects, and passing the coffin. The coffin was given a central role and transformed into a linking object that psychologically connected the people mourning his death with the figure who was lost.

The funeral cortege to Jerusalem became a linking object by the fact that Rabin had fought in the battle to free the besieged Jerusalem. The funeral passed along the road with the remaining monuments of the armored cars, which themselves gave extra meaning as linking objects between society and those who fell defending it.

Likewise, the blood-stained piece of paper on which the "Song of Peace" was written became a linking object on the symbolic level, representing Rabin as a sacrifice of peace. Other linking objects on the personal symbolic level constructed by the mourners were memorial candles, the graffiti on the walls of the building near the assassination site, letters and poems written by children and youth, and the songs they sang. These linking objects provided a continuing attachment to the deceased.

PSYCHOLOGICAL AND CULTURAL ASPECTS OF NATIONAL BEREAVEMENT—A HISTORICAL PERSPECTIVE

Personal and collective bereavement can also be viewed in its social and historical context in Israel. Individuals at every stage customize their behavior according to collective pathways of mourning that evolve over time. In traditional societies, culture and religion shaped the individual's mourning patterns. In contemporary societies, especially those in transition toward modernity, mourning may be problematic.

Witztum and Malkinson (1998) emphasize the influence of the evolving narratives, myths, and collective memory on behavioral patterns. A society requires antecedents; when these are lacking, where the nation is new or in the process of rebuilding itself after a lengthy state of decline or discontinuity, basic myths and images will be created to link it with the past (Steiner, 1971).

These images may possess a complex but selective structure similar to that of myths. Every historical period is mirrored in images and the living mythology it creates of its own past, sometimes borrowing pieces from other periods or cultures. Thus society measures its identity, stability, and ability to progress (or regress) against the yardstick of the past.

According to this approach, a society's understanding of its own past always plays an instrumental role in the beliefs and values of the present. In this sense, the collective memory is actually a recollection of the past and may well be different from historical reality. The factual memory of the past combines with the images of that past to create a new version tailored to the needs and beliefs of the present. In other words, historical events are worthy of remembrance only when contemporary society is motivated to define them as such (Halbwachs, 1980).

As the patterns of heroism and commemoration changed over the years, cracks appeared in the myths. And as these cracks become more pronounced, the voices of personal mourning become louder. This hypothesis is also examined according to the model of stages of mourning. When war was perceived to be a necessity for the existence and security of the state, myths evolved that stressed the heroism and limited the expressions of pain and grief over loss. The halo of a heroic death can be seen as a frequent stage in mourning—denial. Denial on the collective-national level, as on the personal, is intended to help the bereaved continue to function. The fear of expressing pain and grief was a fear of annihilation then associated with the Holocaust, destruction, the end, nothingness.

Where the relationship between bereavement of the individual and of Israeli society is concerned, a possible way to understand the patterns of mourning that evolved after Rabin's assassination is to examine them along a historical continuum. One might compare them with the patterns of collective mourning in Israel after the death of other national leaders. The first such event in the history of modern Israeli society was the the death of the first president, Chaim Weizmann, a much-admired figure who embodied the symbol of new Jewish statehood. A more recent and comparable example was the death of Prime Minister Menachem Begin. Bilu and Levy (1993) describe the reaction of the public in Israel on hearing of Begin's death, and they analyze the attempt to mythologize the figure. Clearly the circumstances of death were different for each of these leaders. Begin's death from a physical disease is not comparable to the trauma of an assassination. But interestingly, the acute and immediate response was similar. In both cases crowds of people accompanied the coffin, visited the grave, lit candles, and gave the appearance of pilgrimage to the tomb of a rabbi. Electronic media played a central role in bringing the funeral to the Israeli public, and the political commentary accompanying the pictures created the story, emphasizing the popularity of Begin as a leader. The same pattern, though even more intense, followed Rabin's death and funeral.

We have already mentioned the central role of the electronic media in reporting the assassination and the unfolding events at every location, including of course the funeral ceremony. This kind of repetition is familiar from the intense stage of mourning, when the mourner repeats over and over the details of the event, finding some release (the cathartic value of repeating details of "the traumatic story"), together with the beginning of cognitive understanding of the "new reality." Electronic media not only deliver information but also construct and shape this "new reality."

Concluding Remarks

People's reactions to the death of a leader include an almost universal initial response of grief and sadness; these were the responses identified after the death in Israel of President Weizmann and Prime Minister Begin. Similar responses have been observed in different cultures, for example in China after the death of Mao Tse Tung and in France after the death of Charles de Gaulle.

Reactions were even more intense when the circumstances of the death were violent and tragic, such as after the assassination of President Kennedy and the death in an automobile accident of England's Princess Diana. In these deaths, the amplifying factors were the traumatic circumstances mediated by a variety of variables forming a common pattern: After the announcement of Princess Diana's death in 1997, streams of people left flowers and their own personal possessions for her in front of the palace where she lived. Thousands wrote her personal letters and poems. Masses queued along the streets during the funeral procession, and millions of viewers "participated" in this tragic experience while watching TV. The resemblance to the pattern of mourning that followed Rabin's assassination is remarkable, especially in the use of linking objects. We assume that traumatic circumstances contribute to the intensity of the reaction and the strong identification with image of the deceased and to preoccupation and rumination long after the death.

It seems to us that the more ambiguous the death event is the more difficult it is for people to grasp the reality of the loss. Denial and false rationalization (like conspiracy theories) are responses parallel to unresolved and complicated grief at the individual level.

Aftermath

The process of collective mourning and the link with individual mourning have evolved over the years into a culture of bereavement, memory, and commemoration. The stages of the mourning process after Rabin's assassination could be the continuation of a multi-year process of national mourning.

At this writing a number of years after Rabin's death, mourning continues, and confusion and denial are still strong. Rabin's grave became a monument, a place for pilgrimage on special dates and for special events. Even the debate over the appropriate style of remembering and memorializing continues. For many people the assassination of Rabin meant the loss of their ideal and shattered their basic belief in themselves. People refer to the sequence of events in terms of life before and after the murder, a pattern of traumatic impact, a prominent finding among the individual cases of post-traumatic stress disorder. Sadly, the wound is still unhealed.

Notes

1. Prof. B. Shamir of the Sociology and Anthropology departments of Hebrew University in Jerusalem, TV interview, *Ha'aretz*, November 8, 1995.

2. Prof. G. Keinan of the Psychology Department, Tel Aviv University, *Ha'aretz*, November 8, 1995.

3. Prof. D. Zakkai of the Psychology Department, Tel Aviv University, *Ha'aretz*, November 8, 1995.

4. Prof. Y. Bilu of the Psychology, and the Sociology and Anthropology Department, Hebrew University in Jerusalem (November 11, 1995).

5. Prof. G. Weimann of the Communication Department, Haifa University, Otot 95.

6. Prof. Eli Bar-Navie of the History Department, Tel Aviv University, *Ha'aretz*, November 17, 1995.

7. The survey queried 199 men and women who had been working at their jobs for at least one year. A week after the assassination, people reported negative effects on their mood (4.4 on a scale of 0 to 5, with 5 being "greatly affected"), their concentration at work (3.3), and the mood of their children (4.0).

References

Bilu, Y., and A. Levy (1993). "The Elusive Sanctification of Menachem Begin." *International Journal of Politics, Culture and Society* 7: 297–328.

Bowlby, R. W. (1980). "Attachment and Loss." Vol. 3: *Loss: Sadness and Depression*. London: Hogarth.

Bronowski, Y. (1996). "Devoted Father with Camera." *Ha'aretz*, December 8.

Halbwachs, M. (1980). *The Collective Memory*. New York: Harper and Row.

Janoff-Bulman, R. (1989). "Assumptive Worlds and the Stress of Traumatic Events: Applications of the Schema Construct." *Social Cognition* 7: 113–36.

Kleber, R. J., D. Brom, and P. B. Defares (1992). *Coping with Trauma*. Amsterdam: Swets and Zeitlinger.

Kushnir, and R. Malkinson (1996). "A National Level Trauma: Behavioral and Emotional Reactions to Prime Minister's Rabin's Assassination." Paper presented at the meeting of the International Studies for Stress and Trauma, Jerusalem, Israel.

Malkinson, R., and E. Witztum (1996). "From 'The Silver Platter' to 'Who Will Remember the Rememberers?' Psychological Aspects of Mourning in Historical and Literary Analyses." *Alpayim* 12: 211–39 [Hebrew].

——— (2000). "Collective Bereavement and Commemoration: Cultural Aspects of Collective Myth and the Creation of National Identity in Israel." In R. Malkinson, S. Rubin, and E. Witzburn (eds.), *Traumatic and Nontraumatic Loss and Bereavement: Clinical Theory and Research*. Madison, Conn.: Psychosocial Press, pp. 295–320.

Menussi, D. (1996). "With God's Help." *Yediot Aharonot*, January 5.

Parkes, C. M. (1972). *Bereavement Studies in Grief in Adult Life*. New York: International University Press.

Rosenbloom, D. (1996). "The Rabin Trauma." *Ha'aretz*, January 12.

Segal, Z. (1996). "Yitzhak Rabin Memorial," *Ha'aretz*, January 15.

Segev, T. (1995a). "Between Facts and Rumors." *Ha'aretz*, December 20.

——— (1995b). "The Words Did Not Kill," *Ha'aretz*, November 15.

Steiner, G. (1971). *In Bluebeard's Castle: Some Notes Towards the Redefinition of Culture*. New Haven, Conn.: Yale University Press.

Volkan, V. D. (1972). "The Linking Objects of Pathological Mourners." *Archives of General Psychiatry* 27C: 215–21.

——— (1983). *Linking Objects and Linking Phenomena*. New York: International Universities Press.

——— (1988). *The Need to Have Enemies and Allies*. London: Jason Aronson.

Weimann, G. (1995). Otot 95.

Witztum, E., and R. Malkinson (1993), "Bereavement and Commemoration: The Dual Face of the National Myth." In R. Malkinson, S. Rubin, and E. Witztum (eds.), *Loss and Bereavement in Jewish Society in Israel*. Jerusalem: Kanna Press and the Ministry of Defense Publishing House [Hebrew].

——— (1998). "Death of a Leader: The Social Construction of Bereavement." In E. S. Zinner and M. Beth Williams (eds.), *When A Community Weeps*. Philadelphia: Taylor and Francis, pp.119–37.

Zertal, I. (1995). "The Rabin Legend." *Ha'aretz*, November 10.

CHAPTER 11

Rhetoric on the Roads of Israel:
The Assassination and Political Bumper Stickers

LINDA-RENÉE BLOCH

In the past, one of the myths Israelis had about themselves was that although their dissenting views might cause them to engage in aggressive rhetoric, they would not stoop to the level of physical violence. With the Rabin assassination, this illusion was shattered. Suddenly, words were perceived as being inseparable from deeds, and verbal violence was considered the culprit that motivated the assassin: Seeking something to blame, the public first accused demagogues of inciting the murder with their rhetoric—rabbinical utterances to which the assassin had supposedly been exposed were imbued with almost mystical powers. Perhaps this is why it was also through words that the public sought to heal.

Although there was a tremendous amount of discussion about this in private as well as on television and radio in Israel, the "People of the Book," as Jews are traditionally known, expressed much of their angst in the form of the written word. The public discourse was manifest in graffiti painted across the plaza where the prime minister was killed; on official and privately sponsored billboards and posters with their mournful announcements framed in black; in sealed and open letters at the murder site, on the grave, in front of the official residence in Jerusalem, and at the Rabin family's private home in Tel Aviv reminiscent of the notes pushed into the crevices of the Western Wall; to newspaper articles, letters, and editorials describing, lamenting, accusing, expounding, analyzing, interpreting, and eulogizing; to banners draped across balconies; and not least, to the bumper stickers on cars. Use of the written word may have satisfied the mourners' desire for a solitary, personal act undertaken in silence, and their emotional need for catharsis and sharing with others.[1]

The subject of this chapter is the impact of Rabin's assassination on one medium of communication that has developed in a manner seemingly unique to Israel: bumper stickers. This mode of expression is so widespread in Israel today that it would be almost unthinkable not to examine it when studying issues of national and political concern. One of the most striking examples of the public's use of this medium took place immediately after the assassination: unquestionably the most common bumper sticker on cars across the country bore the inscription "Shalom, Haver" (Good-bye, Friend). These words were uttered by President Bill Clinton at the close of his official announcement about the assassination of Yitzhak Rabin. The significance of this bumper sticker is discussed below.

The following pages briefly describe the medium of political bumper stickers and their use in Israel until the assassination in November 1995, and look specifically at the impact of the assassination on this medium.

Bumper Stickers: The Medium and Its Use in Israeli Society

The use of bumper stickers in general and their function in expressing socio-ideological views are not widely documented. Outside Israel, bumper stickers seem to be most common in the United States, but their prevalence has earned them little attention there or elsewhere.[2] This is surprising given that, as Stern and Solomon (1992: 169) put it, they are "overt attitudinal comments" in which car owners reveal "something about their attitudes directly in words" and that "examination of bumper stickers can extend our knowledge of the extended self by affording researchers the opportunity to analyze explicit attitudinal comments." C. E. Case clearly agrees: "Public opinion polls can induce people to state 'yes', 'no', or 'maybe' to endless lists of questions on virtually any topic. There is, however, always some question as to the intensity, honesty, or commitment to these expressions of belief, attitude, or opinion. In contrast, using a valuable and visible possession to make a public statement indicates the importance of the messages displayed" (Case, 1992: 118).

Despite the popularity of the medium in both countries, Israeli bumper stickers differ widely from their American counterparts, starting with the fact that in the United States political statements constitute only a small proportion of messages on cars (Case, 1992; Dasenbrock, 1993; Stern and Solomon, 1992), and the number is on the decline (Jankowski and Strate,

1995). Israeli bumper stickers are not as straightforward as those in the United States, they frequently employ complex literary forms (Bloch, 2000), and their interpretation is dependent on a well-grounded understanding of the local political scene. In both countries, political messages are particularly prevalent at election time, though in Israel they exist independently as well.[3]

Nonpolitical bumper stickers of several types have been used in Israel for several years; many are of a commercial nature, frequently advertising products related to motor vehicles. Social concerns such as environmental issues and road safety are also expressed on Israeli cars. To a much lesser extent, other bumper stickers can be seen as well, including those with American-inspired humorous messages (e.g., "When I grow up I'm going to be a Rolls Royce"), those that proclaim membership in or support for a military brigade or corps, religious messages (Shaffir, 1994), and regional and professional stickers often connected to parking permits. All these, however, pale in comparison with the amount and diversity of "political bumper stickers," those that send messages about national ideological issues.[4]

Political Bumper Stickers as an Israeli Phenomenon

Despite the ubiquitousness of political bumper stickers in Israel, the local mass media did not begin paying attention to them until the mid-1990s.[5] The national television channel, for example, discussed the "sticker attack" (*mitkefet stikerim*) some months before the elections (February 21, 1996). Since various political groups made increasing use of the medium in their campaigns, each party's latest bumper sticker frequently inspired news reports and was featured on television and radio.

It is widely believed that political bumper stickers were first introduced to Israel on a large scale in 1977 (Levinson and Ze'evi, 1995). Since then, their use has flourished (Bloch, 2000). The reasons for their appearance and widespread acceptance may be found in Israel's sociopolitical climate and communication culture.

The political split that existed in Israel between the "peace camp" and the clerical-nationalist camp has intensified since the territories known as "Greater Israel" became subject to negotiation, with peace hanging in the balance. Much of the Israeli population is politically active, and its members are keen to discuss politics.[6] On an interactional level, Israelis are renowned for "straight talk" (Katriel, 1986) and even for verbal aggressiveness. Moreover, Katriel has pointed out that Israelis seem to need to air their dissatisfactions in public—primarily about political, social, and economic issues—in a "griping ritual." As she puts it, "The prevalence of griping suggests an overwhelming, culturally sanctioned concern with the public domain, on the one hand, coupled with a marked absence of satisfying participation channels, on the other" (Katriel, 1985: 40).

Since the 1980s the mass-media scene has changed greatly: a second television channel has been added, cable television with community access has penetrated heavily, and local radio stations and newspapers have proliferated (Caspi and Limor, 1992). Some of these channels afford the public far greater opportunities than ever before to participate in the public discourse, and, more important perhaps, their very existence has increased awareness in the possibilities of doing so. However, those who oppose the government in power seem to be more in need of mechanisms to express themselves than those who support the ruling party. Case (1992) argues that bumper stickers provide a way for individuals to contribute actively to the public discourse, thereby disrupting the predominantly unidirectional flow from the mass media to the public.

Several factors seem to account for the creation of additional channels of political expression in Israel: the external crises and internal divisions, each of which fosters the need for public debate; the tendency for outspokenness, political and otherwise, together with the tradition of griping; and a heightened awareness of the possibilities afforded by public communication.

The question arises, however, why this particular mode of expression became popular rather than any other. Jankowski and Strate note that bumper stickers and other media are "meaningful outlets for mass political expression" (1995: 89). Case contends that the "means and methods available to influence the discourse of ideology and symbols have proliferated. Underground newspapers, 'pirate' radio stations, community access television, computer bulletin boards, graffiti, and 'boom boxes' are examples of means though which non-elite groups have relatively uncontrolled access to communication opportunities" (1992: 108).

From the perspective of the medium itself, Smith notes, "Like blank paper in the typewriter or the blank monitor for the word processor, the bumper cries out to be filled with THE WORD and the owner supplies text as best she can" (1988: 148). Certainly bumper stickers are a low-technology medium that costs little to produce, distribute (usually done by volunteers at no cost to the consumer), or use.[7] They are widely accessible to those who affix them to their vehicles and clearly visible to passersby.

Moreover, there is a willingness to show commitment and accountability for the message posted on one's vehicle, with no anonymity unless a car is parked. Yet all this might just as well be said of buttons—which, incidentally, are not especially popular in Israel. Why then did Israelis choose to display their political messages on their cars?

First, it is necessary to understand the place of the car in the Israeli culture. Cars in Israel are very expensive, especially in relation to local earnings, and automobile taxes are as high as the original price of the car. In an Israeli culture based on social democratic and egalitarian foundations, early on the car was regarded as a symbol of luxury, and for many years after the establishment of the state cars were owned only by the wealthy. The rapid increase in family car owners reflected Israel's entrance into the age of accelerated economic development in the 1960s, and its subsequent entrance into the consumer age where what you have represents who you are.

As in the United States, where cars are "powerful symbols that express cultural values such as power, freedom, materialism, success and individualism," (Stern and Solomon, 1992: 169), so they are in Israel as well.

Beyond the symbolic statement made by the car, Stern and Solomon (1992) note that bumper stickers are "a canvas for personal statements" about the self. The car may be considered an extension of a person's own self, or an alter-ego. While most people may be reluctant to mark their own bodies, they are more inclined to mark their vehicles. Indeed, Smith (1988) maintains that a variety of marginal forms of self-expression or "folk poetry"—including buttons, T-shirts, and bumper stickers—are modern genres of badges used to mark and single out people.

Stern and Solomon, citing Belk (1988) and Solomon (1983), claim that "cars and other vehicles . . . often serve as an important extension of the self and a mediator of self-concept." In their study of bumper stickers as a communication medium, they refer to "the dynamics of cars as social canvases on which expressions of the self are displayed against the background context of mass culture" (Stern and Solomon, 1992: 169). One might add to this that they also reflect the local communication culture.

Perhaps not surprisingly, given their reputation as straight talkers, Israelis are also acknowledged to be highly aggressive drivers, a phenomenon that is evidenced daily in the high number of car accidents. The connection between aggressive driving and verbal interaction has not gone unnoticed (Bloch, 1990; Chafets, 1995). Further support for this linkage may be seen in the fact that immediately following the assassination there were calls to reduce violence and aggression. Whether people heeded such calls, arrived at the same conclusion on their own, or were temporarily more subdued, the fact remains that in the four weeks following the assassination there was a 35 percent decrease in the number of road accidents and fatalities. Perhaps it was even the mass media that established the tie between violence or aggression in the political context and the manner in which people conducted themselves toward one another, including on the roads.

Smith maintains that "the bumper is a natural billboard, so we should not be surprised that most of the texts generated to fill it have no particular relationship to the context of the bumper" (1988: 147). In the Israeli case especially, the "what" and "where" may be linked, in light of several factors: the sociopolitical climate and the communication tendencies discussed earlier; the notion that a car may be considered an extension of the self; the fact that bumper stickers reflect the local communication culture; and, finally, the analogy between aggressive driving and communicative interaction.

In view of this, perhaps there is indeed a connection between the medium and the message, particularly in the case of some of the more provocative statements placed on Israeli cars, which might be viewed as a way to issue a challenge.

Although political bumper stickers existed in Israel well before the Rabin assassination, that event had an incontrovertible impact upon the medium. Despite significant differences between U.S. and Israeli bumper stickers, Stern and Solomon's words hold true for both when they make the case that such messages constitute "overt attitudinal comments" in which individuals "are revealing something about their attitudes directly in words—a medium not only visible to other drivers and pedestrian passersby, but also to researchers . . . examination of bumper stickers can extend our knowledge of the extended self by affording researchers the opportunity to analyze *explicit* attitudinal comments. In sum, the stability, visibility, and interpretability of bumper stickers make them a meaningful canvas for researchers to examine" (1992: 169). In Israel, this canvas portrayed attitudes toward the assassination and, in so doing, changed how the medium was used and by whom it was employed.

After the Assassination: "Shalom, Haver." *and Other Bumper Stickers*

By far the most conspicuous effect of the assassination on bumper stickers was the domination of a single message affixed to cars across the nation:

"Shalom, Haver." On the weekend after the assassination, this sticker was distributed primarily by *Yediot Aharonot*, the most widely read newspaper, and dispensed by vendors across the country, frequently without regard for which newspaper a customer had purchased.

In the most superficial of glosses, the words *Shalom, Haver* can be translated "Good-bye, Friend." In Hebrew, these two words create a message of extraordinary simplicity and profundity, almost reminiscent of Japanese haiku. Literally, the word *shalom* can signify "peace," "hello" or "good-bye," and *haver* may mean "friend," "partner" or "comrade." *Shalom* is typically used in Hebrew for both greeting and leave-taking. The phrase can be interpreted in all its meanings and still be consistent in this context: "peace," indicating the goal both Rabin and Clinton had set themselves; "hello," as a greeting that acknowledges anew or perhaps elevates the camaraderie between the two men; and "good-bye," in taking leave at death. *Haver* is no less complex a word and can signify any of the following: "friend," possibly the most common colloquial meaning; "member" of an organization; "partner"; "peer"; and "comrade," as in "comrade in arms."[8] It should be recalled that from a sociopolitical perspective, Israel has its origins in a socialist culture, and this is reflected in linguistic usage. Consequently, in the early days of the state and continuing in some sociopolitical circles for much longer, the term *haver* was common in addressing individuals, often in place of "Mr." and "Mrs.," resembling the use of "comrade" in Communist countries.

Even the use of punctuation in the message "Shalom, Haver" is relevant. By forcing a pause, the comma places emphasis on both words, underscoring the importance of each. Although more than one version of the sticker was put out, the main difference between them was that one contained a period at the end, and the other did not. The version with the period—"Shalom, Haver."—was far more common, and is one of the very few bumper stickers in which the message actually ends in a period. This full stop seems to underscore the terminality of the event.

The grammatical structure is also significant: The possessive is not used, as in *Shalom, my haver* (rendered in Hebrew as either *Shalom, haveri* or *Shalom, haver sheli*). As it stands then, the relationship between the object, the *haver*, and the speaker—the sticker user—remains open to interpretation: it might refer to *my haver* to whom I am saying *shalom*, reflecting a more intimate relationship, which emphasizes the friendship facet of *haver*; but since the possessive form is not specified, the object of the phrase can equally be *everyone's haver*—partner, comrade, and so forth.

The simple phrase *Shalom, Haver* can no longer be heard free of its connotation as a tribute to Yitzhak Rabin. Reminiscent of the synecdochic "I have a dream" that has come to represent Martin Luther King Jr.'s vision of America, here is another phrase—albeit never uttered by Rabin himself—that has come to symbolize another leader's vision for his nation, another person killed for his dream.

The significance of this message, however, does not end with the meaning of the words alone. To more fully comprehend the implications of "Shalom, Haver.," several additional circumstances must be taken into consideration. These may profitably be examined in terms of the classic journalistic questions, what, who, where, why, when, and how, first with respect to this message, and then with regard to its function and that of other stickers that came out after the assassination. In other words, these questions will be answered from two different perspectives: the circumstances that created the most widely adopted Israeli bumper sticker, and the context of this and other messages by consumers at the receiving end.

What

Besides "Shalom, Haver.," the political bumper sticker messages primarily address the burning ideological-political issues of the day, namely peace and related concerns, such as the policy of returning land for peace, security, and reactions of the political parties and leaders regarding these issues. Social and economic issues are superseded by political-ideological concerns in Israel and have, to date, rarely been the subject of political stickers. As the threat to the nation's existence subsides, this seems likely to change.

Other bumper stickers that appeared in direct response to Rabin's assassination included: "Enough Violence!"(Dai La-Alimut!); "Yes to Peace, No to Violence" (Ken LaShalom, Lo La-Alimut); "Rabin, We Are Following You to Peace" (Rabin, Aharekha LaShalom); "Rabin, Hero of the Generation" (Rabin, Gibor HaDor); "Rabin, Now and Forever" (Rabin, Me-Az UleTamid); "There Are Not Many Like Him" (in a play on the Hebrew for "many," *rabim*, the name *Rabin* is juxtaposed with the word *rabim*, meaning "many") (*Ein Rabin Kamohu*) and "In His Death, He Left Us a Legacy of Peace" (BeMoto Tziva Lanu et HaShalom).

Later, during the election campaign, relatively few bumper stickers actually referred to Rabin or the assassination. The few that did were, on the political left: "Someone Is Looking Out for You" (Mishehu Do-eg Lekha) (bearing a picture of both Yitzhak Rabin and Shimon Peres), and on the political right: "For Rabin of Blessed Memory I Grieve, for Bibi I Vote" (Al Rabin Za"l Ani Mitzta'er, BeBibi Ani Boher).

After the assassination, "peace" was the dominant theme, and its meaning on both ends of the political spectrum was renegotiated. On the left, a whole slew of bumper stickers referring to peace appeared, in addition to those already mentioned: "Peace" (Shalom); "By Virtue of Peace" (BeZkhut HaShalom); "The People Have Chosen Peace" (Ha'Am Hehlit Shalom); "The People Are with Peace" (Ha'Am Im HaShalom); "The People Want Peace" (Ha'Am Rotzeh Shalom); "Peace Will Win" (HaShalom Yenatze'ah); "We Are Continuing with the Peace, Friend" (Mamshikhim Im HaShalom, Haver); and "We Want Peace" (Rotzim Shalom). One noteworthy sticker claimed "An Entire Generation Demands Peace" (Dor Shalem Doresh Shalom). It is probably the only instance of a message on a sticker that gave birth to a political movement: after the assassination, and well after the appearance of the sticker "An Entire Generation Demands Peace," a protest group that had gathered weekly at Rabin Plaza publicly labeled itself "The Peace Generation."[9]

In the wake of the assassination, peace took on a new meaning; not only did it represent the peace camp or the political left, but peace became defined as the opposite of violence or aggression by external enemies and also internally, as evidenced by the popular bumper sticker "Yes to Peace, No to Violence." This was a variation on the sticker mentioned above, "Enough Violence!"

Two bumper stickers reflect the different interpretations of the word "peace," implying that there are more ways than one to achieve peace without succumbing to violence. These messages refer to the "Song of Peace" that Rabin himself had sung at the rally just a short while before he was assassinated: "The Song of Peace Has More Than One Tune" (LeShir HaShalom Yesh Od Manginot) and "Peace Has More Than One Song" (LeShalom Yesh Yoter MeShir Ehad). Today, the song is associated with the younger generation twice removed from the late prime minister, with whom Rabin was acknowledged to have had a special relationship. It was this relationship that seems to have inspired the bumper sticker "Rabin, Hero of the Generation," as well as "An Entire Generation Demands Peace."

Closer to the time of the 1999 parliamentary elections, when Jerusalem became a central issue in the Likud campaign, this last bumper sticker prompted the political right to issue a sticker using the same graphics with slightly different colors claiming, "An Entire Generation Demands Jerusalem" (Dor Shalem Doresh Yerushalem, the latter being one of the Biblical names for Jerusalem), as well as "Peace with Jerusalem" (Shalom Im Yerushalayim).

After the assassination, the word "peace" was imbued with almost magical powers; it became the panacea for all ills, which even the nationalist camp could not do without. Although the political right used the word "peace" as a central motif in its election campaign, anyone familiar with Israeli politics could tell that this use differed from its use by the left: the peace policies of the left entail ceding land in exchange for peace a move that would lead to the annihilation of the Jewish people in the eyes of the right.

A whole category of bumper stickers expressed the idea that peace did not have to be defined as the Labor Party conceived it: "This Is Not Peace" (Zeh Lo Shalom) and even "This Is Not Peace, Friend!" (Zeh Lo Shalom, Haver!); "A Different Peace" (Shalom Aher) or "We Want A Different Peace" (Rotzim Shalom Aher); "Good-bye to Peace" (Shalom LaShalom); "Bring Back the Peace" (Lehahazir et HaShalom); "We Want Peace, Not an Illusion" (Rotzim Shalom Lo Ashlaya); "We Want Peace, We Get Terrorism" (Rotzim Shalom, Mekablim Teror); "Peace Through Strength" (Shalom Mitoch Otzma), or "We Want Peace for Generations" (Rotzim Shalom LeDorot)—the implication being that a lasting peace, achieved only through tough negotiations from a position of strength, is more important than the immediate gratification advocated by the "Peace Now" message and the advocates of that movement

Behind the right's reinterpretation of peace was a call for tolerance and understanding, themes previously touted by the left in an effort to foster dialogue between Jews and Arabs. The nationalist camp capitalized on this, advocating the tolerance of alternative points of view, but this time the reference was to sources of internal strife: religious versus secular, right versus left. The concept of unity among the people and internal peace was, in fact, the real theme behind the word "peace," sometimes overtly expressed on bumper stickers: "Unity of the People" (Ahdut Ha'Am); "Unity of Israel" (Ahdut Israel); and even "The People of Israel Will Overcome" (Am Israel Yenatze'ah). Shortly before the elections, this took a more extreme form and became "The People of Israel Will Overcome Not with Peres" (Am Israel Yenatze'ah Lo Im Peres). National unity is considered a precondition and is perceived to be more important than peace with the Arabs. Unity had become of paramount importance to the national religious camp, who felt that they had been turned into scapegoats because the assassin came from their political camp and that they were all being held responsible.

Who

The "who" question refers to the source of the utterance "Shalom, Haver.," as well as to the receiver—who made use of it and of other bumper stickers after the assassination.

"Shalom, Haver" was the signature statement in Bill Clinton's first official speech on learning of the assassination. When the Hebrew phrase is intoned by the president of the United States, it confers a special status on the words for several reasons: first, because Clinton uttered them in person, rather than through a spokesperson; second, because that media-worthy phrase put the assassination and its victim even more prominently on the news agenda; third, because the word *haver* has connotations of friend and partner, it connected Yitzhak Rabin with the leader of the most powerful country in the world; and finally, because Clinton's speaking in Hebrew honored the person, what he represented, and his people.

In the past, political bumper stickers expressing sympathy with political groups not currently in power had been more prevalent. As Case (1992) points out, bumper stickers allow segments of society who feel ignored by the current power holders, and who do not have easy access to the mass media, to express themselves. Indeed the first documented use of a political bumper sticker in Israel was in 1977; the left-wing peace camp issued the "Peace Now" (Shalom Akhshav) bumper sticker at a time when the right-wing Likud was in power (Levinson and Ze'evi, 1995). Bumper stickers might thus be considered to have started as a protest medium.

As the Rabin government took office and the peace process came to light, particularly after the signing of the Oslo Accords, the number of right-wing bumper stickers that voiced objection to withdrawal from the occupied territories dramatically increased. From then until the assassination, the nationalist or right-wing parties, in opposition to the Labor-led government, seem to have conquered the streets of Israel with their messages. Their high visibility may have provided the illusion that supporters of the government and of the peace policies were in the minority and its opponents were in the majority. According to Noelle-Neumann (1974), when people feel they are holding a less-popular opinion they tend to keep their views to themselves (in a "spiral of silence"), whereas those who side with the majority are more likely to reveal their attitudes publicly. Indeed, the bumper stickers served as an unofficial public opinion poll, the results of which conveyed the impression that government supporters were in the minority. This was so true that Rabin was reported to have been stunned by the amount of support he received at his final public appearance, the scene of his assassination.

After the shock of the assassination, those who had supported or sympathized with Rabin's goals felt most personally violated by the tragic event and evinced the greatest need to speak out. Suddenly a multitude of bumper stickers expressing sympathy with the aims of the Labor government appeared in numbers exceeding the quantity associated with the right wing. Many more, though, perceived the "Shalom, Haver." bumper stickers to be politically neutral, to express a reaction to the assassination rather than identification with any political view. Hundreds of thousands of these stickers appeared around Israel, many on the cars of people who had never before affixed any sort of message to their car bumpers.

When "Shalom, Haver." messages initially flooded the country, the negative and more extreme bumper stickers all but vanished, such as "You Chose Rabin, You Got Arafat" (Baharta Rabin, Kibalta Arafat) and "A Terrifying Peace" (Shalom Bałahot). Even an untrained eye could observe the telltale remnants of stickers that had been torn off cars, as did the press. Whether these bumper stickers were removed by the drivers themselves or by passersby right after the assassination is not clear, but right-wing sympathizers seemed to tone down their messages, though they would later escalate the intensity of their objections to the government by exploiting the "Shalom, Haver" theme for their own purposes.

After the wave of terrorist attacks that preceded the elections in 1996, the balance of power between the two camps changed again. Once again the opposition parties felt strong, while the Labor coalition lost confidence. The mood of the public changed (Liebes and Peri, 1998). The Peres government came under attack. As the election campaign heated up, the Israeli left became more vulnerable and right-wing parties increased their use of bumper stickers, joining individuals and extraparliamentary groups. The left reacted accordingly, and the messages from each reflected several levels of intensity. At times, driving the highways of Israel seemed much like attending a political debate, where cars seemed to be responding directly to each other's messages: "Peace," "Peace Now," or "We Want Peace" would be answered by "This Is Not Peace," "We Want a Different Peace," or "We Want Peace, We Get Terrorism." Whereas the right-wing previously had bumper stickers reading "Rabin, Don't Be Hasty!" (Rabin, Al Tehafez), closer to the elections they merely changed the name of the politician and printed, "Peres, Don't Be Hasty!" "Peace Through Strength" was challenged by "Peace Is Security" (Shalom Zeh Bitahon), and "A Strong People Does Not Give In" (Am Hazak Lo Mitkapel) was met with "A Strong People Makes Peace" (Am Hazak Oseh Shalom).

The internal and external dialogue reached its peak when it became a dialectic based on the "Shalom, Haver." sticker. The hideous cycle of terrorist attacks provided impetus for three bumper stickers capitalizing on the "Shalom, Haver" theme: "This is Not Shalom, Friend!"; "Shalom, Friends" (Shalom, Haverim); and "Shalom, Friend II" (Shalom, Haver II). The last two were considered vicious distortions of the original message, because the word "Shalom" was interpreted in both to mean "Good-bye," as in: "Good-bye, Friends" and "Good-bye, Friend II." Both these stickers were considered incitement to violence and threats on the lives of the new prime minister, Shimon Peres, and members of his cabinet. The stickers were reportedly confiscated and banned by the authorities.

Where

It was on the lawn of the White House, where he had received Yitzhak Rabin repeatedly in the preceding few years, the last time barely a month earlier, that President Clinton first spoke the words "Shalom, Haver." That same venue was the backdrop for the groundbreaking handshake between Rabin and Arafat in the peace brokered by the United States and overseen by Clinton himself.

In the eulogy he gave before one of the largest assemblies of heads of state ever to gather, Clinton spoke of his relationship with Yitzhak Rabin as a partner and friend. The American president then apparently added the words "Shalom, Haver" as an afterthought, having heard about the uncalculated success of his first use of the expression. [10]

The second part of the "where" question concerns the actual placement of bumper stickers in Israel. Although the term bumper sticker has been used throughout this paper, Israeli drivers affix them in a variety of places on their cars, including but not limited to their bumpers. They appear anywhere on the rear of the vehicle (though they have occasionally been spotted on the side and front as well), and especially on the back windshield. Frequently a car bears more than one bumper sticker, sometimes featuring the same message repeatedly. Stickers are found predominantly on cars, but they can also be seen on other mobile objects, such as the bookbags and files of students and schoolchildren, most of whom do not own cars, and even on fixed locations, such as doors and walls.

There are also geographic differences in bumper sticker use in Israel, which tend to parallel the geographic distribution of voting behavior. In other words, one part of the country will have a higher proportion of stickers of one type reflecting the voting trends of residents of that area. Thus, in regions with a higher concentration of religious people who tend to vote on the right, there will also be more bumper stickers opposing the return of land for peace and a left-wing government and supporting the right-wing and religious parties. In the Galilee and the Golan, there is a high percentage of stickers opposing the return of the Golan Heights to Syria. In Tel Aviv, which has a secular left-wing majority, there are more stickers calling for peace than in Jerusalem, for example. [11]

Why

Why did the "Shalom, Haver" message come about? Why was it so widely adopted? And why did so many more people begin to place bumper stickers on their cars?

Apparently, Clinton did not at first envisage the effect of his words on the population of Israel. By the time he repeated "Shalom, Haver" at the funeral, he seems to have realized the impact it could have, or else he would not have added it to the beautifully crafted ending of his eulogy after the word "Amen." Furthermore, based on his subsequent actions—at the funeral, his visit to the antiterrorism summit in Sharm al-Sheikh in mid-March 1996, and in meetings with Israeli officials—it seems evident that he intended to produce a clear gesture of support for all the world to see. Bill Clinton and Yitzhak Rabin referred to each other as "partners." They shared a common goal, each for his own reasons, investing inordinate amounts of time and effort in their relationship in order to bring about peace in the Middle East. Even so, Clinton went beyond the call of duty expected in a partnership; the two leaders seemed to have held convivial feelings for one another on a personal level (Peri, 1996).

The elegance of the expression "Shalom, Haver." has already been discussed, but this does not quite explain why the sticker itself should have been so widely adopted. Israel is a country that has withstood external threats on numerous occasions. At such times, the people have come together and acted as one. In previous crisis situations, where the "enemy" constituted a threat to the nation's existence from without, the country was united. The direction of action to be taken was clear: the people of the nation had to stand up and fight against the outside. Now, suddenly, there was an internal threat; only, this time, the people were at a loss as to how to react and what kind of action to take. The frustration was enormous, as this time there was no one to fight, and little to do to release the pent-up emotions. Affixing a bumper sticker to one's car, and in particular the very personal "Shalom, Haver.," which managed to capture the ethos of the tragic situation, constituted taking immediate action. This expressive act contrasted with the monumental apathy that many of Rabin's passive supporters had exhibited prior to his killing. Moreover, to use this bumper sticker was to respond collectively at a time when the population needed to show unity. Using Turner's (1969) concepts, Peri (in Chapter 7), Rapoport (in Chapter 8), and Witztum and Malkinson (in Chapter 10) discuss the liminality of the situation in the aftermath of the assassination and the evocation of spontaneous *communitas*. By marking their cars in a similar manner, people showed a commonality of feeling; the public expression of their emotions on their cars can be seen as a metaphorical touching of one another.

The "Shalom, Haver." bumper sticker apparently inspired people who had never before used a bumper sticker to say publicly and unashamedly that they had been affected by the tragedy of the event. Somewhat like a tattoo on the body, bumper stickers identify cars' drivers as member of a group with, if nothing else, a common desire to express their emotions (Case, 1992). Since affixing a bumper sticker is a voluntary act, Stern and Solomon point out that the absence of a bumper sticker is as significant as its presence, all the more in Israel, where the stickers are distributed free of charge (1992: 169). The question of who did not place the "Shalom, Haver" sticker on his or her car, and why, also merits study (Bloch and Cohen, 1997).

Use of the "Shalom, Haver." bumper sticker expressed different emotions for different people, whether sorrow or mourning for a familiar leader; shared identity, grief, and unity with the rest of the nation; or contrition for not having acted sooner in Yitzhak Rabin's support. The bumper sticker is naturally to be found in the company of messages supporting the left-wing government, but it is also frequently seen on its own, as well as on cars showing support for the nationalist movement. When "Shalom, Haver." appears among bumper stickers supporting right-wing parties, it may also be perceived as an expression of dismay at the act of violence, of respect for a man who unquestionably served his country, and of mourning for one who, whether one agreed with him or not, was the democratically elected prime minister of Israel who did not deserve such a fate.

Finally, it remains to be explained why so many more people began to use bumper stickers; indeed, there appeared to be a sticker frenzy just after the assassination. First the left-wing supporters increased their use, and then right-wing supporters responded, while in the background election day approached. The reason for increased use on the political left seems partially due to the shock and horror felt by people that matters had come to such a state, but also specifically due to comments made by Leah Rabin, widow of the assassinated prime minister, some hours after his death.

Immediately after the assassination, as virtually millions of people decried the events and grieved openly, his widow accused Rabin's supporters of voicing their opinions too late. Where had they been, she asked, in times of need, during the seemingly unpopular and daring moves the late prime minister had made? At least two bumper stickers responded directly: "Rabin, Forgive Us for Our Silence" (Rabin, Sliha SheShataknu); and "We Are Not Silent, It's a Fact!" (Anahnu Lo Shotkim, Uvda!). Interestingly, the latter exemplifies how the printed word is acknowledged to be breaking the silence, albeit soundlessly.

Another outcome of the reproof that supporters of the peace policies had done too little too late was that tens of thousands of people determined to openly support the resolutions of Prime Minister Shimon Peres. In addition to the other media used to express encouragement, the following bumper stickers appeared: "Shimon Peres Is My Prime Minister" (Shimon Peres Rosh HaMemshala Sheli); "Peres, You Are Not Alone" (Peres Ata Lo Levad); another version used "Shimon," his first name; others included: "Peres, You Will Never Walk Alone" (Peres, LeOlam Lo Titz'ad Levad); "Peres, Be Strong and of Good Courage" (Peres, Hazak VeAmatz); "Peres, We'll Continue with You for Peace" (Peres Namshikh Itkha LaShalom); "Peres Is a Prize for the People of Israel" (Peres Hu Pras Le'Am Yisrael); and "Peres Makes Peace" (Peres Oseh Shalom).

Furthermore, in reproaching the public, Mrs. Rabin and others close to the late prime minister also made reference to the Friday-afternoon protests outside the couple's private residence during which people chanted slogans, held up signs, and hurled threatening epithets at Yitzhak Rabin. Unwilling to make the same mistake twice, scores of supporters—frequently organized by party members—congregated silently outside Prime Minister Shimon Peres's private residence (actually located a few hundred feet from the Rabin home) every Friday from when he assumed the role of prime minister until his defeat. There they held up placards and distributed bumper stickers with messages of the left, particularly the Labor Party. Some even referred to the day of the week, declaring: "Have a Good Sabbath, Mr. Prime Minister" (Shabbat Shalom, Adoni Rosh HaMemshala) and "A Sabbath of Peace" (Shabat Shel Shalom).

When

Virtually overnight, after Clinton first uttered the words "Shalom, Haver" at the White House, they became a catch phrase standing for the individual and the collective tragedy of the event. The stickers began to appear late Sunday, the day after the assassination (Levinson and Ze'evi, 1995), and that Friday they were distributed with the weekend edition of *Yediot Aharonot*. Some time after the assassination a new sticker appeared, inspired by the first: "Haver, You Are Missed" (Haver, Ata Haser). *Haver* here clearly refers to Yitzhak Rabin and, indeed, this bumper sticker is frequently displayed on cars alongside the original "Shalom, Haver." message. Indeed, since the assassination there have been numerous other stickers to mark the tragedy, based on the "Shalom, Haver." theme. These include: "Friend, You Are Missed More and More" (Haver, Ata Haser Yoter ve'Yoter); "Time Passes and You Are Missed, Friend" (Hazman Over ve'Ata Haser, Haver); "Friend, I Remember" (Haver, Ani Zoher) and "Friend Do You Remember?" (Haver, Ata Zoher?); "Friend, We Won't Forget and We Won't Forgive" (Haver, Lo Nishkah ve'Lo Nislah); "I Had a Friend, I Had a Brother, I'm Your Brother, Don't Forget" (Haya Li Haver, Haya Li Ah, Ani Ahiha, Al Tishkah). Visually, too, these bumper stickers are inspired by the original message: they use a similar typeface, as well as similar proportions and colors—blue on a white background. Around the time of the anniversary of the assassination, many thousands of these bumper stickers are distributed to the public at large.

As noted, political bumper stickers function well as a protest medium for those who do not support the government of the moment. In addition, they tend to surface most visibly at times of upheaval, when they serve as a barometer to gauge the public mood, reflecting the level of morale and confidence in the leaders. At times of crisis such as a terrorist attack, when some among the public feel that the very foundations of its beliefs have been shaken, bumper stickers are no longer a protest medium alone. At such times, circumstances might call not only for criticism, but alternatively for expressions of support by others. For example, after the series of terrorist bus bombings in early 1996, a spate of bumper stickers appeared. Those on the right condemned the Labor government and its leader with the message, "Step Down from the Defense, Peres—Go Home!" (Sar HaBitachon Peres—HaBaita!).[12] Those on the left expressed messages of encouragement, such as "Terrorism Will Not Win" (HaTeror Lo Yenatze'ah) and "Peace Will Win" (HaShalom Yenatze'ah).

How

Finally, the question remains how the "Shalom, Haver." sticker first surfaced, and how it and other bumper stickers were used after the assassination. Immediately after Clinton's speech, "Shalom, Haver" began to be cited repeatedly by various Israeli public figures, who endowed it with all the power of a verbal symbol, standing for the many complex emotions aroused by the assassination.

But the idea to use the phrase as a bumper sticker was the brainchild of a member of the creative staff of the Gitam advertising agency, a "political" firm that had handled Labor's campaign in the previous elections. Within hours of Clinton's speech, employees of the agency were handing out the bumper stickers at various locations, including the scene of the shooting. Unlike more-political stickers, this one met the needs of high-circulation newspapers to do something special for their clients. *Yediot Aharonot*, the largest newspaper, distributed around 700,000 stickers,[13] and *Ma'ariv*, with the second highest circulation, distributed some 300,000 copies of the sticker "Enough Violence!" (Dai La-Alimut!).

Following the assassination, bumper stickers took on a new role. Language philosophers have used "speech act theory" to distinguish between verbal expressions based on their purposes and their effects (see, e.g., Austin, 1962: 94–101). These are referred to as locutionary acts, illocutionary acts, and perlocutionary acts, and they consist, respectively, of the actual meaning of a message, the specific type of speech act that has been undertaken (e.g., asking, asserting, or warning), and the effect it is hoped that the utterance will produce (e.g., as a result of a warning, special care would be taken).

Israeli political bumper stickers typically concern one of several themes, as discussed earlier, committing similar locutionary acts in a variety of ways. For example, "We Want Peace," "The People Want Peace," "The

People Are with Peace" all mean that peace is the desired outcome for a group of people, though they express this in different ways.

Until the assassination, bumper stickers served one of two functions, or, in the terminology of language philosopher John Searle (1976), performed one of two acts at the illocutionary level: the messages used either "representatives" to assert something (e.g., "The People Are with the Golan"), or "directives" to make demands (e.g., "Peace Now"). Immediately after the assassination a new sort of message appeared, whose message was neither to assert the existence of a general situation nor to demand that some large measures be undertaken. Instead, this category of messages represents a deeply personal, highly specific, seemingly politically independent expression of sentiments; its primary function is emotive rather than the expression of an opinion or need. This category is labeled here "expressive." The term is derived from the class defined by Searle as "expressives," which "express the psychological state of speaker toward a particular state of affairs (e.g., thank, congratulate, apologize, condole, deplore, welcome)" (1976: 10–13). Although the vast majority of Israeli political bumper stickers still do not fall into this category, those that do include "Shalom, Haver.," "Have a Peaceful Sabbath, Mr. Prime Minister," and "Rabin, Forgive Us for Having Been Silent."

At the perlocutionary level, exhibitors of bumper stickers may hope that the needs or opinions expressed will affect future action; ultimately, the motive is to advocate change. In messages such as "Shalom, Haver.," by contrast, the purpose is achieved with the act of expression itself. In other words, it is the mere act of expression that serves the ends.

Conclusion

As long as Israeli society continues to be so sharply divided, and it will be as long as the Middle East conflict does not abate, bumper stickers seem likely to continue to be an important vehicle for conveying the political opinions of the population—albeit not necessarily in representative numbers or proportions. As the political situation changes, new bumper stickers will probably continue to reflect current political issues, as they have since the 1996 elections.

Indeed, the topics continue to be recycled, with the messages hardly changing except for the names, calling to mind the French expression, "The more things change, the more they stay the same." In one instance, a message put out by one side only provided inspiration for a bumper sticker put out by the other when the government changed: "You Chose Rabin and Were Left with an Illusion" (Rabin Baharta Nisharta Baharta) spawned "You Chose Bibi [Netanyahu], You Chose an Illusion" (Bibi Baharta Baharta Baharta).[14] The newer messages will probably continue to resemble the vast majority of the other stickers, constituting either assertions or demands.

As the acuteness of the tragedy of Rabin's assassination attenuates over time, though not its long-term effects on the nation, the expressive form that emerged in response will probably all but disappear. Still, it might be remembered that for a time, the word "peace" almost came to represent respect for one another—even if that other was an anonymous driver. And while the vivid blue of the inscription on bumper stickers bearing the words "Shalom, Haver." may have faded in the strong sun, the message will continue to be indelibly imprinted on the nation's conscience. It will remain a fact that for a brief period, when the tragedy was so overwhelming, an enormous proportion of the country marked their emotions publicly by carrying a highly symbolic message on their cars.

Notes

1. It is noteworthy that words rather than emblems have dominated in Israel, with no symbols becoming preeminent, such as the "peace sign" so prevalent in the United States in the 1960s and 1970s, or the yellow ribbons tied around trees in commemoration of hostages. Some of the more common symbols found on Israeli political bumper stickers—flags, blue skies, Stars of David, maps, and so forth, as well as the use of graphics and colors—have been documented elsewhere (Bloch, 2000).

2. Naturally this does not mean that bumper stickers are not in use in other countries, but only that their use has not yet been documented in the academic literature. Only two studies appear on the topic outside the United States and Israel—one on issues of national belonging in Yugoslavia (Kriznar, 1993) and the other on regional preferences in France (Mailles and Montalieu, 1992).

3. The author has in fact collected bumper stickers since the Fall of 1994, more than a year before the assassination and some eighteen months prior to the 1996 national elections.

4. Although the "Shalom, Haver." sticker might be deemed an apolitical message, I have chosen to consider it political because, first, the phrase came up as a result of a political assassination, and, second, the sticker is most often placed beside other political stickers, most commonly on cars whose owners sympathize with the left.

5. The first article about the use of bumper stickers in Israel seems to have ap-

peared in the weekend edition of the local newspapers affiliated with *Ha'aretz* on December 8, 1995.

6. Average national election turnout is approximately 80 percent, similar to that in many European countries and far higher than in the United States (Arian and Shamir, 1995). For a discussion of American and Israeli tendencies to engage in political discussion and to express their views on a variety of topics, including politics, see Bloch, 1985 and 1990.

7. For $100 or less, anyone can have a personal message printed. Indeed, evidence that private individuals did so can be seen in some bumper stickers with signatures and dates on them.

8. *The Complete Hebrew-English Dictionary* by Alcalay (1990) gives the following translations for the word *haver*: friend, comrade, associate, companion, fellow, member, schoolmate, fellow-pupil, partner, scholar, equal.

9. This is reminiscent of the origins of the phrase "Peace Now" (Shalom Ahshav) Movement, which arose in 1974 after the Yom Kippur War. A group consisting primarily of demobilized soldiers protested the situation and demanded that there be "Peace Now," by way of bumper stickers among other ways. Here, however, the message came after the name of the group, "Peace Now," had already been established.

10. That the phrase "Shalom, Haver" was an afterthought was reported in the popular Israeli press. Support for this comes from videotaped recordings of President Clinton's eulogy for Rabin. At the end of the speech, he cites a portion of the Jewish prayer for the dead in Hebrew, ending with the word "Amen." It is after this, which seems likely to have been the originally intended end point, that Clinton added, "And shalom, haver."

11. The subject of the use of political bumper stickers by Tel Aviv residents has been examined by Tel Aviv University scholar Dr. Rafael Ventura (Drov, 1996).

12. There is a play on words here in the Hebrew, which could also allow for the interpretation a "The Defense Is Depressed, Peres—Go Home!"

13. Some 100,000 copies of the sticker were handed out by Gitam employees (telephone interviews July 16 and 17, 1996, with Gitam staff), and an additional 700,000 were distributed by *Yediot Aharonot*, roughly the weekend circulation of that newspaper. Levinson and Ze'evi (1995) claim that some 500,000 copies of the "Shalom, Haver." bumper sticker were handed out by Gitam, and another half-million were printed and distributed by the newspaper. Whichever figure is correct, an enormous number of stickers were distributed, corresponding roughly to the number of households in Israel.

14. In Hebrew, the two middle words are identical in sound and meaning, while the last two, although homonyms, mean respectively, "chose" and "illusion" in colloquial speech.

References

Arian, A., and M. Shamir (eds.) (1995). *The Elections in Israel: 1992*. Albany, N.Y.: State University of New York Press.

Austin, J. (1962). *How to Do Things with Words*. Cambridge, Mass.: Harvard University Press.

Belk, R. W. (1988). "Possessions and the Extended Self." *Journal of Consumer Research* 15: 139–68.

Bloch, L-R. (1985). "Reactions to Entertainment in Political Broadcasts." Master's thesis, Stanford University.

———— (1990). "Communicating as an American in Israel: The Immigrant's Perception." Ph.D. dissertation, University of Texas at Austin.

———— (2000). "Mobile Discourse: Political Bumper Stickers as a Communication Event in Israel." *Journal of Communication* 50.

Bloch, L-R., and A. A. Cohen (1997). "Sticking or Nonsticking: On the Use of Political Bumper Stickers in the 1996 Israeli Elections." Unpublished ms.

Case, C. E. (1992). "Bumper Stickers and Car Signs: Ideology and Identity." *Journal of Popular Culture* 26: 107–19.

Caspi, D. and Y. Limor (1992). *The Mediators: Mass Media in Israel 1948–1990*. Tel Aviv: Am Oved [Hebrew].

Chafets, Z. (1995). "Fear of Frei-ing." *Jerusalem Report*, October 5, 1995, p. 34.

Dasenbrock, R. W. (1993). "A Rhetoric of Bumper Stickers." In Theresa Enos and Stuart Brown (eds.), *Defining the New Rhetorics*. Newbury Park, Calif.: Sage.

Drov, G. (1996). "'Shalom Haver' in the Lead, Followed by 'The Nation Is with the Golan.'" *Tel-Aviv*, April 5, 1996, p. 18 [Hebrew].

Jankowski, T. B., and J. M. Strate (1995). "Modes of Participation of the Adult Life Span." *Political Behavior* 17: 89–106.

Katriel, T. (1985). "Griping as a Verbal Ritual in Some Israeli Discourse." In M. Dascal (ed.), *Dialogue: An Interdisciplinary Approach*. Amsterdam: John Benjamins.

———— (1986). *Talking Straight: Dugri Speech in Israeli Sabra Culture*. Cambridge: Cambridge University Press.

Kriznar, N. (1993). "Visual Symbols of National Identity: Slovene Bumper Stickers and the Collective Unconscious." *Visual Sociology* 8: 58–63.

Levinson, A., and Y. Ze'evi (1995). "Sticker Now: A Plague." *Kol Ha'Ir*, December 8, p. 10 [Hebrew].

Liebes, T., and Peri, Y. (1998). "Electronic Journalism in Segmented Societies: Lessons from the 1966 Elections." *Political Communication* 15 (1): 27–44.

Mailles, A., and J. P. Montalieu (1992). "Quelles contres interessent les gens d'ici? Une méthodologie de traitment pour les tableaux de contingence bi-spatialiss" [Which regions interest people? A methodology for bispatial contingency array processing]. *Bulletin de Méthodologie Sociologique* 35: 2–21.

Noelle-Neumann, E. (1974). "The Spiral of Silence: A Theory of Public Opinion." *Journal of Communication* 24: 43–51.

Peri, Y. (1996). "Afterwards, Rabin: From Mr. Security to Nobel Prize Winner." In Y. Rabin, *The Rabin Memoirs*. Berkeley: University of California Press, pp. 339–80.

Searle, J. (1976). "A Classification of Illocutionary Acts." *Language in Society* 5: 1–23.

Shaffir, W. (1994). "Interpreting Adversity: Dynamics of Commitment in a Messianic Redemption Campaign." *Jewish Journal of Sociology* 36: 43–53.

Solomon, M. R. (1983). "The Role of Products as Social Stimuli: A Symbolic Interactionism Perspective." *Journal of Consumer Research* 10: 319–29.

Smith, H. (1988). "Badges, Buttons, T-Shirts and Bumperstickers: The Semiotics of Some Recursive Systems." *Journal of Popular Culture* 21: 141–49.

Stern, B. B., and M. R. Solomon (1992). "'Have You Kissed Your Professor Today?': Bumper Stickers and Consumer Self-Statements." *Advances in Consumer Research* 19: 169–73.

Turner, V. (1969). *The Ritual Process: Structure and Anti-Structure*. Ithaca, N.Y.: Cornell University Press.

CHAPTER 12

The Past in Our Present: The Assassinations of Yitzhak Rabin and John F. Kennedy

BARBIE ZELIZER

The past is prologue. So proclaims the entrance hall of the National Archives in Washington, D.C. In the years since that sentence was first uttered, it has been attributed to a wide range of individuals, including William Shakespeare and José Ortega y Gasset, whose presumed moments of declaration have been embellished with fanciful tales and narratives of varying plausibility about what inspired the statement. In fact, we know little about its actual birth, and as time passes we will know even less. Such is the work of collective memory, which changes, alters, and transforms the past as we thought we knew it.

This chapter addresses the initial workings of collective memory related to one specific event: the assassination of Israeli prime minister Yitzhak Rabin. Rabin's assassination in November 1995 shocked not only Israel but the entire free world. The act, committed not by one of Israel's so-called sworn enemies but by a native son with beliefs on the other end of the political spectrum from Rabin's, shook a world only beginning to accustom itself to the newfound cadences of an alternative world in the Middle East. The growing hopes for peace in the region, with which Rabin had come to identify, gave way to the dismay of a state funeral. Visions of the future crumbled, at least temporarily, as a shocked nation found itself suspended between present and past, and public places became sites for collective declarations of memory and mourning. Those declarations communicated concerns about what the nation was as well as what it had been and hoped to be. And watching from afar, the world, particularly the United States, tracked the evolution of those declarations, trying to position an act of imponderable violence within a frame that made sense, however partial and fleeting.

Struggling to give form to a story of shocking proportion, the U.S. media responded by tracking the familiar within the event's singularity. Invoking the coverage of other, more familiar, assassinations, the U.S. media framed Rabin's assassination by paralleling it with an event of particular salience in the U.S. popular imagination—the assassination of President John F. Kennedy in 1963.[1] Although it was not the only event in U.S. history to merit public notice in tandem with Rabin's death—the assassination of Abraham Lincoln also drew discussion—it was a frame favored by the U.S. media. Unlike the Lincoln assassination, Kennedy's death offered an available template on which to shape the coverage of Rabin's killing, making journalism's own collective memory of its earlier coverage a factor in the media's approach to the story of Rabin's assassination.

The Workings of Collective Memory

One of the outstanding features of collective memory is that it offers few previews. We never know where, when, or how an event of the past will emerge; neither can we anticipate alongside which event of the present it will appear. A past event's relevance is generally determined by an array of contesting voices or agents of memory. For instance, the mass slaughter in Rwanda and Burundi has been likened increasingly to the Holocaust; yet officials of the Clinton administration preferred the alternative, and less alarming, frame of a civil war for making sense of the carnage. In 1991, U.S. president George Bush invoked World War II as a way of explaining the Persian Gulf War, though many opponents of the conflict found Vietnam a more apt frame of remembrance. The media have played a central role in shaping our collective memories of the past. Though not the only agents of memory to do so, the media rearrange the past in the popular imagination in ways that lend resonance to the present. And although the media have often been touted as providing the first draft of history, their coverage of events in the present day has positioned them as providers of more than history's first draft. In fact, the media routinely borrow from stories of the past so as to make sense of the present. Watergate, for instance, has regularly resurfaced as a metaphor for irregularities in government such as "Irangate" in the 1980s and the "Nannygate" and "Filegate" scandals of the 1990s. In each case, resonant interpretations of Watergate were rehashed in public discourse, at the same time that the earlier event lent meaning to its later parallels. With the help of the media, then, collective memory pulls together past events of often unpredictable relevance into a frame for understanding the present.

What is collective memory, and why do the media act so readily as its agents? Collective memory refers to the shared dimensions of remembering. Coined by Maurice Halbwachs as a way of accounting for the activity of constituting the past within the present, it is a process "not of retrieval but of reconfiguration [that] colonizes the past by obliging it to conform to present configurations."[2] Collective memory comprises recollections of the past that are determined and shaped by the group in the present, and it presumes activities of sharing, discussion, negotiation, and often contestation. Remembering, when constituted as collective practice, becomes implicated in a range of other activities having as much to do with identity formation, power, authority, cultural norms, and social interaction as with the simple act of recall.[3]

The media are active agents of collective remembering. Not only do they position events in shared memory in innovative ways, but they store memory cues that are displayed when circumstances deem doing so relevant, necessary, or appropriate. The reportage of most current events is shaped through memory work. Sometimes this takes place explicitly—as in magazine retrospectives, anniversary issues, and commemorative documentaries, to name some obvious forms of memory work. But at other times the media draw from the past implicitly, systematically recycling narratives, images, and treatments of a given issue. Often, the similarities in only one aspect of different events can be extended to other areas of their reportage, even those with questionable similarity. Stories about human carnage that have been characterized as examples of civil war, for example, receive media treatments that differ from those accorded stories previously classified as crimes of humanity. By the same token, the prior treatment of a story as civil war reduces the chance that it will be recoded over time as a story about more global crimes. Thus similarities in the form of coverage between dissimilar events can facilitate interpretations of those same events that render them more alike than different.

In such a way, the work of collective memory takes shape. Vehicles of memory—images, memorable phrases, artifacts—act as metonymic cues for broad-ranging interpretations of the past that fit agendas in the present. The appearance of such memory cues can be both unpredictable and ever-changing. Memory work is rarely finite, generally bears illogical and irrational dimensions, and is always the subject of rearrangement. It is through such constraints that the media, like other agents of memory, work at reshaping the present through the past.

The Rabin Assassination in Memory

Like other significant public events, the assassination of Yitzhak Rabin was immediately codified as an event in memory. Within days of his death, bumper stickers bearing statements like "Shalom, Haver" (Goodbye, Friend) appeared on private cars, taxi cabs, and buses in Israel. A postage stamp displaying Rabin's likeness was issued at the end of the month, breaking the customary tradition of waiting a full year after death. And one banner headline in the *Washington Post* predicted on the day of his funeral, "Every Israeli Will Remember . . . How His Heart Stood Still."[4]

Directly upon hearing of Rabin's death, the U.S. media tackled the event, flying to Israel major correspondents from the leading newspapers, newsmagazines, and television networks, all of whom gave the story full play. Fitting the criteria of what news researchers have called the "what a story" category,[5] the event of Rabin's death marshaled immediate media attention. Despite the event's singularity, the media needed to mold the event into a manageable shape so as to establish their authority as spokespeople for its story. They therefore turned an unusually wide-ranging but focused employment of resources to the event at hand. Thus, in form, the media approached the assassination of Rabin in much the same way that they had covered John F. Kennedy's assassination three decades earlier.

Favored not only because it offered a frame for understanding what had happened in Tel Aviv and because it was a memory still alive in the minds of those doing the reporting, the Kennedy assassination was relevant for another reason as well: it offered the media a journalistic template for covering assassinations. Invoking that template helped organize the media's approach to Rabin's death and facilitated the establishment of many similarities between the two events. Significantly, the similarities in form generated similarities in the content and interpretation of the Rabin story.

It is thus no surprise that the assassination of Rabin quickly became seen as Israel's equivalent of the Kennedy assassination. Ultimately, the U.S. president's death was invoked because its coverage had set in place an identifiable, manageable, and proven precedent for the U.S. media working the story of Rabin's assassination.

Similarities of Form: Covering the Assassination of Rabin

The U.S. media covered the Rabin assassination in a way that reflected organizational and institutional decisions to center resources upon the event. The media, particularly television, helped the public come to terms with its grief. They provided a place to mourn together with others, and with it came consolation, unity, and a collective sense of self.[6]

On some levels, Rabin's assassination was enacted much like that of John F. Kennedy three decades earlier, and the U.S. media lost no time in underscoring the comparison. As one U.S. newspaper commented on the day after Rabin's death, "the slaying sent the nation into a state of shock that many likened to the 1963 killing of President John F. Kennedy."[7]

How were the shootings similar? Both Rabin and Kennedy were shot by gunmen—Yigal Amir and Lee Harvey Oswald—in public places in the midst of scheduled November events—Rabin at a peace rally in Tel Aviv, Kennedy during a public procession through Dallas. Both gunmen came from cultures of deep-seated opposition to the targets of the assassination, although Amir, as the *Washington Post* was quick to remind its readers, was "not a disturbed loner in the tradition of Lee Harvey Oswald." Rather, he was a "man sprung directly from a movement with deep roots in Israel's turbulent past."[8] Visual depictions of the two men suggested uncanny physical resemblances: both were in their mid-twenties, were of slight build with short, dark hair, and wore T-shirts. The resemblance was so great that at times the distinction between the two men was discursively erased. For instance, the *New Yorker* commented that Amir had worn "Oswald's crooked smirk on his face" at a brief public appearance.[9]

Both assassinations followed an alteration of extraordinary security arrangements that were made in response to earlier threats on the lives of both leaders. Although the visibility and scheduled nature of the public events—the rally in Rabin's case, the procession in Kennedy's—necessitated media presence in a way that made it easier to cover the continuation of the story, they did not facilitate coverage of the shooting itself. In fact, the media failed to record either assassination: Rabin, like Kennedy before him, was killed out of the media's range.

From the beginning, then, the U.S. media adapted their coverage of the Rabin assassination into a broader story, one that emphasized what the media could cover over what they did not. The assassination narrative was broadened from the coverage of the actual shooting, which the media missed, to the larger story surrounding the shooting, which they were able to cover well. That larger story—which extended for three days, from November 4, 1995, the Saturday on which he was shot, to November 6, the Monday on which he was buried—included other moments during the assassination weekend: the immediate reactions to the assassination, the capture of Amir, the recognition of Shimon Peres as the new leader of government, and Rabin's funeral. In each of these other moments of coverage, the U.S. media performed capably, reinstating their authority as spokespeople for the event. Significantly, this broader assassination narrative echoed the media's performance after the death of Kennedy. In the earlier event, the assassination narrative had also extended for four days—from November 22, 1963, the Friday of Kennedy's death, until November 26, the Monday of his burial—and within that broader assassination narrative the media compensated for missing the actual shooting.[10] The template for covering future assassinations was thereby secured.

Immediately after Rabin was shot, the U.S. media plunged into massive coverage of the event, the sheer volume of which was remarkable. As one newspaper framed it, the "cameras have scarcely blinked since" the shooting.[11] Agendas and schedules were adjusted to accommodate the story.[12] Newspaper stories that started on the front pages with banner headlines, continued at length in subsequent sections of the papers. News magazines—where, as *Time* put it, the event "sent the staff into overdrive"[13]— made the assassination their cover story. On television, CBS, NBC, and ABC each covered the funeral live with VIP anchors who had been sent to narrate the early-morning coverage supplied by Israel Television. Both television and the press showed long lines of mourners outside the funeral bier in Jerusalem, images that recalled similar columns of grieving U.S. citizens after Kennedy's death. Additional broadcasts provided in-depth programming from the scene, such as a town meeting on ABC's "Nightline."[14] CNN provided continuous coverage of the event. And Israel Television's new second channel proved itself on the international scene with a one-hour newsmagazine broadcast by CNN with English translation.

The focused coverage was not always accurate. As with the Kennedy assassination, initial errors were exacerbated by the media's ability to report faster than they were able to gather and confirm information, particularly television. Early reports, for instance, relayed the news that Rabin was only wounded, and CNN's Jerrold Kessler and Wolf Blitzer both reported that Rabin was underdoing extensive surgery when in fact he was already dead.[15] Footage of the peace rally gave various descriptions of where the shooting had occurred.[16] There were conflicting reports about how many times Rabin had been shot. And various claims of responsibility for the shooting were reported, none of which were borne out.[17]

Following the initial shock of the shooting, however, the media worked around their own inaccuracies. Television, though already a proven medium, reached new levels at least in the Israeli context, where, as one observer told it, its "impact has been unparalleled."[18] Similarly, after the assassination of Kennedy the U.S. television medium was perceived to have come of age.[19]

The extraordinary nature of the event was marked by the media in ways that overplayed the departure from routines that covering it required. Reporters made numerous revelations about changed plans. *Time* reporter Lisa Beyer cut short her maternity leave to cover the story.[20] The *Washington Post* ran an ombudsman's column—"Saturday's Story"—that recounted how the newspaper's staff had issued the story against all odds.[21] The staff of *Time* received the Overseas Press Club Award for Best Magazine Reporting from Abroad for its extensive, last-minute reporting of the story.[22] Israeli television reporters wept on camera, in a marked replay of a teary-eyed Walter Cronkite and Frank McGee covering the death of Kennedy three decades earlier.[23] In the *Washington Post*'s view, reporters covering Rabin's death produced "the kind of newspapering they'll remember all their lives."[24] Similar appraisals were made of the Kennedy assassination coverage, which was seen as having raised journalism—particularly television—to new heights.[25]

The similarities of form between the assassinations of Rabin and Kennedy had to do in part with the fact that both assassinations occurred in an era of high media coverage. Certain similarities also derived from a resemblance in the events themselves. But others derived from the fact that the U.S. media now had a precedent to guide their coverage. Although other events—such as the assassination of Abraham Lincoln—might have provided more apt historical comparisons, Lincoln's shooting lacked what Kennedy's assassination had in plenty: wide-ranging media coverage, particularly the visuals provided by television. That similarity of form was sufficient to engender broad-ranging comparisons between the two assassinations that extended to various dimensions of the U.S. media's interpretation of the death of Rabin.

Similarities of Content: Remembering Rabin Through Kennedy

Rabin's assassination was compared to Kennedy's in numerous aspects of the U.S. media's coverage. Like Kennedy's, Rabin's death was earmarked as the material of memory almost immediately, with its resonance compared explicitly to that of the earlier assassination. As one U.S. citizen living in Israel was quoted in the *Washington Post*, "Forever I will remember where I was when Kennedy was shot. Now I will have to remember where I was when Rabin was shot. This is not the way it was supposed to be."[26] The media underscored this shared memorial cogency whenever they could, and Rabin's assassination was seen as provoking in Israelis the same kind of flashbulb memory that Kennedy's death had induced. The *New York Times*, for instance proclaimed that, over and over in conversations, Israelis recalled the assassination of John F. Kennedy and said that, like Americans who were alive in 1963, they would never forget where they were when they heard the news of Mr. Rabin's death.[27]

The media kept the parallel with Kennedy's death intact, even when other agents of memory offered alternative frames for remembering. The following interchange, for instance, took place on CNN:

> Reporter: We've been speculating and talking about in Israeli terms that this is an assassination along the lines of President Kennedy in the United States.
> Response: There are some similarities there, but I think far more it's the case of the assassination of Abraham Lincoln . . .[28]

Although the respondent raised the alternative memory of Lincoln's assassination, the CNN reporters repeatedly returned to the memory cues about Kennedy. Not only did they claim that the assassination was "on a par with the Kennedy assassination,"[29] but they repeatedly asked experts to agree with them, as in the interchange above. The day after the shooting, CNN even broadcast a commentary by correspondent Joe Morton that was titled "Rabin and Kennedy Assassinations Link Countries' Sorrows."[30]

There were three contexts for remembering Rabin's death that emerged in the U.S. media's coverage, all of which underscored a parallel with the assassination of Kennedy: the contexts of family, of nation, and of the international community. In each case, the U.S. public was guided toward an understanding of Rabin's assassination through a comparison with Kennedy's three decades earlier.

The Context of Family: Personal Loss

The personal context for positioning Rabin's death in memory focused on its significance for the basic social unit—the family. Not only did parental images surface in the coverage—one Ethiopian woman in Jerusalem claimed, "Rabin was like a father to me"[31]—but the family unit was routinely invoked as a way of domesticating and concretizing the political and symbolic dimensions of loss. The *New York Times* reported that among the signs being placed on Rabin's grave was one that read simply, "Farewell, Daddy."[32] Even Itzhak Perlman commented that "friends called from all over the world to commiserate, as if we'd lost a close relative, even a parent."[33] Likewise, Leah Rabin was called "Israel's Mother Courage."[34] Rabin's murder, one writer summed up, was "like a death in the family."[35]

Within the context of family, the youth of Israel were thought to have endured a particularly difficult loss. Claiming to have lost a grandfather, young Israelis were seen by the U.S. media as having been emptied of hope by the event.[36] The *New York Times* ran a special story that focused on the youth of Israel five days after the assassination, and Ted Koppel interviewed several young Israelis on ABC's "Nightline."[37] As Kennedy's efforts during the 1960s with the Peace Corps and civil rights had won over the youth of the United States, Rabin's mission for peace was codified as having touched off a spiritual fervor among the youth of Israel. Their poems, graffiti, memorial candles, and tear-stricken faces filled the pages of the press and television screens.

Visual images of Rabin's family and close friends also helped underline the personal aspects of loss. Although an emphasis on Rabin's family, particularly his widow and children, was somewhat out of step with the usual coverage of Israeli political leaders—in that the Israeli media do not traditionally focus on the personal lives of their leaders with same zeal that the U.S. media do—the U.S. media forced a focus on the widow and children in a way that suited the larger assassination narrative. The *Los Angeles Times*, for instance, positioned two articles side by side with secondary headlines "The Widow" and "The Granddaughter."[38]

The parallel here with Kennedy's assassination was striking. Images of Leah Rabin, stricken with grief and surrounded by her children and other family members, eerily suggested an older version of Jacqueline Kennedy. Photos of Leah Rabin reaching out to touch her husband's casket recalled images of Kennedy's widow making the same gesture.[39] Like Jackie Kennedy, Leah Rabin was codified as elegant and strong, dignified and enduring—"larger than life," admired for "her power, her strength."[40] In a piece called "The Woman in Black," *Newsweek* began by noting that Rabin's widow "broke down only once at the funeral."[41] The slain Rabin's home was characterized as "a fortress and an oasis."[42]

The parallel between the two assassinations extended to the family in an explicit fashion as well. The *Los Angeles Times* began a profile of Leah Rabin by remarking that, as a younger woman and diplomat's wife, she had admired Jacqueline Kennedy and tried to emulate her elegant style. She adopted the same haircut and well-tailored suits. She had Kennedy's knack for hospitality. But never did she imagine she would find herself in Kennedy's shoes as the widow of a visionary head of state.[43] Newspapers recounted that the widow, "dressed in black, sat with dignity and composure—the Jackie Kennedy of Israel."[44]

Rabin's children and grandchildren were at the center of this dimension of memory work. Seen as having had a special relationship with the slain leader, Rabin's two children, grown and married, were depicted time and again in shots of mourning. Attention particularly focused on his 18-year-old granddaughter, Noa Ben Artzi Pelossof, who spoke publicly at the funeral of her love for her grandfather. Depicted by one newspaper as "the apple of her grandfather's eye," Ben Artzi "moved the nation and much of the world to tears" with her eulogy.[45] Photographs showed her breaking into tears while making the address. Such photos and narratives again recalled those that had circulated three decades earlier around the death of Kennedy, when pictures of his small children, Caroline and John Jr., filled the press and television, particularly one image of three-year-old John saluting his father's casket. Such memory cues were repeated with Rabin's grieving granddaughter.

In both assassinations, the family context was also seen as breaking apart via a focus on human blood. Pictures and videotapes focused on Eitan Haber, Rabin's longtime close personal aide, displaying a blood-soaked song sheet that Rabin had put in his breast-pocket at the Tel Aviv peace rally. The blood signified both Haber's closeness to the slain leader and the depth of his loss. But for those who remembered the coverage of Kennedy's death, it also recalled the blood-soaked dress of Jacqueline Kennedy as she made her way from Dallas. Just as Kennedy's widow had insisted on wearing her dress so that the world would see what had happened to her husband, Haber pushed a "combination of horror and connection onto the world" when he pulled the sheet, still folded, from his own breast-pocket and read it aloud at Rabin's funeral.[46]

The National Context: Political Loss

As with the death of any head of state, the killing of Rabin was seen as more than just the end of one man's life. It had broader importance as well, marking the end of an era in Israeli politics. In a direct repetition of the phrases connected with Kennedy's assassination, commentators on Rabin's death maintained soberly that Israel, like the United States before it, had "lost its innocence" along with its leader.[47]

Some reports focused on the missions that Rabin had tried to accomplish while alive, and within that scenario he was immediately personified by his most salient cause: peace. "Farewell to a Peacemaker," proclaimed a banner headline to a full-page story in the Los Angeles Times.[48] Although the New York Times wryly predicted that remembrance of the leader would emphasize his peacemaking rather than his hawkish past, in fact many of the media reports codified the intersection between warrior and peacemaker as the feature that made Rabin unique.[49] Time called him a "soldier of peace."[50] He was "a study in contrasts, a traditionalist who brought change."[51] Numerous chronicles recounted that he had finally sung peace songs at the rally for the first time in the evolution of the peace process. His last public words at that rally, wrote the Los Angeles Times, "were the words of a warrior-turned-peacemaker."[52]

In this context, the parallel with Kennedy's killing was particularly salient: "Like the Kennedy assassination," claimed one reader in the Los Angeles Times, "Rabin's quest for peace will be bolstered, not diminished, by his death."[53] Rabin's quest for peace was likened to Kennedy's passion for the space program.[54] Both men's killings were seen as a political loss of the first order.

But the political dimensions of Rabin's death, particularly as they paralleled Kennedy's, also had a darker side, and additional comparisons sneaked into each nation's sense of its future. The Los Angeles Times ran an article, previewed with a box on the newspaper's front page, that wondered about the lingering impact of Rabin's death. Specifically, it questioned whether the assassination would meet the legacy of mistrust and cynicism that had greeted that of Kennedy.[55] In a telling collapse of the visual distinction between the two events, a picture of Kennedy graced the newspaper's front page alongside pictures from Rabin's funeral.

The uncertainty surrounding the cause of the assassination promoted particularly strident discussions of the two killings. "As with Kennedy," said one observer, "the issue is not whether the chief suspect was involved but whether the whole story is really as simple as the initial explanations make it appear."[56] One day after Rabin's funeral, the *Los Angeles Times* ran a piece that addressed that issue directly, when it queried key figures in the investigation of Kennedy's death. G. Robert Blakey, who had served as the chief counsel for the committee in the U.S. House of Representatives that had reopened that investigation in the 1970s, cautioned that if Israel did not allay all uncertainties about the assassination the cost to the nation would be high. "If you don't do this right," he said, "it can plant the seeds of mistrust for a whole generation."[57] The seeds, argued the article, were in place for conspiracy theorists, although Amir's trial was expected to resolve questions that were unresolved in the case of Oswald, who was murdered before he could stand trial.

The Context of International Community: Symbolic Loss

When the discussions of Rabin's assassination turned outward from their familial and national frames, the slain leader was codified as a visionary who had been able to go beyond his own interests and beliefs in order to attend to the common good. In this regard, former U.S. ambassador to Israel Samuel Lewis argued that Rabin was unique among Israeli leaders, and that his death "went beyond the Kennedy assassination parallel."[58]

Rabin was seen as the embodiment of Israel, called by one news magazine simply "Man of Israel."[59] He was "the quintessential Israeli," said another journal.[60] Rabin, an Israeli-born sabra, so embodied contemporary Israel in U.S. eyes that his death was seen as shattering the nation's core. In some cases, this extended to the entire Jewish community, exemplified by one *New York Times* article entitled "Jews Say Their Values Were Torn by a Bullet."[61]

The assassination in such a view generated concerns about Israel's standing in the international community. Charles Krauthammer lamented the "breakdown of civil discourse in Israel."[62] Unspoken assumptions that a Jew would never murder another were shattered, and the U.S. media made much of the point. The *New York Times* quoted observers who pondered, "Has Israel created a new kind of Jew who can kill?"[63] Rabin's killing also shattered assumptions about unfailing Israeli security and assumptions that in politics words did not necessarily lead to violence. In the *New Yorker's* view, "the rhetoric that was the assassin's" had supporters in both Israeli and U.S. Jewish circles.[64]

Significantly, in this frame Rabin's assassination was fit by the U.S. media within its own tradition of upheaval from the 1960s. "We're having deja vu all over again," complained one observer. "JFK, RFK, Martin Luther King, Jr., Malcolm X. . . . Those too young to remember the 1960s now know collective bereavement for the first time."[65] The trauma of a 1960s America was used as a benchmark for explaining Israel's suffering. As one writer commented in the *Los Angeles Times*: "I clearly remember the fateful Friday of John Kennedy's assassination (followed fairly rapidly by the assassination of Robert Kennedy and the Rev. Martin Luther King), and the trenchant comment of Don McLean, whose music gave expression to America's travail in the '60s: 'We think now that we will never laugh again; we will laugh again, but we shall never be young again.' My nation has now become only too normalized."[66]

One article described in detail the way in which U.S. Senator Ted Kennedy sprinkled earth from his older brothers' graves at Arlington National Cemetery onto the grave of Rabin.[67]

Yet the death of Rabin also forced more positive scenarios. Nearly the entire U.S. Cabinet packed onto Air Force One for the funeral. New political categories were forged that brought together old enemies and created new disjunctions between what one journal called those who were "psychologically mobile" and those who were "stonily fixated in the grip of fundamentalist mindsets."[68] Jews and Arabs were among both groups. As one Israeli later said, only after seeing the assembled guests at the funeral did he realize the international impact that Rabin had had.[69] Mary McGrory, writing in the *Washington Post*, offered the view that "great funerals often bring survivors to their senses," as did Kennedy's funeral, when "ex-presidents Eisenhower and Truman made peace with each other after years of hostile silence."[70] In that light, a front-page picture of Leah Rabin and Yasser Arafat sitting shiva together bore witness to the changed political order.[71]

Other Memories, Other Frames

It is worth noting that frames from the past other than that of Kennedy's death were also invoked to further understanding of Rabin's assassination. Some reports invoked the U.S. Civil War: observers worried that the political schisms over Rabin's peace accord could "become a fight between the two sides—civil war."[72] Other comparisons invoked the U.S.

Revolution to suggest that the fight over a nation's collective identity was resurfacing in an Israeli context.

But the frame that was most frequently invoked as an alternative to that of the Kennedy assassination was the assassination of Lincoln. Like Rabin, Lincoln was the first head of state assassinated, and *Newsweek* offered the view that both men were war leaders "whose personal strength held together a divided nation."[73]

In fact, the Lincoln assassination was an apt historical comparison. Discussions about the assassin particularly favored the parallel. Both Amir and John Wilkes Booth, Lincoln's assassin, acted on the basis of political aims. As the *Washington Post* proclaimed of Amir, "This is not Lee Harvey Oswald, a disturbed assassin whose motives we still cannot fathom. This is John Wilkes Booth, a man with a plan."[74] Not surprisingly, then, Amir was called "an Israeli John Wilkes Booth."[75]

In one CNN interview, former U.S. secretary of state Lawrence Eagleburger was particularly adamant about rejecting a comparison between the deaths of Rabin and Kennedy and supporting instead a parallel with Lincoln. "It was the first assassination of an American president," he explained, adding that "Lincoln was a man who was courageous in trying to hold the Union together but at the same time compassionate about how he would handle the South. All of those things are similar to Mr. Rabin. He was murdered by someone who believed in slaveholding and in the splitting of the Union, and Mr. Rabin has clearly been murdered by somebody who thinks that the directions in which Mr. Rabin was trying to take his country, which is toward peace, were inappropriate, and he clearly was a man who wanted war. He and John Wilkes Booth have a lot to answer to for the same kinds of attacks on history."[76] Some readers among the general public held similar views, as one letter to the editor of the *Los Angeles Times* suggested:

> Many compare the assassination of Rabin to that of President Kennedy. Certainly, for those of us who remember, the physical and emotional pains are the same. Yet in historical perspective, it is the assassination of Abraham Lincoln that comes to mind. Both occurred in young countries full of immigrants eager to establish new societies. Both societies were struggling with building new codes of civic behavior while quickly discarding the ways of the old worlds that they left behind. Both leaders were assassinated while being engaged in massive battles to change the course of their nations' histories. And, just like Lincoln's assassination did not stop the emancipation for which he fought, neither will Rabin's death stop the peace process between Israel and its neighbors.[77]

The parallel between Lincoln and Rabin worked on numerous levels and resonated particularly well in considerations of the significance of the assassinations within their larger national contexts.

Nonetheless, the media preferred the Kennedy assassination to that of Lincoln as a frame for making sense of Rabin's death, and they continued to uphold that parallel throughout their coverage. When the Lincoln parallel was mentioned, it was noted generally by officials, politicians, readers, and private citizens, not by the media.

Why did the U.S. media prefer Kennedy's assassination to that of Lincoln as a way of framing the event of Rabin's death? The Kennedy assassination offered the media a way to tell the story that the Lincoln assassination could not provide. Although the Lincoln assassination offered a clearer blow-by-blow parallel with the event itself, the Kennedy assassination made sense both because it offered a familiar frame and because it brought back the intensity of response experienced in the 1960s by many of the people reporting Rabin's death. More important, however, it offered a viable template for reporting that the Lincoln assassination could not provide. The U.S. media's repository of images and messages about the death of a head of state established the familiarity of the earlier event in a way that the media could now recycle, with slight variations. As a frame for making sense of the present through the media, then, Kennedy's death worked more effectively than Lincoln's.

How Is the Past Made to Matter?

In political discourse, the body of the head of state has long been co-opted as a reflection of the state itself.[78] In medieval times, the head of state, usually the king, was thought to have two bodies—one mortal and potentially destructible, the other a mystical creation reflecting the state of his kingdom.[79] A king's death, however, signaled trouble and unrest in the territory over which he ruled. The king's body thereby functioned as a metaphor for the political domain.

In the democratic nations of contemporary times, the death of a head of state does not necessarily lead to the death of the nation-state. Many factors have come over time to modify such a direct linkage, the media among them. Although the media are not the first or only safeguard against civil unrest, they play a crucial role in ensuring that the nation-state does not crumble after its leader dies. The media's coverage of the death of a leader, particularly when he has been assassinated, helps stabilize the transition from one head of state to another. This chapter suggests, however, that the media help effect that transition by fashioning their coverage of contemporary traumas through familiar cues from the past. They help stabilize potential insecurity by invoking rearranged cues from the past into a template that meets present needs. In the case of Rabin's assassination, this meant using the Kennedy assassination coverage to present the difficult story of the Israeli leader's death in a more bearable and potentially meaningful fashion. Although no blatant wrong arises from using the past in such a way to explain the present, using it in times of crisis should nonetheless give pause.

What is less obvious in the use of the past is the media's stake in the practice. The Kennedy assassination was invoked as a frame for understanding Rabin's death because it helped the media cover the story more quickly, more effectively, and potentially more meaningfully. Which memories they invoked in rearrangement, and in what fashion, thus had as much to do with their own agendas and need for self-legitimation as with the event at hand.

Regardless of whether Kennedy's death provided the fullest historical parallel to the assassination of Rabin, it offered the fullest parallel of the event's media coverage. This meant that the U.S. media established Rabin's assassination as a latter-day version of Kennedy's death not only for reasons connected to the journalistic record—that is, because it offered a compelling comparison between two events of the contemporary age. They also established the comparison for reasons central to their own legitimation as spokespeople for the assassination story—because it helped them do their job.

In any public event, the shape of the coverage that the media provide is rarely that which is expected. But all such coverage occurs within templates that are known and familiar—both to the public and to the media who give stories about public life their shape. It would be wise to more closely contemplate the reasons that such templates resurface and the effect that they have on the public imagination.

Notes

Thanks to Selcan Kaynak for assisting me with this paper.

   1. For an extensive discussion of collective memory and Kennedy's assassination, see Barbie Zelizer, *Covering the Body: The Kennedy Assassination, the Media, and the Shaping of Collective Memory* (Chicago: University of Chicago Press, 1992).

   2. Maurice Halbwachs, *On Collective Memory* (Chicago: University of Chicago

Press, 1992 [1951]). The quote is from Patrick Hutton, "Collective Memory and Collective Mentalities: The Halbwachs-Aries Connection," *Historical Reflections/Reflexions Historiques* 15 (2): 314.

3. See Barbie Zelizer, "Reading the Past Against the Grain: The Shape of Memory Studies," *Critical Studies in Mass Communication* (June 1995): 214–39.

4. Barton Gellman, "Mood on Bus No. 7: 'Are There No Limits?'" *Washington Post*, November 6, 1995, p. A19.

5. See Gaye Tuchman, *Making News* (New York: Free Press, 1978), pp. 59–63.

6. For the Kennedy funeral, see Daniel Dayan and Elihu Katz, *Media Events* (Cambridge, Mass.: Harvard University Press, 1992).

7. Marjorie Miller, "Rabin Is Assassinated at Rally," *Los Angeles Times*, November 5, 1995, p. A6.

8. Glenn Frankel, "Past Killings of Jews by Jews Both Unified and Divided Israelis," *Washington Post*, November 6, 1995, p. A19.

9. David Remnick, "The Talk of the Town," *New Yorker*, November 20, 1995, p. 37.

10. For a detailed discussion of this broader narrative, see Zelizer, *Covering the Body*, pp. 49–66.

11. William D. Montalbano, "TV Helped Israel Come to Terms with Its Grief," *Los Angeles Times*, November 9, 1995, p. A14.

12. This was discussed at length in Howard Rosenberger, "From Rabin's Funeral, the Scene and the Unseen," *Los Angeles Times*, November 7, 1995, p. F1.

13. *Time*, "To Our Readers."

14. Ted Koppel, "Nightline: Town Meeting from Jerusalem," ABC News, November 14, 1995.

15. "Rabin Hit by Three Bullets at Close Range" and "Israeli Ambassador to UN Confirms Rabin Shooting," CNN, November 4, 1995.

16. CBS News, November 4, 1995; ABC News, November 4, 1995.

17. "Rabin Hit By Three Bullets at Close Range," CNN, November 4, 1995; NBC News, November 4, 1995.

18. Dan Pattir, quoted in Montalbano, "TV Helped Israel Come to Terms with Its Grief," p. A14.

19. See Zelizer, *Covering the Body*.

20. *Time*, "To Our Readers."

21. Geneva Overholser, "Saturday's Story," *Washington Post*, November 12, 1995, p. C6.

22. *Time*, "To Our Readers."

23. See Montalbano, "TV Helped Israel Come to Terms with Its Grief, p. A14; also see Zelizer, *Covering the Body*, p. 81.

24. Overholser, "Saturday's Story."

25. See Zelizer, *Covering the Body*.

26. Quoted in Gellman, "Mood on Bus No. 7"

27. Douglas Jehl, "A Moment of Disbelief and Uncertainty," *New York Times*, November 6, 1995, p. A10.

28. Wolf Blitzer and Lawrence Eagleburger, "Rabin Assassination Reaction," CNN, November 4, 1995.

29. Wolf Blitzer and Walt Rodgers, "Rabin Assassination Reaction," CNN, November 4, 1995.

30. "Rabin and Kennedy Assassinations Link Countries' Sorrows," CNN, November 5, 1995.

31. Quoted in Gellman, "Mood on Bus No. 7."

32. Joel Greenberg, "Grief and Guilt Soak Gravesite Like the Rain," *New York Times*, November 8, 1995, p. A13.

33. David Remnick, "Talk of the Town," p. 40.

34. Tom Post and Christopher Dickey, "The Woman in Black," *Newsweek*, November 20, 1995, p. 63.

35. Steve Lipman, "Who Are We?" *Tikkun*, January/February 1995, p. 58.

36. Quoted in Greenberg, "Grief and Guilt Soak Gravesite Like the Rain."

37. Alan Cowell, "From Young Israelis, An Outpouring of Emotion," *New York Times*, November 9, 1995, p. A10; "Nightline: Town Meeting from Jerusalem," ABC News, November 14, 1995.

38. The headline of the main story was "Farewell to a Peacemaker," *Los Angeles Times*, November 7, 1995, p. A9.

39. For example, see picture appended to Carla Power and Gregory Beals, "Grandfather, You Were the Pillar of Fire," *Newsweek*, November 20, 1995, p. 60.

40. Dalia Philosof, cited in Marjorie Miller, "Leah Rabin: 'Larger Than Life,'" *Los Angeles Times*, November 7, 1995, p. A9.

41. Post and Dickey, "The Woman in Black."

42. Miller, "Leah Rabin: 'Larger Than Life.'"

43. Ibid.

44. Marjorie Miller, "Peres Appeals for Unity as a Shocked Israel Mourns Rabin," *Los Angeles Times*, November 6, 1995, p. A1.

45. Marjorie Miller, "The Keeper of Rabin's Flame," *Los Angeles Times*, November 7, 1995, p. A9.

46. Jim Hoagland, "'Pillar of Fire,'" *Washington Post*, November 7, 1995, p. A13.

47. Mary Curtius, "Israelis Confront the Heart of Hatred," *Los Angeles Times*, November 7, 1995, p. A1.

48. "Farewell to a Peacemaker," *Los Angeles Times*, November 7, 1995, p. A9.

49. Clyde Haberman, "Recalling a Peacemaker, Hard Crust and All," *New York Times*, November 6, 1995, p. A1.

50. "Soldier of Peace" (cover story), *Time*, November 13, 1995, p. 56.

51. Michael Parks, "A General Who Wanted Peace," *Los Angeles Times*, November 5, 1995, p. A1.

52. "Final Address Echoes Words of a Peacemaker," *Los Angeles Times*, November 5, 1995, p. A6.

53. Joan C. Hatt, "Letter to the Editor," *Los Angeles Times*, November 7, 1995, p. B8.

54. Ibid.

55. "Lingering Impact of Assassinations," *Los Angeles Times*, November 7, 1995, p. A1.

56. Richard T. Cooper, "Rabin's Death, Like J.F.K.'s, Could Breed Skeptics," *Los Angeles Times*, November 7, 1995, p. A5.

57. Ibid.

58. Samuel Lewis, "Samuel Lewis Explains Reasons for Israeli Shock," CNN, November 6, 1995.

59. Kevin Fedarko, "Man of Israel," *Time*, November 13, 1995, p. 69.

60. Wendy Orange, "Rabin Is Dead," *Tikkun*, January/February 1996, p. 48.

61. Pam Belluck, "Jews Say Their Values Were Torn by a Bullet," *New York Times*, November 6, 1995, p. A13.

62. Charles Krauthammer, ". . . And Paid with His Life," *Washington Post*, November 10, 1995, p. A29.

63. Belluck, "Jews Say Their Values Were Torn by a Bullet."

64. Remnick, "Talk of the Town," p. 37.

65. Letty Cottin Pogrebin, "Yitzhak Rabin: A Meditation," *Tikkun*, January/February 1996, p. 70.

66. Shlomo Riskin, "Israel, the Morning After," *Los Angeles Times*, November 6, 1995, p. B2.

67. Elisa Ben-Rafael and Joab B. Eilon, "The Golden Bowl Is Broken," *Tikkun*, January/February 1996, p. 43.

68. Wendy Orange, "Rabin Is Dead," *Tikkun*.

69. Quoted in Nomi Morris, "Soul Searching," *MacLean's*, November 20, 1995, p. 73.

70. Mary McGrory, "Leah Rabin's Lament," *Washington Post*, November 7, 1995, p. A2.

71. The picture appeared on the front page of the *New York Times*, November 10, 1995. It also appeared with the article "We Became More Than Friends," *Time*, November 20, 1995, p. 81, and appended to Post and Dickey, "The Woman in Black."

72. Miller, "Peres Appeals for Unity as a Shocked Israel Mourns Rabin," p. A10.

73. Evan Thomas, "Can Peace Survive?" *Newsweek*, November 13, 1995, p. 43.

74. Charles Krauthammer, ". . . And Paid with His Life."

75. Patt Morrison, K. Connie Kang, and John Dart, "Sorrow Unites Those Still at Odds over Peace Effort," *Los Angeles Times*, November 5, 1995, p. A5.

76. Lawrence Eagleburger, "Rabin Assassination Reaction," CNN, November 4, 1995.

77. Hanna Hill, "Letter to the Editor," *Los Angeles Times*, November 7, 1995, p. B8.

78. Ernst H. Kantorowicz, *The King's Two Bodies: A Study in Mediaeval Political Theology* (Princeton, N.J: Princeton University Press, 1957); also see Mike Featherstone, Mike Hepworth, and Bryan S. Turner (eds.), *The Body: Social Process and Cultural Theory* (London: Sage, 1991). see also Chapter 9 in this volume by Haim Hazan.

79. See Bryan S. Turner, "The Anatomy Lesson: A Note on the Merton Thesis," *Sociological Review* 38 (1990): 13. For a consideration of discussions about the body of John F. Kennedy, see also Barbie Zelizer, "From the Body as Evidence to the Body of Evidence," in Katharine Young (ed.), *Bodylore* (University of Tennessee Press, 1993), pp. 225–44.

PART IV

The Ongoing Crisis of Legitimacy

The Latitude of Acceptance: Israelis' Attitudes toward Political Protest before and after the Assassination of Yitzhak Rabin

EPHRAIM YUCHTMAN-YAAR

AND TAMAR HERMANN

Democratic Citizenship and Political Protest

The proliferation of citizens' initiatives, social movements, and other manifestations of extraparliamentary public political participation in Israel from the mid-1970s through the 1980s and 1990s marks a change in the Israeli political culture since the first decades of statehood.[1] This change[2] makes one ask a critical question: whether such grassroots activities are potentially harmful or beneficial to Israeli democracy. Previously, Israeli democracy had been characterized by a highly centralized, party-oriented political system, in which extraparliamentary criticism was relatively scarce and was considered destructive to the democratic well-being of the fledgling state, because it implied less than full control by the authorities over the political arena.

The question of active public participation in political decision-making in democratic systems has always been of scholarly and practical interest. Broadly speaking, one may distinguish between two principal approaches to this issue. The first approach, represented by political thinkers such as Schumpeter[3] and Kornhauser,[4] advocates limited public interference in state affairs, on the grounds that in a democracy, the appropriate occasion for the public to express its political preferences is election day and ordinary decision-making, particularly in the "high politics" of foreign and security affairs, should be left to the representative government. In contrast, the "participatory democracy" approach, represented in the writings of Rousseau and at present by Pateman,[5] among others, is based on the acknowledgment that the functioning of a viable, authentic democracy requires active forms of citizenship. It should be noted, however, that the advocates of this approach disagree about the recommended forms of public political participation. While most favor legal forms of participation only, some go as far as to say that even illegal forms of grassroots activity should be acceptable in certain circumstances.[6]

The scholarly debate aside, the public itself is often divided over this question. In Israel, as several studies have pointed out, the notion of citizen participation is quite deeply rooted.[7] While some Israelis consider straightforward protest against official policies a threat to the democratic order or a symptom of delegitimization of the representative system, the majority regard grassroots political activism as a fundamental element of a genuine democratic order or, at least, an effective and legitimate way to overcome what they see as the authorities' frequent unresponsiveness to demands from below. Hence, the majority of Israelis endorse the idea of political protest or the "politics of provocation," and a considerable percentage of the population sometimes takes part in such activities.[8]

Since the launching of the Oslo process, all observers who care about the stability of Israeli democracy have paid much greater attention to the legitimacy, efficacy, and relevance of grassroots protest.[9] This process, foremost because of the steep material and nonmaterial costs it involves, has evoked an increasingly heated debate within Israel and elicited an unprecedented wave of protest, legal and illegal, from both the left and the right. The turmoil culminated in a tragic moment of truth on November 4, 1995: the assassination of Prime Minister Yitzhak Rabin by Yigal Amir, an activist in the extraparliamentary radical right. The assassination exposed the difficult question of the limits of acceptable forms of civic participation in a democratic system. The dilemma was exacerbated by widespread charges that the leaders of right-wing opposition parties, by implicitly and explicitly encouraging antigovernment protest activities— particularly those focusing on Mr. Rabin—had created an atmosphere that directly or indirectly instigated the assassination.

Therefore, the main purpose of this chapter is to examine Israelis' attitudes toward political protest in the context of the assassination of Yitzhak Rabin. We focus on two related questions. First, did the assassination bring about significant changes in attitudes toward political protest among the population at large and how long-lasting have these changes been? Second, were there systematic group differences in these attitudes before and after the assassination and, if so, what were the major inter-group cleavages that produced the disparities in their reactions—political, sociodemographic, or both?

Former discussions of political protest often focused on the distinction between legal and illegal protest and between violent and nonviolent forms of illegal protest.[10] We examine an additional analytical distinction, which we consider equally significant: the distinction between those who uphold the right to protest as an integral part of democratic functioning and those who oppose all kinds of protest—legal and illegal, nonviolent and violent—on the grounds that antigovernment protest is altogether undesirable.

To address the two aforementioned questions, we built several hypotheses regarding the propensity to protest before and after the assassination, at the aggregate level and the cross-sectional level.

Hypothesis 1: Shock Effects

As mentioned above, the first question addressed in this chapter is whether the assassination of Prime Minister Rabin has affected the legitimacy of political protest in the eyes of Israel's Jewish citizens. It is commonly agreed that the assassination created a huge shock wave that rocked all of Israeli society. This effect was manifested by widespread spontaneous expressions of mourning by ordinary citizens as well as manifestations of sorrow and revulsion among the political leadership across the political spectrum. The atmosphere of a nation appalled and aggrieved was intensified by relentless mass-media coverage of the murder and its aftermath

On the basis of the literature on political assassinations,[11] it is reasonable in these circumstances to expect the Israeli people to respond in the short term by perceptibly dampening their endorsement of antigovernment protest activity for two main reasons. First, political protest was perceived to be closely associated with, if not a catalyst of, this traumatic assassination. Second, the manifestations of protest and the right-left antagonism that formed the backdrop for the assassination were perceived as threatening and detrimental to Israeli national unity. The question, however, is whether this immediate shock effect applied to all forms of political protest—legal and illegal, violent and nonviolent, etc.—to the same extent. One possibility is that Israelis displayed such panic that they drastically withdrew or downscaled their support for all forms of protest, including legal ones. Alternatively, the commitment to the democratic value of active participation may have been so deeply rooted that even immediately after the assassination, despite the shock, the people withdrew their support only from illegal or violent protests and adhered to the democratic path of legal forms of protest.

As for the long-term effects of the assassination, the aforementioned literature suggests that the immediate public shock after such an event tends to dissipate over time until the general features of the political culture are eventually restored. However, the extent to which these observations are applicable to this case is not quite clear, mainly because the political cleavages that nourished the climate of political protest before the assassination have not disappeared and the salience of the right-left antagonism has continued to govern the Israeli political discourse. On the other hand, the general elections that took place in May 1996, about seven months after the assassination, resulted in the replacement of the Labor-led government by a new coalition government headed by Likud and its allies on the right. This crucial turn of power, by changing the specific meaning of "antigovernment protest," undermines our ability to contemplate the possible effects of the passage of time on attitudes toward protest and to distinguish between these effects and the change in government.

The hypothesis presented above, regarding the shock effect and the recovery, refers to the Israeli public *en bloc* and disregards potential differences in the initial (i.e., preassassination) attitudes of various population groups toward political protest. It also overlooks the possibility that the assassination had different short- and long-term effects on the attitudes of such groups. The following hypotheses are meant to refine the first one in this respect.

The Preassassination Propensity to Protest

Given the nature of the political confrontation over the peace process that preceded Rabin's assassination, and the fact that perceptions of security affairs overshadow all other issues in determining political attitudes across the entire political spectrum of Israeli society,[12] it was reasonable to expect that support for political protest, particularly illegal protest, would depend on or at least correspond to attitudes toward Rabin's government and, especially, its peace policy. Surveys conducted for the Peace Index Project[13] indicate that opponents and supporters of the peace process can be differentiated in two complementary ways: by sociodemographic characteristics and by voting behavior. With regard to the first criterion, it has been consistently observed that support for the peace process corresponds most strongly with higher education and income, Ashkenazi origin, and older age—that is, with the strongest groups in Israeli society. Opposition to the process, in turn, was found to be more in concert with lower levels of income and education, Mizrahi (Sephardi) origin, and younger age— that is, with a weaker position in the Israeli power structure (in the sense of command of material and political resources).

With respect to the sociopolitical dimension, supporters of right-wing parties and especially those who back the far right—who in many cases belong to the country's weakest socioeconomic groups—are clearly less supportive of the peace process, particularly as conducted by the Labor government, than are supporters of parties on the left. The Peace Index surveys also reveal that opposition to the Oslo process was strongly correlated with higher levels of religious observance[14] and voting for orthodox and, especially, ultra-orthodox parties.

The distribution of attitude toward the Oslo process according to voting preferences between January 1995 and October 1995 clearly shows that voters for orthodox and ultra-orthodox parties are very close in their attitudes to the voters of the secular far right (percent, $N = 3,459$):

	Pro-Oslo	In between	Anti-Oslo
In 1996, will vote for:			
Secular far right	7.0	10.3	81.6
Ultra-orthodox	9.2	9.2	81.5
Orthodox	3.9	18.2	77.9
Right	14.0	25.1	60.8
Left	73.1	21.6	5.3

We used these findings to define three types of voting patterns among Israeli Jews: left (Meretz and Labor), right (Likud, Third Way, and Yisrael Ba'aliya), and far right (Moledet, National Religious Party, Shas, and United Torah Judaism).

On the basis of these considerations, we hypothesized as follows.

Hypothesis 2: The Preassassination Propensity of Weaker Groups

Weaker groups in Israeli society are fundamentally less inclined than stronger groups to express support for any kind of antigovernment protest because of their greater vulnerability in the system and alienation from it. By the same token, because of their greater identification with the political right, these groups could be more supportive of illegal protest. We cannot anticipate *a priori* which of the two tendencies will prevail.

Hypotheses 3: The Preassassination Propensity of Anti-Oslo Groups

It is almost trivial to suggest that the sociopolitical groups that opposed Rabin's government in general and the peace process in particular, as characterized above, were more inclined toward antigovernment protest. However, it is not clear to what extent these groups were willing to express overt support for illegal and, especially, violent forms of protest. Given the climate of political turmoil before the assassination and the implicit delegitimation of Rabin's government by the leaders of the parties on the right, we expect to find that significant numbers of their followers leaned toward support of nonviolent illegal protest but that very few went as far as to endorse violent forms of protest.

The Postassassination Propensity to Protest

The following hypotheses (4 and 5) suggest that the two factors mentioned above—the group's position in the power structure and intergroup differences in sociopolitical orientation—might have generated different reactions to protest activity following the assassination. Notwithstanding our hypothesis regarding the shock effect of the assassination on the public as a whole, we would expect to find that the event left differential impacts—that is, affected some groups more powerfully and in different ways and degrees than others. In this context, two hypotheses were formulated.

Hypothesis 4: The Guilt-by-Association Syndrome

The immediate reaction of groups likely to be associated with the assassin and with the sociopolitical origins of the antigovernment campaign that preceded the assassination, would be more inclined, at least overtly, to denounce all forms of protest, especially illegal ones. The groups within Israeli society that were most likely to exhibit this syndrome were supporters of parties on the far right; opponents of the peace process, people of Mizrahi origin, and young orthodox males — those who shared salient sociopolitical traits with the assassin.

Hypothesis 5: "Weaker"-Group Vulnerability

We expected the inclination to reject all forms of antigovernment protests following the assassination to be more pronounced among weaker social groups than among stronger ones. This is because weaker groups feel more vulnerable in situations of social unrest and instability, such as that created by Rabin's murder, because these situations may threaten their already dismal well-being. Moreover, weaker groups are less likely to make "fine" distinctions, such as between legal and illegal forms of protest, thus opting for the safety of "no protest" at all.

Method

To test these hypotheses, we used a research design composed of the following elements: (1) comparison of attitudes toward antigovernment protest at four points in time; (2) an operational definition of the different attitudes toward political protest as the dependent variable; (3) specification of presumably relevant independent variables. The procedure is described below.

TIMES OF ATTITUDE MEASUREMENT AND DATABASE

Since the main purpose of this chapter is to detect change, the analysis below pertains to four specific points of measurement: September 27, 1995, about five weeks before the assassination (hereafter: t_1);[15] November 8, 1995, four days after the assassination (t_2); October 29, 1996 (t_3), about one year later; and December 30, 1997 (t_4), about two years afterwards. The findings are based on data collected by means of telephone interviews conducted on these four dates. Each survey encompassed slightly over 500 respondents aged 18 and above, who constitute a representative sample of the adult Jewish population of Israel, including settlers in the occupied territories and kibbutz members. The surveys were conducted as a part of the aforementioned Peace Index Project.[16]

DEPENDENT VARIABLE

Our major dependent variable is Israelis' attitudes toward antigovernment protest. To measure this variable empirically, we asked the respondents in the four surveys the following three questions:

> In your opinion, should citizens who consider the government's policy on the peace process harmful to Israel's national interest have the right to (possible answers — *Yes* or *No*):
>
> 1. Protest in lawful ways (e.g., initiate petition campaigns or hold demonstrations with official permits)?
>
> 2. Participate in nonviolent acts of civil disobedience (e.g., demonstrate without a permit, initiate a popular tax boycott, refuse to perform military service)?
>
> 3. Participate even in violent acts of civil disobedience (e.g., forcibly resist the evacuation of settlements in the occupied territories)?

We assumed that the logic underlying the answers to these questions, taken together, is transitive in terms of Guttman's Scale, as follows: support for illegal protest activity also implies support for legal protest activity but not vice versa; in other words, not everyone who supports legal protest activity necessarily supports illegal activity but everyone who supports illegal protest activity probably supports legal protest. Similarly, support for violent illegal protest ostensibly implies support for nonviolent illegal protest, but the reverse is not true. Finally, those who oppose legal protest *ipso facto* oppose illegal protest.

On the basis of this logic and the answers to the three aforementioned questions, we distinguished among four types of attitudes of Israeli citizens toward protest activity:

Type A: Totally antiprotest citizens (those who answered No to all three questions).

Type B: Law-abiding citizens (those who answered Yes to question 1 and No to questions 2 and 3).

Type C: "Soft-core" nonconformist citizens (those who answered Yes to questions 1 *and* 2, but No to question 3).

Type D: "Hard-core" nonconformist citizens (those who answered Yes to all three questions)

An empirical examination of the relationships among the answers to the three questions at the four points of measurement, as reflected in this fourfold taxonomy, yields results that strongly support the assumption of transitivity. For example, in September 1995 only 3.5 percent of all cases deviated from the pattern of Guttman's scale. Similar results were found at the three other points of measurement.

Based on these results, we operationalized the concept of attitudes toward protest in two complementary ways:

As a quantitative measure, i.e., on a scale from 1 (opposition to all forms of protest) to 4 (support of all forms of protest). We used this measure to calculate, for example, the mean scores and variance of the level of support for protest at each time of measurement for the entire sample and for different subgroups.

As a qualitative measure, distinguishing among four types of attitudes toward protest. This enabled us to refine the quantitative analysis, since the same degree of propensity to protest in terms of the mean scores on the scale may represent different profiles in terms of the different types of protest.

INDEPENDENT VARIABLES

As mentioned, we used two sets of independent variables: sociodemographic and sociopolitical. The first set was composed of sex, age,[17] education,[18] income,[19] and ethnic origin.[20] The choice of these specific variables was based largely on the results of previous research that consistently demonstrated strong correlations between most of them and Israeli political attitudes, social attitudes, and social cleavages.[21] The second set of variables included religiosity,[22] attitudes toward the Oslo process,[23] and voting behavior.[24]

The following analysis, predicated on our research questions and hypotheses, takes place on two levels: aggregate and cross-sectional. At the first level, we present overall trends of change in Israeli public opinion regarding the acceptability of various kinds and levels of political protest. The cross-sectional level describes the degree of support that these attitudes command among various sociodemographic and sociopolitical subgroups.

Empirical Findings

AGGREGATE TRENDS OVER TIME

As the first step in the analysis, we compared the mean scores of the general public's attitudes toward political protest at each of the four points

TABLE I

Mean Scores of Attitudes Toward Protest over Time

	t_1 N = 507	t_2 N = 506	t_3 N = 509	t_4 N = 505
Means	2.25	1.96	2.01	2.02
S.D.	(.71)	(.50)	(.51)	(.57)

NOTE: The scale ranges from 1 ("low") to 4 ("high"). All differences between the means of t_1 and subsequent points times of measurement are significant ($p < .001$) by the t test; all other paired comparisons are not.

of measurement. Table 1 indicates a significant decline in the mean score of the protest scale from t_1 (2.25) to t_2 (1.96) and subsequent times, but no significant changes since then—that is, from t_2 through t_3 and t_4 (2.01 and 2.02, respectively). These results are consistent with the hypothesized shock effect of the murder and with our consideration of the factors that might have impeded a quick recovery of the preassassination level of support for protest. In other words, the decline in this support that occurred immediately after the assassination has lasted for at least two years and therefore seems to be more than a short-term reaction. It is also worth noting the sharp decline in the variance of the protest scale, from .71 at t_1 to .50 at t_2, with relatively small changes afterwards. These results indicate that the Israeli public has apparently become more homogeneous in its attitudes toward political protest since Rabin's murder. However, it remains to be seen if this trend is also reflected in the distribution of these attitudes by types of protest.

Examination of changes over time by the proportions of the four types of protest (see Table 2) reveals that the overall decline between t_1 and the subsequent points of measurement resulted from an increase in the proportions of the no-protest and "legal protest only" types (A and B) and a decrease in the proportions of the "illegal nonviolent" and "illegal violent" types (C and D). Thus Type A climbed from 5.5 percent at t_1 to 12.6 percent at t_2 and Type B from 73.8 percent to 80.3 percent. Type C declined from 10.5 percent to 5.3 percent and Type D from 10.2 percent to 1.8 percent. Note that Type D declined more steeply than Type C, apparently because violent protest was associated with Rabin's murder. Table 2 also reveals that the changes in the attitude distribution immediately after the murder proved quite durable afterwards. Nevertheless, we call attention to the observation that the proportion of Type A receded slightly one year later (t_3), from 12.6 percent to 9.6 percent, and remained at that plateau

TABLE 2

Proportions of Types of Protest over Time

(Percent)

	t_1	t_2	t_3	t_4
Type A	5.5	12.6	9.6	9.8
Type B	73.8	80.3	82.4	80.2
Type C	10.5	5.3	5.3	7.8
Type D	10.2	1.8	2.7	2.2
Total	100%	100%	100%	100%

NOTE: All differences between the proportions of each type at t_1 and the other three times of measurement are statistically significant ($p < .001$) except for the difference between the proportions of Type C at t_1 and t_4. All other paired proportions are not statistically significant.

through the end of the following year. Similarly, support for illegal non-violent protest (Type C), which declined from 10.5 percent at t_1 to 5.3 percent at t_2, climbed again to 7.8 percent at t_4. To be sure, none of the changes between t_2 and subsequent times of measurement are statistically significant. However, they may indicate the potential of at least a partial recovery in support of political protest, including its illegal forms, with the possible exclusion of its violent manifestations.

Notwithstanding the pattern of changes in the proportions of each type of attitudes over time, perhaps the most salient finding in Table 2 is the persistent dominance of Type B—support for legal protest only—at all points of measurement. Thus even during the preassassination period, when the support for both types of illegal protest reached its peak, nearly three-quarters of the public expressed support for legal protest only. Technically speaking, the persistent dominance of this one type implies that the distributions in each of the four points of measurement are highly skewed, so that the amount of variation that remains unexplained is very small indeed. This is particularly the case at the three times of measurement after the assassination, when, as noted, the variance of the protest scale declined considerably.

Cross-Sectional Trends before and after the Assassination

The preceding aggregate analysis provides an overall picture of Israelis' attitudes toward various types of protest over time. However, such an analysis may conceal potential differences among the attitudes of major so-

TABLE 3
Mean Scores of the Protest Scale by Point in Time and Group

	t_1	t_2	t_3	t_4	t_1-t_2
Education:					
Low	2.23	1.92[a]	2.00	2.00	−.31[b]
High	2.29	2.09	2.04	2.07	−.20[b]
Ethnic Origin:					
Mizrahi	2.28	1.90[a]	1.97	1.99	−.38[b,c]
Ashkenazi	2.23	2.01	2.04	2.03	−.22[b,c]
Sex:					
Women	2.24	2.02[a]	2.02	2.04	−.22[b]
Men	2.27	1.90	2.00	2.01	−.37[b]
Income:					
Low	2.29	1.93	1.93[a]	1.99	−.36[b,c]
High	2.18	2.02	2.06	2.06	−.16[b,c]
Age:					
Young	2.32[a]	2.01[a]	2.04	2.05	−.31[b]
Old	2.12	1.89	1.97	1.96	−.23[b]
Religiosity:					
Orthodox	2.62[a]	1.90[a]	2.04	1.97	−.72[b,c]
Traditional	2.20	1.89	1.93	1.93	−.31[b,c]
Secular	2.18	2.02	2.06	2.07	−.15[b,c]
Voting:					
Left	2.06[a]	1.94	2.05	2.06	−.13[b,c]
Right	2.39	2.03	1.98	1.95	−.36[b,c]
Far Right	2.76	1.98	2.03	2.07	−.77[b,c]
Oslo:					
Pro-Oslo	2.02a	1.93	2.01	2.07	−.09[b,c]
In between	2.29	1.97	1.97	1.96	−.31[b,c]
Anti-Oslo	2.47	2.04	2.05	1.99	−.44[b,c]

NOTE: With regard to the variables of the three categories—religiosity, voting, and attitudes toward the Oslo process—we also ran Duncan tests to compare each pair of subcategories. Accordingly, with regard to religiosity the differences between the orthodox and the secular and between the traditional and the secular are significant, while the difference between the orthodox and the traditional was not. With regard to voting, the difference between the means of all categories were significant. With regard to attitudes toward Oslo, the differences between the means of all pairs were also significant.

[a] The difference between means at t_1 and at t_2 among the specific-variable subgroups is significant by the t test.

[b] The difference between this subgroup's means at t_1 and t_2 is significant according to the t test ($p < .01$)

[c] The difference between these subgroups' individual changes between t_1 and t_2 is significant on the basis of two-way variance analysis in which time was entered as an independent variable. The interaction term indicates whether the difference between the degree of change (t_1-t_2) of the relevant subgroup is statistically significant.

ciodemographic and sociopolitical subgroups at the different times of measurement. For example, a moderate increase in support for a specific attitude may in fact be the result of a small decrease in support for that attitude among members of one group and a large increase in support among members of another group. The cross-sectional analysis findings are presented in Tables 3 and 4.

Turning first to the quantitative analysis in terms of the protest scale, the figures in Table 3 reveal that the patterns of change observed at the aggregate level recurred in *all* categories of the sociodemographic and sociopolitical variables. Thus each category shows a significant decrease in the scores of the protest scale between t_1 and each of the subsequent times, with no significant changes between t_2, t_3, and t_4. However, the degree of decline between t_1 and t_2 was uneven, some groups showing larger or much larger changes than others. This may be seen in the right hand column of Table 3, which presents differences in the mean scores between t_1 and t_2 for each subgroup of the independent variables. (We focus on t_1 and t_2 because only between these two points of measurement did major significant and consistent changes occur.)

As the figures in the right-hand column of Table 3 make clear, the changes between t_1 and t_2 follow the same direction across all subgroups, as suggested by our shock-effect hypothesis, and the differences in the degree of change correspond to our weaker-groups and guilt-by-association hypotheses, although not all of these differences are statistically significant. Considering the socioeconomic variables first, it appears that the degree of decrease in the level of approved protest following the assassination was consistently larger among the weaker groups than among the stronger groups. Thus in the low and high education categories, the decreases between t_1 and t_2 were −.31 and −.20, respectively. Similarly, the change in the low income category was −.36 as against −.16 at the higher income level. Similar trends can be observed in differences between Mizrahim and Ashkenazim (−.38 vs. −.22), younger and older respondents (−.31 vs. −.23), and men and women (−.37 vs. −.22).

The most salient decline, however, occurred among groups that were generally associated with the intensive anti-Rabin campaign during the period before the murder: the far right, the orthodox, and opponents of the Oslo process. Thus the decrease in the mean scores on the protest scale was −.72 among the orthodox as against −.31 and −.15 among the traditional and the secular. Corresponding decreases were −.77 among the far right, −.36 among the right, and −.13 among the left. Finally, the change

TABLE 4

Proportions of Types of Protest by Group and Time

EDUCATION

	Low		High	
	t_1	t_2	t_1	t_2
Type A[a]	6.4	16.0	3.2	3.2
Type B	73.7	77.8	75.0	86.3
Type C	9.8	4.8	12.1	7.3
Type D	10.1	1.4	9.7	3.2

ETHNIC ORIGIN

	Mizrahi		Ashkenazi	
	t_1	t_2	t_1	t_2
Type A	9.0	17.3	3.5	9.1
Type B	67.5	76.2	78.4	83.2
Type C	10.5	5.4	10.3	5.1
Type D[a]	13.0	1.0	7.8	2.6

SEX

	Men		Women	
	t_1	t_2	t_1	t_2
Type A	5.9	16.7	5.0	8.6
Type B	71.6	77.7	76.1	82.7
Type C	12.3	3.9	8.8	6.6
Type D	10.2	1.7	10.1	2.1

INCOME

	Low		High	
	t_1	t_2	t_1	t_2
Type A	7.4	16.0	3.2	7.9
Type B	69.9	77.3	80.0	83.6
Type C	9.6	4.8	11.4	6.2
Type D[a]	13.1	1.9	5.4	2.3

AGE

	Young		Old	
	t_1	t_2	t_1	t_2
Type A	3.8	10.2	8.9	16.4
Type B	71.6	80.5	77.9	79.8
Type C	13.4	7.5	5.8	2.2
Type D	11.3	1.7	7.4	1.6

RELIGIOSITY

	Orthodox		Traditional		Secular	
	t_1	t_2	t_1	t_2	t_1	t_2
Type A[b]	2.9	15.6	7.3	20.4	5.6	7.6
Type B[a]	54.3	78.1	73.8	71.1	79.1	85.5
Type C	21.4	6.3	10.4	7.9	7.6	3.8
Type D[a]	21.4	0.0	8.5	0.7	7.6	3.1

VOTING

	Left		Right		Far right	
	t_1	t_2	t_1	t_2	t_1	t_2
Type A[a]	8.4	11.3	5.9	13.9	0.0	11.6
Type B[b,c]	82.5	83.3	64.7	74.7	48.8	69.8
Type C[c]	6.0	5.0	14.3	6.3	25.6	11.6
Type D[a,c]	3.0	0.4	15.1	5.1	25.6	7.0

OSLO

	Support		Middle		Oppose	
	t_1	t_2	t_1	t_2	t_1	t_2
Type A	8.2	12.1	6.4	12.5	3.9	12.8
Type B	84.1	83.4	69.1	78.6	64.6	75.5
Type C	5.5	4.0	14.9	7.1	12.4	7.4
Type D[c]	2.2	0.4	9.6	1.8	19.1	4.3

[a]Significant difference between category 1 and 2 between t_1 and t_2.
[b]Significant difference between category 2 and 3 between t_1 and t_2.
[c]Significant difference between category 1 and 3 between t_1 and t_2.

amounted to −.44 within the anti-Oslo group as against −.31 and −.09 among those holding a middle position and those supporting the Oslo agreement, respectively. Of course, it is difficult to tell from these findings whether the decline between t_1 of t_2 reflects a genuine change of heart among these groups or whether it was merely an expression of social desirability.

Another way of viewing the changes in attitudes toward protest over time at the group level of analysis is to examine these changes in terms of the distributions of the four types of protest. After all, as noted above, the quantitative changes in the levels of the protest scale may result from different processes, as indicated by the changes in the relative frequency of each of the four protest types over time. The data pertaining to this inquiry for t_1 and t_2 are provided in Table 4 and indicate that the pattern of aggregate changes in the proportions of the four protest types between t_1

and t_2 applies to all the sociodemographic and sociopolitical subgroups—that is, all subgroups evince increases in the proportions of types A and B and decreases in the proportions of types C and D. Moreover, in each case the decrease in support for Type D (illegal violent protest) exceeded the decrease in Type C (illegal nonviolent protest).

Notwithstanding these uniform trends, the degrees of change between t_1 and t_2 in the proportions of the protest types were not the same across groups. The most salient and systematic difference in this regard pertains to the pattern of change in Type A (no protest). As Table 4 shows, the increase in the share of this type was larger in the low-income, low-education, and Mizrahi groups, as well as among the orthodox, the far right, and the opponents of Oslo, than among their opposites. Thus the increase in Type A amounted to 9.6 percent in the low-education category as against 0.0 percent in the high-education category. Corresponding figures were 8.6 percent and 4.7 percent in the low-income and high-income categories, respectively; 8.3 percent vs. 5.6 percent among Mizrahim and Ashkenazim; 12.7 percent vs. 2.0 percent among orthodox and secular; 11.6 percent vs. 2.9 percent among far right and left; and 8.9 percent vs. 3.9 percent among anti-Oslo vs. pro-Oslo respondents. Also note the difference between men (10.8 percent) and women (3.6 percent). Taken as a whole, these figures suggest that the weaker groups and those perceived as associated with opposition to the government's peace policy were more inclined than the other groups to adopt the safest outlet, that which delegitimizes even legal types of protest. Notwithstanding this observation, Table 4 shows that these groups—particularly the far right, the orthodox, and opponents of the Oslo process—also withdrew their support of illegal protest more drastically, as suggested by the guilt-by-association hypothesis. However, as the subsequent findings of the cross-sectional analysis at t_1 point out, these groups had much more room than other groups to effect this specific reduction.

Cross-Sectional Analysis at Specific Points of Time (t_1 and t_2)

After exploring the changes that occurred between t_1 and t_2, we now focus on the groups' initial attitudes toward protest—that is, before the assassination. These differences are important because, as our hypotheses indicate, certain groups were expected to outrank others on the protest scale. Examination of the mean scores of the various groups at t_1 (see Table 3 above, left-hand column) shows that the differences by education, ethnic origin, sex and income are not statistically significant. However, there were significant differences by age and particularly large differences by levels of religious observance, voting preferences, and attitudes toward the Oslo process. These differences are consistent with our hypothesis regarding the preassassination propensity of antigovernment and antipeace groups to engage in political protest. For example, the mean score on the protest scale was 2.62 for the orthodox as against 2.20 and 2.18 for the traditional and the secular, respectively. Similarly, the mean score of the far right exceeded that of the right, which in turn exceeded that of the left (2.76, 2.39, and 2.06, respectively), while the score of Oslo opponents was higher than that of in-betweens and Oslo supporters (2.47, 2.29, 2.02).

These quantitative differences reflect the salient preassassination tendency among the orthodox, the far right, and Oslo opponents to support both forms of illegal protest. Among the orthodox, 42.8 percent supported both types of protest, as against 18.9 percent of the traditional and 15.2 percent of the secular. The corresponding figures on the right-left axis were 51.2 percent on the far right, 29.4 percent on the right, and 9.0 percent on the left. Similarly, 31.5 percent of Oslo opponents approved of illegal protest, as against 24.4 percent of in-betweens and 7.7 percent of Oslo supporters.

As for the preassassination propensity of weaker groups to engage in antigovernment protest, it should be recalled that we had no unidirectional hypothesis. In other words, we suggested that these groups might either reject all sorts of protest more vehemently or exhibit a stronger propensity to illegal protest. The observation that none of the differences in the scores among the sociodemographic subgroups were statistically significant seems to confirm that neither of these potential tendencies was dominant. However, it may be worth noting that in four of the five sociodemographic variables (age, origin, sex, and income), the propensity to protest was higher among the weaker groups than among the stronger, even if only one of the four (age) is statistically significant.

As for the distribution of attitudes toward protest immediately after the assassination (t_2), we witness a general tendency toward convergence of the means across the subgroups. This convergence apparently reflects the aforementioned differential degrees of change among the subgroups between t_1 and t_2. Thus at t_2 the extreme groups in terms of their scores on the protest scale at t_1, such as the orthodox and the far right, converted toward the other groups in their willingness to express support for protest. This process is reflected in the previously mentioned decrease in the overall variance of the protest scale from .71 at t_1 to .50 at t_2 (see Table 1).

However, despite the general tendency of intergroup convergence after the murder, several significant differences in the mean scores of the protest scale were obtained at this time of measurement, as at t_1, but the pattern of these differences does not correspond perfectly to that obtained at t_1. (Compare the means in the relevant columns of Table 3.) Before the murder, the variables that yielded the major differences were sociopolitical: voting preferences, attitudes toward the peace process, and degree of religiosity. After the murder, the effects of voting and attitudes toward Oslo disappeared, while religiosity partially reversed its direction of influence. Thus at t_1 the mean scores on the protest scale for the orthodox, the traditional, and the secular were 2.62, 2.20, and 2.18, respectively, and at t_2 they were 1.90, 1.89, and 2.02. This change seems consistent with our guilt-by-association hypothesis—that is, the orthodox reacted more extremely to the assassination by withdrawing almost all their support from illegal modes of protest, many opting for the no-protest alternative. Notice then the negligible proportion of secular respondents who opted for this outlet (see Table 4). Apparently, the guilt-by-association syndrome also accounted for the disappearance of the differences that were observed at t_1 among subcategories of the voting and the pro-/anti-Oslo variables, owing to the sharp decrease in the mean scores of the far right and the right, as well as in those of the anti-Oslo and the in-between groups.

Additionally, three sociodemographic variables that did not show significant effects at t_1—education, ethnic origin, and sex—became significant at t_2. An examination of the direction of these effects indicates that respondents of low education and of Mizrahi origin were less prone to protest than those of high education and of Ashkenazi origin. As for the effect of sex, men scored lower on the protest scale than women, because support for illegal protest decreased more strongly, and support for "no protest" increased more strongly, among men than among women, a finding consistent with the guilt-by-association hypothesis. The only variable that showed significant differences that moved in the same direction in both times was age, the young outscoring the old on the protest scale, although the difference between the two groups was much smaller at t_2 than at t_1. Notice that the lower scores of the low-education and the Mizrahi groups derive not only from steeper decreases in support for illegal protest between t_1 and t_2 but also from a higher proportion among them than among the high-education and Ashkenazi groups in respondents who chose the no-protest option. (Compare the relevant columns in Table 4.) These results are consistent with our weak-groups hypothesis.

Multivariate Analysis

The final step in our empirical analysis is an examination of the relative influence of all independent variables on attitudes toward protest at t_1 and t_2, with the variables controlled for each other by means of regression analyses (see Tables 5 and 6). Such an analysis is pertinent because quite a few of the independent variables are intercorrelated, particularly the three variables of sociopolitical nature—religiosity, voting, and pro-/anti-Oslo attitudes. (See Appendix for the correlation matrix for all variables.) The regression equations for t_3 and t_4 are not statistically significant (F = .7664; F = 1.427, see Appendix).

The standardized regression coefficients for t_1, as shown in Table 5, indicate that the strongest effect on attitudes toward protest was exerted by the public's voting preferences (Beta = .278), followed by attitudes toward Oslo (Beta = .151), with both effects in the expected direction. None of the other variables, including religiosity, yielded significant coefficients, although the age variable comes very close with a coefficient of .106 and a significance level of .053. That the religiosity variable did not yield a significant coefficient despite its appreciable gross effect is probably due to its relatively high correlation with the voting and Oslo variables. (See the correlation matrix in the Appendix.) In any event, the results of the regression analysis indicate that sociopolitical variables were more important than sociodemographic variables in determining the public's attitudes toward the use of antigovernment protest before Rabin's assassination. The total extent of variance explained by these variables (16.2 percent) may not seem very impressive, but considering the highly skewed distribution of the protest scale, as noted above—with more than 70 percent of respondents choosing the legal-only option at t_1—it is not negligible.

As for the results of the regression analysis for t_2, several observations seem in order. First, the total degree of explained variance is somewhat smaller at this time (11.5 percent) than at t_1. This finding should be expected in view of the much smaller variance of the protest scale at t_2, as noted above (see Table 1). Second, more variables seem to have significant if small effects at t_2 than at t_1, despite the smaller amount of explained variance. This is due mainly to the sharp decrease in the effect of the political variables, especially voting preferences, after the murder. Thus the metric coefficient of this variable declined from .299 at t_1 to .107 at t_2, and that of attitudes toward Oslo decreased from .126 to .070. Third, the relatively strong

TABLE 5

*Regression Analysis of Effects of Sociodemographic and Socio-
political Variables on Attitudes toward Protest (t_1)*

(Metric and standardized coefficients, N = 326)

	B	Beta
Constant	1.331 (.253)	
Education	−.136 (.091)	−.085 (.134)
Ethnic origin	.013 (.085)	.009 (.879)
Sex	−.006 (.078)	−.004 (.935)
Income	.149 (.082)	.100 (.071)
Age	.162 (.083)	.106 (.053)
Religiosity	.053 (.065)	.050 (.416)
Voting	.299 (.071)	.278 (.000)
Pro-/anti-Oslo	.126 (.051)	.151 (.013)
R^2	16.2%	

F = 7.664   p < .0001

effect of religiosity seems to act in the opposite direction of our initial hypothesis concerning this variable, since at t_2 the orthodox respondents scored lower on the protest scale than the secular. This indicates that the finding regarding the gross effect of the religiosity variable, as discussed above, is not spurious. In other words, after Rabin's murder, the orthodox were apparently more inclined than the secular to suppress their overt support of protest.

Overall, the results of the multiple regression analysis suggest that the public's attitudes toward antigovernment protest before the assassination were dominated by the political controversy between right and left, as reflected in the configuration of political-party alignments. In other words, individuals formed their attitudes mostly in accordance with the positions of the parties with which they identified. After the assassination, as all parties condemned the murder and those on the right attempted to disassoci-

TABLE 6

*Regression Analysis of Effects of Sociodemographic and Socio-
political Variables on Attitudes toward Protest (t_2)*

(Metric and standardized coefficients, N = 336)

	B	Beta
Constant	1.458 (.180)	
Education	−.143 (.061)	−.127 (.020)
Ethnic origin	−.110 (.055)	−.108 (.047)
Sex	.087 (.054)	.086 (.108)
Income	.047 (.057)	−.046 (.411)
Age	.106 (.056)	.103 (.058)
Religiosity	.127 (.046)	.180 (.006)
Voting	.107 (.051)	.145 (.038)
Pro-/anti-Oslo	.070 (.038)	.111 (.067)
R^2	11.5%	

F = 5.293   p < .0001

ate themselves from it, party affiliation lost much of its explanatory power, thereby reinforcing the influence of individuals' sociodemographic characteristics.

Summary and Discussion

The two major issues of concern in this chapter are (1) the level of support for different forms of protest before the assassination of Prime Minister Rabin and the extent to which this support changed shortly after the assassination and in ensuing years; and (2) the extent to which support for antigovernment protest generally and specific types of protest particularly, both before and after the assassination, correlate systematically with the sociodemographic and sociopolitical traits of various segments of the Israeli population.

With respect to the first question, we confirmed that the overwhelming majority of Jewish Israelis, both before and after Rabin's assassination, endorsed the idea of political protest as a legitimate means of citizen participation. However, this extensive support was limited at all points of measurement to protests conducted within the limits of the law—that is, legal protests only. This finding may be interpreted as indicative of the health of Israeli democracy at the grassroots level, particularly as it marches hand in hand with meager support for the no-protest option and a weak support for illegal protest activity. Nevertheless, one cannot overlook the disturbing finding—from the democratic point of view—that in the preassassination period a significant minority—over 20 percent—supported the use of illegal forms of protest and about half of this minority sanctions violent means of protest.

In the aftermath of the assassination, Israelis almost uniformly reduced their overt support of illegal protest activity by more than half and lowered their endorsement of violent forms of protest to nearly zero. The decline in support for illegal protest activity in the aftermath of the assassination resulted in more than an upturn in categorical rejection of all forms of protest activity. Although such a reaction did occur (from 5.5 percent at t_1 to 12.6 percent at t_2), we also witnessed a significant increase in support for legal protest only (from 73.8 percent to 80.3 percent at the two points in time). In other words, even the immediate shock effect of the assassination did not shatter Israelis' commitment to the democratic value of extraparliamentary citizen participation by legal means. The dual observation that the level of support for legal protest remained high after the assassination, while support for illegal protest has not recovered from its sharp post assassination decrease, indicates that the assassination generated in the public mind a close affinity between violent manifestations of protest and illegalism per se. Perhaps paradoxically, the assassination seems to have reinforced democratic legalism in Israel at the grassroots level.

Notwithstanding these aggregate trends, we found noticeable differences among population sectors in their endorsement of various types of protest, particularly in the preassassination period. Clearly, the most distinctive factor in this regard is voting preferences. As we anticipated, support for illegal protest activity at that time was noticeably higher among those who had voted for orthodox and far-right parties and somewhat higher than average among voters for parties of the right (mainly the Likud). Furthermore, opposition to all types of protest activity was practically nonexistent among supporters of all opposition parties on the right, religious and secular alike. The weakest preassassination support for both forms of illegal protest activity and the greatest support for legal protest only were evinced by voters on the left (Labor and Meretz)—that is, supporters of the parties that formed the coalition government and spearheaded the peace process. It is worth noting in this context that the greater effect of voting preferences as against the Oslo variable suggests that support of illegal protest against the government was not motivated by the Oslo issue alone. Supporters of the right, and particularly of the far right, apparently challenged the legitimacy of Rabin's government in the belief that it was not a "Jewish" government. One of the ways this sentiment was voiced was in overt accusations of its depending on the votes of Arab parties to assure its survival in the parliament.

Consistent with our guilt-by-association hypothesis, these rightist groups also evinced the largest decrease in support for illegal types of protest immediately after the assassination; thus, the shock effect was apparently strongest among them. However, given the strong preassassination disposition of these groups toward antigovernment protest, one might expect this propensity to recover at least partly with the passage of time. How, then, can we explain the observation that two years after the assassination, they have maintained the low levels of support for protest that they manifested immediately after the assassination? The main reason for this pattern, we suggest, is the change in government after the 1996 elections— that is, the formation of a right-wing coalition led by the Likud. Because these groups consider the new government "theirs," they have remained quite dormant as far as antigovernment protest is concerned.

How, if so, can we explain the weak level of support for antigovernment protest among voters on the left and supporters of the Oslo process after the 1996 elections? After all, the Likud government has adopted a drastically different policy toward the peace issue, subjecting the peace process to a considerable slowdown if not an outright halt. There are two plausible answers to this question. (1) The left has a fundamentally lower propensity to illegal protest, especially in its violent forms. (2) Even if highly dissatisfied with the incumbent government's policies, the left is probably constrained by the antiprotest climate created in the aftermath of the assassination, a constraint that did not exist when the right was disaffected by the peace policy of Rabin's government.

On a more general level, the implications of our findings for Israeli democracy seem to transcend the specific focal question in this chapter, the impact of Rabin's assassination on the attitudes of Israeli Jews toward protest activity. First, it appears that despite the antagonism and deep cleavages that characterized the Israeli political arena both before and after the assassination, the tragic event has not undermined the legitimacy of the political system, as indicated by the overwhelming public support for the use of legal means as the only legitimate way to express citizens' dissatisfaction with the government. This is further manifested by weak support for the two antithetical positions of total rejection of political protest and support for violent protest. Both of these attitudes are antidemocratic, although their sources are clearly different: opposition to any form of protest may imply strong sociopolitical alienation or passivity, owing either to lack of political efficacy or to doubt about the capacity of the democratic system to cope with protest. Support for violent protest, in contrast, implies the opposite: a sense of efficacy combined with lack of faith in the rules of democracy. Both positions, as demonstrated, were quite uncommon in Israel in the mid-1990s.

Appendix

Regression Analysis of Effects of Sociodemographic and Sociopolitical Variables on Attitudes toward Protest (t_3)

(Metric and standardized coefficients, N = 370)

	B	Beta
Constant	1.095 (.165)	
Education	.019 (.063)	.016 (.765)
Ethnic origin	–.052 (.060)	–.048 (.388)
Sex	.045 (.056)	.042 (.421)
Income	–.062 (.060)	–.058 (.304)
Age	.058 (.058)	.053 (.317)
Religiosity	.018 (.043)	.024 (.679)
Voting	—	—
Pro-/anti-Oslo	.030 (.037)	.047 (.411)

F = 0.704   p < 0.669

Regression Analysis of Effects of Sociodemographic and Socio-political Variables on Attitudes toward Protest (t_4)

(Metric and standardized coefficients, N = 350)

	B	Beta
Constant	1.821 (.150)	
Education	−.043 (.055)	−.043 (.436)
Ethnic origin	.032 (.057)	.032 (.579)
Sex	.057 (.050)	.062 (.252)
Income	−.050 (.054)	−.053 (.358)
Age	.080 (.058)	.079 (.173)
Religiosity	.058 (.037)	.095 (.120)
Voting	—	—
Pro-/anti-Oslo	−.002 (.033)	−.004 (.944)

F = 1.427   p < 0.193

Correlation Matrix for All Variables (t_1)

(N = 326)

	Voting	Oslo	Income	Ethnic origin	Sex	Religiosity	Education	Age	Protest scale
Protest scale	.352	.283	.093	.097	−.028	−.163	−.026	.164	1.000
Age	.178	.087	−.079	.251	−.121	−.098	−.055	1.000	
Education	.057	.125	.331	.266	.097	−.088	1.000		
Religiosity	−.505	−.371	−.117	−.195	.094	1.000			
Sex	−.024	−.033	.042	.044	1.000				
Ethnic origin	.202	.166	.126	1.000					
Income	.074	.097	1.000						
Oslo	.506	1.000							
Voting	1.000								

Correlation Matrix for All Variables (t₂)

(N = 336)

	Voting	Oslo	Income	Ethnic origin	Sex	Religiosity	Education	Age	Protest scale
Protest scale	.352	.283	.093	−.132	.118	.121	−.171	.139	1.000
Age	.178	.087	−.079	.113	−.008	−.008	−.099	1.000	
Education	.057	.125	.331	.153	−.020	−.111	1.000		
Religiosity	−.024	−.033	.042	−.183	.127	1.000			
Sex	−.024	−.033	.042	−.019	1.000				
Ethnic origin	.202	.166	.126	1.000					
Income	.074	.097	1.000						
Oslo	.506	1.000							
Voting	1.000								

Notes

1. S. Lehman-Wilzig, *Public Protest in Israel* (Ramat Gan: Bar-Ilan University, 1992) [in Hebrew]; T. Hermann, "Do They Have a Chance? Protest and Political Structure of Opportunities in Israel," *Israel Studies*, vol. 1, no. 1, pp. 144–70.

2. In terms of Wildavski's categorization of political cultures, this was a change from a hierarchical, collectivist political culture to a competitive-individual one. See A. Wildavski, "Choosing Preferences by Constructing Institutions: A Cultural Theory of Preference Formation," in Arthur Asa Berger, ed., *Political Culture and Public Opinion* (New Brunswick: Transaction, 1989), pp. 21–48.

3. J. Schumpeter, *Capitalism, Socialism and Democracy* (London: George Allen & Unwin, 1943).

4. W. Kornhauser, *The Politics of Mass Society* (New York: Free Press 1959).

5. C. Pateman, *Participation and Democratic Theory* (Cambridge: Cambridge University Press, 1970).

6. F. Fanon, *The Wretched of the Earth* (Harmondsworth: Penguin Books, 1967).

7. G. Wolsfeld, "The Politics of Provocation Revisited: Participation and Protest in Israel," in E. Sprinzak and L. Diamond, eds., *Israeli Democracy Under Stress* (Boulder and London: Lynn Rienner, 1993), pp. 199–220.

8. According to the responses in a Peace Index survey conducted in August 1996, 17 percent had signed a political petition in the previous two years, 28 percent had placed political stickers on their cars or political placards on their homes, 11 percent had participated in one political demonstration or more, and 9 percent had donated money to a political organization.

9. See, for example, *Between Protest and Civil Disobedience*, round table organized by the Israel Democracy Institute, Jerusalem, April 26, 1996.

10. For a discussion of legalism and illegalism generally and in Israeli society particularly, see E. Sprinzak, *Every Man Whatsoever Is Right in His Own Eyes— Illegalism in Israeli Society* (Tel Aviv: Sifriyat Poalim, 1986) [in Hebrew].

11. James F. Kirkham, Sheldon G. Levy, and William J. Crotty, *Assassination and Political Violence* (New York: Preager, 1970); Havens Murry Clark, Carl Leiden, and Karl M. Schmitt, *The Politics of Assassination* (Englewood Cliffs, N.J.: Prentice-Hall, 1970).

12. Asher Arian, *Security Threatened: Surveying Israeli Opinion on Peace and War* (Cambridge: Cambridge University Press, 1996); Yochanan Peres and Ephraim Yaar-Yuchtman, *Between Consent and Dissent: Democracy and Peace in the Israeli Mind* (Jerusalem: The Israel Democracy Institute, 1998) [in Hebrew].

13. The Peace Index Project is conducted by the Tami Steinmetz Center for Peace Research at Tel Aviv University. As part of the project, monthly and annual public opinion surveys have been conducted since June 1994. The aim of the project is to assess in real time developments in Israeli public opinion on issues related to the unfolding peace process.

14. See Tamar Hermann and Ephraim Yuchtman-Yaar, "The Religious-Secular Cleavage and the Oslo Peace Process," *Peace in Brief,* no. 1 (Jan. 1998), p. 3.

15. Observers of the Israeli political scene generally agree that the confrontational dialogue between right and left reached a peak in the weeks before the assassination. This, of course, raises the question of the use of this point of measurement as a baseline. Nevertheless, empirical data collected about six months earlier show that the distribution of attitudes toward political protest at that time was very similar to the findings obtained in September 1995. In other words, this period was not unique with regard to levels of support for political protest among the Jewish population in the preassassination era.

16. The fieldwork was conducted by Modi'in Ezrahi.

17. The respondents were divided into two age groups: young (18 to 45) and old (45 +).

18. This variable was divided into two subcategories: low (up to 12 years of schooling) and high (more than 12 years of schooling).

19. This variable was divided into two levels: those reporting a household income of approximately or less than the average income of a four-member Israeli household in the preceding month (low income) and those reporting a household income higher than this average (high income). The interviewees were informed of the average figure as provided by the Israel Central Bureau of Statistics.

20. Ethnic origin was measured according to the prevalent distinction between those of European or American origin (Ashkenazi, first and second generations) and those of Middle Eastern or North African origin (Mizrahi, first and second generations). Third-generation Israelis, those whose parents were born in Israel, were enumerated as Ashkenazim, since preliminary analysis of our data indicated that the attitudes of this group (about 16 percent of the adult population) are much closer to those of Ashkenazim.

21. See, for example, Peres and Yuchtman-Yaar, *Between Consent and Dissent.*

22. This variable was trichotomized into the following categories, based on interviewees' self-labeling: orthodox (including ultra-orthodox), traditional, and secular. These categories also constitute a scale of degrees of religiosity. For the

scaling properties of this variable, see Peres and Yuchtman-Yaar, *Between Consent and Dissent*.

23. This variable was divided into those who supported the Oslo process, held an in-between position, and opposed the process.

24. See note 14.

CHAPTER 14

At the Last Moment

GADI YATZIV

At the last moment, historically speaking, before becoming passé in that sector of the Israeli public from which he emerged and which, to a large extent, he represented, Rabin was shot and killed. Two legitimate, fairly similar interpretations suggest themselves. It could be said that Rabin was killed because, at the last moment before he and his generation became passé, he managed to leave an indelible historical imprint on the life and collective image of Israeli society. People are not expected to leave such a definitive imprint in their old age, and when they do, they may evoke unrestrained anger and resentment—about both the substance of the imprint and its timing; hence he was despised and thus assassinated. It could also be said that a historical miracle occurred: at the last gasp of the generation whose distinguishing features were modernity, rationalism, and enlightenment in an era when these were vanishing, Rabin, the representative par excellence of that generation, outdid himself and reached a level of Herzlism and Ben-Gurionism for which he will be remembered by history; but he only achieved that status at the very last moment, and it was the tragic, but coincidental, event of the assassination that left a dramatic mark.

In other words, the Oslo agreement through which Rabin made his imprint on Jewish and Israeli history was written and signed at the last moment, at the height of social processes that almost prevented it from happening, threatening to eliminate people like Rabin from the political ring and almost driving Israeli democracy off the tracks of rationalism. Thus Rabin signed the Oslo agreement and shook Arafat's hand even though elementary sociological analysis would have concluded that events like that could not take place.

In this chapter I seek to identify the social processes that threatened but did not obstruct the event; speculate about why the event was not prevented; and examine the impact of Rabin's assassination on changing the course and direction of these processes.

The Oslo Accord

The Oslo Accord has far-reaching historical significance that many Israelis still find it difficult to discern. When Israelis today discuss the agreement, they are usually referring to the stages it sets for creating a temporary respite and constructing confidence-building measures. Also, all Israelis and Palestinians know that the "important subjects"—the issues around Jerusalem, the right of return, the location of the borders, and the fate of the Jewish settlements—are not in the Oslo Accord, but were postponed to the "final status talks."

The importance of the Oslo Accord does not lie in these matters, and Yitzhak Rabin understood that well. This agreement created and formulated a historic compromise between two peoples, one that had tarried for too many years. In it, the government of Israel and the PLO agree to recognize each other as the legitimate representatives of two nations, each of which has legitimate claims over the same land, which is the homeland of both. These nations also agree to reach some permanent arrangement, to eschew violent means and to enter into negotiations that will gradually evolve into a permanent arrangement in which peace will prevail.

All other matters related to the Oslo Accord, including the intermediary stages and the expectation of permanent status talks, have less, if any, importance at all in the future. Some problems will sort themselves out, others will not be solved in this generation, and a large number of controversial issues will appear to future generations as strangely trivial. The crux of the matter is already achieved, the reason that violence and bloodshed prevailed between the two national movements, and this could not have been accomplished without the authority and resoluteness of Yitzhak Rabin. For that resoluteness, he paid with his life.

The Process of Derationalization

Rabin would not have recognized those who mourned at his grave, or his political opponents who suspended activity for several days, supposedly in shock over the assassination. Those who mourned were his enthusiastic supporters, but not his type: for them, the Oslo Accord was not the least of all evils, the product of a rational, sober, and cold assessment; one does not express mourning by gritting one's teeth in silence and suppressing one's anger. The peace of these mourners was a wonderful, gala party; their mourning was expressed in weeping, heart-wrenching and bitter, in community singing and candle-lighting. Had Rabin lived for one more term, these mourners would have been his potential supporters, the ones he would have had to win over, those he would have had to learn how to connect with, and it is doubtful that he would have managed.

Even his political opponents were unknowns to him. Rabin had no idea of the depth of their hatred; he never for a moment realized that they considered him—"Mr. Security"—the most despicable of traitors. He did not discern that Israel, like most Western societies, was undergoing a process of derationalization.

The process of rationalization used by Max Weber to characterize modernization (Weber, 1947), was born in the Western world some 250 years ago together with the process of creating a range of secular, "public dreams" (or ideologies) that are attainable with the end of the absolute, exclusive reign of religion as a source of meaning. From among this range, "modern man" could choose the public dream he wanted and work rationally toward its realization. The dispute over the preferred public dream or secular ideology—the important things in life that one should aim toward—takes place through arguments from the field of substantive rationality, to use Weber's term. The debate over the most efficient way to accomplish each goal takes place through arguments from the field of formal rationality, in his words. The price paid by the individual for his devotion to accumulating instrumental knowledge regarding realization of his dream, and his exclusive connection to the world through this type of knowledge is an "iron cage" (on this process according to Weber, see Bendix, 1962). Rationality and the desire to realize a public dream thus entered the world as twins. Each draws its significance from the other, and when one expires so does the other. Israel in the mid-1990s was a society with few public dreams, like most other societies in the Western world; and the more impoverished the dreams, the less room they occupy on the public agenda; hence the need diminished for rational arguments in this discourse, both essential and formal, while the patently irrational elements in the Israeli public discourse multiplied.

Despair about rationality and the appeal to irrationality are characteristic not just of Israeli society, of course, but they are more visible and likely to reach the public agenda of societies that live in the shadow of an existential threat, are in a constant state of tension, and draw on a variety of sources to rationalize and defend their existence. Israel is one such society, and therefore the increasing role of irrational factors is more visible than it is in many other countries. In particular, the process has become more conspicuous in the context of the subject at hand—the Israeli public discourse on the conflict in our region.

The current version of the discourse, begun right after the Six Day War, was conducted between two rival secular ideologies, both led by secular citizens, and both receiving massive support from religious doves and hawks. The doves demanded an end to the occupation and domination of the Palestinian people, and recognition of their right to self-determination—the right by which the Zionists lay claim to a Jewish state. The hawks demanded realization of the vision of the Greater Land of Israel and restoration of past glory in territorial terms. The ongoing political claims in the early 1960s and 1970s were derived from these total ideologies. The ideological debates slowly and gradually retreated into both "pragmatic" and irrational arguments. Pragmatic arguments are waged by individuals who worry about their fate and use arguments based on personal security. Under no circumstances should the distinction be blurred between security arguments, even when they relate to the security of the entire nation, and arguments that relate to objectives that can be applied only to collectivities or nations, such as the argument for restoring the religious-nationalist glory. Security arguments are always personal, from the sphere of the individual; and arguments related to collective identity of the nation (against the domination of one people by another, or in favor of an expanded Israel) are always from the public sphere.

Alongside the pragmatic-personal arguments, more and more nonrational elements began to appear in the public discourse: songs, slogans, plays, drawings, and also arguments that do not pretend to persuade, but only to express emotion. All these began in earnest during the Lebanon War ("We'll fight for Sharon/and return in an *aron* [coffin]"), but have stepped up their pace since then. As in the Western, democratic world, in Israel the number of those who belonged to one of two categories of the "nonrational" increased: the religious fundamentalists and the postmodern seculars. Those of Gush Emunim (the bloc of the faithful) represent the former group, but the latter had no clear representative for a long time, although their spirit was pervasive among the younger generation until those even younger came along—the generation of singer Aviv Geffen—and surprised the adults with the force of their passion and support. Note that all these nonrational elements—songs, slogans, and even jokes—did not exist in parallel with the public discourse, but constituted a crucial, integral part of it.

Yitzhak Rabin did not, of course, metamorphose into Aviv Geffen. He maintained the rational discourse, but he and those like him are a vanishing breed, in Israel in particular. Had Rabin not acted when he did, but waited for another term of office, the number of rational discussants who remained might not have been sufficient to choose him as a leader. The newly prominent politicians are Benjamin Netanyahu and Ehud Barak, whose power is not based on any particular ideology or principle, but on their ability to invent a quasi-reality through "media mavens" or to create a "hyper-reality" (Baudrillard, 1983) in whose invented terms it is relatively easy to manipulate the public opinion required for electoral purposes. Rabin was unable to do this. Nevertheless, in his very last days, at the very last moment, he realized that his most vocal supporters, those unequivocally dedicated to him, belonged to the camp that Aviv Geffen and others represent. It was these he convened in a mass rally in support of his peace policies, and it was they, not others, who were there when Rabin tried, for the first and last time in his life, to participate in the public discourse through song.

The Public Discourse

The public discourse about the Jewish-Arab conflict after the signing of the Oslo Accord was not essentially different from the discourse that preceded it, but its rules became clear and visible, and people were more aware of the power-orientation of each discourse. As if for the first time, many Israelis became aware of the connection between the knowledge communicated in each discourse and the power that bearers of knowledge hold over each other, described as "discourse formation" by Michel Foucault (1971, 1974, 1993). It seemed at the time as if Rabin and his colleagues were the only ones who had not realized that the rules of public discourse had changed, and they alone did not discern the power-orientation that was then apparent to all.

In all his years in politics, Rabin knew the modern public discourse as it is commonly understood: Some parts of the public formulate arguments and counterarguments with the aim of persuading others to vote according to their views on election day. Obviously Rabin and his colleagues also understood that forms of persuasion are not always rational, that a "public image" must be created for every leader, that separate staffs must be set up for different segments of the population, and that the mass media have an enormous impact. Nevertheless, they had no deep understanding that public discourse is actually a process of signification of the important concepts in our lives, that it is a social process in which meaning is bestowed upon language, through which we create our world and persuade others. The discourse, according to Foucault and others, persuades people who take part in it, even before the first rational argument is sounded. According to this approach, we are all "graduates" of various types of discourse, and each is forced on us by virtue of the knowledge of those who conduct it, the meanings bestowed upon the language, directions convenient to those with knowledge, and meanings and associations that conform to their interest; thus at an early stage, we lose our freedom of choice, although this is ostensibly conferred by the rational arguments at a later stage. This is precisely how Rabin's most bitter adversaries in Israel understood the discourse, and this understanding gave them a powerful edge.

Immediately after the signing of the first Oslo Accord, Rabin's foes began a major struggle to ascribe hostile meanings to all terms related to the agreement. The accord was interpreted as surrender and humiliation, evoking the memory of collaboration with the Nazis. Rabin himself, it was explained to the public, is a traitor, a *moser* or *rodef*—one who sells out his people and homeland. Rabin was contemptuous of this slanderous propaganda. He scorned it and its producers, trying to relate to the public discourse as he remembered it from the past. It was evident from Rabin's reactions that he had no understanding whatsoever that the public discourse was not in addition to or parallel with the slander, but that the smear campaign was the public discourse itself in its new visible format.

Rabin did not understand the depth of hate and abhorrence he engendered in his opponents because he lived by an obsolete notion of the nature of public discourse, one astonishingly similar to that used by Jürgen Habermas to describe and justify his concept of "public sphere" (Habermas, 1989). "Public sphere" is relevant because it gives the concept "discourse" a meaning entirely different from that conferred by Foucault (Habermas, 1985, 1987). In addition, the concept is relevant because at the root of the Habermasian approach is an assumption shared by Rabin's generation, namely that one believes differently in the public than in the private domain, and agreement is always possible in the public domain if one operates according to the best rational argument. The power-orientation of the public discourse in Israel might have become patently evident in any case, and the concepts of Rabin and his generation about the worthiness of the discourse might have become obsolete and abandoned regardless of the Oslo papers. It is reasonable to assume that matters would have thus evolved since this format of public discourse has emerged in the world in general. Thus, in this context one can also appreciate the fact that at the very last moment, before all the power that could be mobilized by a mud-slinging campaign could function as public discourse, Rabin managed to push through the Oslo Accord in the public discourse known to him from earlier days, and to conduct "discursive communication" in the public domain, at least for several days, of the type recommended by Habermas (for more about "discursive communication," see Yatziv, 1985).

Israeli Democracy

The deep trauma caused by the assassination of the prime minister did not stem from the sense of terrible fracture in Israeli democracy, but from pain over the death of the man beloved by many, from anger at the "takeover of the religious," and especially from enormous fear over the fate of the peace process, which had been wreathed with beautiful hopes. Almost all Israeli citizens know and respect the law that declares Israel a democratic country. And yet democracy in Israel has no normative standing deeply rooted in public awareness. Democracy in Israel lacks the axiomatic dimension that exists, for example, in English-speaking and Scandinavian countries. In those countries, democracy underlies all social proceedings, and no one would dare call into question its moral and procedural validity. In Israel, however, democracy is a law like any law. Nothing more. Perhaps this derives from the youth of the democratic state, just over 50 years old. It is certainly related to the two features of Israeli democracy that could be erased or even entirely eliminated if Rabin's historical initiative is realized: Israeli democracy has fewer beneficiaries than other democracies, and fewer supporters as well. This shortcoming of Israeli democracy casts a shadow on its value and prevents it from being revered as a value by many citizens.

Formal democracy prevails, of course, only in the territories that were sovereign to Israel before 1967; it does not exist in the territories conquered in the Six Day War. Israel's effective borders, however, do include these territories, because anyone with intelligence must accept, even intuitively, Weber's classic definition of the borders of sovereignty as the borders of legitimate monopoly on the use of physical power. According to this widely accepted definition, there are many within Israel's borders—almost half the population—who do not benefit from a democratic government. In some cases, the phenomenon reaches apartheid proportions, with residents of Jewish settlements enjoying the democratic rule of law to which their Arab neighbors are not entitled. This intolerable situation was, of course, the product of circumstances entirely different from those that created South African apartheid, and if the Oslo Accord signed by Rabin is implemented, this could also vanish from the face of the earth.

The formal democracy that prevails inside the Green Line (the pre-1967 borders) is regarded by ultra-Orthodox Jews, whose electoral power has expanded since the Six Day War, as the "law of the gentiles" that will change in some vague, rosier future. For them, in any case, democratic law is no more sacred than, for example, the laws of traffic or construction or taxation, which are subject to continual amendment. Indeed, regarding the key issue in Israeli public discourse and that over which Rabin was assassinated—settlements in the occupied territories—many religious Zionist rabbis claim that the laws of democracy have no preference over the laws of Halakha, as they interpret it; indeed, the Halakha takes precedence. In addition, it can be assumed that Israel's large proportion of first-generation immigrants from undemocratic countries in eastern Europe and the Middle East also contributes to the skepticism of many Israelis about the advantages of democracy and the importance of obeying its rules.

If we add to these the increasing size of the "educated mob" (Yatziv, 1997) in Israel who doubt the efficiency of the democratic order for arriving at wise decisions, and who generally mock the politicians that democracy places in charge of the wisdom of these decisions, we can conclude that the status of democracy in the consciousness of Israeli citizens is precarious and unstable—quite far from the expectations of democracy's proponents. Nonetheless, in his days as prime minister, Rabin managed to take advantage of the opportunities that Israeli democracy still afforded to pass one of the most important decisions in the history of Israel. It is highly doubtful that a prime minister these days could pass a decision of this magnitude, and one also wonders if Rabin could have done so had he delayed for several years. This is especially true in light of the crisis of legitimacy in which Israeli society in general, not just its government, is plunged.

The Crisis of Legitimacy

Rabin signed the Oslo Accord even though the agreement itself expedited and underscored the crisis of legitimacy—its causes and characteristics—which would probably have beset Israeli society in any case. This agreement, an attempt to give long-term stability to Israel's status in the heart of a hostile Middle East, brought to the surface the potential areas of tension regarding the Zionist state. Rabin managed to pull it off almost at the very last moment and signed the agreement before these sources of tension reached the Israeli agenda, where they would create, at a minimum, considerable shock waves.

Most sociologists currently understand a "crisis of legitimacy" to be "the failure of the political order to generate a sufficient level of commitment and involvement on the part of its citizens to be able properly to govern them" (Giddens, 1990: 742). All explanations for this crisis related to the inability of the modern state to provide citizens with benefits they were promised by the various parties, especially by those in power when they were running for office.

The term itself was coined by Habermas and developed by Offe (Habermas, 1976; Offe, 1984, 1985). Habermas refers primarily to the contradiction between the necessity of democratic-capitalistic regimes to meet the needs of the citizen-voters, including the poor who pay low taxes, and the unwillingness of the wealthy to have their taxes pay for the welfare of the poor. This insoluble dilemma, in the opinion of Habermas, leads the government to foster that "inadequate" level of commitment and involvement among citizens to which Giddens refers. From another starting point, this situation is described by the theory of "state overload" (Brittan, 1975; Nordhaus, 1975). Here too the explanation refers to the breach of government promises, which generates apathy and lack of trust among citizens, but here the problem begins with the government's taking on too many tasks. In both cases, the term "crisis of legitimacy" applies, but Habermas seemed to be a kind of neo-Marxist, while the others are ultra-liberals.

The crisis of legitimacy characteristic of the connection of many Israeli citizens with their government after the signing of the Oslo Accord touches on various areas. Looking at this issue might enable us to redefine the concept in the general sociological literature. The Israeli phenomena cited below may well be true of other societies, and could be generalized and categorized differently.

The crisis of legitimacy that followed the signing of the Oslo Accord stems from at least four sources, all serious and never refuted even by those who deny their validity, and these are all applicable to other societies as well. First, as in both aforementioned theories, many believe that the Oslo Accord reflects the breach of a promise. Recognition of the PLO and a willingness to make territorial concessions on the Golan were not the policy position of the Labor Party before the elections, which Rabin headed. Second, many Israeli citizens were distressed at the thought that there might be an unbridgeable gap between the validity of the decision of the national public discourse and the slim majority that carried the day. It was commonly known that Rabin had won the previous elections because the two small right-wing parties had not received enough votes to win a seat in the Knesset. Had every vote counted in the Israeli electoral system, it would not have been possible to form the coalition that chose to sign the Oslo Accord. Thus one of the most fateful decisions in the history of Israel—perhaps in the history of the Jewish nation—was made on a hair's breadth plurality. This fact was viewed as patently illegitimate by some citizens, though no one claims that the process was illegal. Third, the question of relations between the state of Israel as the representative of the national Jewish movement and the PLO representing the Palestinian national movement, and also the question of territorial concessions that Israel is willing to make, were viewed by many Jewish Israelis as a "Jewish issue." Although the decision must be made within state institutions, some argued that Jews alone should participate in the decision because it concerns relations between Jews and Arabs, notwithstanding the fact that Israeli Arabs are citizens with equal rights. A significant portion of the slim majority in support of Rabin included Israeli Arabs, and this too was perceived as illegitimate by many of his opponents. Fourth, between the long-term, hoped-for results of the Oslo Accord and the immediate, painful, and tragic results loomed an abyss of bloodshed that could not be halted. This bloodshed cannot be explained away, even when government spokespersons articulate all the reasonable explanations in the world. Thus the accord was considered illegitimate because it catalyzed an escalation of terrorist activity in the heart of Israel, and the government who defended and signed the accord was perceived to be illegitimate.

The Israeli crisis of legitimacy in the early 1990s was deeper and broader than the mid-1970s crises in Western countries discussed by Habermas. In the West, the confidence of citizens in the government's ability to rule according to its promises was eroded. In Israel, the confidence of many Israelis in *the right* of the government to rule and carry out its policies was eroded. Nevertheless, although the scope of the crisis of legitimacy during this period cannot be precisely fixed, it is likely that most Israelis did not recognize it. However, the minority who felt this way and protested was not small, and it was very vocal. Rabin related to this significant, vocal minority as if it did not exist.

Not Post-Zionism, but Postmodern Zionism

Anyone who was listening during Rabin's final years could have heard the deep currents of the legitimacy crisis underlying all four claims described above. Almost suddenly, these deep currents became relevant and even critical and quite dangerous for the stability of Israeli society. When Yitzhak Rabin shook Yasser Arafat's hand, almost immediately, as if there had been no prior warning—although it seemed that he did so almost reluctantly—he undermined the validity of the basic assumptions on which the Zionist movement grew and the state of Israel was established. For this, in particular, many will never forgive him.

The first basic assumption was the modernity of Jewish society in Israel, from the early days of the Zionist enterprise some one hundred years ago until today. According to this assumption, everyone has the right to choose his or her private and public dreams; and people as a group choose the best public dreams to realize. That people's public dreams are realizable is the essence of modernity. Those who realize their dreams are capable and resourceful individuals with the power to change the world—to take bad situations and make them good. The ability of people to change situations is so great that they even succeeded in gathering those dispersed among many countries of the earth for almost two thousand years, bringing them to a remote land inhabited by another people for generations and establishing an independent nation state there.

The second basic assumption is that Jews cannot continue to live as a minority among the gentiles. Assimilation is impossible, despite the early illusions of Theodor Herzl and others, and insularity or isolation within gentile countries is also not tenable. This was the assumption of Zionists, and they marshaled weighty historical facts to support it. The expulsion from Spain was the classic example of Zionist propaganda to support this claim. The Holocaust was the ultimate proof, final and definitive, which ostensibly ends all arguments. The large Jewish population in America is considered a temporary success whose hour of tragedy is yet to come.

The third basic assumption is that a nation-state is a solution to the anguish of the Jews and an option for continuing the orderly evolvement and nurturing of Jewish tradition. Zionism was born at a time when the nation-state was the aspiration of many peoples, and self-determination related primarily to the right of collectivities to set themselves apart as nations and demand sovereignty. Herzl published *Der Judenstaat* at a time when many nations in the multinational empire in which they evolved and lived were raising similar demands, and all these demands seemed reasonable and legitimate.

The fourth basic assumption is that there is a connection between the willingness of the Arabs to accept the Jewish state and their economic and social development. The Zionists assumed that the ignorance, social and cultural backwardness, distance from the centers of civilization, and submissive attitude to the colonialist powers are what led the Arabs to refuse to accept the Jews as peers in the Middle East. When the "processes of modernization" would take root here, the hour of Jewish-Arab reconciliation would also arrive.

The fifth basic assumption was that Israel's military advantage would cause the Palestinians to concede their country. This assumption was formulated in many ways while fostering various levels of expectation: Zeev Jabotinsky spoke about the "iron wall"; David Ben-Gurion tried to create this wall; and Rabin believed, for example, that if Israel were to "break their bones," they would stop demonstrating and running an intifada.

All these assumptions have been fundamental to the generation of Israelis of whom Rabin was a premier spokesman, their bread and butter—eaten several times a day—and this shaped the cognitive map of the generation and set the coordinates of that map, the trends, and the milestones defined as political objectives. Put simply, these were the unquestioned assumptions according to which they lived (in the incisive language of Rachel, poet of the second aliya: "This is the way, there is no other, to go to the finish"). Everyone who knew Rabin even superficially would not question that these basic assumptions were the infrastructure of his world view and the basis of his approach to the roots of the Jewish-Arab conflict.

Especially since the signing of the Oslo Accord, the number of those who question the validity of some or all of these assumptions has increased. If the leadership of the nation as embodied by Rabin no longer aspires to the maximum goals but is willing to accommodate the constraints of reality—without maintaining the iron wall or relying on "the qualitative edge"—perhaps there is something faulty about all the basic assumptions on which Israelis were raised.

The assumption of modernity is dissipating, not necessarily in the writing of thinkers called postmodern, but in the spirit of the younger generation who do not probe their attitude toward modernity. The assumption that dreams are realizable, not just media entertainment or raw material for some virtual reality, is again not axiomatic. Some thinkers who tried to express this mood claim that "the subject is dead" and that "the author is dead" (on postmodernism and the social sciences, see Rosenau, 1992), but the younger generation simply distances itself from all public dreams intended for realization and focuses on its private dreams—behavior that Rabin's generation would view as treason. This generation does not aspire to realize beautiful ideas, but to realize the potential in life that is possible for each.

The assumption that Jewish life cannot continue in the Diaspora is repudiated anew every day. One can today live a full Jewish life in most countries of the developed world: one can identify as a Jew without any harm occurring; one can identify as an affiliated or unaffiliated Jew, and Jewish culture of all kinds is fostered and earns the respect and sometimes even material support of others; one can choose to belong to any of several movements of Judaism whose legitimacy is not called into question; in the Diaspora of today, one can be a Jew and feel physical, economic, and social security. All of this is possible in the Diaspora to a greater extent than it is possible in Israel.

The assumption of the eternity of the nation-state, and even continuity of the effective existence of the nation-state in the coming period, is slowly crumbling. Today the nation-state is increasingly understood to be exactly the same as all social frameworks created by people from time immemorial—a temporary phenomenon suitable only in its era. The processes of globalization and the reverse trend of social-tribal-national-cultural-religious associations undermine the foundations of the nation-state. People know that new technologies will solve problems old and new—economic, ecological, military, scientific, medical—on a global scale. To this end, international authorities should be set up that will chip away, gradually but steadily, certain portions of the sovereignty of nation-states. But people within the nation-state are slowly splintering into homogeneous groups along ethnic or voluntary lines, and the significance of the nation-state is gradually dissipating. As is evident from the history of Israel, this process has not necessarily been harmful to the Jewish people, who will probably prosper and survive even in a new order, but it does diminish the relevance of the state of Israel to the fate of the Jew, at the same time that some of its "security" problems (such as a definitive drawing of borders) may become obsolete.

The assumption that there is a connection between modernization in the Arab world and the Arabs' willingness to reconcile themselves to the existence of Israel has been proven completely false, even though some still believe that "if only we were dealing with real democracies" reconciliation would have come long ago. This is utter foolishness, even when implied again and again by the prime minister, and practically illegitimate in light of previous experience. The problems that divide Israel from the Arab world are real, and no government in the name of being "progressive" or "modern" can gloss over them or give up on their solution. This assumption, it should be emphasized, was pervasive among most schools of thought in the Zionist movement, but is also vanishing with the passing of Rabin's generation.

The assumption that the iron wall will break Arab rejectionism—formulated by Jabotinsky, tried by Ben-Gurion, and accepted unquestioningly by most of Rabin's generation—was perhaps the first basic assumption that Rabin put to an empirical test. When he realized that it repeatedly failed this test, he decided as a rational person to consider the alternatives and chose the one he considered best—the Oslo Accord.

Thus the basic assumptions of Zionism were proven false, one after the other, over Rabin's shoulder or behind his back; yet as a classic Zionist and conservative, shaped by the generation of his parents, he still contributed more to strengthening the Zionist enterprise and increasing the chances of its survival than others of his or previous generations. This was possible because Zionism itself was not dismantled or abandoned by most citizens of Israel. Zionism, in its basic meaning, according to which there is one Jewish nation with rights identical to those of all nations, the most important being its right to gather in the territory where the nation was born, remained the founding ideology, the meta-narrative of most Israelis. The only difference was the attitude of most Israelis (and most citizens of Western countries) toward every meta-narrative or total ideology. People today are less Zionist just as they are less liberal, less socialist, and less nationalist in most democratic countries, and they are less willing to sacrifice private matters on behalf of a public dream. Because life itself is a very private matter, it is hard to galvanize most of the younger generation, even in Israel, to sacrifice themselves on behalf of any idea, let alone that of the Zionist enterprise. In this situation, and before this weakness was revealed to the world, at the very last moment, Rabin signed the Oslo Accord, based on mutual recognition of the two nationalist movements of each other's rights.

Summary

Rabin was assassinated very near the borderline between two periods, almost at the last moment before Israeli society crossed over to the next stage. A sociologist who takes into consideration Rabin's temporal proximity to this borderline and analyzes the possible impact of the new period from the other side of the border would never have expected Rabin to make the peace that he did. At any rate, Rabin made this peace, and its significance is far-reaching, beyond what is currently believed by most Israelis.

Rabin made a rational peace, a peace that can logically be evaluated in terms of the profit and loss incurred by both sides. He did it on the cusp of an era in which such a peace would not have been an option. In a later period, perhaps this peace would never have happened, but would have awaited a more gradual ripening over many years, until it fell on the inhabitants of the region like a dried-up fruit, when it would make no difference whether there was or was not peace. It could also be that in the absence of a rational peace based on mutual concessions, an irrational peace would have befallen Israel—unilateral surrender to the unconventional warfare of the other, for example, or an irrational eruption of terrible hostilities, religious or otherwise, that is incomprehensible in our current conceptual systems.

Rabin managed to transfer the content and principles of the peace he was making onto the track of Israeli public space one moment before this space was exposed as a power-hungry jungle of the type usually concealed behind screens of alleged culture, which are torn and discarded as unnecessary in the new era. In the public space to which Rabin was accustomed, rational arguments for and against the issues on the public agenda would be laid out and all power exercises well concealed, to the extent that the winner of the discourse, at least in matters relating to the nature of public space, seemed to be the best rational argument. This belief accorded some legitimacy to the public discourse and encouraged citizens to participate. After signing the Oslo Accord, Rabin did not succeed in extending this to deliberations about the Oslo Accord; hence the character of the public discourse as a power struggle over the meaning of all the basic concepts in our language was exposed in all its ugliness.

Rabin managed to use the formal structures of Israeli democracy to win approval for the Oslo Accord in the state institutions, even though in the eyes of most Israelis the democratic mechanisms were virtually inapplicable to the conflict in the region. He managed this despite the deep crisis in legitimacy pervasive in Israeli democracy, and the crumbling of most of the basic assumptions that Rabin's generation considered essential to the Zionist enterprise and defense of their collective right to exist in the region and in the country. From across the borderline between the two eras, it is hard to say with certainty and confidence that today he would have been successful.

The borderline near which Rabin was assassinated does not divide, as some claim, the Zionist from the post-Zionist era. On both sides of that line, Zionist spaces still exist that are valid and well established. The borderline near which Rabin was assassinated and that now divides eras in the entire Western world to which Israel belongs, but is still not developed in the world to which Arab countries belong, can be called, albeit with some difficulty, the borderline between the modern and the postmodern periods. The difficulty stems from the fact that the concept "postmodern" has as many meanings as the writers and thinkers who define it. Nonetheless, the state of Israel beyond that line is another country: It is an Israel divided between citizens with completely different conceptual systems and emotional baggage, not just between citizens with different claims about and interpretations of the same goal. The Israel of today does not belong to the group of natural democracies in which the fundamental concepts of democracy are axiomatic and incontrovertible, but rather it is a conditional democracy—contingent upon circumstances, religious affiliation, and changing leadership. Israel is not populated by a rational majority, but by many groups disdainful of democracy, ultrafundamentalist messianists, and cynical seculars who believe that nothing in the world is worth killing for or dying over. This postmodern Israel is not the country of the Palmach generation, though one of its preeminent representatives bequeathed to it a peace with which it will live for many years.

The collective identity of Israel from this side of the borderline may, of course, change over time and absorb the peace that Rabin made in various degrees. Beyond these uncertainties, two assumptions still suggest themselves: first, that the peace will take root one way or another because it represents powerful global interests, and no Israeli interest, caprice, or belief—or the Arab equivalents—can prevent it. Rabin understood what his adversaries were late in understanding but others understood before him—that the region is important to international power brokers who will not relinquish it to an endless series of wars. In making peace, Rabin supposedly represented the "world interest" and hence won the praises of the world. Second, this was apparently why Rabin was so hated by his political adversaries and assassinated. From Israel's point of view, the "world" is the reality in which Israelis live and grapple with its constraints. Rabin was hated by those who perceive the world beyond the Jewish people as a naturally evil phenomenon. Rabin was hated and assassinated by those for whom reality does not exist; but the reality in their mind's eye shatters all the basic cultural concepts that Rabin and his generation had accepted as givens.

References

Baudrillard, J. (1983). *In the Shadow of the Silent Majorities*. New York: Semiotext(e).

Bendix, R. (1962). *Max Weber: An Intellectual Portrait*. New York: Anchor Books.

Brittan, S. (1975). "The Economic Contradictions of Democracy." *British Journal of Political Science* 15: 168–89.

Foucault, M. (1971). *Madness and Civilization*. London: Tavistock.

—— (1974) [1966]. *The Order of Things*. London: Tavistock.

—— (1993). "About the Beginning of the Hermeneutics of the Self." *Political Theory* 21 (2), May: 193–227.

Giddens, A. (1990). *Sociology*. Cambridge: Polity Press.

Habermas, J. (1976). *Legitimation Crisis*. Cambridge: Polity Press.

—— (1985). *The Communicative Action*. Trans. T. McCarthy. Boston, Mass.: Beacon.

—— (1987). *The Philosophical Discourse of Modernity*. Cambridge: Polity Press.

—— (1989) [1962]. *Structural Transformation of the Public Sphere*. Cambridge: Polity Press.

Nordhaus, W. D. (1975). "The Political Business Cycle." *Review of Economic Studies* 42 (2): 169–90.

Offe, C. (1984). *Contradictions of the Welfare State*. Cambridge, Mass.: MIT Press.

—— (1985). *Disorganized Capitalism*. Cambridge: Polity Press.

Rosenau, P. (1992). *Post-Modernism and the Social Sciences*. Princeton, N.J.: Princeton University Press.

Weber, M. (1947). *The Theory of Social and Economic Organization*. Oxford: Oxford University Press.

Yatziv, G. (1985). *Social Lexicon*. Tel Aviv: College of Management Press [Hebrew].

—— (1997). *Introduction to Normative Sociology*. Tel Aviv: College of Management Press [Hebrew].

CHAPTER 15

Rabin: Between Commemoration and Denial

YORAM PERI

The Sacrifice of Isaac as a Nation-Constitutive Myth

Nations have different attitudes toward the past and their collective memories. If the United States began "without history" in the words of Daniel Bell (1975) and "Americans have been cast as slightly more amnesiac than other populations" (Kammen, 1991), the Jews were at the other extreme. "With their dispersal the Jews became a people of memory. To be Jewish is to remember" (Valensi, 1986: 286).

According to Pierre Nora, "The Jews' daily adherence to traditional ceremonies of tradition, turning them into a 'people of memory,' absolved them from concern for history until their opening up to the modern world imposed on them the need for historians" (1993: 6). The intensive occupation with historical memory in the twentieth century stems from the fact that the Zionist movement—as its leaders love to say—"restored the Jewish nation to history." Nevertheless, the official Israeli historiography is losing its influence despite the large number of history scholars and improved research tools, while the "agents of memory" are gaining ground (Shapira, 1994).[1]

The extensive intellectual, cultural, and even political occupation with questions of collective memory and commemoration occurred in Israel in the 1990s parallel with, or perhaps following, another cultural phenomenon of the era: myth wrecking (Ben-Yehuda, 1995: 285–87) or myth shattering (Zerubavel, 1995: 232). The constitutive myths of Israeli society have been undergoing a process of deconstruction, sometimes even an attempt to destroy them completely. This is the process of postmodernist societies a la Lyotard, in which the "grand narratives" collapse, intertwined with specific social and cultural process cultural changes that have occurred in Israeli society, as described in several chapters of this book. The formation of the various cultural groups, combined with the weakening of the hegemonic status of the established Ashkenazi elite, challenged the meta-Zionist narrative and led to the diversification of texts and counternarratives describing the past.

Studies of Israeli society that describe how the changing cultural context, ideological climate, and social psyche have led various groups to reread the old myths and reprocess the collective memory share a common feature—the diachronic dimension of the research. Thus Ben-Yehuda (1995) examined the changes that have occurred in the Masada myth of A.D. 66; Zerubavel (1995) looked at the changing of the Tel-Hai myth of 1925; Shapira (1994) studied the battle of Latrun of May 1948, and so forth. The assassination of Yitzhak Rabin, in contrast, tragically provides the researcher with a unique opportunity to follow closely the initial, amorphous formation of an original narrative, examining how the lava of the dramatic event first solidifies and settles in the collective consciousness, and how the various forces that shape the collective memory work. This is processing the past in a different sense, by shaping the present as it will be perceived and remembered in the future. In these terms, "remembering Rabin" does not mean simply remembering, but refers to socially constitutive action.

Furthermore, researchers on collective memory follow Durkheim's basic perception that "moral unity is the ultimate object of commemoration" (1912). Wagner-Pacifici and Schwartz explain that researchers of collective memory, from Halbwachs on, described the process whereby commemorative monuments integrate the glory of society's past with present concerns and aspirations. "Commemoration," they write, "is governed by a kind of pleasure principle that produces a unified, positive image of the past. But suppose a society is divided over the very event it selects for commemoration, how is commemoration without consensus, or without pride, possible?" (Wagner-Pacifici and Schwartz, 1991: 379).

Rabin's assassination as a divisive event thus affords us a close look not only at the formation of a primary historical memory, but also at the struggle taking place—"live" or "on-line" in modern media parlance—among interpretive communities over the canonization of this narrative. An in-depth examination of this case study permits us to see the various mnemonic agents in action, locate the techniques used by the mnemonic communities, perhaps even compare the two analytical approaches that Schwartz describes so well: on the one hand, social reconstructionism, which states that present needs, problems, and interests are the dominant factor in remembering the past; on the other hand, the argument that it is the past that enables us to understand the present (Ben-Yehuda, 1995: 273). Observing the attempt to canonize the hegemonic narrative can theoretically enable us to examine a current event that has not been completed: to pass beyond Zelizer's argument that the collective memory is unpredictable (1995), to ask whether the creation of a lasting collective memory is at all possible in contemporary societies or whether that kind of tradition was a characteristic product of religious-traditional and national-romantic societies.

The tragic event of Rabin's assassination is of unique importance in the study of historical memory because it relates to a collective memory that shapes the collective identity. This kind of memory requires dramatic events to serve as symbolic milestones in the collective history. These milestones, like those in the life of the individual, grow to mythical dimensions and become paradigms of the collective past (Zerubavel, 1994: 44). These are what Shils refers to as the "great moments" (ibid.), or, in the words of Claude Levi-Strauss (1966: 259), the "hot moments" to which society attributes deep meaning.

The Rabin myth that developed after the assassination is highly significant in that it is part of the nation-constitutive myth. Although the murder took place nearly 50 years after independence was declared, it is an integral part of "the nation's formative period," a period cloaked in an aura of sanctity (Eliade, 1963: 34). This myth narrates the formation of the sociopolitical order that builds the community as a meaningful entity in space and time in the consciousness of each of its members. It binds people together in a common and integrative belief in a shared past. Thus myths can play an important part in shaping personal identities within a process of nation-building (Smith, 1991). This myth serves as a basis for the "invented tradition" (Hobsbawm and Ranger, 1983), on which the "imagined political community" is built (Anderson, 1987; Bhabha, 1990). This myth is fostered by the various "state cults" because it gives them legitimacy (Azaryahu, 1995: 8–10).

Nation-constitutive myths are created by commemoration, and examination of Rabin's commemoration from the very moment of the assassination reflects the particular way in which his myth was formed. It emerged clearly from the various texts—verbal, graphic, visual, dramatized and others—describing Rabin, the murder, the mourning and the patterns of commemoration. The most outstanding is the "leopard's leap" description, to use Walter Benjamin's term, leaping from one historical point to the next. The highlights of Rabin's rich life that were mentioned in the mourning ceremonies and the various commemorative events were the War of Independence in 1948, the Six Day War in 1967, and the peace process in the 1990s. And what are leaps of 20 or 30 years to a nation whose history includes leaps of centuries and even millennia?[2]

The fact that in November 1995 Israel was still dealing with the War of Independence story is reflected in the description of Rabin's death, portrayed not as a passive act of weakness but as an act of heroic sacrifice, of supreme courage, the fall of a soldier on the battlefield. The term "fall" is used for soldiers; ordinary civilians simply "die." Certainly the term "fall" is not normally used to describe the death of a murder victim. Rabin fought fiercely in battle, and in this battle he died as a hero. His death was an active one, one of courage and glory. He was fighting "the battle for peace," which followed directly from the War of Independence and continued with the breaking of the stranglehold of the Arab states in 1967. Rabin referred to himself as "a soldier of peace," and that was how King Hussein eulogized him at the funeral: "Yitzhak Rabin lived as a soldier and died as a soldier for peace." This image continued in the collective memory.

Rabin's burial site also reflects the fact that he fell in battle. He was not buried like the first prime minister, David Ben-Gurion, on the edge of the Negev desert; or like Prime Minister Menachem Begin, who asked to be buried with his forefathers on the Mount of Olives, the sacred burial place of Jewish tradition; but on Mount Herzl, a few steps away from the military cemetery. Here lie the fighters who served under him during the War of Independence as well as IDF soldiers who fell in all the wars since (Yoram Bilu, *Ha'aretz*, April 23, 1996). Rabin's "falling in battle" permitted him to be regarded in the same way that soldiers who fall in action are seen in Israel, with its rich and highly developed culture of mourning and bereavement (see Malkinson, Rubin, and Witztum, 1993).

The modern cult of the fallen in battle began during the French Revolution and the German wars of liberation, with the formation of the citizens' army and the consolidation of the modern nation-state. The death of a soldier became a sacrifice, and the personal loss was compensated for by the national gain: Not only the belief in the goals of war justified dying for the homeland, death itself acquired a transcendental, superhuman image (Mosse, 1990). The death of an individual acquired value, because with his death he guaranteed the life of the nation, and the blood that was spilled on the battlefield became the blood of the nation's birth.[3] "The fallen in battle became saints following in the footsteps of Jesus," writes Mosse describing the iconography of war, "and the cult of the fallen supplied them with martyrs." Just as religious sacrifice mediates between man and god, so death on the altar of the homeland is a sacrifice that mediates between the individual and the nation" (Mosse, 1990: 84–85).

The cult of the fallen began in Israel in the 1920s, the nation's formative years, as part of the strategy for inventing the new Israeli community. In the early years of the state, the cult of the fallen was directly related to the War of Independence. Their commemoration played an important part in fostering the myth of heroic sacrifice. "The myth creates and explains the collective commitment to commemorating the fallen and also provides the symbolic meaning of commemoration in the sociocultural totality. The cult of the fallen was immediately linked to the constitutive myth of the state of Israel" (Azaryahu, 1995: 113).

The Israeli cult of the fallen was based on the ethos of patriotic sacrifice of the modern nation-state and on the Jewish tradition of self-sacrifice in the name of God and national heroism. However, as has already been noticed in many other cases, it provided legitimacy to the hegemonic status of the elite groups by virtue of their relatively high "blood donation" to society. Blood is a powerful and emotion-laden symbol in the cult of the fallen. Blood represents life, and the sacrifice of blood expresses the sacrifice of the lives of the fallen, who devoted their lives to the nation. As with national myths in Europe of the late-nineteenth century, and again in the mid-twentieth, Israel's invented national tradition began to foster the myth of blood after the battle of Tel-Hai and the death of Joseph Trumpeldor, the fighting pioneer who settled in the North and fell defending his settlement in 1920. There blood was linked with work, sustaining the cult of the pioneer—a soldier working on the land, dying at his post while defending the homeland: "Presenting the sacrifice as a special conceptual mixture of 'blood-hero-homeland' established it as a supreme value" (Brug, 1996: 210). These things were expressed in the blood-curdling words of Yitzhak Sadeh, the venerated leader of the Palmach fighters: "The building blocks of this country are the bodies of the comrades-in-arms, the cement is the blood of those with a common cause" (Sadeh, 1953: 53).

As the Israeli-Arab conflict continued and the number of victims grew, blood acquired a more powerful meaning in the Israeli symbolic order. It even became a decisive factor in legitimizing Jewish rights to the country, more than the historical right or the divine promise. Land on which Jewish blood had been spilled became holy and could not be given to Arabs. A people who spills its blood over land becomes its owner. The settlers turned this principle into a political tactic when they pressed for a new settlement to be established everyplace where "Jewish blood" was spilled. This is the concept of "buying the land with blood." It is not surprising that one of the most dramatic moments in the week of mourning Rabin was the moment when Eitan Haber, Rabin's close aide, pulled out of his pocket the piece of paper with the words of the "Song of Peace" stained with Rabin's blood.

Another sanctified object that is part of the cult of the fallen is the altar. Thus Masada was described as the main altar in the cult of the myth of heroism and sacrifice (Brug, 1996), and the fallen were defined as a sacrifice on "the altar of the homeland." The altar of 1948 was the establishment of the state. Five decades later, Rabin's blood was spilled on the altar of peace. It was said of the fallen of 1948 that "in dying they bequeathed us life," and it was said of Rabin that "in dying he bequeathed us peace." Thus the images surrounding Rabin's death complement those of the War of Independence.

Rabin's murder could easily be identified with another image—the biblical sacrifice of Isaac. This myth was so central in the ethos of the reawakening nation "that there is hardly a poet in modern Hebrew literature who does not use this theme" (Carton Blum, 1996: 232). In the poetry of Rabin's contemporaries, the 1948 generation, treatment of the myth of revival and redemption became intertwined with new motifs: the sacrifice of Isaac became a metaphor for a personal experience (ibid., 235). Although he died when a younger generation of writers was already making new use of the motif of the sacrifice of Isaac, the story of Yitzhak Rabin's death also illustrates the generational link to the writers of 1948. And his first name, Yitzhak (Isaac), helped foster the motif of sacrifice in describing the story of his life.

In addition to the cults of independence and the fallen—the two major state cults in Israel (Azaryahu, 1995: 214)—a third cult became interwoven into the construction of Rabin's memory, that of the mythic hero. Seeking to foster the new Zionist myth, the Zionist movement restructured the image of Bar Kochba, the mythic hero who dared to revolt against the foreign ruler, the all-powerful Roman Empire, in A.D. 132–35—60 years after the destruction of the Second Jewish Commonwealth. Thus Trumpeldor was mythicized according to the model of the contemporary hero: the antithesis of the ghetto Jew, a brave fighter and pioneer, a man firmly facing the world, a man of the soil, one who gives his life for the good of the many.

In Frye's (1961) terms, Trumpeldor was posthumously raised to the level of a "hero of romance." He is a human hero with high social power whose characteristics are greatly superior to those of the average man, as if he had acquired for a set period some of the characteristics of the gods themselves and thus gained the status of a son of the gods. Trumpeldor, for example, is described in the poem called "Joseph Still Lives": "He is not dead, he lives on/The hero of Tel-Hay!"[4]

In the process of building the Israeli nation, other figures also achieved heroic status, most on the basis of actions in the realm of security, but none of them rose to the level of the mythic hero as Rabin did. After his death a process of sanctification began, reflected in the explicit use of the concept "hero": a newspaper headline, "The People Weep over Their Fallen Hero"; the official government death notice, "A True Hero of Peace"; a poem by Nathan Yonathan, "That Man," which almost became the anthem of the Rabin mnemonic community—"Where can we find others like that man, who was like the weeping willows"; and the words of the bodyguard who was with him in the car on the way to the hospital, "Even in his last moments Rabin behaved like a brave soldier and hero."

But there were also signs of an attempt to make him more than a high-mimetic hero, to portray him "larger than life"—as a genuine mythic hero. An almost unprecedented visual expression of the mythic figure cult appeared in the portrait of Rabin placed at the memorial ceremonies. It is customary to place a picture of the dead at memorial ceremonies, but Rabin's portraits were enlarged to vast dimensions. Another salient expression of this was in relating to him as someone still alive in the world above, appealing to him directly to continue acting from there. A great deal of use was also made of supernatural motifs emphasizing his link with sanctity, divinity, and nature. Pleas like "Guard me from above, because I'm afraid now" appeared on stickers and posters. One song said, "Be strong up there." One poster bore the text, "He who makes peace in the heights," making explicit use of a line from a prayer addressed to God. Were it not for the nonetheless secular character of these religious motifs, it might seem as if a process of deifying Rabin began a few days after his death.[5]

Rabin's spectrum of commemoration spanned four fields: a spontaneous field (from below), an institutional field (from above), artistic representation, and the mass media. Complex interactions existed among the fields, and patterns and images moved from one to another. Patterns of commemoration that emerged spontaneously were adopted by institutions and organizations. Elements that appeared on the improvised memorial were incorporated into the official monument. Particularly complex were the relations between the media and the other fields owing to their growing role in contemporary society. In Chapter 7, I described the media's role in shaping the mourning ceremonies during the first week. Television played an equivalent part in setting the nature of the memorial days, especially the first anniversary of the murder, when the political establishment was only half-hearted in its wish to mark the day.

Materials that became "realms of memory"—videotapes of Rabin's life, CDs of the songs played during the mourning period, photograph albums, memorial books—all had their source in the media and served as raw material for artistic commemoration. Memorial exhibits included piles of newspapers from the week of mourning and a large TV screen that repeatedly broadcast the events of the week of the assassination. "The main existence of the realms of memory," states Nora, "is to stop time, to delay the process of forgetting. To fix a certain state of affairs, to give death immortality, to concretize the spiritual, to trap the maximum meaning within the minimum signs" (1993: 16).

As described in some of the chapters in this book, the spontaneous commemoration, where private memory most mingled with social memory, was marked immediately after the assassination by a multiplicity of genres, and diverse expressions of the meaning of the memory existed side by side. Thus contradictory statements appeared on the wall of graffiti at Rabin Square (his "temple"). For example, one slogan expressed a magical perception of memory as a driving force ("Rabin, speak to God for us," or "Keep on and bring us peace from above"), in contrast to the perception that, according to Gershom Scholem, expresses the traditional rabbinical attitude toward memory—that it is not a magical power that transforms things, but something that raises images into awareness and relates to the unique historical identity ("We will remember you always," or "Why did this happen to us") (Omer, 1996).

The message conveyed by the artistic field was much more uniform, represented in pictures mostly expressing the iconic dimension of the memory. An analysis of the motifs that appeared in various exhibitions shows clearly that most of these artists belonged to the same mnemonic community—the one socially, politically, and ideologically aligned with Rabin. Hence they emphasized the space of meanings identified with the liberal-democratic camp. The motif of Rabin's death as a martyr on the altar of peace was more dominant than other motifs such as "a Jew murdered by a Jew" or "the unity of the people." There is, though, one exception. The monument at Rabin Square—which was built one year after the assassination—does include the motif of the unity of the nation, in the form of a steel chain surrounding broken basalt blocks. It expresses the need for bonds to strengthen the social unity that was shaken by the assassination.

The field of Rabin's commemoration is extremely varied. It includes places named after him (buildings, institutions, streets, squares, special memorial sites, monuments, commemorative plaques in military camps, and so forth). Influenced by popular culture there was a spate of memorabilia (candles, medallions, T-shirts, coins, stickers, posters, pictures, his image stamped on various articles). Hundreds of thousands of "quality" goods were produced (books Rabin wrote, collections of his speeches, books about him, photo albums, tapes of TV broadcasts, CDs about his life, albums of songs performed during the mourning week, photograph albums, films, and so on).

Another form of commemoration is the devotion of special time to his memory, such as minutes of silence, memorial events, seminars, and conventions. There is a regular gathering at Rabin Square on Friday afternoons of a group calling itself "the Guardian of Peace and Democracy, November 4, 1995." There are specific activities dedicated to his name, such as marches, research prizes, and awards for educational work. Of course there was also a spate of commercial activity exploiting the commemoration—people sold and produced everything from phone cards, stamps, and medallions to T-shirts. Since 1995 the spontaneous commemorative activity (which has even included naming babies after him) has not halted, although it has diminished.

A textual analysis of these commemorative items reveals the desire to avoid, to the degree possible, political or ideological memorialization of the assassination and its circumstances. If there is an attempt to give some meaning to the murder, the main motif that appears is unity of the people and, to a lesser extent, the need for tolerance. The good qualities of Rabin the man are referred to, and little mention is made of the political background of his actions. Someone who did not know how and why Rabin was assassinated could not learn of it from these memorial items.

In many cases the boundaries between the spontaneous and the institutional fields were blurred. This happened not only in the organizational dimension, when initiative from below brought organizations to hold ceremonies, but also in other dimensions such as visual design. For example, the visual language used in the institutional memorial ceremonies was full of statements taken from the language of the spontaneous field. Rabin's portrait, flowers, candles, phrases such as "Shalom, Haver," the dove as a symbol of peace, and other symbols taken from the spontaneous field appeared in stylized, polished, and organized form in the allocation of space in official ceremonies. The blurring of boundaries between the spontaneous and institutional commemoration enabled the establishment to instill various messages into the products of popular cultures, similar to the use that secular state cults make of traditional religious artifacts.

But it was in the institutional field that the problematic nature of Rabin's commemoration was most acutely expressed. Because commemoration means canonizing the constitutive myth, the struggle over the meaning of the murder and the contents of the memory emerged full blown, revealing the difficulty of reaching agreement over a shared narrative. This difficulty was compounded because whereas in the past the state had undertaken the role of "guardian of the memory" (Zerubavel, 1994: 64) and there was "a tendency of the ruling elites to monopolize the memory" (Shapira, 1994: 40) and shape the past according to present needs, now they have lost control of the collective memory. Today, commemoration becomes "an anarchic process in which the elite and counterelite take part, but to the same extent so do diffuse, almost random, forces" (ibid.). Indeed, Israel at the beginning of the twenty-first century has no one unifying political myth or hegemonic power for the whole nation, but various mnemonic communities competing over the shape of the collective memory.[6]

The Politics of Memory

MOBILIZING THE ASSASSINATION — BETWEEN APPROPRIATION AND DENIAL

"Control of society's memory largely conditions the hierarchy of power," writes Connerton (1989: 1). Shortly after Rabin's assassination, the mnemonic contention began between the commemorative communities. At first, it was over the meaning of the assassination, and—in the absence of agreement on this—the actual commemoration became the focus of the battle: one side seeking to commemorate Rabin and the other wishing to blur his memory. Those in the Rabin camp saw (and still see) him as a victim on the altar of peace, and to them the aim of the commemoration was first to continue on the road to peace for which he served as a symbol, and second to strengthen the principles of Israeli democracy. The clerical-nationalist camp would not agree to base the collective memory of Rabin's assassination on these meanings. The secular-nationalist camp agreed to linking his memory with the theme of national unity or the need for tolerance and strengthening democracy, but they could not accept "Rabin's path to peace," which meant relinquishing not only parts of the homeland but also its definition of the collective identity and national culture.

The clerical bloc, for its part, has trouble identifying with Rabin's legacy if it is translated into one of peace (Bnei Akiva, the religious youth movement, announced that it would boycott a youth rally if the "Song of Peace" were played there). But it also has difficulty placing the *polis* above the *ethnos* and legitimizing universalist secularist democracy. Even the one motif on which Rabin's memory might have been based in the past—his contribution to security—could no longer be accepted by the countermnemonic groups, since after the Oslo accords Rabin was perceived by some as having endangered the security of the state.

There was some difficulty in the process of constituting Rabin's memory even within the mnemonic community close to him. This sprang from the incompatibility of the components gathered in the Zionist repertoire described in the previous chapters. The early attempts at memorialization made by Rabin's mnemonic community in the first month after his death were harshly criticized by other mnemonic communities, who claimed that the act of commemoration was an attempt by the Labor Party to capitalize on the murder for its own political interests. ("A blatant and even vulgar attempt to obtain the maximum political profit from Rabin's assassination," wrote Yoram Beck, a right-wing publicist, in "Bolshevism Is Alive and Kicking," in *Ha'aretz*, October 14, 1996.) Similar accusations were voiced mainly by right-wing politicians. In a TV interview, Yitzhak Zuckerman, editor of the ultra-Orthodox *Ha'Shavua*, noted, "The word 'Yitzhak Rabin' has become a mantra used as provocation against a certain section of the public" (August 26, 1996). It was the sharp reaction against the peace camp's commemoration attempts that caused the Labor Party to avoid invoking Rabin's assassination in the subsequent election campaign. Thus blurring the memory became the preferred strategy of the left as well as the right, to the distress of Rabin's close friends, for whom his personal memory lives so vividly.

THE CONTENTION OVER NATIONALIZING THE MEMORY

Another manifestation of the struggle over the commemoration focused on the question of nationalizing the memory. The dilemma here was who would be the guardian of the memory after the wave of spontaneous commemoration. Would the state declare the slain leader a secular saint and institutionalize his memory? The fact that the Labor Party was in power during the first months after the assassination enabled it to mobilize the state machinery during the mourning period. But after Labor lost the elections of May 1996, the question returned and became more acute as the first anniversary of his death approached in November 1996. The party elected then had no political interest in using the state mechanism for commemorative purposes.

Moreover, Rabin's camp itself was steeped in a quandary that impeded its demand to nationalize the memory. This camp wished to turn Rabin into a national martyr, but at the same time it wanted to make him the hero of one political camp, a role model for an entire movement and particularly for the party. A social movement has many reasons for wanting to turn into a political myth a member killed in its service—not to mention its leader: "The myth of a movement aims to make the man's death meaningful in the eyes of his friends. . . . The victim exemplifies commitment to the ideas of the movement, and by implication shows the strength of the idea that people are ready to sacrifice their lives for it. . . . The myth provides an opportunity to translate the abstract ideology into a concrete symbol . . . [and] turns complex ideas that contain internal contradictions and difficult problems into something applicable, something concrete. Outwardly, it serves the aims of recruiting new supporters by setting a model" (Feige, 1996: 303).

After its defeat in the elections, the left needed more than ever a figure who would become a political myth and serve as a symbol of the movement, one with unifying and drawing power. To make him a national hero at the same time would only be possible if his national representation included the specific attributes of the movement. And it was clear that the parties now in power would not agree to this. They could not accept the left's demand that the state nationalize Rabin in the garb of the movement.

If Rabin's movement had nevertheless sought to turn him into a national hero, it would have had to let the other mnemonic communities—if they so wished—determine the meaning of the assassination. It would have had to content itself with "a Jew murdered by a Jew" or "a blow to the unity of the people" and do without the figure of Rabin as a symbol of peace and the movement. This it could not do. The result was that real nationalization was not possible, as reflected in a series of issues, such as the pattern of commemoration on the first anniversary, setting an official memorial day, the wording of the inscription on his gravestone, that text to appear on the memorial candle, and so forth.

One of the most effective patterns of remembrance is a memorial day. Removing a specific unit of time from the chronological, linear sequence and making it a part of cyclic time strengthens the symbolic, mythic, and sacred dimensions of this time unit. Marking a certain date in the year as a "memorial day" is an effective way of creating a *lieu de memoire* and makes it possible to choose from the inventory of the past various items for reconstruction of the memory. Historical holidays offer rituals of remembrance that create "a shared network of practices around which are clustered the common memories of the people as a whole" (Yerushalmi, 1988: 40).

The ritual calendar was a source of vitality and strength to the Zionist ethos. As Funkenstein wrote, "The nation state replaced the sacred liturgical memory with secular liturgical memory—days of remembrance, flags and monuments" (1990: 21). It is natural, therefore, that some months after the assassination the question arose whether an official memorial day should be set for Rabin. The ministerial committee for state ceremonies and symbols decided in the negative, and this decision aroused considerable ire among the public, although again political interests were evident. In a survey conducted by the newspaper *Shishi* (November 1, 1996), most respondents (59 percent) said that the day of the assassination should be declared a national day of mourning, and 37 percent were against such a commemoration. But further analysis shows that 84 percent of the people who vote for left-wing parties and only 48 percent of right-wing voters agreed; 49 percent of the latter did not.

The public pressure included petitions in newspapers addressed to the president and even an appeal to the Supreme Court, which was rejected. Instead of an official day there was a memorial-day broadcast by the media. There were also memorial events run by private and public bodies. Even the chief rabbis published the three psalms and two paragraphs of the Mishna to be recited on that day, but there was still a feeling that these things were not enough. *Ha'aretz* complained in an editorial that the significance of the assassination—the threat to Israeli democracy—was missing from the memorial ceremonies. The ceremonies "mainly eulogized Rabin the man, the commander, the grandfather, the statesman, and were not used adequately to illustrate the terrible meaning of the assault to the democratic way of life" (October 27, 1996). The demands on the government to hold an official memorial day continued unabated until finally, on December 4, 1996, a group of Knesset members proposed a bill to mark an official memorial day, which received the support of the coalition. In summer 1997 the law was passed.

The fact that no official memorial day had been set in the first year after the assassination also made it difficult to decide on the content of the ceremonies. The state holds an annual ceremony for presidents and prime ministers who have died, and it was expected that the same would be done for Rabin. At such a ceremony, the president, prime minister, speaker of the Knesset, chief rabbi, or similar national figures customarily speak. But as the anniversary of Rabin's death approached, the family opposed the idea that President Ezer Weizmann and Prime Minister Benjamin Netanyahu would speak. Leah Rabin blamed Netanyahu for his role in the incitement that preceded the murder and Weizman for his negative attitude toward Rabin, which was even reflected in his eulogy. However, representatives of the state could not fail to appear at the memorial ceremony, if only because their absence would discredit them in the eyes of the public.

A compromise solution was found. Two ceremonies were held on the anniversary, one at the graveside and the other in the Knesset Assembly. The former was partisan in nature, and the family were able to choose who would attend; the latter was official. At the first, no representatives of the "accused" spoke, but only members of the movement and the family; at the memorial session in the Knesset, three people spoke: Prime Minister Netanyahu, Knesset Speaker Dan Tichon (Likud Party), and the head of the opposition, Member of the Knesset (M.K.) Shimon Peres. A critical reading of the speeches reveals the subtexts as well as the whole political debate over the meaning of the assassination. Peres spoke of Rabin's legacy of peace, Prime Minister Netanyahu emphasized the need for national unity, and Knesset Speaker Tichon spoke of the need to preserve democratic rules.[7] The same pattern of two ceremonies was repeated in November 1997.

Another compromise, even more problematic in terms of setting a memorial day, related to the actual date. The date etched in the memory of the secular Rabin camp was November 4, which was the 11th of Heshvan on the Hebrew calendar. Since the custom in Israel is to mark anniversaries by the Hebrew calendar, and the 11th of Heshvan fell on October 24 in 1996, the question arose which date to use. The power of tradition tipped the scales in favor of the religious practice, but some events were also held on November 4 (for example, the Labor Party's memorial rally). The lack of a single memorial date again revealed the division and blurred the memory. The same debate occurred the following year.

This splitting of the memorial day into two dates is liable to blur the memory even more in the future. Close to the first anniversary, a Gallup poll examined whether Israelis remembered the date of the assassination. Even then, only 41 percent remembered the date of the event, which was described by sociologist Moshe Lissak, winner of the Israel Prize, as "the gravest event in the history of Jewish settlement in Israel" (*Pi Ha'Aton*, October 1996). Eighteen percent remembered that it was in November but could not say what day, 35 percent did not remember the date at all, and 6 percent were mistaken. Thus almost half the public did not remember the date of the assassination (*Ma'ariv*, September 18, 1996).

The tension between the attempt to objectivize Rabin and his friends' endeavor to preserve the meaning of the murder as they understood it was revealed time after time. A photograph of Rabin hanging in the meeting room of the Knesset Committee on Defense and Foreign Affairs referred to the date of his "death," which infuriated many Knesset members. "Rabin did not die, he was not even killed in action, he was murdered. Assassinated. Any other statement is an attempt to whitewash the truth," said Meretz Party M.K. Dedi Zucker (*Ma'ariv*, October 16, 1996). An event that was given broader public exposure related to the inscription on the new monument in Rabin Square in Tel Aviv. The family wanted to engrave the text, "Peace will avenge him." This is a saying charged with symbolic meaning and powerful emotions. It has strong religious connotations and is based on the familiar Jewish saying "God will avenge him," referring to the murder of Jews by gentiles and commonly used in reference to national heroes who were killed by the enemy. The phrase "Peace will avenge him" does four different things: it sanctifies peace and gives it divine status; it adds an element of religious martyrdom to the murder victim; it places the assassin as an enemy of the people—and because his name is not mentioned hints at the entire camp from which he came; and this leads to the fourth point—it calls for vengeance. This kind of explicit challenge was unacceptable to the clerical-nationalist camp.

The Rabin family gave in to pressure and softened the text to "Peace is his legacy." The mention of peace as a factor in his assassination remains, but the sanctified, mythic nature has gone. Even people on the right could identify with such an abstract reference to peace. At the same time, it is not only the attempt at deification that has disappeared but also the finger-pointing and the call for political action.

Israeli society has in the past experienced similar dilemmas concerning the canonization of leaders, with varied results. In one case the figure became a national hero; another remained the hero of a movement. During the prestate period there was a salient difference between the case of Trumpeldor and that of Zeev Jabotinsky and Berl Katzenelson. In the first, the memory became the property of all the political movements, and Trumpeldor became a national model. The process of mythicization, turning the historical event into a national myth, or in Schwartz's terms, the shift from chronologization to commemoration (Schwartz, 1982), was possible because each political movement could emphasize a different dimension of the hero: his being a pioneer working on the land (the left) or a fighter (the right). Unlike Trumpeldor, the other two figures remained "founding fathers" of specific political movements: Zeev Jabotinsky of the Likud (Herut) Party and the right wing, and Berl Katzenelson of the Labor camp (Mapai).

After the establishment of the state a more interesting process took place in relation to the two outstanding prime ministers of the left and the right, David Ben-Gurion and Menachem Begin. On each side, the main reason for nationalizing their memories was the opposing political camp's need for legitimization. Ben-Gurion, the Labor leader, was hated by the right, but when Menachem Begin rose to power in the political upheaval of 1977 and sought to divest himself and his party of the stigma of political outcasts, he adopted Ben-Gurion's trappings of *mamlacktiut* (statism) and positioned himself as Ben-Gurion's successor. Thus Ben-Gurion's image was softened by his political rival, who transformed him from the leader of a movement to the leader of the nation.

The same thing happened, to a lesser degree, with Menachem Begin and the left. In the election campaign of 1992 the Labor Party appropriated Begin in order to strengthen Rabin's legitimacy in the eyes of traditional Likud voters and supporters (see Bilu and Levy, 1993). This tendency increased in the years that followed. The heads of this camp, Rabin and Peres, needed to broaden the support for their peace policy, and this led them to make extensive use of the argument that it was Begin in the Camp David agreements who first recognized the legitimate rights of the Palestinians and returned Sinai to Egypt in exchange for peace. They praised him for his political wisdom and courage and presented their acts as a continuation of his policy.[8] Thus the left's historical dispute with Begin was blunted; had he not started an unnecessary war in Lebanon, Begin might even have attained the stature of Ben-Gurion by the end of his life.

What direction will Rabin's memory take? Will he also be adopted by the cultural camp that opposed him in the last stages of his life? Or will he remain only the leader of a movement, as happened to Yigal Allon, his commander in the Palmach? Rabin's funeral cortege was very much like that of Herzl, and he was even buried not far from Herzl in the part of the cemetery reserved for the leaders of the nation. But what will happen to Rabin's monument? Will it become a national monument like that of Herzl? Or will its fate be like that of the monument in Kibbutz Hulda erected in 1929 in memory of the builders and defenders of the Jewish community, which over time was forgotten even by members of the Labor movement (Shamir, 1994: 49). Only time will tell. What is clear at the present stage of history is that hyper-politicization, a defining characteristic of Israeli society, has also led to politicization of the memory, and this is what obstructs and perhaps entirely prevents the victim of assassination from becoming a sanctified national hero.

A further difficulty is Rabin's canonization by the Israeli left. This relates to the left's aversion to the culture of martyrdom. Rabin could have been the first martyr of the Israeli peace camp, after long years in which settlement and security were the ground that bred martyrs. After 1967, martyrology became the language of the clerical-nationalist camp. Rabin provided an opportunity that Peace Now activist Emil Gruenzweig—killed in 1983 by a grenade thrown at a demonstration—could not provide: a hero all his life whose tragic death made him a martyr. But there is an intrinsic difficulty in this process. It is true that even democratic and liberal societies supported by modern movements cultivate political myths, and that civilian cults are part of the symbolic order of secular democracies—of the Israeli left as well. Nevertheless, there is a difference between the cult of blood and land of the clerical-nationalist camp and the attitudes of the liberal-democratic camp.

If we examine the more extreme representatives of these camps, or those nearer to the ideal type—Gush Emunim on the one hand and Peace Now on the other—the difference is obvious. The former actively cultivated the memory of those who fell in the struggle over settlement in the territories, creating complex patterns of commemoration and making broad political use of them. The latter refused to do this with regard to its own "saint," Emil Gruenzweig (Feige, 1996: 311–12). If the former can be defined as "a church built on the blood of martyrs," the latter speaks in the name of liberal humanist values, avoids larger-than-life symbols taken from the monumental Jewish and Zionist history, objects to transcendental concepts, is reluctant to develop hagiographic sentiments, and presumes to oppose mythological thinking with modern values.

Even the unofficial anthem of the movement, "The Song of Peace," expresses the preference for modern pragmatism over the dictates of memory with the lyric "Don't look back/let the fallen be." The Peace Now movement marks the extreme of the antimythical pragmatic culture in contrast to the central stream of the liberal-democratic camp (such as supporters of the Labor Party), but Rabin's historic move brought the central stream closer to the cultural order that marked the more extreme group. At the rally where Rabin was assassinated, "The Song of Peace" became the main motif, the song that is identified above all with his murder. Amos Oz, the celebrated author and Labor ideologue, gave dramatic expression to the difference between the political and cultural camps: "Yitzhak Rabin was assassinated because he turned his back and our backs on the graves and chose life. Don't sanctify his memory. Don't sanctify his grave. Sanctify life and justice and freedom and wisdom and reality, because it was for them that Yitzhak Rabin was murdered" (*Yediot*, March 2, 1996).

Perhaps there was a dialectic process at work. The more the clerical-nationalist camp developed and fostered the cults of blood and land, the more the liberal-democratic wing distanced itself from those cults, which in the past had been an integral part of its culture, too. The cult of martyrdom increasingly suited the settlers' political interests and ideology, while the members of the secular democratic camp, who had adopted the new Israeli civilian ethos, felt less and less comfortable with it.

THE COLLECTIVE MEMORY AND THE FAMILY MEMORY

The canonization of Rabin's memory encountered another difficulty: the contradiction between the collective and the private memory, especially the family memory. Unlike large societies such as India, where Gandhi was assassinated, and the United States, where Kennedy was murdered, Israel's collectivist, familial, and open character caused Rabin's murder to be felt by thousands as a personal loss, and his memory to become a private one. It is unlikely that the private memories will dissipate in the near future. Rabin had a strong personal impact, and his image returns to many like a flash-bulb memory. This is the route from the private to the collective memory, and what turns social memory into something personally meaningful.

A central role in the process of remembering and commemorating was played by the family, especially Rabin's widow, Leah. Her private pain, made public by television, penetrated almost every home in Israel just as the eulogy of Noa, Rabin's granddaughter, was the most poignant moment of the funeral. "The contribution of those close to the victim is purer, in the sense that it is a direct expression of their private pain and memory, although it assumes that they have a message for the public, including those who did not know the deceased; a message based on his personal attributes, or on his being a representative of many others, apart from the fact of his being a victim," writes Sivan (1991: 130).

Leah Rabin's dominance and her political character helped shape the memory of Rabin from the day after the assassination, suggesting that the state and its representatives lost their monopoly on defining the collective memory. Assertive, extroverted, and with a strong public and political presence, Leah Rabin surprised many by her public appearances during the week of mourning, going against the tradition that mourners seclude themselves in their homes. She assumed the role of family head in those days and supported an appearance by her two grandchildren on a TV talk show during the shiva.

In the symbolic aspect of her activism, Leah Rabin was no different from some other widows such as Jehan Sadat or Jacqueline Kennedy. But what stood out in the role she played was its political tone. She harshly blamed the religious right for the assassination and pointed her finger at the Likud, its leader Netanyahu, and the religious camp, including Bar-Ilan University. She refused to shake hands with Netanyahu at the funeral, and after Labor's defeat in the elections she responded, "I'm walking around today with the feeling that Rabin was murdered again" (*Ma'ariv*, May 31, 1996), adding that she "felt like packing her bags." This statement was sharply criticized, not only by the clerical-nationalist camp but also by some of Rabin's supporters.[9] She was also criticized for some other statements and actions, such as her opposition to the appearance of the president and prime minister at the memorial service at Mount Herzl cemetery (Ruth Gavison, *Yediot*, January 1, 1996), her objection to the election of President Weizman to a second term in 1998, and particularly the argument she used against Weizman—that he had a negative attitude toward Rabin and his memory.

The widow's actions illustrate some of the dilemmas of the commemoration. She demanded that the state foster the Rabin ethos and place his commemoration high on the national agenda, while at the same time she found it hard to forgive those she saw as accomplices, and presented the political dimension of the assassination in a way that was unacceptable to the clerical-nationalist camp. This also found expression from time to time in the four years after the assassination. In 1999 the City of Tel Aviv decided to clean the walls of city hall of the thousands of graffiti written since the assassination and to devote one wall to a "clean" memorial. The artist who did the work wrote the following text on the memorial wall: "Rabin was murdered by a young Jew wearing a skullcap." This text aroused fury in religious and right-wing circles, who said it was a generalization that castigated an entire population. In the light of this harsh criticism, the mayor decided in November of that year, a week after the dedication of the new memorial site, to delete this sentence. The affair stirred up public debate on the question of whether it was right for the sake of collective memory to mention the fact that the assassin had come from a certain social group and in the name of its ideology. In this debate, Leah Rabin, as usual, was adamant an unequivocal in favor of the original text and against the deletion. "I don't see myself as a symbol of consensus, but as a victim of the lack of consensus" (interview on TV channel 2, October 24, 1996).

Leah Rabin expected the assassination to be nationalized, but her political involvement in the process of remembrance and commemoration reinforced Rabin's image as partisan in the eyes of the rival camp. A few days after the assassination it was suggested that she be proposed for the presidency of Israel. In that role she would have created a "living statue" whose commemorative effect is one of the strongest (Volkan, 1990), but could such a political personality achieve the national status that is required of the president? Not surprisingly, this idea did not gel, but speculation arose that she might appear on the Labor list for the Knesset, which would be more natural in view of the nature of her activities. For the same reason, the suggestion raised after the Labor Party's return to power that Leah Rabin be appointed Israel's ambassador to the United Nations, was sharply rejected

The problematic nature of national commemoration, as opposed to personal-family commemoration, was also reflected in the actions of other members of the Rabin family. Noa, the granddaughter, won the sympathy and love of the entire world with the eulogy she gave at the funeral. But her book of memoirs and celebrity lifestyle opened her to criticism and diminished her status as a "living statue" (Eleonora Lev, *Sefarim*, October 30, 1996; Amir Oren, *Ha'aretz*, May 10, 1996). The position of the family in some of the national commemorative events met with criticism from political rivals—for example, when the Knesset decided to fund a special office for the widow for her public activity. The very criticism demonstrates the difficulty of establishing a process of canonization in such a divided society.

The entrance into the political arena of Yuval, the son, who had jealously guarded his privacy in the past, also reflected the dilemma. Instead of his mother's appearing on the Labor list for the Knesset elections of 1996, he was placed in the honorary position of 117 out of 120 (the last ten places, although they do not have a chance of winning a seat, are bestowed upon former presidents, prime ministers, and other special figures in the movement). Later, Yuval Rabin was chosen to head the organization Dor Shalem Doresh Shalom ("an entire generation demands peace"; see Chapter 1). Three years later, in the 1999 elections, his elder sister, Dalia, was elected to the Knessett on the new Center Party list. In the context of Israeli politicization, the active public role played by the Rabin family hindered the objectivization of Rabin, diminished the possibility of greater nationalization of the memory, and hampered construction of his image as a national hero.

The forces blurring the memory used various strategies, such as allowing school officials a free hand in addressing Rabin's legacy on the first memorial day. A circular sent to principals by the director-general of the Ministry of Education stated: "Teachers will hold discussions in the classrooms in accordance with the age of the students, their level of development, and awareness of public events. Emphasis should be placed on the commitment to democracy as a way to resolve social and public disputes. They should also demonstrate how these principles are reflected in everyday life and relationships between people, in mutual tolerance and adherence to the proper rules of behavior and mutual respect."[10] Not a word about peace.

Another strategy that aroused a storm of protest was used at the first anniversary of the assassination, then abandoned, then used again more forcefully as the second and the third anniversary approached in 1997 and 1998. This was the conspiracy theory, according to which Rabin was not murdered by Yigal Amir but by someone else, perhaps by a plot of the General Security Services (GSS). This theory lost the public's interest soon after the murder. But when it was revealed that Avishai Raviv, an active member of extreme right-wing organizations and a friend of Yigal Amir, was a GSS agent, the conspiracy theory revived and won supporters among clerical-nationalist groups. It did not gain wide public acceptance, however, especially after the Commission of Inquiry headed by former chief justice Shamgar rejected it, and the press did not give it extensive exposure.

On the eve of the second anniversary, however, the conspiracy theory gained surprisingly broad credence in right-wing circles. Statements made by Knesset members from the clerical right, glaring headlines in the newspapers, and finally suggestions by cabinet ministers that the matter be investigated gave the theory new legitimacy and respectability and aroused fury among the left. In response, the government even revealed some classified parts of the Shamgar report that dealt with the issue. But even this information did not douse the fire. It was hard to escape the conclusion that stirring up the theory that the GSS, Shimon Peres, or Rabin himself had initiated the assassination plot in order to implicate the right worked to the advantage of those who sought to discredit the memory of Rabin during that sensitive period of the memorial day. This conclusion is strengthened in view of the fact that the story recurred in a very similar manner in 1998.

Summary: The Past Is Not Past

The peace camp's attempt to turn Rabin's memory into one of the pillars of the Israeli peace ethos and to impart this ethos to the whole of society has so far been unsuccessful. Following the 1996 elections, the growing alienation of the media and the cultural elite from the new political elite made it difficult to commemorate from above. The Rabin commemorative stamp, for example, which is a formal visual expression of the basic state ethos, did not include the concept of peace and referred only to Rabin's contribution to security.

There are also forces that act continually to create countermemories. On the first memorial day, ultra-Orthodox newspapers published articles mocking what they called "the mourning celebrations" or "the mourning festival." An article in *Ha'Shavua* explained why "Rabin will be remembered as a most negative figure in the national consciousness." In the Shas newspaper *Yom Le'Yom,* the secretary of the parliamentary faction, M.K. Zvi Yaakobson, attacked the chief rabbis, who ordered the reading of parts of the Mishna and Psalms on the memorial day (*Ha'aretz*, October 27, 1996). Right-wing ideologue Hillel Weis claimed that the sacrifice on the altar was not Isaac, but the kid, and called the left wing "auto-anti-Semites": "The shamelessness of Jews who are ashamed of their Jewishness" and therefore blame ultra-Orthodox or religious Zionist Jews . . . is a scorpion that stings itself" (*Ma'ariv*, October 25, 1996).

In January 1997 the head of the Zo Artzenu movement, Moshe Feiglin (whose partner in leading the movement, Benny Elon, was elected to the Knesset from the Moledet Party), said, "There is no difference between Baruch Goldstein and Yitzhak Rabin. The difference is only that Goldstein murdered 39 Arabs and Rabin murdered 16 illegal immigrants on the ship *Altalena*." At that time, a derisive pamphlet about Rabin was distributed among Knesset members noting "all his sins from the *Altalena* to the treacherous act of Oslo." On the second anniversary of the assassination, the editor of *Kfar Habad,* Aharon David Alperin, accused the Labor Party and its leader, Ehud Barak, of cynically using a big commemorative event as a weapon against the government and Prime Minister Netanyahu. "The incitement against Netanyahu is worse than against Rabin" (*Kfar Habad*, no. 782, June 11, 1997). The criticism of the memorial ceremony and the memory became sharper, more overt and outspoken over the years. Toward the third memorial day, in November 1998, most of the Russian-language press broadly criticized what it called the "personality cult" of Rabin, comparing it to cults practiced in the Soviet Union (a summary of this attitude appeared in *Yediot Aharonot*, November 12, 1999).

In the absence of agreement on the meaning of the assassination, the lessons to be drawn from it, or the content of "Rabin's legacy," public discourse has shifted to anther question—the memory itself. The debate is now between those who argued that it is Israel's duty to remember and those who seek to forget: "Any remembrance entails its own forgetfulness, as the two are interwoven in the process of producing the commemorative narratives" (Zerubavel, 1995: 214). Instead of diving into the essence—the substance of the memory of Rabin—public debate centers on questions of remembering: Should we remember? How can we remember? and so on. Slogans like "Remember and Do Not Forget" and "Rabin—We Will Not Forget" appear on posters, stickers, and graffiti, as well as in speeches and lectures, and at conventions. The first memorial rally in Rabin Square in November 1996 was organized under the banner "We Will Not Forget." The sticker that was prevalent at the time of the assassination had been "Shalom, Haver" (Goodbye, friend). On the first anniversary the sticker read "Haver, Ata Haser" (We miss you, friend), and on the second anniversary the sticker said "Haver, Ani Zocher" (I remember, friend).

But more important is that instead of discussing the meaning of the assassination, the debate focuses on the private figure of Rabin the man. In other words, the actual remembering became ritualized. Just as the Rabin cult immediately after the murder was designed to channel the catharsis in the absence of real political action, so too the ritualization of the memory is designed to make up for its weakness or even its lack of content. Discourse shifted from representation of the assassination to representation of the representation. Virtual reality rather than historical reality became the focus of discussion: not what we should learn from the assassination, but whether we have learned a lesson; not what we should do in light of the murder, but whether we have done it—without defining "it."

The development of Israeli society—the divisions between the two major political camps, but more important, the collapse of the master narrative and the loss of a common text owing to the crystallization of the various cultural enclaves—leads to the conclusion that the society is entering a new era in which there will no longer be one narrative. The difficulty in forming a narrative around Rabin's assassination is just one expression of this broad phenomenon. So how will Rabin's assassination fit into the many different narratives in the future? Which of the narratives will become more salient? And which will have staying power (Zelizer, 1995: 217)?

The initial reaction of transforming Rabin into a saint immediately after the assassination was thwarted for the reasons explained above, first and foremost hyper-politicization. Postmodernist culture treats heroes cynically and critically. Bilu and Levy (1993) believe that in Israel hagiography will remain the province of the religious, not of politicians. But the new Israel of the peace era has no other hero, even if Rabin's attempt turns out to be a failure and happened too early or too late (see Chapter 14 by Yatziv). The failure of Rabin's commemoration in the first years cannot tell us anything about the future. And we have already seen that historical figures can change radically in the ongoing process of the formation of collective memory (Schwartz, 1991a and 1991b). What, then, will be the fate of the memory of Rabin's assassination?

At the end of the first year, *Ha'aretz* wrote, "Rabin's assassination is not 'a scar in the flesh of the nation,' it is an open, bleeding wound that has no cure" (editorial, October 24, 1996). Even after years have passed, "memorial structures" will certainly remain (Tanaka, 1984); these are the representations of the object that remain in the memory, even if they are no longer "warm" or evocative of the traumatic event. The Yitzhak Rabin Center for Israel Studies, Rabin Square in Tel Aviv, and his grave on Mount Herzl in Jerusalem, which has become a pilgrimage site as "the most impressive spatial representation of secular religion in Israel" (Bilu, *Ha'aretz*, April 23, 1996), will function as powerful mnemonic sites. But what will be the content of this memory? What will be its meaning?

Theoretically, Rabin's commemoration could have been based on spheres other than the political. Indeed, in a discussion of intellectuals at the Israel Democracy Institute, the historian Michael Hed suggested "erecting the monument, the monumental statue, to Rabin's memory in spheres related to the rule of law, the relationship between the individual and society . . . [s]pheres that touch the boundaries of political discussion, not its totality" (minutes of the discussion, September 18, 1996). But this suggestion ignores the basic character of the Israeli culture, its overpoliticization. As long as this characteristic remains unchanged, the fate of the commemoration and the memory depend on developments at the heart of the political sphere.

Just as holy places and saintly cults need agents of memory, so do heroes. They too need "moral entrepreneurs [who] seek public arenas and support for their interpretations of the past" (Wagner-Pacifici and Schwartz, 1991: 382). Therefore, another central variable that will influence the memory is the future role in Israeli society of the elite of the peace camp, the liberal-democratic wing of Rabin's political movement. The social position of the agents of memory is critical, as Schudson says about the memory of Watergate: "There is no great mystery about why liberal and conservative versions dominate the public memory rather than radical left or ultra-conservative interpretations: they have been officially sanctioned by the political establishment" (Schudson, 1992: 65–66). If the agents of Rabin's memory stand at Israel's helm, the prospect of his commemoration will increase, as indeed happened after the Labor victory in the 1999 election.

Related to this is another development, one that will determine the fate of Israeli society, just as it will determine the future of Rabin's memory: the fate of the peace process. As long as Israeli society is torn in its attitude toward peace, the countermemory that demythicizes Rabin will continue to operate. Commemoration or denial of Rabin and the nature of his image in the future will depend largely on whether the state of Israel manages to free itself from the burden that the ongoing occupation places upon it and enter an era of peace. If there is peace, with all its internal social implications, Rabin, who paved the way to a new era and laid the foundation for peace, will become a national hero. If not, he will continue to be the protagonist of one part of the nation and the antagonist of others.

No matter how hard we try, it is still too early to understand the full significance of Rabin's assassination for Israeli society. What is clear is that the murder will not fade away. "The past is not dead," remarks a character in William Faulkner's *Requiem for a Nun*, "it is not even past." The philosopher Arthur Danto sought to create a "perfect historian," whom he called "the ideal chronicler." This creature would know everything that was happening, even in people's minds, at any given moment. But Danto understood that this knowledge would be insufficient, that there is a need for a characteristic beyond perfect chronicling. "It is impossible to know the whole truth about any event except in retrospect, and sometimes long after the event happens" (Danto, 1965: 245) Alas, even Danto's "ideal chronicler" cannot come equipped with knowledge of the future. Only the future can reveal the full meaning of Rabin's assassination. And even then the narrative will remain ambiguous and polysemic, with many different interpretations.

Notes

1. For purposes of this discussion, I will avoid entering into the debate between historiographers and narrativists over the representation of the facts that compose the myth: whether the collective memory contradicts history or complements it, and how the conflict between these approaches can be solved (Schwartz, 1991a,b; Schudson, 1992: 218–19). An article by Olick and Robbins reviews extensively the state of the art of studies on collective memory and refers to many of the issues discussed in this literature. It also contains a rich list of sources (Olick and Robbins, 1998).

2. A fine illustration of this appeared in an exhibition by Guy Raz, "The City Square," shown on the first anniversary of Rabin's assassination in the Kibbutz Gallery in Tel Aviv. The exhibition consisted of memorabilia from 1948 (photographs of Rabin as a Palmach fighter, boxing), the Six Day War medal of 1967, and items symbolizing the murder (candle wax on the paving stones of Rabin Square). See the exhibition catalog, "Memory as a Candle of His Life," by Idith Zertal.

3. See Hubert and Mausse, 1964; this subject is examined in Zerubavel, 1994, and in Azaryahu, 1995: 111–36.

4. This is the fourth type of hero, higher than the third type, which Frye calls high/low mimetic. The two lower types are the narratives of irony and low mimetic. For a modern secular society it is hard to invent a hero belonging to the fifth level, which is Frye's highest level. This is the mythic hero who is a real god.

5. Indeed, some describe Rabin's mythological "resurrection": "And thus Rabin was transformed into a saint by the fatal bullets. He rose again and his spirit returned to stir the youth" (Shlomo Giora Shoham, *Ma'ariv* supplement on the 30th day of mourning, December 1, 1995).

6. An extreme and dramatic example was the new interpretation by Jehoshaphat Harkabi of the Great Revolt against Rome in 66–70 C.E. After hundreds of years in which it was portrayed as an act of bravery, Harkabi presents it as utter stupidity, an irresponsible act of national suicide. Harkabi did not hide his political motivation for evoking the memory of this historical event and interpreting it

anew: "People are not as sensitive and resistant to criticism of a past event as they are to an attack on political attitudes in the present. Therefore it is easier to begin with criticism of the past as a preface to criticism of the present. This is also an indirect method of demonstrating the need to distinguish clearly between political vision and dangerous fantasy. In this way people can draw their own conclusions concerning present policy out of the political insight they have acquired concerning past events" (Harkabi, 1986: 289).

7. The media, especially television, emphasized the first ceremony on Mount Herzl, which was more dramatic and poetic and had become engraved on the public consciousness. The fact that two ceremonies were held on the same day detracted from the nationalization of the memory. The philosopher Asa Kasher commented on the absence of the president and prime minister at the ceremony: the president's symbolic silence was appropriate because it expressed the shame of the state over the murder of its prime minister. Prime Minister Netanyahu's silence was also symbolic, since it symbolized the failure of the system, which had replaced the prime minister not in the polling booth but by a bullet (Ma'ariv, November 1, 1996).

8. From private conversations with Rabin.

9. For example, Teddy Proyce, Davar Rishon, January 15, 1996.

10. Special circular from Ben Zion Dal, director-general of the Ministry of Education, to educational institutions, October 8, 1996.

References

Anderson, Benedict (1987). *Imagined Communities*. London: Verso.

Azaryahu, Maoz (1995). *State Cults*. Sede Boker: Ben Gurion University Press [Hebrew].

Bell, Daniel (1975). "The End of American Exceptionalism." *The Public Interest*, no. 41: 193–224.

Ben-Yehuda, Nachman (1995). *The Masada Myth: Collective Memory and Mythmaking in Israel*. Madison: University of Wisconsin Press.

Bhabha, Homi K. (1990). "Dissemination: Time, Narrative and the Margins of the Modern Nation." In Homi K. Bhabha (ed.), *Nation and Narration*. London: Routledge, pp. 290–322.

Bilu, Yoram, and Andre Levy (1993). "The Elusive Sanctification of Menachem Begin." *International Journal of Culture, Politics, and Society* 7: 297–328.

Brug, Muli (1996). "From the Top of Massada to the Heart of the Ghetto." In David Ohana and Robert S. Wistrich (eds.),

Carton Blum, Ruth (1996). "Yitzhak's Fear: The Myth of the Sacrifice of Isaac as a Test Case in the New Hebrew Poetry." In David Ohana and Robert S. Wistrich (eds.), *Myth and Memory*. Tel Aviv: Hakibbutz Hameuchad, pp. 203–27 [Hebrew].

Connerton, Paul (1989). *How Societies Remember*. Cambridge: Cambridge University Press.

Danto, Arthur C. (1965). *Analytical Philosophy of History*. Cambridge: Cambridge University Press.

Donner, Batia (1996). *Map of a Memory*. Exhibition catalog, Eretz-Israel Museum. Tel Aviv [Hebrew].

Durkheim, Emile (1965) [1912]. *The Elementary Form of the Religious Life*. New York: Free Press.

Eliade, Mircea (1963). *Myth and Reality*. New York: Harper and Row.

Feige, Michael (1996). "Let Them Go: The Attitude of Gush Emunim and Peace Now to the Martyrs of Their Movements." In David Ohana and Robert S. Wistrich (eds.), *Myth and Memory*. Tel Aviv: Hakibbutz Hameuchad, pp. 304–320 [Hebrew].

Frye, N. (1961). "Fictional Modes and Forms." In Robert Scholes (ed.), *Approaches to the Novel*. San Francisco: Chandler, pp. 31–40.

Funkenstein, Amos (1990). "Collective Memory and Historical Consciousness." *History and Memory*, no. 1: 5–26.

Halbwachs, Maurice (1992) [1941]. *On Collective Memory*. Chicago: University of Chicago Press.

Harkabi, Jehoshaphat (1986). *Fateful Decisions*. Tel Aviv: Am Oved [Hebrew].

Hobsbawm, Eric, and Terence Ranger (eds.) (1983). *The Invention of Tradition*. Cambridge: Cambridge University Press.

Hubert, H., and M. Mausse (1964). *Sacrifice: Its Nature and Function*. Chicago: University of Chicago Press.

Kammen, M. (1991). *Mystic Cords of Memory: The Transformation of Tradition in American Culture*. New York: Alfred A. Knopf.

Levi-Strauss, Claude (1966). *The Savage Mind*. Chicago: University of Chicago Press.

Malkinson, Ruth, Simon S. Rubin, and Eliezer Witztum (1993). *Loss and Bereavement in Jewish Society in Israel*. Jerusalem: Kana.

Mosse, George L. (1990). *Fallen Soldiers: Reshaping the Memory of the World Wars*. Oxford: Oxford University Press.

Nora, Pierre (1993). "Between Memory and History—The Problem of the Place." *Zmanim*, no. 45: 5–19 [Hebrew].

——— (1996). *Realms of Memory: The Construction of the French Past*. New York: Columbia University Press.

Olick, Jeffrey K., and Joyce Robbins (1998). "Social Memory Studies: From 'Collective Memory' to the Historical Sociology of Mnemonic Practices." *Annual Review of Sociology* 24: 105–40.

Omer, Mordecai (ed.) (1996). *Graffiti in Rabin Square*. Tel Aviv: Tel Aviv Museum of Art.

Sadeh, Yitzhak (1953). "Comradeship in Arms." In *Around the Bonfire*. Tel Aviv: Hakibbutz Hame'uchad.

Schudson, Michael (1989). "The Present in the Past Versus the Past in the Present." *Communication*, no. 11: 105–13.

——— (1992). *Watergate in American Memory*. New York: Basic Books.

Schwartz, Barry (1982). "The Social Context of Commemoration: A Study in Collective Memory." *Social Forces* 61 (2): 378–402.

——— (1991a). "Mourning and the Making of a Sacred Symbol: Durkheim and the Lincoln Assassination." *Social Forces* 70 (2): 343–64.

———— (1991b). "Social Change and Collective Memory: The Democratization of George Washington." *American Sociological Review* 56 (2): 221–36.

———— (1996). "Rereading the Gettysburg Address: Social Change and Collective Memory." *Qualitative Sociology* 19 (3): 395–422.

Shamir, Ilana (1994). "Monuments to the Fallen in Israel's Wars: Commemoration and Memory." Ph.D. dissertation, Tel Aviv University [Hebrew].

Shapira, Anita (1994). "Historiography and Memory: The Case of Latrun 1948." *Alpayim*, no. 10: 9–41.

Sivan, Emmanuel (1991). *The 1948 Generation: Myth, Profile and Memory*. Tel Aviv: Ma'arachot [Hebrew].

Smith, Antony D. (1991). *National Identity*. Reno: University of Nevada Press.

Tanaka, V. (1984). "Dealing with Object Loss." *Scandinavian Psychoanalysis Review*, no. 7: 17–33.

Valensi, Lucette (1986). "From Sacred History to Historical Memory and Back: The Jewish Past." *History and Anthropology* 12 (2): 283–305.

Volkan, Vamik D. (1990). "Living Statues and Political Decision Making." *Mind and Human Interaction* 2 (2): 46–50.

Wagner-Pacifici, Robin, and Barry Schwartz (1991). "The Vietnam Veterans Memorial: Commemorating a Different Past." *American Journal of Sociology* 97 (2): 376–420.

Yerushalmi, Yoseph Hayim (1988). *Zakhor: Jewish History and Jewish Memory*. Seattle: University of Washington Press.

Zelizer, Barbie (1995). "Reading the Past Against the Grain: The Shape of Memory Studies." *Critical Studies in Mass Communication* 12 (2): 214–39.

Zerubavel, Yael (1994). "The Death of Memory and the Memory of Death." *Alpayim*, no. 10: 42–67 [Hebrew].

———— (1995). *Recovered Roots, Collective Memory and the Making of Israeli National Tradition*. Chicago: University of Chicago Press.

INDEX

Index

In this index an "f" after a number indicates a separate reference on the next page, and an "ff" indicates separate references on the next two pages. A continuous discussion over two or more pages is indicated by a span of page numbers, e.g., "57–59." *Passim* is used for a cluster of references in close but not consecutive sequence.